D1715710

Montesquieu's System

of

Natural Government

Montesquieu's System

of

Natural Government

by Henry J. Merry
1970

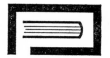

Purdue University Studies

West Lafayette, Indiana

Standard Book Number 911198-23-7
Library of Congress Catalog No. 77-94841
Printed in United States of America
© 1970 by Purdue Research Foundation

To
My Father and Mother
Earl and Lillian Merry

Preface

My study and re-study of Montesquieu's political theory have been the result of a series of inspirations. The first that I now recall, and undoubtedly the most enduring and propelling, came during a seminar conducted a number of years ago by Professor Carl J. Friedrich on constitutional reason of state. He awakened in me a profound interest in Montesquieu and his inspiration carried me beyond that immediate problem into the broader field of constitutional development. This motivation was fortified by studies of American constitutional law, particularly analyses of the relationship of Congress and the Supreme Court, at first under the guidance of Professor Arthur E. Sutherland. From these beginnings I inquired more and more into the separation of powers and related doctrines, while continuing the viewpoint of social psychology as well as that of political and legal philosophy. These further studies convinced me that there is much more than usually recognized to not only these doctrines but also to Montesquieu's many-sided explanation of governmental arrangement and sociological interaction.

For this series of inspirations, I am deeply thankful to Professors Friedrich and Sutherland and to many others who also have guided and encouraged me. In the final stages of putting the results of the study into book form, I benefited immeasureably from consultations with Dr. Robert Shackleton, the Bodleian Librarian and author of the definitive biographer of Montesquieu, and with Professor John Plamenatz of All Souls College, who was my superviser of studies during a recent sabbatical leave at Oxford. I am much indebted to Professor Plamenatz for his thorough review of the final manuscript and for his many helpful comments and criticisms.

While the guidance of these eminent scholars has aided me to avoid many pitfalls, the opinions expressed and the errors and deficiencies which remain are of my own doing and responsibility.

Henry J. Merry

Hammond, Indiana
October, 1969

CONTENTS

Introduction

This study seeks to show that *L'Esprit des Lois* and other works of the French philosopher, Charles-Louis de Secondat, Baron de la Brède et de Montesquieu (1689-1755), despite their broad reach, diverse subject matter, and apparent lack of unity, have a meaningful coherence from the viewpoint of modern political theory. More specifically, I will undertake to explain that Montesquieu's work embodies a systematic analysis of the complex interactions of political life, that he finds the central psychological spirit of a nation in the conflicts of social classes and social forces, and that *L'Esprit des Lois*, like many recent studies of political systems,[1] makes the inter-relationship of governmental institutions, political infrastructures, and sociological environment, the focal point of both the method of inquiry and the theory of government.

What I will present is not, of course, the usual picture of Montesquieu. Surveys of political thought ordinarily give him little space and then seem to be more intent upon fitting him into an assumed American ideology than in reporting his own system.[2] Mostly, he is made to stand for a legalistic doctrine of separating legislative, executive, and judicial functions. Occasionally, he is associated with anti-monarchical liberalism, sociological jurisprudence, or climatic determinism[3] — and even these are only phases of what I believe to be his theory of natural government. But, generally, anthologies and commentaries limit Montesquieu to a few paragraphs of his analysis of the English constitution and then use these excerpts to support the traditional American beliefs about the structure of our government. For a century or two we have taken his cryptic warnings against the concentration of three powers in one body and by inversion and extension turned them into rationalistic doctrines of separation of powers and checks and balances with little regard for most of what he says in a positive way about the distribution of political authority. By this process of forced selection and conversion, we have used the authority of a disinterested liberal philosopher to praise the general pattern of a constitution which arose out of our national political struggles. The artificiality of this interpretation of both Montesquieu's work and our constitutional development has become increasingly evident. Less and less does it enter into our studies and conclusions about the psychology of even our own political system.

Montesquieu warned against such narrow interpretations of *L'Esprit des Lois*. The Preface refers to the "infinite number of subjects" contained in the work and promptly begs the reader not to judge the labor of twenty years by a few hours of reading nor to approve or condemn the entire book by a few isolated phrases. Moreover, he suggests that the diverse particulars are related in a meaningful way. "Here a great many truths will not make themselves felt until we see the chain which connects them with the others. The more we reflect upon the details the more we will sense the certainty of the principles." Thus, Montesquieu believes that common ideas underlie his inquiries into the relation of political laws to such seemingly disparate subjects as education, climate, slavery, family morals, social classes, commerce, population trends, religion, community mores, and civil laws.

These diverse relations may appear to have little coherence as long as we allow Montesquieu to stand for only such limited doctrines as the separation of powers and the influence of climate. Yet these two ideas mark the principal lines of interpretation. On the one hand, the English and American political historians, like Blackstone, Pollard, Trevelyan, and Holmes,[4] were pleased to find remarks that seem to flatter their constitutions even while they questioned his analysis of the British government. On the other hand, the sociologists, like Comte, consider Montesquieu's statements about climatic influence to be the forerunner of a modern emphasis upon sociological factors in political systems.[5] Such narrow interpretations have tended to give *L'Esprit des Lois* a reputation for disunity. For instance, some commentators consider the historical books at the end of the volume to be digressive. These cannot be reconciled easily with the doctrine of separating legislative, executive, and judicial powers, nor with climatic determinism, but what should be questioned is not the relevance of these books, which Montesquieu himself said were necessary in this undertaking, but rather the sufficiency of the specific theories of interpretation.

Perhaps it is coincidence that recently each one of four or five commentators has taken a broader view of Montesquieu, but there does seem to be a growing recognition that his ideas about politics and government are not as simple as we have believed. A 1948 lecture suggests that he may not have been mistaken in his analysis of the British constitution.[6] Then, for comprehensive appraisal, an unusually definitive and scholarly biography of Montesquieu appeared in 1961.[7] This work by Robert Shackleton, now the Bodleian Librarian, resulted from thorough research in many areas. About the same time, Werner Stark, the sociologist, made a penetrating study of Montesquieu's epistemology with emphasis upon his sociology of knowledge.[8] The recent studies by David Lowenthal and John Plamenatz for surveys of political thought have gone considerably beyond the usual treatment; they recognize Montesquieu's contributions to economics, sociology, and psychology as well as to various aspects of politics and government.[9] This trend probably will continue because the present emphasis of political scientists upon the relations of government to the social system and the total environment will make us much more sympathetic to the great bulk of *L'Esprit des Lois* and its inquiries into various facets of social psychology.

This study of Montesquieu's ideas about the political systems is based upon a comprehensive and, hopefully, a penetrating inquiry into *L'Esprit des Lois* and his other works. In general, the purpose is twofold. One, I have tried to test the hypothesis that there is considerably more to his system of government than the separation or balance of legislative, executive and judicial powers and the influence of climate. My finding here is that his political theory is much more complex than these well known doctrines. Two, I have tried to see whether there is underlying *L'Esprit des Lois* a basic principle or proposition that will give substantial unity to the whole work. In this matter, I believe that there is fundamental coherence, and that this lies essentially in the natural interrelationship of governmental processes and the diverse forces which arise from the national society and its environment. Montesquieu, I believe, is urging that political rulers respect the sociological and psychological differentiation of the society and that this respect be assured through the socially relevant distribution of authority and a general spirit of toleration and moderation among the conflicting classes of the nation. The underlying theme is mostly in the realm of social psychology, and it involves the relation of political decision to the whole intrasocietal and extrasocietal environment. Throughout *L'Esprit des Lois* the subject that appears with greatest persistence is the relationship of government to the three political classes. The idea that social class conflict is an essential element of a viable political system can bring even the two final historical books of *L'Es-*

prit des Lois into a meaningful association with the other twenty-nine books of the work. Accordingly, the essential principle of Montesquieu's theory of liberty-assuring government may not be, as we often believe, the functional separation of legislative, executive, and judicial powers, but rather the joint or interdependent distribution of political control among the monocratic, aristocratic, and democratic classes of the society. This study of Montesquieu's work also argues that *L'Esprit des Lois* is designed for Frenchmen and seeks to explain the kind of government that is most natural for France. Yet Montesquieu proceeds with such breadth and depth of analysis that his work is an inspiring guide for the study of any or all political systems.

What Montesquieu describes or prescribes I call "natural government" because he assumes that conformance to nature is the highest ideal or value for government. In this assumption, he is in harmony with much of the intellectual thinking in France at the time and with a good deal of the thought in the West since then. He gives nature a sociological and psychological meaning, and he bases the legitimacy of government upon its relevance to the attitudes and behavior of the people who form the corresponding social system.

When we look to the whole scope of Montesquieu's political studies, we find that they contain much that is relevant to present day theories of social science and political system. The neglected books of *L'Esprit des Lois,* which often have been called digressive because they do not fit with the rationalistic doctrine of the separation of powers, actually investigate the social roots and environmental influences of government with greater breadth and depth than hardly any present day analysis. In fact, if the reader will go to the other portions of *L'Esprit des Lois* before he looks at the chapter on the English constitution, he is likely to find that Montesquieu's ideas about mixed government are considerably more sociological and psychological than any theory about the complete or partial separation of legislative, executive, and judicial powers.

Here, we will look first at other aspects of his political system so that when we reach his analysis of the British government we may have a better perspective on what he has in mind when he calls it the ideal constitution. The main points of our study will be Montesquieu's theories of human and social action; his separation of politics from commerce, religion, and civil interests; his comparative analyses of the political capabilities and responsibilities of the three classes of society; his ideas on assuring political liberty in respect of both the citizen and the constitution; and the theory of the structure and spirit of naturally mixed government.

We will start with his thoughts about man in society and these are much more explicit in *Les Lettres Persanes* than in *L'Esprit des Lois*. That early work may seem to be just so much spicy satire on Persian and Parisian manners, but it contains many serious inquiries into man's relations with God, the church, society, government, and man himself.

Notes

1. David Easton, *The Political System* (New York, 1953); *A Framework for Political Analysis* (Englewood Cliffs, N. J., 1965), and *A Systems Analysis of Political Life* (New York, 1965); David Easton (Ed.) *Varieties of Political Theory* (Englewood Cliffs, N. J., 1966); Gabriel A. Almond and G. Bingham Powell, Jr., *Comparative Politics — A Developmental Approach* (Boston, 1966) and H. V. Wiseman, *Political Systems — Some Sociological Approaches* (New York, 1966).

2. For instance, William Ebenstein, *Great Political Thinkers* (New York, 1951) 420-430, quotes only from *The Spirit of the Laws* and nothing from the sociological inquiries in Books IV-VII and Books XIV-XXIII, or from the final six books; and John Hallowell, *Main Currents in Modern Political Thought* (New York, 1948), 140-150, is even more limited. Other commentators limit themselves to the paragraphs on separation of powers, Leslie Lipson, *The Great Issues of Politics* (Englewood Cliffs, 1960), 299; Alpheus T. Mason and Richard H. Leach, *In Quest of Freedom* (Englewood Cliffs, 1959), and Alan P. Grimes, *American Political Thought* (New York, 1960), 106.

3. George Sabine, *A History of Political Theory* (New York, 1961, 3d Ed.) 551-60; Julius Stone, *The Province and Functions of Law* (Cambridge, Mass., 1961) 400-1; Howard Becker and Harry Elmer Barnes, *Social Thought from Lore to Science* (New York, 1961), II, 551.

4. William Blackstone, *Commentaries on the Law of England.* (London, 1811), I, 146; A. F. Pollard, *The Evolution of Parliament* (London, 1920), 235-9; C.M. Trevelyan, *History of England* (London, 1926), 511 fn.; Max Lerner (Ed.) *The Mind and Faith of Justice Holmes* (New York, 1954), 381.

5. Auguste Comte, *System of Positive Polity* (London, 1876), IV, 568-570.

6. Charles Morgan, *The Liberty of Thought and the Separation of Powers* (Oxford, 1948), 13.

7. Robert Shackleton, *Montesquieu A Critical Biography* (Oxford, 1961).

8. Werner Stark, *Montesquieu Pioneer in the Sociology of Knowledge* (London, 1960).

9. David Lowenthal, "Montesquieu" in Leo Strauss and Joseph Cropsey, *History of Political Philosophy* (Chicago, 1963), 485; and John Plamenatz, *Man and Society* (New York, 1963) I, 253-298.

Chapter I

The Natural Relations of Man in Society

Political theorists traditionally like to begin with questions about human nature, such as, whether man is good or bad, or rational or irrational, and what man ought to be. But Montesquieu gives no simple answers to such questions. For him, man is naturally alive with a variety of conflicting tendencies amid a host of confusing situations so that human life is a constant problem of making choices in face of inner and outer pressures. Accordingly, I will endeavor in this chapter to explain Montesquieu's ideas about the natural conflict in man's attitudes, about the natural contradiction of the human mind, and about the continuing struggle against the many forces which tend to alienate man from his natural inclinations.

The Natural Conflict of Human Attitudes

We can, without too much trouble, find in Montesquieu's works a number of statements that suggest a pessimistic view of mankind, but these may be merely aspects of a complex pattern of human nature. His best known remark on the character of man appears shortly before the famous analysis of the English constitution. There he declares that "constant experience shows us that every man invested with power is apt to abuse it."[1] Yet that potential tendency does not exclude a general trend of moderate behavior among the common lot of man. The remark concerns a person holding power, while an analysis of human nature logically should begin with a man who does not have the added element of political authority. We should consider whether the abuse springs from the power which convention has supplied or from the dispositions which nature itself has given.

The traditional device among political theorists for examining the character of man in the absence of political power has been the so-called state of nature, and Montesquieu uses it briefly in the second chapter of Book 1 of *L'Esprit des Lois*. But like other parts of Book I it is more of a formal prologue to conform to the established style of treatises on government than a substantive part of his undertaking, which really begins with Book II or even Book III. Moreover, in *Les Lettres Persanes* he scoffs at the theorists who ponder the origins of society (94).[2] If men did not form societies, he says, there would be need for reasons why they kept apart, but to explain why they associate in communities is absurd when they are born dependent upon other men. "The son comes into the world beside his father and stays there, and this is both the definition and the cause of society." There may be gaps in that argument, but the short account of a state of nature in the first book of *L'Esprit des Lois* includes an express attack upon the Hobbesian idea that man is naturally warlike.[3] In Montesquieu's account, man's first thoughts are of preservation and nourishment, but he does not seek these ends by fighting. Rather he avoids contact. At that time, man is impotent, fearful, and apprehensive, and he fancies himself not equal but inferior. He begins to associate with his fellow men when he sees that fear is reciprocal or mutual. Montesquieu identifies four stages of sociability. These are marked by the pleasure of an animal at being near another of his species, the attraction of the sexes, the advantage of uniting acquired knowledge, and the desire to live in society. But at this point in his account society takes a new or added meaning and causes men to lose their sense of weakness. Montesquieu declares that, when men enter the state of society, a condition of war arises between man and man and between nation and nation. Thus, the national societies suddenly appear in full force and number, heavily engaged in internal and external conflicts. Incidentally, Montesquieu's references to the interdependence of man in the early stages of association and to the emergence of war in the later periods have an interesting correspondence to Plato's descriptions of the rudimentary *polis* and the luxurious *polis* in the Republic.[4]

What we have then is a compound disposition. Montesquieu seems to say that men have a natural inclination to form societies, but that, when they have associated together, the society itself brings out aggressive tendencies. Yet he says little about why societies exist; he is much more interested in why they differ and how the conflicts within and among men can be alleviated without inappropriate coercion. Basically, he presupposes that men are in society by nature and not by contract or coercion and that man has both social and aggressive tendencies.

There is another remark, fairly well known, which taken alone might give a wrong impression of Montesquieu's ideas about the individual character of man. He observes in the work on the Romans that "men have had the same passions at all times."[5] But the context of the remark makes it applicable to only a certain kind of political conflict. We should not forget that Montesquieu had a legal training and that lawyers customarily use the language of universal principle while they are thinking only of particular situations. The context of Montesquieu's observation about the uniformity of passions is a comparision of the political strategy of Servius Tullius of Rome and Henry VII of England. Montesquieu is arguing that at a certain point in its history Rome was forced to change its government, and he fortifies his proposition by saying that modern history furnishes an example of what happened. Then, in line with his frequent practice of combining rationalistic and empirical support, he inserts the generalization that, while occasions differ, the causes of change are always alike because men have the same passions at all time. Next, he finds empirical verification in the similarity between Roman and modern history, and this is a specific bit of political strategy. He notes that just as Henry VII increased the power of the commons in order to degrade the lords, so Servius Tullius extended the privileges of the people in order to reduce the power of the senate. Hence the similarity of passions concerns the interaction of the three political classes of each society. The remark clearly has this limited context because the comparability of Roman and modern history is the subject of both the sentence preceding and the sentence following the generalization about common passions. Moreover, the whole discussion suggests that the passions which are most fundamental to Montesquieu are those which concern the political conflicts of the one, the few, and the many, and this assumes that each society has three such political classes. When we look into the varied analyses of *L'Esprit des Lois*, we will find that nothing is more common or more basic to the many parts of that work than the conflict of these three political classes.

Montesquieu's ideas about the natural conflict of human attitudes and relations come out dramatically in *Les Lettres Persanes*. That work presents two ways of life, viewed from a number of positions and described in varying terms. Now it is a conflict of sense and reason, then a choice of happiness or duty, another time a conflict of activity and indolence, or motion and restraint, and quite often the contrast is between natural behavior and artificial convention. The two ways of life provide the continuity and the characters of the work. The Persian visitors to Paris are at the same time undertaking foreign travel to gain wider knowledge and maintaining a steady flow of thoughts about the sensuous pleasures of their home life. One remarks at the start that they are leaving behind "the delights of a tranquil life" for the "the laborious search for wisdom." This is a choice for every man. Also, the two principal letter writers personify two sides of man. Usbek is somber and serious while Rica is gay and spirited. Usbek grieves that each day makes him more depressed in mind and body while "Rica enjoys perfect health; his strong constitution, youth, and natural cheerfulness render him superior to every affliction." Montesquieu may be reminding his countrymen that they should be happier and more spirited than the Persians because of their greater social intercourse, but, as the letters proceed, Rica increases his natural gaiety while the French seem to be losing theirs.

With its diversity of approach and indirectness of answer, *Les Lettres Persanes* provides no simple statement of Montesquieu's view of mankind, and it may even suggest that there is some merit in natural conflicts and contradictions. Montesquieu's general attitude is shown by a fragmentary comment which may not be incorporated into any full work: "It is well that there has been in the world some good and some bad; without that, one would be driven to leave this life."[6]

Not surprisingly, commentators look at the same material and give different verdicts. One of the best recent analyses of the *Lettres* finds that Montesquieu has a rather optimistic view, saying that the work concerns "those human societies which are grounded upon the principle that man as a rational creature has an innate sense of justice and natural goodness."[7] Since *L'Esprit des Lois* is patently less cynical than the earlier work, this comment may be further support for the idea that Montesquieu assumes that men generally have a substantial degree of reason, sense, and justice even though they may tend to abuse political power.

Biographers of Montesquieu, notably Robert Shackleton, Henri Barckhausen, and Joseph Dedieu,[8] do not portray him as pessimistic as Machiavelli, Hobbes, or even Burke, nor as optimistic as Rousseau, Comte, or Marx. Also, they deal less with his theory of man than with his position among his contemporaries. For instance, Shackleton finds that Montesquieu's "principal intellectual aim" in *Les Lettres Persanes* was to destroy prejudice, and also that he is in some degree a *philosophe* and a deist but with a belief in Christian ethics.[9] The consensus seems to be that Montesquieu was not a revolutionary in either religion or politics but was a reformer with a deliberate and circumspect viewpoint.

I have found that he combines acute perceptiveness with a careful choice of words and that he has good balance as well as broad interests. The difficulty of getting at his ideas arises largely, I believe, from the assumptions of contradiction in the human mind and of natural conflict in social behavior and from his unwillingness to make absolute choices in order that he may avoid logical extremes. His method of analysis is not satisfying to those who want ideological consistency and sharpness, and it frustrates those who want unqualified answers, simply stated. But his works are rich with the thousands of events that he draws upon to produce a vast mosaic that has greater and greater depth as you study it more and more.

Werner Stark, the social philosopher who has made the most exhaustive study of Montesquieu's epistemology, sees in Montesquieu a somewhat pessimistic view of man. His appraisal varies a bit as his analysis progresses.[10] At first, he emphasizes the statements of antisocial tendencies; then he notes the admittedly mixed character of Montesquieu's man; next, he recognizes that man is shown to practice sociability; and finally, he returns to the antisocial inclinations and asserts that while they may be latent at times, the social order never entirely subdues them. He draws upon Montesquieu's statements about man's self-interest, passion, pride, and natural malignity. Since Stark is more penetrating in his analysis of this matter than most commentators, I will examine his conclusions in more detail.

Montesquieu does say that man can be unjust, but he adds that "no one is gratuitously wicked" (83). Man does not do injustice for its own sake. There must be a determining cause, he says, and he is clear that the cause is self-interest. In part this is epistemological. Montesquieu explains that man sees his own interest more easily than he does the principles of justice. Stark also points out the remarks in the essay *De la Politique* that men act out of caprice or passion and that sometimes they simply act without our being able to say why.[11] But action that springs from passion or interest may or may not be bad, and there are places where Montesquieu points to its good effects. Again, such actions and their motivations may be bad only in excess.

Stark makes much of Montesquieu's remarks about pride, glory, and envy. *Les Lettres Persanes* says that we have a desire of glory that is as natural as the instinct of preservation (89). This is a manifestation of pride, and elsewhere Montesquieu observes that pride is usually the cause of all moral effects.[12] Also, he suggests that pride is a desire to be happier than our fellow men and that this trait involves envy, which may arise in part from an overestimate of the happiness of other men. Here Montesquieu may be worried about excesses. Too much pride and too much desire of glory may deceive a man about his own interest. As long as the feelings are natural, they may be unobjectionable; it is when they are artificially accentuated that they have evil consequences. Much of *Les Lettres Persanes* is a condemnation of the artificialities of man, society, religion, and politics.

Stark draws attention to the remark about "our natural malignity" which Montesquieu makes in his *Essai sur le Goût*. There he is talking about the elements of comedy and our pleasure in the dramatization of what we dislike in others. That *Essai* analyzes the pleasures of the soul or mind in respect of both the things of nature and the things of art. Montesquieu calls attention to the pleasures of order and of variety, and he asserts that the mind loves both symmetry and contrast. Still more, he attributes particular sentiments to a diversity of causes.[13] Rather than having a pessimistic view of man, the *Essai* recognizes much that is optimistic. Even more precisely, it shows that Montesquieu has no simple view of man, that he sees in human attitudes and behavior a great variety of beliefs and actions. It shows Montesquieu's love of observation and the great variety of human life.

Another of Stark's reasons for putting Montesquieu in the man-is-bad class is the description in *Les Lettres Persanes* of the misery of human condition. But Montesquieu does not consider this to be natural, and he stages a many sided attack on the artificialities which he thinks are the causes. This will be explained further in the next section but we may note here that he places a good deal of the

blame upon the pessimistic concept of man found in Christian theology, such as its effort to find consolation in the necessity of evil
and the idea that man is born miserable (61, 93). Clearly, Montesquieu does not accept the full measure of original sin. Also, while
he assumes the conflict of soul and body, he is a bit disturbed that
the human mind is a contradiction itself (33), and he strives repeatedly to help man out of the unhappy dilemma of social life. His
answer is to look less to reason and more to feeling. But this must
be taken in the context of eighteenth century France where both
the old and the new philosphy wanted man to be a strictly reasoning soul. For Montesquieu this would mean more and more restraint upon the senses and feelings that naturally make man active
and noble.

Montesquieu may be a bit deceiving to scholars of the eighteenth
century because he does not have the attitude toward sense, interest
or passion, which is deemed to be common among the intellectuals
of the French enlightenment. When Montesquieu calls a man a
being of sense or feeling, he does not mean that man lacks moral
propriety. In fact, he may assume that morality and sympathy are
in the senses and not in the calculations of reason. This comes out
quite dramatically in Usbek's letters on feminine manners. He admits that the French women appear to lack shame, but he insists
that they stop short of violating the conjugal vow. They all "bear in
their hearts a certain impression of virtue, naturally engraved,"
which education may weaken but cannot destroy. "Though they
may decline the external duties which modesty exacts; yet, when
about to take the last step, nature returns to their help" (26). Another dramatization of respect for natural capacities is the account
of a slave who rebels strenuously against being converted into a
eunuch for Usbek's harem (41-3). Likewise, Montesquieu prefers
those with natural modesty. "I have known some people to whom
virtue was so natural that they themselves were scarcely sensible to
it." They did "their duty without any constraint . . . carried to it as
by instinct." These "are the men I love, not those virtuous persons
who themselves seem so surprised" at being virtuous that they believe all others ought to be equally astonished (50).

The esteem of natural passion is evident also in the study of the
Romans. "There is nothing so powerful," he says, "as a republic in
which laws are observed not through fear, not through reason, but
through passion."[14] This was the case of Rome and Sparta and he

explains that through a passion of observance all the strength of a faction is joined to the wisdom of a good government.

There are occasional traces of utilitarianism among his ethical attitudes. The book on religious doctrine (XXIV) promptly looks to social consequences. Then his legal analyses anticipate phases of the sociological jurisprudence, penal reform, and utilitarian standards later expressed by Beccaria, Bentham, and Ehrlich.[15] Beccaria, in setting forth the principles of legislation that became part of Bentham's theory of reform, specifically acknowledges the contribution of Montesquieu.[16] Happiness may not be the only social goal in *L'Esprit des Lois,* and it may not be expressed with the mathematical possibilities found in Bentham, but stress upon social consequences and psychological impact is evident in the books on the judiciary, liberty in fact, and slavery (VI, XII, XV). In arguing that slavery is bad, he declares that it is not useful to either the master or the slave. Yet his explanation of this shows that he has not abandoned entirely the ethics of virtue and good will. He asserts that the slave does nothing through a motive of virtue and that unlimited authority causes the master to lose moral virtues.[17] What seems most fundamental is the attitude toward free will. Montesquieu says in effect that slavery is bad because it allows the slave no free will and the master too much.

Probably the most telling characterization of man in *Les Lettres Persanes* is in the analysis of justice and interest. Clearly justice is the highest value in that work and in what we know of Montesquieu's writings until he began preparations for *L'Esprit des Lois.* Its superior status reflects the way in which it is conceived. Montesquieu declares that justice "is always the same, whoever contemplates it, whether God, or an angel or, finally, man" (83). Even more, God must necessarily be just because otherwise "he would be the worst and most imperfect of all beings." He has no need for disregarding justice because he has no need of anything, in contrast to man who departs from justice out of need and interest. Yet man has a duty to be just, "even if there were no God, we ought to love justice." If we were free of the "yoke" of religion we would not be free of that of justice. Montesquieu's definition of justice to be *"un rapport de convenance* actually existing between two things" may seem to make justice relative but I believe that it precludes subjectivism as well as abstract universalism and permits the development of sociological objectivity.

Yet, Montesquieu recognizes a natural tendency to be just in some definite even though limited degree. On one hand, he asserts that justice is eternal and independent of human conventions, and he finds solace in that idea. If justice were dependent upon human compacts, he says, this would be a "terrible truth" which should be concealed from ourselves because we are surrounded by men stronger than we are, who could injure us in many different ways, usually with impunity. "What a satisfaction to us to know that there is in the heart of all these men, *un principe interieur* which fights in our favor." Without this, he adds, we should be in continual fear, we should pass by men as by lions, and we should never be assured for one moment of our goods, honor, and life (83). On the other hand, Montesquieu acknowledges that men, even without the added factor of political power, do act at times in an unjust manner. In the first chapter of *L'Esprit des Lois* he reiterates the abstract concept of justice, calling it "relations of possible justice" among "intelligent individuals," but he promptly adds that neither this invariable law nor those of the divine or the physical worlds will keep man from committing error. For this reason, human laws and inferentially worldly sanctions are needed to assist in maintaining order. Through this opening he presents the whole remaining part of that work.

Les Lettres Persanes gives two reasons for man's acts of injustice. One is that men do not always perceive the relations of justice and the other is that, when they do see them, they prefer their own interest, which they see much better. In another metaphor, he says that justice may raise its voice, but it scarcely can make itself heard in "the tumult of the passions" (83). Yet man does not do injustice without a reason and this is always *"une raison d'interet."* Unlike God, man has a motive to be unjust; he explains, man is not self-sufficient and needs many things. Thus, he assumes that man is caught between a sense of justice and a sense of interest. The latter may often be the stronger, but this depends, presumably, upon the situation so that man is still faced with conflicting dispositions.

I believe that Montesquieu's remark that "interest is the greatest monarch on earth" (106) is an example of his tendency to exaggerate when he is attacking contemporary political opponents. His statement about the monarchy of interest may be directed at Voltaire, d'Argenson, and other advocates of the theory of enlightened absolutism,[18] as well as being a justification of human laws gener-

ally. Where Voltaire argues that absolutism is not necessarily despotic, Montesquieu holds in effect that since it may be, there is need
for limitation and counteraction. Also, I believe, he applies the idea
that sense interest may be stronger than rational virtue to aristocratic and democratic power groups as well as to the monarch. This
need not mean interest is their only motive, only that they may
need to be mutually restrained by such means as the tripartite
parliament.

How Montesquieu reconciles man's natural attitudes toward both
interest and virtue or justice is dramatized in the captivating story
of the Troglodytes, to which he devotes five letters (10-14). This
arises when Usbek is asked "whether the happiness of mankind consists in pleasure and sensual gratification or in the exercise of virtue." He reponds with the fable of the Troglodytes. The ancient
members of this Arabian tribe resembled beasts more than men.
Brutal and ferocious, with no principle of equity, they killed their
king, then elected magistrates and in due course massacred them.
Next, consulting "their own savageness," each one agreed to submit
to no person and to "follow his own interest without any attention
to that of others." Then came poor crops, disputes, and disease, and
they "were destroyed by their own wickedness and fell victims of
their own injustice."

Only two families escaped. They were headed by "two very extraordinary men" who were humane, knew justice, and loved virtue. They worked together for mutual benefit, had abundant crops,
"led a life of peace and happiness," and trained their children in
the ways of virtue. They impressed upon the children "that the interest of individuals was always to be found in that of the community, and that to attempt to seek it separately was to destroy it."
Also, they asserted that virtue should not be considered either burdensome nor painful and "that doing justice to others is acting
charitably to ourselves" (12). They lived a delightful rural life with
nature supplying their desires as well as filling their needs. Their
prosperity was the envy of nearby barbaric tribes, who soon attacked them. Peace overtures failed, and a long seige was withstood.
Many Troglodytes were killed, but each died for a double cause:
not only to avenge some particular death but also for the common
interest. Eventually, their virtue triumphed over barbaric injustice.
But despite this victory, the Troglodytes decided to leave their lea-
derless condition and choose a king.

The new king tells them why they gave up their self-rule. He explains, "your virtue begins to be too heavy for you." Without a head, "you are constrained to be virtuous in spite of yourselves," otherwise "you cannot subsist, but must sink into the miseries of your ancestors." Self-rule "seems too hard a yoke for you; you like better to be subject to a king, and to obey laws less rigid than your morals." The idea that the laws of a prince may be less rigorous than the self-restraint needed for pure democracy may enter into Montesquieu's theory of mixed government. Also, we may find here his assumption that people are interested primarily in economic activity and well-being. The king explains that by accepting his rule, "you know, that then you may gratify your ambition, gain riches, and languish in slothful luxury, and, provided you avoid falling into great crimes, you will have no want of virtue" (14).

The story of the Troglodytes may be interpreted in a number of ways, but in any approach it does seem to show two sides of man. On the one hand, there is in human nature an element of justice and virtue, so that man finds pleasure and satisfaction in having regard for the common interest. On the other hand, there is in human nature an element of competition and self-interest so that man finds great difficulty in imposing restraints upon himself and is happier when a king sets reasonable limits upon social behavior. The fable is an attack upon the Hobbesian concept of man, but it is also a criticism of the idea of a purely virtuous man. Montesquieu seems to dislike either polar position. Man is not so purely virtuous that he does not need some restraining force. While he has the reason to be his own guide, he tires of using it except for a few large issues, and eventually he prefers to be directed in what is rational for living in society.

Stark says that the story of the Troglodytes has an unhappy ending, apparently because they decide to live more by their senses than by their reason.[19] Stark takes solace in their earlier achievement of governing themselves because this apparently means to him that they have the capacity for rational living. But I think that this misses the main point of the story and its possible connection with *L'Esprit des Lois*. The Troglodytes believe that they will be happier under a ruler who governs by reasonable laws than in trying to live under their own restraint, and this is what Montesquieu is trying to tell the French people in both *Les Lettres Persanes* and the later work. Montesquieu seems to admire the sense driven activity

of a people who do not burden themselves with all the petty restraints of rational virtue. He believes that people should freely devote themselves to economic pursuits which will bring them greater
rewards and happiness. He associates rational virtue with excessive
restraints upon natural activity, and he seeks to lessen the burden
of man's constraint by encouraging the people to act more in response to their feelings and interests. Montesquieu may be suggesting that people prefer to live in an economically open monarchy
under law rather than in an absolute democracy under their own
virtue.

The attitude toward monarchy and democracy in the story of the
Troglodytes should be joined with Montesquieu's comments upon
these forms of government in the later part of *Les Lettres Persanes*
(102). There he puts European rulers into three groups: the emperor; the kings of France, Spain, and England; and the princes of
Germany and Italy. Then he observes that most European governments are called monarchies but doubts "whether there ever was
one truly so" or that one could subsist long without being
corrupted. "It is a state of violence, that always degenerates into
despotism or into a republic." He means a democratic republic because he adds that "power can never be equally divided between
the people and the prince." He says that "the balance is too difficult to be preserved" and when power increases on one side it must
decrease on the other, but, he concludes, "the balance is generally
in favor of the prince, who is at the head of the armies." The idea
of the prince and the people being in an irreconcilable conflict re-
minds one of the observation in Plato's *Laws* that monarchy and
democracy are the two mother forms of government and that to
have liberty, friendship, and wisdom, you must have some of
both.[20] *Les Lettres Persanes* does not suggest such a solution by
mixture; it seems directed at changing individual attitudes rather
than reforming official institutions. Even the latter day Troglodytes
give up self-rule for the laws of a prince. But one question to be
considered in making our way through *L'Esprit des Lois* is whether
Montesquieu there is trying to solve this dilemma by means of both
institutional arrangements and sociological circumspection.

The Contradictions of the Human Mind

The basic epistemological dilemma between the relativity of sense
knowledge and the inaccessibility of rational absolutes appears with
force in *Les Lettres Persanes*. The problem is first considered when

Usbek, one of the Persian visitors at Paris, is puzzled by the religious rules on the eating of pork, the touching of corpses, and the washing of bodies (17). He says that he cannot conceive how any inherent quality can render these things either pure or impure. "Dirt appears filthy to us; yet in itself it is no more so than gold or diamonds." He reasons that, since we regard things to be unclean or impure only because they are naturally repugnant to us, the senses ought to be the sole judges of purity or impurity. But, he argues, things do not affect all men the same way and what gives an agreeable sensation to some may disgust others. He concludes that our senses here cannot serve as a rule unless each one may decide according to his own fancy. So he writes to the divine mollah, Mohammed Ali, asking whether this point of view would not upset the distinctions and fundamental points of the religious law. The answer of the divine mollah invokes "the traditions of the doctors . . . that pure foundation of all intelligence" (18). He calls Usbek an unhappy man, encumbered by worldly interests, with no eye for heavenly things. Usbek, he says, cannot see the reason for the impurity of certain things because he does not know "what has passed between God, the angels and men" and because he has not read the history of eternity and knows only a small portion of the divine library. In other words, eternal truth is largely beyond the ordinary man's reason, and Montesquieu leaves us with the dilemma of absolute knowledge being unknowable to most men and knowable sense experience being relative in character.

Thus an effort to pin down Montesquieu's theory of knowledge may be no more successful than the attempts to find a single ethical position. The whole matter may be epitomized by the remark in *Les Lettres Persanes* that "the mind of man is a contradiction to itself" (33). At the time Usbek is telling how Christian princes, who are permitted to drink wine, are not wronged by it, while oriental chieftains, who are forbidden the usage, drink to a degrading excess. But, as noted in the previous section, man appears to be a paradox in many situations. Montesquieu's whole life must have been a series of struggles in which he tries to solve the great and simple dilemmas of the human intellect. He repeatedly confronts himself with the polar alternatives familiar to philosophers, but he never quite makes the final choice between the one or the other. Rather, he tries to find some way of reconciling or combining the two. The earlier and intermediate works tend to present or to dramatize the issues and to view them more rationalistically than empirically while *L'Esprit des Lois* is most concerned with endeavoring to find solutions of an operational, sociological and psychological character.

The most penetrating analysis yet made of Montesquieu's epistemology gives no simple answers. Professor Stark weighs many factors before reaching his conclusions and then he recognizes that there are contrary opinions. He calls *L'Esprit des Lois* "a book of description, not of reasoning" and he finds Montesquieu to be more empirical than Locke. At that point, Stark is talking about Locke's political philosophy and the contractual origin of society, and he argues that "Montesquieu omits this original contract which is beyond the possibility of observation." I would say that *L'Esprit des Lois* is fundamentally prescriptive because, at crucial points in developing a political system, Montesquieu shapes the presentation into an attack upon contemporary antagonists, particularly those who advocate absolute sovereignty and the alliance of church and state in France. It seems to me that Stark virtually admits the prescriptive character of *L'Esprit des Lois* when he says that Montesquieu does not allow the facts to have all their own way on certain occasions.[21]

What makes *L'Esprit des Lois* prescriptive rather than normative and yet more objective than subjective, in my opinion, is its implicit proposition that, if France wants a government that conforms to the reason in nature, then this is what is required. Montesquieu's recommendation is not the product of mere introspection but is very much the result of observing the physical, moral, and cultural environment and examining the way in which governmental action is related to multiplicity of forces which affect social behavior. Montesquieu looked at the French scene with considerable detachment. He was not a participant in the circles of Versailles, and he even withdrew from the salons of Paris.[22] At Bordeaux and at the Chateau de la Brede, he had a provincial vantage point from which to view the French monarchy. Also, he was a participant in the increasing commerce of that area, and he had a stake in the new economic activity. Bordeaux looks out more than in, and the vineyards of the Brede estate drew Montesquieu into the ways of trade. The book on taxes gives a detailed analysis of an English import tax upon wine, and his analysis of economic matters goes far beyond his personal interests. *L'Esprit des Lois* devotes an uncommonly large portion of its attention to such matters, and Montesquieu seems to have more sympathy for the wealthy newcomer to the nobility than for the decadent hanger-ons who dissipated all but their titles.

Montesquieu's whole analysis of government may be much more objective than appears on the face of *L'Esprit des Lois*. There is a basic distinction between the process of research and that of writing. He may include in the final work only illustrations that support his propositions, but this does not mean that he disregarded other examples or that he began his research with these propositions. He may have undertaken considerable study before drawing the generalizations which he presents and supports in *L'Esprit des Lois*. His research may have considered a much broader and even more diversified body of empirical data than appears in his published works.

The manner of prescribing varies, and it is usually indirect. One of his favorite ways of showing a preference is to assert that an idea conforms to reason, is conducive to liberty or moderation, or corresponds to nature or the nature of things. Likewise, negative prescriptions may take the form of warnings of danger to liberty or of inappropriateness to the nature of things. Another means of making prescriptions involves the selection of historical instances. What is preferred is shown to be an aspect of the government of classical Athens, the Roman Republic, the ancient Germans newly arrived in France, or the contemporary government of England. On the other hand, condemnation is expressed by using examples from China, Persia, or Turkey. In both positive and negative situations, Montesquieu is drawing upon the prejudices of his French readers; his likes and dislikes toward these countries are theirs. But the effect is to pass judgment upon aspects of the prevailing French government. Likewise, in respect of religion, the unwanted practices of the Catholic church at Rome or in France are described to be elements of Mohammedanism. The indirection is a way of circumventing the censor, but it may also make the prescription more appealing to his fellow Frenchmen. Montesquieu is definite and even dogmatic about what he dislikes but rather indefinite and varying about what he prefers in its place. This presents problems of interpretation because what he condemns may not be a good guide to what he favors. For instance, his warning against concentration of powers does not tell the essential aspects of his ideas about distributing powers.

While *L'Esprit des Lois* is aimed primarily at France, it is so comprehensive and fundamental in its method that it provides a means of analyzing the political system of many, if not all, national societies, and of ascertaining how any particular government may be brought into relationship with its physical, moral, and cultural environment. The prescriptive aspects of *L'Esprit des Lois* do not make it a subjective undertaking because Montesquieu supports with empirical illustration or even verification the means by which to determine what is natural for France. He does not prescribe a scheme or rule by laying down a universal value, such as one that monarchy is the best type of political system, but rather he sets forth the diverse ways in which any type of government should relate to the sociological and psychological situation in which it exists.

Professor Stark reconciles some of the differences among Montesquieu's methods with the proposition that a turn from rationalism to realism occurred with the European and English travels during 1728 — 1731. Logically, travels have this effect, particularly upon one who is as sympathetic to observation as Montesquieu clearly was. Stark asserts that Montesquieu was more Cartesian in his youth than in his later years, pointing out that there are tendencies toward rationalism in general, toward determinism, and toward sociological mechanism in the earlier writings which are less apparent in the later works. Quite probably Montesquieu did undergo changes of this sort. But even in his youth he had a deep interest in empirical methods of thought and experimental verification. He became a member of the Academy of Bordeaux in 1716 and entered into discussions of natural history. He engaged in experiments on plants and animals during at least 1718, and in the next three years, 1718 to 1721, he wrote discourses on the causes of echo, the functions of the renal glands, some aspects of the physical history of the earth, and certain qualities of bodies.[23]

Moreover, I believe that the principal change in his attitude toward rationalism and sociological empiricism may have occurred during 1725. In that year he started to write a treatise on duties which would give a comprehensive answer to ethical problems.[24] Inspired by Cicero and perhaps Pufendorf, the project was intended to make justice the key to ethical duty. But the premise may have proved inadequate to the problem. At least he abandoned it, and all that remains is a digest of thirteen chapters.

This apparent disappointment in a metaphysical venture may

have caused Montesquieu to think more about actual social and political relations. If a change of heart or mind did not occur then, it
quite likely did a year or two later when he began his travels to
Italy, Hungary, England, and other countries. A change did take
place, and his writings of the 1730's as well as *L'Esprit des Lois* are
more realistic and less rationalistic than the works of the
mid-1720's. In brief, the principles of speculative justice give way to
observations of sociological and psychological forces.

Whether or not Montesquieu is a rationalist involves, of course,
the many meanings of "reason." At times, reason is associated with
virtue and stands for some kind of deliberate restraint, but Montesquieu shows a dislike of rational virtue when it hinders the natural
inclinations and happiness of the French. Moreover, when he is
engaged in sociological inquiries, he makes "reason" the mental
tool by which particular experiences are brought into some kind of
order rather than a source of knowledge or a moral principle. His
ethics sometimes is rationalistic but more often sensationalist. In
Les Lettres Persanes he asserts that "There are some certain truths,
of which it is not sufficient to be persuaded, but men must be made
even to feel them"; and these include "moral truths" (11). In another letter, on the training of a daughter, he remarks, "Is all to be
expected from the force of reason and nothing from the sweetness
of custom?" (62) But note that he requires both persuasion and
feeling and both reason and custom. In the philosophical climate of
the time, sense gains by being treated equal to reason. Thus, Montesquieu is in part a pioneer in the trend toward romanticism even
though he is far from a complete or even an acknowledged romanti-
cist. He shows an undercurrent of sympathy for feeling, instinct,
sense, and even passion a few times. Also, his rationalism is largely
instrumental, negative, or formal. When he values reason, he may
be questioning the dogmas and faith of divine right rather than
placing rationalism above empiricism. Thus, reason may stand for
the inner principles of natural order which it helps to ascertain, so
that even when Montesquieu talks about reason he may be giving
priority to the generalizations which bring man into closer
harmony with his physical and cultural environment.

"Nature," even more than "reason," is a multiple-meaning word
which has been a favorite of Western philosophers and historians.
For political theorists it most often means something between the
supernatural and the conventional. Montesquieu uses it this way in
some situations. But, when he speaks of conformance to nature or

the nature of things, he probably means the whole sociological and psychological environment in so far as it is relevant to the matter at hand. He assumes, as did many scholarly Frenchmen of his time, that nature is a universe of particulars and that valid generalizations are to be found and supported by applying reason to the diverse phenomena. He declares in the preface to *L'Esprit des Lois* that he has drawn his principles, not from his prejudices, but from "the nature of things," and the whole of his work may demonstrate what this embraces. The phrase is used in diverse situations, and its particular meaning may depend upon the context. The first sentence of *L'Esprit des Lois* defines laws in general to be "the necessary relations arising from the nature of things," and the ensuing discussions concern the essence of universal realms. Later in the work "the nature of things" is made a standard of political validity or a basis of legitimacy. This is the case in the analysis of the spirit of democracies in Book III. Then, in Book XV, slavery is said to be rightful only when it originates in "the nature of things," and this is satisfied by only two conditions: a very hot climate and a very despotic government. Likewise, the idea of "the nature of things" may be a key to historical movement, as Montesquieu remarks about Charles XII. "The casualites of fortune are easily repaired; but who can be guarded against events that incessantly arise from the nature of things?"[25] Whatever the context, the term seems to stand for the set of particulars that is empirically relevant to the idea under verification. *L'Esprit des Lois* and even *Les Lettres Persanes* are in some ways like law case books which set forth many separate opinions about particular cases. There are gaps and uncertainties because the general pattern is in continual evolvement.

The way in which Montesquieu uses several methods to develop and support general principles is evident in his explanatory statements in the Preface to *L'Esprit des Lois*. His declaration that he "laid down the first principles" and "found that the particular cases follow naturally from them" suggests both intuitive conception and empirical verification. Then the statement that every law is connected with another or depends upon a more general one indicates a test of coherence as well as a deductive method. Next, his assertion that he drew his principles from the nature of things could refer to an inductive method. Also, there is emphasis upon empirical inquiry and testing in the declaration that the "more we enter into particulars, the more we shall perceive the certainty of the principles on which they are founded." Moreover, the empirical data that he examined may have been much more extensive than that which appears in *L'Esprit des Lois* because he says that he does not mention all of the particulars for fear of fatiguing the reader. Thus, what may seem like hand-picked examples to support given ideas may come from a larger collection which was brought together without much preconception and which was found in its entirety to support the propositions for which he gives only one or two illustrations in the finished work.

While a number of methods appears throughout his work, Montesquieu seems in general to favor an empirical method of some type and to rely mostly upon a broad array of observable data even though he supplements this with reasoning from general accepted values in order to gain greater acceptability.

The combination of rationalistic and empirical methods appears in his definitions of law in the third chapter of Book I. Here he says that law in general is "human reason" and that political and civil laws of a nation "ought to be only the particular cases in which human reason is applied." This suggests that positive law is deduced from general principles, such as those of classical natural law. But, then, the definition of the spirit of laws declares in effect that laws should be related to various objects, most of which are largely sociological in character. This would seem to require deriving laws from factual situations or forming them for certain consequences. In either event, it means that laws should be made relevant to the empirical environment as well as deduced from reason. This may seem to be inconsistent, but more likely Montesquieu is setting up joint standards. Like the bicameral legislature, which requires approval of both houses for positive action, so the joint standards of law require the satisfaction of both sets of values. Political legislation should not offend human reason, and at the same time it should not be indifferent to the environment.

Montesquieu seems to have conflicting attitudes toward mathematical models. *Les Lettres Persanes* scoffs at the followers of Descartes who reduce everything to geometrical or arithmetical patterns. Usbek ridicules those who explain the mystery of "divine architecture" by a few simple mechanical terms, those who would reduce all knowledge to five or six truths, and those who see in the Pont-Neuf, or a superb chateau, or a magnificent garden, only a few mathematical dimensions (97, 128, 135, 145). These remarks may be satire on Descartes' first laws of motion and the contemporary stress upon mathematical rules.[26] But, while Montesquieu generally is antagonistic to mathematical formalism or polar alternatives and instead prefers multiple observations, he does use simple mathematical models in some situations. A number of times he expresses economic propositions as mathematical variables, and he makes national defense largely a matter of geometry and geography. He also uses simple mathematical patterns in crucial aspects of his political analysis. For instance, he says that there are an infinite variety of governments, but he sets forth a simple typology of governments. The comparative analysis in Books II — X is based largely upon three or four types, and later he deals largely with only two kinds, variously identified.

Then, the English constitution is reduced to the simple pattern of three parliamentary elements with express disregard for whether it actually gives its potential of liberty. Yet empirical connection is not entirely lost because the trichotomy of parliament matches the trichotomy of classes which he finds in the national society; and the three parts of both parliament and society are not inert geometric objects but groups of people in mutual conflict. The model may be as much organic as mechanistic, but in general Montesquieu does not follow either analogy for long. Largely, his analysis of political life is sociological and psychological. The simple geometrical patterns seem to appear only when he is deep in political antagonism. The typology of governments is probably an indirect attack upon Voltaire, d'Argenson, and others who preferred absolute monarchy.[27] They argued that absolutism is not necessarily despotic and could be enlightened, but Montesquieu assumes that absolutism is apt to be despotic. He feels so strongly on this point that, when he discusses the corruption of the special spirit of governments in Book VIII, he says the absolutism of the few and that of the many is despotic even though he had defined despotism to be rule by one. Then, the tripartite parliament is another way of attacking the absolutism of the French monarchy and at the same time avoiding the separate recognition which the clergy had in the old French Estates-General.

Montesquieu is more interested in particulars than he is in universals, but he reduces the infinity of particulars to a more or less manageable number of categories. This is done in various ways and the result is a few score of second, third, and fourth level generalizations. Some of these general types are neatly grouped and identified, while others are in varying stages of disorder and disguise.

Nations are loosely classified for many of the analyses in *L'Esprit des Lois,* and the criteria for identifying the general types include some qualities of a nonpolitical character. These qualities embrace physical factors, particularly the climate, the location, size, type of terrain, and altitude. In Book XVIII nations are classified by the principal types of occupation. Montesquieu makes a distinction between savage and barbarous nations, the former being generally hunters and the latter herdsmen or shepherds. Also, he finds that whether or not a people cultivate the land may affect its political qualities and tendencies. Again, the volume of laws is said to vary with the way in which a nation procures its subsistence. In this last analysis, Montesquieu identifies four types of national occupation: hunting, pastoral, cultivation of land, and trading.[28]

The way in which a national society divides into classes is probably the most important categorization in *L'Esprit des Lois.* Certainly, it is the most persistent and most pervasive. It appears at the start of Book II and reappears again and again and has its most penetrating analysis in the final two books of the work. Primarily, there are three classes, often referred to as the monarch, the nobility, and the people. These classes separately are the bases of three types of government, and jointly they are the basis of the tripartite parliament which Montesquieu calls the fundamental constitution. Subdivisions of the aristocracy and of the nonprivileged people enter into Montesquieu's political analysis. The distinction between the social and the professional nobility is implicit at many points, and at least once he expressly recognizes the difference between the nobility of the robe and that of the sword.[29] The people generally form an egalitarian basis of democracy, and Montesquieu also asserts that equality is necessary in the commercial classes; but he recognizes that there may be two kinds of poverty classes which need special consideration.[30]

Variations in the degree of generalization appear in Montesquieu's identification of the forces at work within a society. The *Essai sur les Causes* reduces all forces to two categories which it calls physical and moral. The study of the greatness and decline of the Romans, which is expressly a consideration of causes, sometimes reduces the forces to a single spirit, other times puts them in two categories, but, for a good deal of the time, leaves them innumerable and indefinite. The works of the intermediate period result in the doctrine that each nation has a general spirit arising from five, six, or seven general causes. Then, the definition of the spirit of the laws in the final work points out nearly a score of law-related objects. Yet all of these classifications deal with much the same kind of phenomena, whether they are categorized in two, six, or twenty types. The rather interchangeable use of "cause" and "relation" helps to explain the meaning of each. Causes may be close to correlations, and relations may include an element of motivating action. In both, there is an evident factor of interaction or mutual influence.

The way in which Montesquieu classifies government in relation to the activities of a society is illustrated by his comments upon the capitularies or decrees issued during the second dynasty of the French monarchy. He observes that some of those decrees related to "political government, others to economical, most of them to ecclesiastical polity, and some few to civil government."[31] Here are four kinds of government based upon different aspects of the society. This is not applied expressly in *L'Esprit des Lois*, but the classification underlies much of the work. The manner in which Montesquieu separates the political, economic, religious, and civil orders will be discussed in Chapter III. His observations that the capitularies of the ninth century dealt with four types of order shows how he draws upon the pre-feudal history of France for principles which are quite modern in their tendency to increase the particularization and the secularization of government. Governmental functions are divided in other ways at different places in *L'Esprit des Lois*. The best known division is that among legislative, executive, and judicial processes, but even more fundamental is the implicit division between control and action. Control includes the electoral and representative functions as well as legislation and oversight. Action includes executive, administrative, and judicial functions and subdivisions of these. This last includes the several functions of the nobility of the robe which had been institutionalized in the *Parlements* of Paris and provincial cities.[32] The various parcels of authority over control and action are allocated among social and professional groups on a joint and a separate basis respectively.

The particularization of governing authority and practice reflects in part the differentiation of positive law. Montesquieu not only puts divine and natural law into the background, but he also divides human or positive law into a number of distinct realms. At first, he says that man-made laws consist of religious, moral, political, and civil laws, but he says little about the religious and moral types until Books XXIV — XXVI. Political and civil laws receive much attention, and with the law of nations they provide one basis for separating the authority of a government. This trichotomy appears at the start of the chapter on the English constitution. Political laws and the law of nations are usually distinct.[33] The civil legal realm often includes laws on domestic relations and economic regulation, but at times it may mean only laws concerning private property and the security and privileges of the person. When Montesquieu makes a distinction between the civil order and the economic one, the former concerns mostly property and personal relations while the economic realm deals with matters of commerce and money. When he discusses the administration and adjudication of criminal laws, he looks separately at private and public crimes (Books VI and XII). Then the analysis of servitude is divided into civil, domestic, and political realms in Books XV — XVII.

His presuppositions about the diversity of law and social order may reflect current intellectual tendencies, such as described by Ernst Cassirer in his study of the Enlightenment. Among these is the idea that nature "implies the individuality, the independence, and the particularity of objects" and "signifies the integration of all parts into one all-inclusive whole of activity and life."[34] Montesquieu also reflects, I believe, both of what Cassirer calls an attempt to merge the intellectual sciences and the physical ones and the shift of direction from looking beyond nature to inquiring into nature itself for the secret laws of mankind.[35] Montesquieu may not consider reason to be the sole means of knowing or believing, but he gives reason the necessary instrumental role of generalizing and classifying the particulars of nature for the processes of explanation and verification.

There is one aspect of natural order and action to which Montesquieu gives special attention. This is the idea that an object acquires its character from both its intrinsic and its extrinsic relations even when they may conflict. Plato remarks at one point in the *Republic* that a political society has inner and outer relations,[36] but he does not develop the thought in an express manner. Likewise, other leading political theorists have given it little more than implicit recognition. Montesquieu sets it out expressly and then works it into his theory of socially responsible government. His interest in the idea seems to have developed during his intermediate period or perhaps during the early preparation for *L'Esprit des Lois*.[37] The most explicit statement is in the *Essai sur les Causes*. That declares that every being has two values: an intrinsic one and a value of opinion.[38] The immediate subject is education, and the *Essai* asserts that each man has a particular education which he receives from his family and other immediate associates and a general education which he receives from the external society. In *L'Esprit des Lois,* the doctrine of dual meaning appears at crucial points. It says that political liberty consists in "security, or, at least in the opinion we enjoy of security" and that tyranny is of two sorts, one arising from oppression and the other "seated in opinion."[39] Opinion definitely suggests external relations and particularly those with other persons. Montesquieu probably considers a conflict of internal and external factors to be natural and even socially useful as long as one force does not restrain the other in an unnatural or unsociable degree.

Montesquieu's assumption of relational pluralism in any universe or realm is suggested by his remark in the preface to *L'Esprit des Lois* that "many truths will not appear till we have seen the chain which connects them with others." Aside from making truth plural, this indicates that the validity of an idea depends less upon conformance to a single superior truth than upon the interdependent harmony of the community of ideas or truths in which it exists.

The proposition that the essence of structural form and social behavior is the relation of diverse things to each other is one idea that seems to have remained with Montesquieu throughout his whole career of authorship. *Les Lettres Persanes* defines justice to be "the proper relationship really existing between two things" (83). *Le Traité des Devoirs* describe justice to be a general relation while other virtues are particular relations. *L'Esprit des Lois* defines both laws and the spirit of the laws to be types of relations.[40]

With all his delight in the plurality and diversity of objects, Montesquieu says that he is more interested in the order of things than in the things themselves. This is declared halfway through *L'Esprit des Lois,* but it is stated even more pointedly in the earlier *Essai sur les Causes.* There he observes that education consists in giving us ideas and "good education in putting them in proportion." He adds for emphasis that lack of harmony may mean stupidity or even folly.[41] The plurality and variety may be the basis of orderly arrangement. As Professor Stark points out "this very diversity of functions and interests and preoccupations is the guarantee of ultimate harmony."[42] If the multiplicity of objects and elements does not assure harmony, at least it is a helpful condition. When there are more units and elements to combine, the probability of an acceptable arrangement increases. The breaking down of issues also reduces antagonisms and allows more ways of balancing interests.

The type of order is not clear. Montesquieu is not consistently metaphysical, organic, or atomistic. In *L'Esprit des Lois* he gives little express recognition to the metaphysical existence of a complete whole or universe. The first chapter declares that there is a prime reason and invariable laws in the divine, physical, and intelligent worlds. But he promptly asserts that these are not adequate to keep man in proper order and must be supplemented by human laws. This is what *L'Esprit des Lois* is all about. His concept of social relations also appears to grow. His description of primitive or early society might be interpreted to be atomistic, but such an order does not remain long. Society is quickly assumed to consist of different classes, and, while he sometimes urges equality within one or more of the classes, he never departs from the idea that society is stratified. One commentator has suggested that the confusion of *L'Esprit des Lois* arises from the attempt to describe an apprehension that is essentially organic with methods of the physical and mechanical sciences.[43] He points out that the methods of the biological sciences had not been much developed at the time. But I would say that Montesquieu probably would not have been satisfied to employ merely biological methods. I believe that he was seeking something more appropriate to the social sciences and with his ideas of mixed society as well as mixed government, neither the physical sciences nor the biological sciences alone could furnish an appropriate method. Moreover, Montesquieu's idea of society is not organic in a full sense. He is much concerned with the various parts, and he has less interest in the character of the whole as a single entity. Even the relations of the parts to the whole are less meaningful to him than the relations of the parts to each other. The character of a part is often determined more by its relation with other parts than by its relations to the whole unit. These tendencies would seem to make the organic analogy rather inappropriate, and the term "relational pluralism" is suggested to identify Montesquieu's idea of structure and operation.

L'Esprit des Lois is in many respects a transitional work bridging metaphysical and sociological attitudes toward the analysis of political systems and not surprisingly, it uses old terms in new and varying ways. Such traditional words as monarchy, aristocracy, and democracy receive several meanings in the course of the volume, and key terms of theoretical analysis, such as nature, reason, cause, relation, principle and spirit have some applications which are not common at the present time and differ even from many earlier writings. Montesquieu is similar to most theorists who seek changes in that he casts new ideas in traditional language to make them more acceptable. Also he tends to be journalistic, adopting contrasting terms, when what he has in mind is more complex, and using absolute terminology, when his thought is only relative. His tendency to be dogmatic about what he dislikes also makes for difficulties in interpretation. Also, Montesquieu, like many Western political commentators, may describe in legal terms what is merely expedient, prudent, or political. Likewise, he uses indirect means of expression to avoid censorship.

Montesquieu's view on natural movement also may be transitional. Commentators differ on his theory,[44] perhaps because his statements are mostly observational. He sees, not simple mechanistic motion, but conflict and struggle even in the physical world, and, when he considers in turn matter, plants, animals and men, he finds less and less invariability.[45]

The relations which Montesquieu assumes to constitute the basic elements of a universe or realm are essentially channels of action and reaction. Throughout his writings there is an emphasis upon uneasy motion and the need for man to be in an active struggle. Invariable laws of motion may exist, but they allow room for a substantial degree of accident, free will, conflict, and change. *Les Lettres Persanes* asserts that the earth "suffers an internal and perpetual conflict among her principles; the sea and land seem to be at eternal war; each instant produces new conjunctions" (113). Thus, the analysis of the physical realm focuses upon the plurality of elements, their diversity, their conflict, and the capacity of the struggle to produce changes. Likewise in *L'Esprit des Lois*, the essential factors of plurality, diversity and interaction stand out in his few remarks about the physical realm. The first chapter of that work acknowledges that the world is "formed by the motion of matter," subject to rules which are "a constantly established relation." He declares further that between one moving body and another, "the motion is received, increased, diminished, or lost according to the relations of the quantity of matter and velocity." In conclusion, he adds that "each diversity is uniformity, and each change is constancy." The mind of man also involves the motion of struggle. *Les Lettres* observes that "the human mind is contradiction itself" (33) and the study of the Romans declares that "there is a strange inconsistency in the mind of man."[46] Again, one of the *Pensées* says that "what causes most of the contradictions of man is that *la raison physique* and *la raison morale* are seldom in accord."[47] *L'Esprit* says man has both a physical and an intelligent side.[48] Repeatedly, Montesquieu seems to suggest a tension between man's potential capacity and his actual behavior.

Man's Natural Activity and Its Enemies

Montesquieu is much less concerned with whether human nature can be called rational or irrational than with protecting and strengthening the natural inclinations that man does have. The common underlying effort of *Les Lettres Persanes* and *L'Esprit des Lois* is a many-sided battle against the forces that would alienate man from his natural attitudes. The first work rather dramatically identifies the enemies of man's natural activity, and the later work brings forth several prudent ideas about how to moderate the conflict. But the identity of the natural inclinations themselves must be determined largely from the descriptions of the antagonistic forces.

In endeavoring to identify the aspects of human nature which Montesquieu strives to protect, we should recognize first of all that, while he lived in an era that is often identified with the natural right theory of government,[49] he bases little of his political thought upon the natural rights of individuals. His account of the state of nature is quite cursory, and he derives society from psychological tendencies rather than from prior rights or contract. He does say that slavery is contrary to natural right, once because it endangers equality and another time because it denies liberty[50], but he supplements this dogmatic pronouncement with the circumstantial judgment that natural reason may justify slavery in two situations — a very hot climate and a very despotic government. The closest he comes to basing political rules upon natural rights is in the discussion of conquest, and there natural rights pertain more to the people collectively than to particular individuals.[51]

When Montesquieu defines government, the emphasis is upon its relevance to the dispositions of the people. In *Les Lettres Persanes* he considers "which government is most conformable to reason" and says that "the most perfect is that which arrives at its end with the least difficulty" and "which leads men in a way which best suits their disposition." Yet, he is talking about means and not ends. He is not condoning disobedience but arguing that in a country like France, punishment that is moderate and proportionate to the crime, is more conducive to obedience than cruel sanctions. "If, under a mild government, the subjects are as obedient as under a severe one, the first is preferable, because it is more conformable to reason and because severity is a foreign motive" (80). Likewise, Book I of *L'Esprit des Lois* says that the most natural government is "that which best agrees with the humor and disposition of the people in whose favor it is established." In these observations, Montesquieu, I believe, is more concerned with the duties of legislators than with the rights of individuals as such.

⌐ The natural attribute of man which receives the most profound defense in *Les Lettres Persanes* is the human capacity of free will. One of the letters doggedly makes four attempts to reconcile the free will of man with a Supreme Mind (69). First, it says that God is limited by himself out of necessity and that he lacks those perfections, such as the power to alter essences or break promises, which would imply greater imperfections, such as the power to deceive men. Second, the letter asserts that God could not possibly know all of man's action because what has not happened cannot be foreseen. Here, Montesquieu says that "the mind is the maker of its own determination" and often acts "only to make use of its liberty." This, of course, assumes more than proves free will. Third, Montesquieu says that God knows all that he wishes to know and that while God can see everything, he prefers to leave man to man's own way of acting. God's position is likened to that of a monarch who does not know what his ambassador will do on a certain matter but who, if he wishes, could order the ambassador to act in a prescribed way and be assured that the ambassador would so act. This distinction between potential capacity and actual behavior appears also in some analyses of man. The final attempt to solve the conflict of God's power and man's freedom involves the humility of man before God. Montesquieu finds precedents in the Koran and in the Books of the Jews. They make the dogma of absolute prescience unnecessary on the ground that God is too immense, too infinite, and too grand a spirit to be concerned with man's future decisions. Montesquieu argues that we should be constantly adoring and constantly humble; we can see God only in his commandments. This seems to seek a solution in psychology where it could not be found in logic. It sets God apart from the problem and assumes more than proves the freedom of human will.[52] Still there is no doubt but that free will is a fundamental premise of Montesquieu's theory of natural government.

This is evident also in his rejections of accidental, physical, and

animal determinism. The study of the Romans declares that fortune does not rule the world,[53] and the start of *L'Esprit des Lois*
denounces "blind fatality." Some commentators have held that
Montesquieu espouses a physical determinism. For instance, R. G.
Collingwood says that Montesquieu "conceived of human life as a
reflection of geographical and climatic conditions, not otherwise
than the life of plants."[54] But Collingwood fails to take into account much of *L'Esprit des Lois* and other works. Montesquieu
gives considerable attention to sociological and psychological factors, such as the mores and manner, the religious life, and a broad
array of economic forces. When Montesquieu does compare human
beings to plants, it is not climate but cultural influences that he has
in mind. He remarks in *Les Lettres Persanes* that "men are like
plants that never flourish if they are not well cultivated" (122).
Clearly his interest is what man does with the physical conditions.
L'Esprit des Lois devotes more than twice as much discussion to cultural, economic, and religious influences upon society than it does
to physical forces.

Moreover, the possibilities of physical or animal determinism are
countered in the first chapter of *L'Esprit des Lois*. It asserts that
man lives in both a physical and an intelligent realm, implying that
the latter is substantially independent of the former. The *Essai sur
les Causes* speaks of a *raison physique* and a *raison morale* and the
conflict of the two persists in Montesquieu's writings. Further,
Montesquieu regards the "moral causes" to be more determinative
than the physical ones. This is stated explicitly in the *Essai sur les
Causes,* with supporting reference to the uniformity of Jewish culture despite the diverse geographical location.[55] It is also implicit
in a number of situations, to be discussed shortly, in which he recommends laws to counteract what he calls the evil effects of climate.

Probably the foremost test of human value in *L'Esprit des Lois* is
whether man is engaged in socially relevant activity. Montesquieu
repeatedly attacks indolence and passivity. He assumes that man is
naturally inclined to be active and productive and that, while social
gain is not inevitable, it does result from man's interest-motivated
activity. He declares that "nature is just to all mankind, and repays
them for their industry." Likewise, nature "renders them industrious by annexing rewards in proportion to their labor."[56] Presumably, it does not matter whether the motive is rational or irrational,
social duty or self-interest. Also, Book XVIII, on the relations of
laws to the terrain, declares that lands are cultivated not in propor-

tion to their fertility but in proportion to the liberty of the people. This is coupled with an optimistic view of human history. "Mankind by their industry, and by the influence of good laws, have rendered the earth more proper for their abode." He tells how rivers have been made to flow where there had been marshes and arid land, and he points out the contrast between "destructive nations which provide evils more durable than themselves" and "the actions of an industrious people which are the source of blessings after they are no more." Likewise, he condemns monasticism, or as he calls it "monkery," because it is conducive to indolence and he asserts that penances ought to be joined with "the idea of labor, not with that of idleness."[57]

The high value which Montesquieu places upon the natural activity of man is evident from the scope of the attacks upon the forces that alienate man from his inherent dispositions. *Les Lettres Persanes* is repeatedly critical of social formalities, the deceptive tendencies of man's own pride and imagination, and the artificialities of theological and political arrangements.

The preference for natural behavior over conventional modes appears in several of the satirical letters on the life of the Persian and French aristocracies. Usbek's first letter to his wives declares that natural graces are preferred to borrowed charms and that the simplicity of nature is superior to the ornaments of dress (3). At a dramatic performance in Paris, Rica observes more acting among the audience than upon the stage (28) and finds himself the center of attention as long as he wears his Persian clothes or his foreign ornaments, but without these the French hesitate to believe that he is Persian (30). Again, Rica pictures the French as knowing their way no better than the blind man who guides him through the streets of Paris (32). Usbek reports that the Parisians are addicted to the coffee houses on the belief that drinking coffee makes them four times wittier. He is shocked that these "clever minds" render "no useful service to their country and amuse their talents with puerilities." Some of them quarrel in the vulgar tongue. Others dispute in a barbarous language, presumably scholastic Latin, and seem to live only for subtle distinctions and obscure reasoning (36). Rica, on another occasion, scoffs at the excessive preoccupation with witty conversation. He reports that two men are forming an association for the production of wit and that they rehearse social conversation with signals for congratulating each other. This, Rica concludes, will give them a place in the Academy within six months and then they will be judged witty whatever they say (54).

The manner in which man's pride tends to alienate him from his natural self is dramatized by the comments upon religious symbols. Montesquieu presents man in a paradox of wishing to live by ideals and at the same time creating ideals in his own image. Rica tells Usbek that "we never judge of things but with a private view to ourselves" and that he is not surprised "that the Negroes paint the devil in the most glaring whiteness and their gods as black as a coal" or "that the Venus of some nations should be represented with breasts pendent to her thighs." Rica comments further that when he sees "men who creep upon an atom, the earth, which is but a point in the universe, propose themselves as the immediate models of providence, I know not how to reconcile so much presumption with so little sufficiency" (59). Another example of man's exaggerated pride is the law against suicide, and Rica sharply attacks the argument that suicide disturbs the providential order. "Do you think," he asks, "that my body, when become a blade of grass, a worm, a green turf, would be changed into a work of nature less worthy of her, and that my soul disengaged from all its earthy part, would become less pure." These ideas, he adds, "have no other source but our pride. We are not at all sensible of our littleness" (76). This is similar to the fourth explanation of God's omnipresience and man's free will, mentioned previously. But later, he seems to agree with Locke that the divine command against suicide is the basis for the inalienability of certain rights (104). A less metaphysical example of how men tend to live in their imagination is the report to Usbek that one of his female slaves wishes to marry a eunuch, and the comment, "To be always in dreams and fancies; to live only imagination" (53). Then later, Usbek associates the power of mental imagery with the ups and downs of population trends. "Sometimes the fertility of a people," he remarks, "depends upon the minutest circumstances in the world" (119).

Religious charms and superstitions may accentuate the power of the imagination over man's reason and sense. Rica suggests this when he acknowledges that the religious amulets and talismen which he carries at all times have no more power than other things. He insists that they have no less power than other objects and that without confidence in "mysterious letters" we would be in a continual fright. Yet, presumably even our fears may be equally imaginary. Rica declares: "Men are indeed unhappy! They constantly float between fallacious hopes and absurd fears; and, instead of adhering to the dictates of reason, they form to themselves either monsters that intimidate them or phantoms that seduce and mislead them" (143).

There is also stinging criticism of artifice in church organization and theological doctrine. Montesquieu calls members of religious orders "dervishes" and ecclesiastical conformity "casuistry." One cleric tells the Persian travelers that no one is a heretic unless he wishes to be because he need only offer a subtle distinction to his accusers. Any distinction, he says, will render the man pure and orthodox (29). Also, there are two kinds of sin: mortal sin which absolutely excludes one from paradise and venial sin which offends God but does not preclude beatitude. The distinction is indispensable, Usbek says, because most Christians wish to enter heaven as easily as possible. The sin is not the act but "the knowledge of him who commits it." There are many acts of "a doubtful nature" and "a casuist can give them a degree of goodness." If a casuist "can persaude the man to believe they are harmless, he entirely takes away all their evil" (57). Rica's account of a library tour suggests that Scriptures are researched not for what to believe but for authority on what the researchers do believe (134). Elsewhere, Usbek quotes a church official that his brethren are tormented constantly by an envy to convert others to their opinions and that this is as ridiculous as trying to whiten the face of Africans. One remark may disclose much of Montesquieu's complaint. "We trouble the state, we torment even ourselves, to make men receive points of religion which are not fundamental" (61).

Another of *Les Lettres Persanes* blames Catholic taboos, dogmas, and practices for the reported decline in European population (117). It charges that celibacy and chastity vows have been "the loss of more men than ever have been destroyed by the plague or the most bloody wars." It suggests that monasticism encourages indolence and inactivity and says that a man can make full provision for himself by "learning five or six words of a dead language." Montesquieu claims that Protestant countries are more populous, accept higher taxes, cultivate the lands better, and have a more prosperous commerce than Catholic ones. "Trade gives life to everything" among the former "but monkery carries death among every thing belonging to the others" (117).

The way in which political despotism suppresses man's natural inclinations is probably the most direct connection between *Les Lettres Persanes* and *L'Esprit des Lois*. The early work makes no express distinction between monarchies and despotisms, and it associates the tyrannical tendencies of unlimited rule by one with the term monarchy. But the travelers criticize despotic rule in various ways from the start to the finish. Usbek, even before he reaches Paris, writes of his astonishment at the weakness of the Osmanli empire. He attributes this condition to its severe methods and predicts that it will be conquered within 200 years (19). The next three letters might seem to be a diversion because they dwell on the problems of disciplining Usbek's wives and slaves. However, the letters may be intended to dramatize the plight of any person under despotic rule. A Frenchman under a grand Bourbon as well as an oriental slave could have exclaimed: "Good God, how many things are necessary to the happiness of one man" (22).

The principal evil of despotism is its repression of man's natural attitudes. Rica acknowledges that in Persia human behavior is forced to be uniform. He declares that "in this state of slavery, both of heart and mind, it is their fears only that speak." They have only this one language in contrast to that of nature, which expresses itself so variously (63). These comments anticipate the proposition stressed in *L'Esprit des Lois* that fear is the moving spirit of despotic government. At other points in *Les Lettres Persanes* Usbek describes the French monarch as despotic, that is, governing his family, his court, and his state in the same way (37) and forcing the court, the city, and the provinces into his own mold (99). The confounding of domestic, civil and political orders is one of the distinguishing features of despotism, to be emphasized in the later work. The oppressive effect of despotism upon man's natural inclinations for productive activity is described rather pointedly in Book XIII of *L'Esprit des Lois*. There, after saying that nature repays mankind for their efforts and renders men industrious by giving them rewards in proportion to their labor, Montesquieu declares that "if an arbitrary prince should attempt to deprive the people of nature's bounty, they would fall into a disrelish of industry; and then indolence and inaction must be their only happiness."[58]

The object of censure in *Les Lettres Persanes* is not merely the French monarchy, but even more its alliance with the church. Montesquieu calls the Pope a greater magician than the king (24), because, while the latter makes money of paper, the Pope controls the monarch with another piece of paper. This refers to the *Bull Unigenitus* of 1713,[59] which was directed at the Jansenists. Montesquieu is partial to them as he is to the Huguenots. Rica with obvious sympathy describes how the Jansenists are undermining the king from their positions at the royal court, in the capital, in the army, and in the laws courts. Strangely, while the tourist sees the Jansenists everywhere, he says that the king may never discover them because they "have a general existence" and "nothing of individuality"; they are like a body without members. Rica observes that "it is heaven that would punish this prince for not having been sufficiently moderate towards his conquered enemies, whose genius and appointment are superior to his own" (24). This shows Montesquieu's sentiment for middle-class dissenters and his esteem of moderation in political action.[60]

Les Lettres Persanes discloses some basic ideas about the ends and means of government while criticizing legislators for making the laws "too refined" and following "logical ideas rather than natural equity." Montesquieu observes that some lawmakers have shown great wisdom in giving fathers broad authority over their children. "Nothing contributes more to the ease of magistrates, nothing more prevents the courts of justice from being crowded, nothing more firmly establishes tranquillity in a state, where morality *(moeurs)* always makes better citizens than laws can make" (129). This is probably not intended to mean that government should emulate patrimonial authority. At least, the first book of *L'Esprit des Lois* rejects the parental analogy and asserts that government should look instead to the humor and disposition of the people.

The artificiality of those French nobles who merely cling to the king is the subject of particularly biting satire. But this is probably not directed at the nobility of the robe, which Montesquieu tends to esteem in *L'Esprit des Lois.*

Usbek assails the French monarch for using the great nobles for personal servants and for granting honors without regard to merit. This part of the aristocracy is pictured to give little and cost much. *"Un grand seigneur* is a man who sees the King, who speaks to ministers, who has ancesters, debts and pensions" (88). The process of royal favoritism is lampooned and later the whole system of royal pensions is attacked (124). Criticism is not limited to the decadent old aristocracy. It also extends to the politically ambitious *nouveau riche.* Rica describes a tax-farmer to be short on breeding and education but long on wealth and impertinence (48). Montesquieu may be suggesting that the French monarch is bringing the wrong kind of aristocracy into the functions of reigning and ruling. In *L'Esprit des Lois,* we will see that he prescribes that the king share administration with the nobility of the robe.

Equally relevant to the Bourbon rule in France is the letter on the influence of women at the royal court. Usbek remarks that the test of western kings is their selection of "their mistress and their confessor." The women, he says, form a sort of republic, whose members continually aid each other like a new state within the state. The remark that to see what moves ministers, magistrates, and prelates, one must know the women who govern them (107) seems particularly relevant to the Paris and Versailles of the eighteenth century.

But what makes despotic government really bad is the character of the king's chief minister, and here Montesquieu probably has Richelieu in mind. In *Les Lettres Persanes,* Rica writes his friend Rhedi that "there is scarcely a king so bad, but his minister is still worse" (127). Whatever evil the prince does, he says, has almost always been suggested to him by the minister; and on this basis, he says that the ambition of the prince is never so dangerous as the servility of his counselors. Rica calls sincerity the soul of the good minister. Unlike a private person, a minister cannot hide his deficiencies. He has as many judges as the people he governs. The greatest evil is not serving the prince badly but, a thousand times worse, is "the bad example he sets." The ill effect of a bad minister is described as if it occurred in India, but the resemblance to France is apparent. Usbek writes of "a nation by nature generous, debauched in an instant, as it were, by the bad example of a minister." He elaborates. "I have seen a whole people, amongst whom generosity, probity, candor, and uprightness had long been considered as qualities natural to them, become all of a sudden the most despicable people upon the face of the earth" (146). The most virtuous men, he says, have done the most unworthy things and have violated the first principles of justice on the frivolous pretext that they had been mistreated. Montesquieu's apprehension that a despotic minister may cause the people to foresake their natural ideals and affections is an underlying theme throughout much of *L'Esprit des Lois,* and the work develops several ways of distributing authority and mod-

erating its exercise so that such consequences do not fall upon the
people.

There are political implications also in the final group of letters
(146-161) even though on their face they concern only Usbek's authority over his harem. The letters seem designed to tell the French
people that oppressive government cannot withstand natural law
and civil attitudes. Usbek has received word that discipline in his
seraglio is growing weaker and weaker, and he writes his chief eunuch to exercise unlimited power. "Command with as much authority as I do myself" (148). Such an unqualified delegation of authority to a single official is portrayed in *L'Esprit des Lois* to be the essence of despotic government.[61] But before the letter arrives, the
chief eunuch dies. Another is appointed with a new grant of unlimited power. "I put the sword into your hand; I entrust you with
what is of all things most dear to me, that is my revenge. Enter
upon this employment, but enter upon it without either compas-
sion or feeling. I have written to my wives to obey you implicitly"
(153). The cryptic note to the wives tells them that the new chief
eunuch has full authority to "make you live under so rigorous a
yoke, that you will regret your liberty, if you do not regret your virtue" (154). Yet, Usbek then writes to a friend that he is in the
midst of confusion and despair, enjoying only his anxieties, and
that the eunuchs themselves, "shameful refuse of human nature,"
know less misfortune than Usbek himself (155). The idea that in a
despotic government even the despot feels enslaved is expressly asserted in *L'Esprit des Lois*.[62] Still, despotism cannot stand against
the natural force of moral character, and *Les Lettres Persanes* ends
with both tragedy and high ideal. The new chief eunuch rules with
such tyranny that Usbek's favorite wife, Roxanna, commits suicide,
and her final note contains words that could have been uttered by a
Frenchman to his despotic king: "I lived indeed in servitude, but
still I was always free. I reformed your Laws by those of Nature and
my mind always kept its independence."

Notes

1. *L'Esprit des Lois* (hereafter referred to as *Lois*) XI, 4. The translation of Thomas Nugent (Hafner edition, New York, 1949) has been used with exceptions noted.

2. *Les Lettres Persanes* (hereafter referred to as *L.P.*) In this chapter the particular letters quoted or otherwise drawn upon are designated by the parenthetical numbers in the text. Translations have been taken from *Persian Letters,* sixth edition, Alexander Donaldson, Edinburgh, 1773. The letter numbers have been made to conform with those in Roger Caillois *Oeuvres Complètes de Montesquieu* (hereafter referred to as Caillois I or II) (Paris, 1951), I, 133-373. Translations have been checked against the French text in Caillois I.

3. *Lois,* I, 2.

4. Plato: *Republic,* II, 369-375.

5. *Considérations sur les Causes de la Grandeur des Romains et de leur Décadence* (hereafter referred to as *Romains*) I, Caillois II, 71. David Lowenthal (Tr.) *Considerations on the Causes of the Greatness of the Romans and Their Decline by Montesquieu* (Macmillan, New York, 1965), 26.

6. *Pensée* 1029. Caillois I, 1272.

7. A. M. Boase, "The Interpretation of *Les Lettres Persanes*" in Will Moore, *et al.* (Ed.) *The French Mind — Studies in Honor of Gustave Ridler* (Oxford University Press, 1952), 154.

8. Robert Shackleton, *Montesquieu a Critical Biography* (Oxford, 1961) ; Henri Barckhausen, *Montesquieu, Ses Idées et ses Oeuvres* (Paris, 1907) ; Joseph Dedieu, *Montesquieu, L'homme et l'oeuvre* (Paris, 1943) .

9. Shackleton, *op. cit.* 41, 386, 352, 353.

10. Werner Stark, *Montesquieu, Pioneer of the Sociology of Knowledge* (London, 1960), 45-51. Some shifts of emphasis occur when he analyzes Montesquieu's basic doctrine of society, *ibid.* 52-72

11. Caillois I, 115.

12. Stark, *op. cit.,* 46; L.P. XLIV.

13. *Essai sur le Goût dans les Choses de la Nature et de l'Art,* Caillois, II, 1240-1263.

14. *Romains,* IV; Caillois, II, 85; Lowenthal, *op. cit.,* 45-6.

15. Julius Stone, *The Province and Function of Law* (Cambridge, Mass., 1961), 400-1, 272-3, 400-1; Eugen Ehrlich *Fundamental Principles of the Sociology of Law,* translated by Walter L. Moll (New York, 1962) 473.

16. Cesare Beccaria, *An Essay On Crimes and Punishment,* (London, 1767), 4.

17. *Lois,* XV, 1.

18. Peter Gay, *Voltaire's Politics, The Poet As Realist,* (New York, 1965), 100 — 111.

19. Stark, *op. cit.,* 54.

20. Plato, *Laws,* 693, 756.

21. Stark, *op. cit.,* 6, 8.

22. Shackleton, *op. cit.,* 194-243.

23. Stark, *op. cit.,* 7, 34; Shackleton, *op. cit.,* 20-26, 400, 401.

24. Shackleton, *op. cit.*, 68-75; *Analyse de Traité des Devoirs*, Caillois I, 108-111.

25. *Lois*, X, 13.

26. See for Descartes' ideas on motion, Lucien Levy-Bruhl, *History of Modern Philosophy in France* (Chicago, 1924), 26-29; for Montesquieu's reaction against Descartes, see Stark, *op. cit.*, 1-12.

27. See fn. 18, *supra*.

28. *Lois*, XVIII, 10-14.

29. *Ibid.*, XX, 22.

30. *Ibid.*, XX, 3.

31. *Ibid.*, XXVIII, 10.

32. Shackleton, *op. cit.* 46-8, 82-4.

33. At one point the law of nations is called the political law in its relation to other countries, *Lois*, X, 1.

34. Ernst Cassirer, *The Philosophy of the Enlightenment* (Princeton, 1951), 3-21, 41.

35. *Ibid.*, 13, 14, 20, 21, 37, 38.

36. Plato, *Republic*, IV, 428 (Cornford's translation, Oxford, 1941, 119; paperback edition, 121).

37. Montesquieu began definite work on *L'Esprit des Lois* during 1734, Shackleton, *op. cit.*, 228.

38. Caillois, II, 57.

39. *Lois*, XII, 2; XIX, 3.

40. *L.P.* LXXXIII: Caillois, I, 110; *Lois*, I, 1,3.

41. Caillois, II, 57.

42. Stark, *op. cit.*, 131.

43. Levy-Bruhl, *op. cit.*, 26, 146-9

44. Shackleton, *op. cit.*, 258-260. Shackleton suggests that Montesquieu might have been a disciple of Malebranche more than of Descartes, and he also notes that G. Lamson believes that *L'Esprit des Lois* is constructed in accordance with Cartesian methods while Sir Isaiah Berlin says that Montesquieu does not apply Cartesian methods.

45. *L.P.* CXIII; *Lois*, I, 1. The possibility that Montesquieu at one point abandoned the belief that motion is essential to matter, is indicated in one *Pensée*. See Shackleton, *op. cit.*, 73. Another remark connects the billard-ball type of motion with the denial of free will, *L.P.* LXIX. Montesquieu's thought has been called "counter-optimistic," Henry Vyverberg, *Historical Pessimism in the French Enlightenment* (Cambridge, Mass. 1958) 158.

46. *L.P.* XXXIII; Romains XXII, Caillois II, 199.

47. *Pensée* 1208, Caillois I, 1302. See also *Lois*, I, 1.

48. *Lois*, I, 1.

49. M. Judd Harmon, *Political Thought from Plato to the Present* (New York, 1964), 317; Frederick M. Watkins, *The Age of Ideology — Political Thought, 1750 to the Present* (New York, 1964), 13.

50. An anti-slavery argument is based upon the equality of man in *Lois*, XV, 7, and upon the liberty of man, in *Pensée* 1935, Caillois, I, 1467. See also *Lois*, XV, 2.

51. *Lois*, X, 2, 3.

52.   Another argument for free will appears in *Pensée* 2175, Caillois I, 1565. This comes from Polignac and argues that absence of free will would make a mockery of the commandments.

53.   *Romains*, XVIII, Caillois, II, 173; Lowenthal, *op. cit.*, 169.

54.   R. G. Collingwood, *The Idea of History* (Oxford, 1946), 79.

55.   Caillois, II, 60.

56.   *Lois*, XIII, 2.

57.   *Ibid.*, XVIII, 3,7; XIV, 7; XXIV, 12.

58.   *Ibid.*, XIII, 2.

59.   See Shackleton, *op. cit.*, 344-9; L.P. XXIV, CI; Caillois, II, 1217-1231.

60.   *Lois*, XXIX, 1.

61.   *Ibid.*, II, 5; III, 9, 10; IV, 3; V, 13, 14, 15; VIII, 10.

62.   *Ibid.*, III, 9, 10; V, 14; XIX 17, 19; XXIV, 2.

Chapter II

The Natural Relations of a National Society

L'Esprit des Lois assumes the political divisions of the historical world, and it deals with a wide range of diverse entities, including China, Turkey, and India, as well as western countries from classical Athens to contemporary England. But it considers them to be societies more than states, and when we need a single term for them, I will call them "national societies" even though some may be more strictly cities or empires. The term "national" is preferred to "political" because it may embrace civil and other relations as well as political ones. Montesquieu assumes that any society, like any natural being, consists of internal and external relations, and he strives to identify the general types of interactions which arise from the natural inclinations of its people. This is manifest in his concern for the natural activity of the society, his doctrine that each nation has a general spirit arising from diverse causes or relations, and the autonomy which he gives to the mores and manners of a society in contrast to its particular laws. These three aspects of his concept of a national society will be discussed in this chapter.

The Active Society and Its Enemies

Montesquieu's conception of a national society may have changed somewhat during his lifetime, but throughout he considers a national society to consist of natural interactions among its members and he strives to maximize natural activity within the social order. He assumes that the liberty of an individual depends upon a predictable social order, and he admonishes the legislators to respect the spirit of the nation because "we do nothing so well as when we act with freedom and follow the bent of our natural genius."[1] Thus, the political system should protect and even stimulate the internal and external relations of the national society. His ideas of natural government, I believe, are designed to safeguard the active society from its enemies, particularly from religious intolerance and political despotism. We will look first at his idea that a national society consists of natural relations and then at his efforts to invigorate the activity of a national society.

Montesquieu's penetrating interest in essential relations is well attested. It extends throughout his whole career and is particularly noticeable in his definitions of justice and law. As noted previously, *Les Lettres Persanes* defines justice to be an appropriate relation and *Le Traite des Devoirs* called it the one general relation.[2] The first chapter of *L'Esprit des Lois* mentions the invariability of "possible relations of justice," and most of the work inquires into the relations of laws to human and social conduct. *L'Esprit des Lois* promptly defines laws in general to be "necessary relations arising from the nature of things" and the laws of the Deity to be relations between a prime reason and different things and the relations among different things themselves. Then, it explains that God is related to the universe, and his laws are related to his wisdom and power; that the rules of the physical world are a constant relation; and that the intelligent world has relations of justice antecedent to the positive law. In the third chapter, the three principal types of positive law, that is, the law of nations, the political law, and the civil law, are each defined to be a certain kind of relation. That chapter borrows definitions of the political state and the civil state which do not speak of relations expressly.[3] However, *L'Esprit des Lois* develops, not these, but Montesquieu's own definition of the government most conformable to nature, and the standard for this is the particular attitude that is best related to the disposition of the people.

The definition of the spirit of the laws, at the close of Book I of *L'Esprit des Lois,* makes the relations of laws to other objects the central theme of the whole work. Each of the three sentences of this definition declares in one form or another that the laws ought to be related to specified objects.[4] These objects are virtually an index to the thirty remaining books of *L'Esprit des Lois*. They deal with ecological as well as political subjects and also extend over much of the field of social psychology. Each book or two deals with the relation of laws to a particular subject, and the general types of relations provide a rough pattern of *L'Esprit des Lois*. Books II — X deal with the relation of laws to the nature and principle (or special spirit) of different kinds of government; Books XI — XIII concern the relation of laws to types of liberty; Books XIV — XXV inquire into the relation of laws to climate, terrain, mores and manners, commerce, money, population trends, and religious doctrine and polity; and Books XXVI–XXXI investigate the sources and relations of different kinds of laws, with particular emphasis upon civil law. The definition of the spirit of the laws seems to be a more specific formulation of the doctrine of general causes, which Montesquieu developed during the 1730's.[5] Where he had six or seven objects he now has a score or so. Also, we may feel that there is improvement when he uses "relations" more than "causes" throughout much of *L'Esprit des Lois.*

The theory that a national society is a system of internal and external relations reflects the belief among eighteenth-century Frenchmen that nature is a universe of particulars, imbedded in which is the body of rational laws which govern the physical and human worlds.[6] At the start, Montesquieu declares that he has taken his principles from "the nature of things" and throughout *L'Esprit des Lois* he invokes "the nature of things" as a source and standard. However, he may differ from his fellow French intellectuals in the extent to which he considers that the particulars of nature, whether divine, physical or human, consist of relations.

The proposition that a national society consists of an identifiable pattern of active relations gives unity and coherence to the diverse subject matter in *L'Esprit des Lois* and Montesquieu's other political studies. This principle of structure and function is being called "relational pluralism" or "relational diversity" even though Montesquieu does not use the expression. It means, in part, that every being, system, or universe, whether divine, physical, or human, is composed of and characterized by a diversity of intrinsic and extrinsic relations and that each object or force within that society is both distinctly separate from and inherently related to each other.

Montesquieu assumes that a national society exists within a framework of three universal realms, the divine, the physical, and the intelligent, each with its own body of invariable law. For the world of human intelligence he calls the universal law the "possible relations of justice," but I believe that it is much like a metaphysical version of natural law. It may be a recognition of the Stoic idea of law and justice which Montesquieu describes in *Les Lettres Persanes* and which he planned to develop in the *Traité des Devoirs.*[7] But in *L'Esprit des Lois* it appears only briefly in the first chapter and at a few other places. It is never entirely abandoned but it is mostly in the background. The three kinds of invariable laws are not sufficient to control mankind in all respects, and there is need for human laws, which means that there is need for physical or economic coercion. Most of *L'Esprit des Lois* is concerned with the manner of making and applying of positive laws.

The relation of a national society to natural law is not too clear in *L'Esprit des Lois*. What are called the laws of nature in Book I are hardly more than primitive psychological tendencies. Later, there are references to natural law in the discussions of conquest, slavery, the succession of property, and some phases of domestic relations.[8] More important, I believe, is the pervasive effort to make the civil mores and the civil law take the place of much of what Montesquieu's predecessors, notably Jean Bodin, had added to the natural law. Bodin had enlarged its scope to embrace some of the property law which had been known as customary law.[9] This gave it greater moral standing against the king but reduced its precision. Montesquieu's endeavor to make the civil law replace at least part of the natural law is evident in some of the chapters of Book XXVI. There, he argues "That the Order of succession or inheritance depends on the Principles of political or civil Law and not on those of the Law of Nature" and later he declares that these are civil law matters. More directly, he explains "Cases in which we may judge by the Principles of the civil Law in limiting the Principles of the Law of Nature."[10]

The framework within which national societies exist includes also the positive law of nations. Montesquieu discusses this mostly in Books IX and X, where he analyzes the impact of such laws upon the defensive and offensive forces of a nation.[11] But he seems to assume that the external relations of a national society are not only legal but also embrace principles of morals, economics, and the communication of diverse ideas.[12] In general, I believe, he considers each national society to be part of a larger system, which affects its intrinsic character whether the system is loose or rigid, whether universal, continental, or regional. In other words, he may give greater respect to the civil qualities of the family of nations than to its political aspects. At one point, Montesquieu mentions a general political law applicable to all societies,[13] but he does not develop the matter. Also, he says in Book I that positive laws include those of morals and religion, but the idea is dropped at once, and there is no analysis of such laws until Books XXIV — XXVI when it is mixed with explanations of natural and divine laws. There may be a universal moral law in Montesquieu's comments upon natural religion, but these are limited to a few basic ideas about respecting God, family, and fellowmen and doubting the power of sacrificial rites.[14]

Montesquieu sometimes speaks of "sovereign" or "sovereign power" to mean a monarch or a despot,[15] but his use of the more abstract term "sovereignty" is rare and then a bit strange. Once he says that the best attribute of "sovereignty" is the pardoning power. His near avoidance of the term is evident in his use of *le monarque* in one instance to mean the supreme power of the people in a de- mocracy.[16] These tendencies may reflect his antagonism to con- cepts of absolute power. We will see that he prefers that legislative power be distributed jointly and that administrative power be shared with certain elites. Also, in external affairs, he sees the power of a nation to be not legal independence of other nations, but rather a set of actual forces which depend in part upon those of other nations. He declares that "all grandeur, force and power are relative" and he cautions that efforts to increase the "real gran- deur" might cause the "relative" power to diminish. He points out that during the reign of Louis XIV, France was at its highest pitch of relative grandeur because neither Germany nor Italy had united, while England and Scotland were still divided, and, in addition, the Spanish monarchy was increasingly weak. He also counsels that an impotent neighbor probably should not be disturbed because sub- duing such a state may diminish relative power.[17] Thus, he seems to consider relative power more important than "real" power.

While democratic and aristocratic republics are defined in Book II of *L'Esprit des Lois* in terms of the social location of "supreme power," Montesquieu clearly opposes the concentration of power in any class. Book VIII asserts sharply that the spirit of any kind of government, whether monarchical, aristocratic or democratic, is corrupted when one class or person attempts to bring all power within its exclusive grasp. Montesquieu rather definitely rejects any kind of absolute or monistic sovereignty, whether by one, by few, or many. He is, of course, much involved in attacking the divine right theory of monarchy, expounded by Bossuet,[18] and the absolutism, favored by Voltaire.[19] In fact the vigor of his opposition carries him into some dogmatic remarks against pure or unmixed types of government. He opposes not only divine and dynastic sovereignty but also oligarchic and popular sovereignty of an absolute type.[20] Repeatedly he condemns the Decemvirs of Rome, and his opposi- tion to popular absolutism, even though more indirect, seems to be just as strong and to be reiterated as much.[21] He appears to be against legal and even moral sovereignty as long as it is monistic or absolute. He might perhaps be said to advocate a sociological sovereignty and to give absolute character to the concept of national society[22] in his eagerness to refute the myth of divine right sovereignty. But sooner or later he subdivides the sociological forces to such a degree that there is more conflict than absolutism in his idea of a national society.

Likewise, when Montesquieu uses the term "state," he usually intends something relatively concrete rather than abstract. A good deal of the time he does not use the word but rather speaks of either specific entities, like Rome or England, or general types, such as republic or despotisms. These are employed as concrete models or analytical ones, respectively, but sometimes specific entities, particularly Athens or China, appear to be ideal types of mixed republic or pure despotism. Also, Montesquieu seems to use such terms as government, nation, people, or country, more than state, and may employ them interchangeably because he makes little or no effort to distinguish them.[23] Basically, *L'Esprit des Lois* is not a study of states but of societies and governments or even more fundamentally a study of the relations of societies and governments. This is so whether the particular focus is a city, an empire, or a country. The view that a nation is a social rather than a juridical being is a factual approach which eliminates much of the idealism often associated with the concept of a state. Such a way of explaining or developing a concept of a political system, allows the national society to have a higher standing than the state or government and also to be more natural and less artificial than the state or government. In all, I would say that Montesquieu does not derive the validity of government from a metaphysical concept, such as the state, sovereignty, or the general will, but rather that he makes legitimacy a matter of quantitative empirical relationship; that is, a political decision is valid to the extent that it is relevant to the natural activities of the people of the particular national society.

I believe that Montesquieu does not presuppose or develop any ideal type of national society apart from a specific environment. Nor does he seem to assume any chosen nation or society which could embody eternal ideas for posterity or even for a given period. The national societies in his analysis are limited in time and space, and any particular national society is only one among many. Each has external relations with the others, and it is limited in character by its connections with other societies.

Just why there is a plurality of societies and not a single, universal society is more assumed than explained. In Book I the step from a general state of nature to particular societies is one quick leap. Elsewhere, Montesquieu points to the difficulties of ranging everyone under a single rule.[24] The general import of *L'Esprit des Lois* would seem to be that a number of national societies arise because of the difficulties of making and applying laws for a large, diversified community. This rather than the variance of climate[25] would seem to be the more fundamental explanation because the territories of many nations do not coincide with regions of climate. Likewise, his discussion of the universal laws of nature and the positive laws of particular states suggests that the former might suffice for social relations that are simple in scope and character but that as society becomes more complex, natural law is inadequate and a supplementary system of positive laws becomes highly convenient, if not necessary.

Furthermore, the national societies are as diverse as they are numerous. Each one differs from all others even though two or more may have some traits in common.[26] The uniqueness of each society is an essential aspect of his theory of natural government. In this respect, Montesquieu may differ from Hobbes, Locke, Rousseau, and others whose formulae of legitimacy do not incorporate the diversity of social forces.[27] Montesquieu does recognize general types and principles but the total message of his analyses and explanations seems to be that the ideal standards for any national society are to be found in its own unique attributes and situation. His investigations of diverse types of relations identify the various factors which permit each national society to get closer to its own natural forces and to express its distinctive general character.

The political life analyzed in *L'Esprit des Lois* is primarily not the conflict of the individual and the state, but the diverse struggles between the civil society and the political apparatus. Montesquieu is deeply concerned with the liberty of the national civil society. He sees that society to be full of divisions and variety, but what is to be protected from political despotism is the society more directly than the particular individuals. The liberty of a particular citizen comes largely from participation in a free society, and a society is free when it has a working legal order that agrees with "the nature of things." His emphasis upon the national civil society, in contrast to both the state and the individual, is one of the ways in which *L'Es-*

prit des Lois seeks to avoid the conflict between prince and people which *Les Lettres Persanes* pictured as virtually irreconcilable.[28] The civil mores and behavior of a nation provide the basis of a theory of government, or a political system, which rejects the metaphysical absolutism of both divine and popular right sovereignty and which places legitimacy in the combined effect of diverse sociological and psychological forces.

Montesquieu's emphasis upon the particularity of societies could mean, I believe, that each nation is capable of developing its own sense of order, social values, natural or customary law, and a distinct standard of legitimacy for political law and authority. He expresses his ideas on the comparative autonomy of a national society in one of his travel notes. Montesquieu writes that "the mores and the customs of the nations which are not contrary to morality cannot be judged as some better than the others." He asks, "By what rule could they be judged," and he gives the answer that there "is no common measure except as each nation makes its own mores the rule by which it judges all the others."[29]

The idea that the national society can develop its own source of legitimacy need not mean that it is tradition bound. Montesquieu may anticipate Burke to some degree, and he may open the door for a fuller attachment of the state to history, but he does not carry the matter very far. His aim is to make society free of the outside controls implicit in the doctrine of absolute and divine right monarchy. Any judgment of Montesquieu should take into account that France had been moving contrary to the general trend of social development. Change in French politics during the past century or two had led to despotism. But this does not mean that Montesquieu viewed change to be degenerative or that he esteems the past as such. The key choice is not between conservatism or progressivism but rather between what is natural and what is unnatural. The circumstances were that the government of the past was more natural in Montesquieu's view than the political system introduced by Richelieu or even that of Louis XI.[30] The admiration of the past may make Montesquieu appear conservative, but this is circumstantial, and his ideal is neither the past nor the future but the basic forces of nature. To allow these fuller play there is scarcely need for political prophecies or programs of new and striking dimension but merely the removal of prejudices and artificialities.

Montesquieu believes that a national society has a natural

rhythm which is both spontaneous and regular. One of *Les Lettres Persanes* remarks that "nature proceeds slowly and economically" (114). He is discussing the relations of the sexes, but he has similar ideas about social relations generally. In the work of the Romans, he approves the hesitance and reluctance of the Romans to add territories after the Punic wars. "It was not yet the time for seizing conquered countries," and when the Romans did proceed, he thinks they were proper in using a slow method of conquering.[31] In *L'Esprit des Lois* he declares that "Politics are a smooth file, which cuts gradually, and attains its end by a slow progression." He also gives some credence to the thought that nature will repair whatever is amiss; and he suggests that one should be restrained in making changes rather than trying to alter everything. "Such is the nature of things that the abuse is very often preferable to the correction, or at least, that the good which is established is always preferable to the better that is not." Moreover, the damage from particular events is less important than the continuing forces of the general causes that make up the movement of the political society. "The casualities of fortune are easily repaired but who can be guarded against events that incessantly arise from the nature of things."[32]

The theory that recurring interactive motion is natural and rational is further indicated by the proposition that a mixed system of government provides a political society with the means of inspecting and correcting itself. Montesquieu asserts, in his study of the Romans, that their government was admirable because "from its birth, its constitution found itself such, whether by the spirit of the people, the force of the senate, or the authority of certain magistrates, that all abuses of power could always be corrected." In contrast, he observes that Carthage perished because she would not let even Hannibal undertake the necessary retrenchment of abuses. Athens fell, he says, "because her errors appeared to her so sweet that she did not wish to cure them." Even the contemporary Italian republics, which he says boast of the perpetuity of their governments, "have no more liberty than Rome had in the time of the Decemvirs." The contemporary example of a government with a self-correcting mechanism is England. It has a governing body "which examines it continually and which continually examines itself." Its errors never remain long before "the spirit of attentive vigilance." "In a word, a free government, that is to say, one that is constantly agitated, cannot maintain itself if it is not, by its own laws, capable of correction."[33] Thus, the key to freedom is not inaction or static repose of separated political powers. Rather the key to freedom is conflicting action itself. The equating of free government with constant agitation would seem to limit any effort to call Montesquieu simply conservative minded. Moreover, the natural forces of constant agitation and conflict, which give rise to inspection and correction, are the forces which *L'Esprit des Lois* seeks to preserve and strengthen through such institutions as the administrative intermediaries, the depositary of laws, and the three class legislature. Montesquieu was a political reformer as well as a historian,[34] and his search for generalizations of natural motion was a quest for both an explanation of history and a guide to legislative wisdom.

In his opposition to absolute power, Montesquieu appeals to many viewpoints. One of his lines of persuasion is directed at those who believe in the theory of climatic influence. He is often given the credit for the modern introduction of that doctrine, probably because he is the first among the comparatively few writers recognized in survey courses to give expression to the subject of climate. However, the theory of climatic influence is not a product of *L'Esprit des Lois,* but rather one of the givens for Montesquieu. Clearly, he did not originate the doctrine. Aristotle, Bodin and others had expressed it.[35] Moreover, he did not introduce it to his own day and country. Belief in climatic influence had considerable currency when he was writing his masterpiece.[36] Aside from a general interest in the subject, scientists, doctors, and others were stirred by the epidemics in Europe and England during the 1730's to undertake further studies of the effects of climate upon man and society. The work which most influenced Montesquieu may be *An Essay concerning the Effects of Air on Human Bodies* by the English doctor, John Arbuthnot. This was published in 1733 and translated into French in 1742. It is a systematic treatment of the pros and cons of climatic influence. The numerous similarities between this work and Montesquieu's treatment of climate have been detailed by Joseph Dedieu.[37] While the extent of the influence is not certain, there is little doubt but that Montesquieu derived a good deal of this theory from the English doctor.

The idea that climatic influences are reasons for legislation rather than alternatives to it seems implicit in the opening sentence of the book on climate. "If it be true that the temper of the mind and the passions of the heart are extremely different in the different climates, the laws ought to be relative to the variety of those tempers."[38] Incidentally, this is a good example of Montesquieu's neutrality on many prevailing issues. He makes no choice between the mind and the heart as the source of human knowledge or action, and the conditional character of the statement indicates that he is neither accepting or rejecting the doctrine of climatic influence in any final way. He says in effect that, if there is such a principle, then legislators should consider it. Also, this statement shows that he may not consider all men to have the same passions, as he said in a certain context in the work on the Romans.

Montesquieu's purpose may be less to declare that climate has influence than to argue that its effect is limited and that it can be counteracted. At the least, if he is to make legislators responsive to social behavior and human objectives, he must overcome the belief that social conditions are merely the result of climate and other physical factors. In denying the full measure of physical determinism, his method is to bring the legislative process and the law-related forces into the common realm of social psychology. The much criticized remark that the English are prone to commit suicide may be an attack on political impatience. The Romans, Montesquieu explains, did not kill themselves without a cause, but the English are apt to commit suicide without any imaginable reason so that in England a civil law which branded suicide with infamy would simply punish the effects of madness. This trait of the English, he infers, is only one manifestation of a climate distemper which causes them to dislike everything. They may not wish to change governments because they are under law rather than a prince, he says, but they find no rest in any situation, can hardly be lulled to sleep, have little patience with negotiations, and win wars but lose the peace.[39]

The belief in climatic influence also becomes a weapon against religious determinism. Montesquieu weakens or reduces the hold of supposedly sacred beliefs by showing that they originated for geographical or other physical reasons. When viewed in this light, traditional taboos are likely to lose much of their force. At the same time, he undermines religious theories of history and authority. The belief in climatic influence is used to broaden the vision and to strengthen the will of the legislators so that impediments to the natural activity of man and society will be removed. Not only does Montesquieu give the legislators objectives and more positive goals, but he also paves the way for action. He assumes that men are by nature freely active and socially tolerant, and he attributes any contrary behavior to incidental rather than essential causes. For instance, he attacks monasticism for its unnecessary and unnatural qualities. Above all, it is an enemy of the active society, hindering man's natural inclination toward activity. *L'Esprit des Lois,* in calling "monkery" a cause of indolence, points out that it had its origin in the warm countries of the East where men are more inclined toward speculation than action. He believes that legislators should take counteraction. "In order to surmount the laziness of the climate, the laws ought to endeavor to remove all means of subsisting without labor." He criticizes the church still further with the assertion that the southern countries in Europe have done quite the reverse, encouraging rather than discouraging monasticism.[40]

Montesquieu views psychological forces so much above physical ones that he passes judgment upon climatic influences and speaks of "the vices of the climate."[41] It is evil when it causes indolence as it is likely to do in hot areas, particularly when, as in India, the religion exalts passivity in thought. Good legislation would seek to induce activity, and presumably Montesquieu believes that this can be done. "The more physical causes incline mankind to inaction," he declares, "the more the moral causes should estrange them from it." The high value of productive effort is indicated clearly when he observes that agriculture is the principal work of mankind and that the more that climate inclines a man to shun this labor, "the more the religion and the laws of the country ought to incite him to it."

He criticizes a law of India, which might be, in fact, a monarchical decree of France, because it gives the lands to the princes and destroys the spirit of property among the individual subjects, thereby augmenting "the evil effects of the climate, that is, the natural idleness."[42] If Montesquieu indirectly is accusing that French ruler of governing France as if it were in a hot climate like India, he is surely calling its action unnatural and inappropriate. A little later, he gives another plan for increasing productive effort. He observes that lazy nations are generally proud and he argues that pride be used against indolence by giving awards to husbandmen who excel in agriculture and to artists who lead in their professions. He notes that such practice succeeded in establishing the famous Irish linen manufacture.[43] Again, Montesquieu esteems not just the landed noble but even more the new economic classes, competitive trade and successful enterprise.

The use of laws to counteract climatic influences is demonstrated

also with respect to incontinence. "All nations," Montesquieu explains, "are equally agreed in fixing contempt and ignominy on the incontinence of women. Nature has dictated this to all." He points out that nature has placed boldness in one sex and shame in the other and that together they furnish a basis for legislative action. "When the physical power of certain climates violates the natural law of the two sexes, and that of intelligent beings," he says, "it belongs to the legislature to make civil laws, with a view of opposing the nature of the climate and re-establishing the primitive laws."[44] This example of civil laws to counteract climate and reinforce natural laws is a striking illustration of how ethical, physical, psychological, and sociological factors enter into Montesquieu's theory of a natural political system.

He also draws upon the prevailing doctrine of climatic influence to explain in part the diversity and peculiarity of national traits. He assumes three general types of climate, that is, hot, cold, and temperate. He associates despotisms mostly with hot regions and, in a less clear way, connects cold areas with varying degrees of liberty.[45] But his real aim here, I believe, is to suggest that the climate of France, being temperate, provides no justification for the French being under a despotic government. They do not live in a hot climate, nor are they oriental in cultural, religious, or political background. For them, despotism is neither natural nor rational. Book XVII, on the relations of laws and climate to political servitude, seems to be particularly designed to show that there is no excuse for despotic rule in France. Most of that book contrasts Asiatic and European countries, physically and politically. For instance, it explains that Asia has no temperate zone, while Europe had an extensive one, and that in Europe there are graduated or small differences between neighboring powers so that "each resembles the country adjoining it." In contrast, Asiatic countries differ greatly and they are either quite strong or quite weak, each alternative being conducive to slavery. The European nations are similar in strength, and this aids liberty for all. Asia has been subdued thirteen times whereas Europe has known, Montesquieu says, only four great changes since the establishment of Greek and Phoenician colonies. These are the conquest by the Romans, the inundations of the barbarians, the victories of Charlemagne, and the invasion of the Normans. He points out that the Romans had less difficulty in conquering Asia than in subduing Europe and that in Europe the destroyer nations were inevitably destroyed themselves. Montesquieu makes a still further contrast. The northern European nations conquered as freemen while the people of northern Asia conquered as slaves; that is, the natural conquerors of Asia, the Tartars, were themselves enslaved through being governed by a despotic emperor.[46]

Political servitude is made implicitly inappropriate for France by showing its connection to the size and the geography of a country. Asia has always had great empires, unlike Europe. This, Montesquieu explains, is because Asia has larger plains, the barriers are less formidable, and the divisions between mountains and seas are more extensive than in Europe. Accordingly, he says, power in Asia ought to be despotic because, if slavery were not severe, there would be divisions inconsistent with the nature of the country. The situation in Asia is contrasted with that in Europe where, "the natural division forms many nations of a moderate extent," and where "the ruling by laws is not incompatible with the maintenance of the state."[47] In fact, he says that ruling by laws is so favorable to the situation in Europe that otherwise the state would fall into decay and become a prey to its neighbors. The natural division in Europe, he says, "has formed a genius for liberty that renders every part extremely difficult to be subdued and subjected to a foreign power, otherwise than by the laws and the advantage of commerce."[48] Such analysis and language seem well designed to stir his fellow Frenchmen into dissatisfaction with the oppressive rule under which they lived.

The superior force of moral causes over physical ones is implicit in a number of statements which assert a direct correlation between lack of productivity of the soil and the industry and fruitfulness of a society. Montesquieu declares that: "Countries are cultivated not in proportion to their fertility, but to their liberty."[49] He observes that, if we divide the world between the most fruitful areas and the most unproductive, we would find in most ages "deserts in the most fruitful parts and great nations in those where nature seems to refuse everything." The explanation for this is that areas of good soil are the natural targets of invasion and that invasion brings desolation and depopulation. The almost uninhabitable countries of the North are always well populated and the most temperate parts of Persia, Turkey, Muscovy, and Poland have never recovered fully from the devastations of the Tartars. Another supporting example is that a country with barren soil produces the best soldiers. The German troops raised in areas where the peasants are rich are said to be inferior to other soldiers. "Military laws may provide against this inconvenience by a more severe discipline." Other examples are given of how geography affects the belief of liberty through the psychological consequences. England is evidently the subject of the statement that the inhabitants of islands have a higher regard for liberty than those of the continent because the former can more easily preserve their own laws. Again, those countries which reclaimed flooded lands, such as Holland, ancient Egypt, and two provinces of China, have a mild and moderate government because continual care is necessary for the preservation of such areas. His esteem of industry, progress, and laws is evident in a single sentence: "Mankind by their industry, and by the influence of good laws, have rendered the earth more proper for their abode."[50]

The General Causes of the National Spirit

Montesquieu seems to have developed much of his system of natural government through the increasing particularization of the idea that each nation has a unique general spirit arising from diverse general causes. These last range from climate to religion, and they have the same wide scope as the relations of laws and objects which enter into his definition of "the spirit of the laws." In fact, the titular concept of *L'Esprit des Lois* appears to be an elaboration of the theory of a national spirit from general causes. Montesquieu explicates both types of spirit largely through the specification and illustration of the law-related objects embraced by the general causes. The interchangeable way in which he uses "causes" and "relations" tends to show what he means by each. Both seem to be active correlations between the government and the social system. The doctrine of a national spirit from general causes gives an underlying coherence to *L'Esprit des Lois* as well as furnishes a pattern for the natural interactions between political functions and the physical, moral, and cultural environment. At the start, the doctrine may have been a theory of historical movement, but in *L'Esprit des Lois* it becomes mostly a guide for legislators in determining what is rational and enduring. This study is concerned mainly with the bearing of the doctrine upon the character of a political system and its origin, development and application will be considered in this section.

Montesquieu's ideas about a national spirit from a diversity of forces were developed or formulated in the lesser known works which he wrote during the years 1725 to 1740. This is an interesting period of his life because the decade beginning with 1725 was a transitional one.[51] At the start he is much concerned with universal justice and the ethics of mankind while at the end of the decade he is deeply immersed in empirical analysis of the history and the politics of national societies. Yet, his writings of this period are not unrelated to his better known volumes, *Les Lettres Persanes* and *L'Esprit des Lois.* The lesser known works grew out of some of the problems dealt with in the *Lettres,* and they anticipate some of those in *L'Esprit des Lois.* The latter volume may have had its beginnings in these lesser known works. Montesquieu himself said that *L'Esprit* was the labor of 20 years. The intermediate works tend to fall into two groups.[52] One group was written in the mid-1720's prior to Montesquieu's travel in Europe and England. The second group was written during the 1730's.

The principal work of the 1720's was the start of a general treatise on duties. The first thirteen chapters of this were the subject of an address by Montesquieu before the Academy of Bordeaux in 1725. Beyond that, the work was not completed and even that manuscript has been lost.[53] However, there is a summary analysis which had been prepared for distribution to the academy members. This is now included in the complete works of Montesquieu as the *Analyse du Traité des Devoirs.* Another work written at about the same time is the essay *De la Politique.* This was associated with the *Traité des Devoirs* in the presentation to the Academy of Bordeaux.[54]

The works written during the 1730's include three that contribute directly to the doctrine of general causes. The most important of these is the *Considérations sur les causes de la grandeur des Romains et de leur décadence*[55] published in 1734. This is a landmark in the development of the philosophy of history. It consists of 22 short chapters which draw various generalizations from aspects of Roman history as others had presented it. A second work was also printed in 1734: the *Réflexions sur la Monarchie Universelle en Europe.*[56] But this was immediately withdrawn from circulation, probably because of remarks about the French government.[57] A third work of considerable interest is the *Essai sur les Causes qui peuvent affecter les esprits et les caractères,* written between 1736 and 1742 and not published until 1892.[58] This essay has two parts: one dealing with physical causes and the other with moral causes. The principal theme is that moral causes may overcome physical ones. Montesquieu also wrote a number of other short works, and he left hundreds of one sentence or one paragraph fragments which may have been intended for some essay or book. The majority of these have been incorporated in his complete works under the designation *Mes Pensées,* but there are many others grouped under the title *Spicilège.*[59] Several of these morsels pertain directly to the doctrine of general causes as well as other ideas and propositions developed or adapted in *L'Esprit des Lois.*

The theory of a national spirit arising from general causes is in some ways two fairly distinct ideas which developed at different times. There is first the contention that each nation has a general spirit which is peculiar to that nation. Then, there is the proposition that the national spirit arises from the types of diverse forces which Montesquieu terms "general causes." The ways in which the two parts of the theory are set forth in the two groups of intermediate works will be considered in that order.

The concept of a general spirit for each national society appears in Montesquieu's writings before the identification of its causes. At first, the general spirit is rather mysterious and may have been aimed at superseding the mystique which Bodin, Bossuet, and others gave to state sovereignty and divine right monarchy.[60] The target may have been also the art of politics suggested by Machiavelli and further extolled by the *philosophes.*[61] The effect of Montesquieu's concept is to suggest that a political society is moved by the national spirit rather than by the wisdom, divine or secular, of the monarch, or by some external determinism.

In his antagonism Montesquieu carries his argument to a degree of anti-politics which is hardly characteristic of him. The *Analyse du Traité des Devoirs* asserts that nothing hinders justice more than *"la Politique",* and it calls politics "this science of ruse and artifice" which proceeds from injustice and which has no use for reason.[62] Montesquieu declares further that "the majority of consequences result from means so singular or depend upon causes so imperceptible or so distant that they cannot be foreseen." Politics, he says, "is useless in seeing future events" because revolutions seldom occur as predicted. He cites various historical events to prove the unpredictability of developments. For instance, the Huguenots put Henry IV on the throne, but they were beaten by his son and annihilated by his grandson. Their total ruin was connected with accidents that could not be foreseen. Political leaders, he declares, have little success because they do not know mankind. They assume that all men follow the straight and narrow, whereas men are usually moved "by caprice of passion" and "they do only what they said they would not." Likewise, "what ruins the great politicians is that the reputation that they have of excelling in their art discourages nearly every one from negotiating with them."[63]

The theory of a national spirit may have been an antimonarchical device conceived and formulated when Montesquieu considered a monarchy to be despotic, as he assumes in *Les Lettres Persanes*. This was before he worked out the distinct concepts of monarchy and despotism which he uses in *L'Esprit des Lois* to mark the difference between a limited monarchy and an unlimited rule of one. The theory that a nation is moved by a general spirit is antimonarchical in the anti-despotic sense because it undermines the doctrine that a nation should be controlled by an enlightened despot or that it is controlled by divine or dynastic wisdom. The proposition that the concept of the national spirit, in all its inscrutability, was designed to supersede the prevailing myths of monarchy, has some support in the fact that the idea of a general spirit was developed before its causes were identified. Neither *Le Traité des Devoirs* nor *De la Politique* makes any attempt to identify the causes; in fact, both assert that the causes cannot be foreseen or perceived. The mysterious character of the national spirit was probably necessary if the mystique of absolute monarchy was to be countered and the prevailing myths of national monarchy superseded by respect for the forces of national society.

Peculiarly appropriate, then, are the terms with which Montesquieu first explains the idea that each society has a common spirit or character. In the essay *De la Politique* he uses language that is commonly associated with eternal and universal concepts for his first recorded explanation of a single spirit from a multiplicity of causes. "In all societies, which," he says, "are only a union of spirit, there arises a common character." The essay explains that this "universal soul assumes a manner of thinking that is the effect of a chain of infinite causes, which multiply and combine from century to century." It is this "alone which governs" and "all that the sovereigns, the magistrates, or the people can do or imagine, whether they appear to check this tone or to follow it, always relates to it, and it dominates until the final destruction."[64] Even here Montesquieu assumes a nation to be a combination of one, few, and many, and each of the three powers is deemed to be subordinate to this "univeral soul" and "common character" which arises from the "union of spirit." The use of these expressions as well as "infinite causes" suggests rational generalization on top of empirical observation.

But Montesquieu is talking about the spirit of a nation and not the spirit of all mankind. The spirit is the product of events during a series of centuries and thus is limited in time. A limitation in space seems equally implicit. He speaks of societies in the plural and, while this may refer to all societies, it concerns them as particulars and not as one single generality. What he says here makes sense only when applied to a single society, and, accordingly, the "univeral soul" is universal only within a particular nation. His method of taking concepts and language commonly associated with the universal or the eternal and applying them to national societies, which are inherently limited in time and space, may not be the consequence of error or confusion. It may be part of a design to undermine the appeal of absolute monarchy by attributing the progress of a nation in history to something inherent in the national society itself rather than to the external forces of divine wisdom or monarchical sovereignty. Looked at for a contribution to the history of political ideas, this would mean an effort to replace theological and legal values with psychological and sociological ones.

The works of the mid-1730's also reflect an antimonarchical attitude. The *Réflexions sur la Monarchie Universelle en Europe*,[65] printed in 1734, and immediately withdrawn, argues that a universal monarchy for Europe has become impracticable. It may have been directed at Louis XIV's dream of being the only sovereign in Europe. Later, *L'Esprit des Lois* says that a great prince (obviously the Sun King) was happier in being the most powerful ruler in Europe than he would have been as the only sovereign.[66] The *Réflexions* reviews the various efforts that have been made to form a single government for Europe, particularly those in which one monarch would rule, and asserts that such an arrangement has become still more impracticable because of the difference in the military and economic power of the various European countries. However, it does maintain that the European powers are mutually dependent.[67]

The study of the Romans has antimonarchical implications, even though it may be best known for its pioneer contributions to the philosophy of history.[68] That treatise seems to be the first in

which Montesquieu expressly uses the term "general spirit" in relation to a national society. This occurs in an argument that human
political authority is inherently limited, which could be directed
against the contentions of Voltaire, Bossuet, and others for absolute
monarchy. Montesquieu declares that in this world a human authority cannot be in all respects despotic; "the most immense power
is always limited on some side." His supporting examples of despotism are oriental, just as they usually are in *Les Lettres Persanes* and
L'Esprit des Lois. "If the grand seigneur imposes a novel tax upon
Constantinople, a general outcry will immediately disclose to him
limits that he had not known."[69] This suggests that social mores
are stronger and more dominant than political authority, and such
a theory is assumed in many portions of his latter study. The work
on the Romans includes another and still more pointed example of
this social phenomena. "A king of Persia might well constrain a son
to kill his father, or a father to kill his son, but to oblige his subjects to drink wine, he could not do so." The implication here that
social rights are stronger than individual ones is evident also in discussions of liberty in *L'Esprit des Lois.* Clearly Montesquieu is making psychological forces superior to political ones. A prince may be
able to command an individual but he cannot compel a whole people to change their customs, mores or manners. The distinction between the control of an individual and the control of a group bears
upon the problem of determinism and also upon the meaning of
liberty. He assumes that the society or the group has freedom
against the political authority and that, while the individual is free
to change his way, the motion of a society is determined by its own
mores. In this context, Montesquieu sets forth his principle of a national spirit. "There is in each nation a general spirit upon which
power itself is founded; when it strikes against this spirit, it strikes
against itself and necessarily arrests itself." Thus, the general spirit,
as the controlling power of a national society, could supersede the
force of divine right or dynastic monarchy. Likewise, it may answer
the dilemma posed by *Les Lettres Persanes* on the degeneration of
monarchy into either tyranny or anarchy. The general spirit of the
nation could take precedence and authority over both the king and
the individuals.

The idea that the national spirit is the natural product of a system of interrelations is suggested by an observation in the study of
the Romans. This deals with the harmony of diverse social elements
and says that "union in a body politique" is a "very equivocal

thing."[70] The "true union is one of harmony" which makes all conflicting parties "concur in the general good of the society" just as
"the dissonances in music concur in the total accord." Such a union
"is like the elements of the universe, eternally bound together by
the action of some and the reaction of others." Thus, Montesquieu
assumes that there are general, enduring, and somewhat harmonious relationships within the apparent confusion of particular social
events. This may reflect in part the contemporary belief in the ra-
tionality of natural motion.[71] Also, it might anticipate the theory
of a natural harmony of particular and general interests, later asserted by the Physiocrats and the early English utilitarians,[72] but
Montesquieu seems to rely more upon the counteraction of diverse
and conflicting interests to assure common good and political liberty. Moreover, we will see that in *L'Esprit des Lois* he proposes a
system of laws, institutions, and attitudes to protect and support natural tendencies. He might concede a natural harmony in the civil
order, but not in the political order.

While the concept of a general spirit for each nation is emphasized in the works of 1725 and to some degree in the study of the
Romans, there is in those early treatises comparatively little identification or explanation of the specific causes of the spirit. The plurality of the causes was recognized from the start but their identity
was perhaps purposely vague, and the process of specification did
not begin for some time and then was slow and irregular. *Le Traité
des Devoirs* remarks, as noted before, that most political events result from imperceptible causes, and the essay *De la Politique* attributes the national soul to "a chain of infinite causes."[73] The study
of the Romans seems to have no consistent classification of causes.
The *Essai sur les Causes* gives separate treatment to physical and
moral causes and describes the latter to include "the combination of
laws, the religion, the mores and the manners."[74] A fairly consistent identification of the general causes appears in two fragments,
now called *Pensées,* reportedly written during the 1730's. Each frag-
ment lists five general causes with but one variation. The first declares that states are governed by religion, general maxims of government, particular laws, mores, and manners.[75] This is noteworthy for the omission of climate. The other *Pensée* adds climate but
omits maxims of government.[76] These six causes and a seventh
(precedents) make up the final formulation in *L'Esprit des Lois.*

The reduction of the vague multiplicity of unidentified causes to
a small number of general causes gives the doctrine additional force

because of the implication that what is general is rational and enduring. The idea that the generalization of causes is more rational than particular causes is suggested by the *Essai sur les Causes*. Its opening sentence makes this point. "The causes become less arbitrary to the extent that they have a more general application." Specifically, "we know better what gives a certain character to a nation than what gives a certain spirit to an individual, what modifies a sex than what affects a man, what forms the genius of the society which make up a living race, than that of a single person."[77] This may seem to give more meaning to the abstract generalization than to the concrete particulars but the sense of it is more likely that what is uniform and recurring in the particulars has more meaning than what is irregular and unique.

Along with the specific identification of the general causes, Montesquieu gives attention to the manner in which the causes are related to each other. He does not set down any scale of priority or any hierarchy of value for the causes. Rather, he indicates that their relative force varies from country to country and that a change in one affects the others. The first *Pensée* that designated five things which govern a nation declares that they "are all in mutual relation with one another" and that if you change one, "the others follow slowly, which leaves above all a kind of dissonance."[78] Thus, the potentially disharmonious general causes give rise to a single national spirit by a process of mutual accommodation. Montesquieu seems to presuppose such a natural tendency at many points in the development of his theory of natural government. In the second *Pensée*, he sets forth a working principle of active equilibrium. "In proportion as, in every country, one of these causes acts with more force, the others in the same degree are weakened."[79] He indicates that one general cause may characterize a particular society, but I believe that this does not mean that there is only one general cause in any particular nation. One force may be more important than others in a specific country, but I believe that he assumes that each nation has all general causes in some degree of potentiality and that the difference in the make-up of the combination helps to explain the diverse character of various national societies. The interaction of the general causes is another manifestation of the logic of relational pluralism. The pattern of interaction embodies the basic premises that any realm is composed of a plurality of diverse elements and that each constituent element has a separate, distinct character even though it is at the same time essentially related to each other element.

Though the express recognition in *L'Esprit des Lois* of the doctrine of a national spirit from general causes is limited to a few paragraphs in Book XIX, it comes at a strategic and engaging point. Book XIX may be the keystone of *L'Esprit des Lois*. But it also has more than its share of the mystique. Its ideas are as profound and as vague as any in Montesquieu's writings. The book expressly concerns "the laws in relation to the principles that form the general spirit, the mores and the manners of a nation," and its subjects range from a declaration of primary interest in order to an investigation of political party behavior in England. More than half of the book examines the power of the mores and the manners, clearly the two general causes which are the least specific and the most pervasive.

There may seem to be a disconnected array of subjects in Book XIX, but I believe that they all concern the recurring problem of political change and social order. The doctrine of general causes may be the key to Montesquieu's answer to that problem. At the start of the book, he declares that in the "crowd of ideas which presents itself to my mind, I shall be more attentive to the order of things that to the things themselves." We will see that the order is a complex, moving one and that Montesquieu endeavors to bring general regularity to it. For instance, the first three chapters concern the order of things, the preparation of people's minds for the reception of "the best laws," and the psychological tyranny which results when political leaders disregard the beliefs and opinions of the people. All of these discussions are relevant to the problem of psychological order and change within a society. Then the next chapter presents the doctrine of general spirit, and this is brought into relation with the issue of order and change by the paragraph on the interaction of the general causes and by the argument in the fifth chapter that the legislators should be cautious in changing the general spirit. Moreover, the next half dozen chapters (6-11) talk about the natural forces of change, the sociability of the Athenians (and inferentially the French), the power of pride and vanity, the aim of a happy mixture of vices and virtures, and a final reminder that political and moral vices are not the same. All of this pertains to the particularly fundamental problem of how far and in what way the legislators should attempt to change the existing pattern of ideas within a national society. The remainder of Book XIX, which is the larger in size, concerns the relations of the two most indefinite general causes, that is, mores and manners, with laws, and sometimes with religion. This is one of Montesquieu's most penetrating analyses of the relationship of the political and cultural systems.

There is a problem of translation in Book XIX, particularly with the word *moeurs,* which Nugent traduces variously as morals, manners, and customs. This, I believe, may confuse it with other terms that Montesquieu uses, such as *coutumes* and *morales,*[80] which would seem to have a superior claim on the words customs and morals, respectively. Accordingly, I will consider *moeurs* to be mores; *manières* to be manners; *morales,* morals; *coutumes,* customs; and *usages,* usages, regardless of the context.

The way in which the seemingly diverse subjects of Book XIX do relate to the single problem of psychological order and change will be explained more thoroughly by considering the specific content of the particular chapters.

Montesquieu's comprehensive recognition of environmental influences is definitely indicated by the way in which he investigates the order of things. The declaration of interest in the order of things, at the start of Book XIX, is followed by an express determination to be circumspect in his observation and study. "I shall be obliged to wander to the right and to the left, that I may investigate and discover the truth." This anticipates the declaration at the start of Book XXIX, that he wrote *L'Esprit des Lois* for the primary purpose of showing legislators that they should be guided by the spirit of moderation. Likewise, his remark about investigating both left and right, but presumably not confining himself to either, is similar to the mythological story in Book XXX about the sun warning Phaeton to drive his chariot in the middle without ascending too high nor too low or too much to the right or left lest he encounter disaster.

The psychological bent of Montesquieu's thinking is evident here because the second chapter of Book XIX expressly asserts that "it is necessary the people's mind should be prepared for the reception of the best Laws." This might suggest the use of propaganda, but, more likely, Montesquieu is urging legislators to respect the established ideas of the people. The supporting illustrations concern the dislike of ancient Germans for Roman legal procedure, even though it was designed to assure justice. "Liberty itself has appeared intol-

erable to those nations who have not been accustomed to enjoy it."
This indicates that liberty depends upon common attitudes of a
people and that social habit is more determining than calculated
reason. Another illustration is the inappropriateness of popular
government among people who cannot imagine living without a
king. This need not mean that Montesquieu favors crude forms of
judicial procedure nor that he sees no place for popular government. Rather, I believe, his point is that liberty is not an absolute
idea the same everywhere but something relevant to the social psychology of the respective nation.

This interpretation is supported, I suggest, by the subject matter
of the next chapter. This identifies two sorts of tyranny, "one real,
which arises from oppression" and the other "seated in opinion,"
but the discussion is limited to the latter. This kind of tyranny, he
says, is sure to result "whenever those who govern establish things
shocking to the existing ideas of a nation." For support, Montesquieu recalls how Caesar, the Triumvirs, and Augustus, despite
their regal power, respected the Roman dislike of kings and preserved all the outward appearances of equality. He points out that
the resolve of the Romans to have no king merely meant that they
retained their republican manners. Another example of the importance of public psychology to acceptable government concerns
Augustus and the banishment of an actor. Montesquieu explains
that the laws of Augustus were so severe they exasperated the Romans, but when Augustus recalled Pylades, the banished comedian,
the discontent ceased. "A people of this stamp have a more lively
sense of tyranny when a player is banished than when they are deprived of their laws."[81] Thus, with all of his emphasis upon government under law, the importance of a separate judiciary, and the
need of established legal procedure, Montesquieu still believes that
government must be relevant most of all to the mores of the people.

Having discussed the primacy of order, the people's preparation
for "the best laws," and the psychological tyranny of disregarding
the existing ideas of a nation, Montesquieu then presents the proposition of a national spirit arising from general causes, much as it
was formulated in the two Pensées mentioned previously. In Book
XIX, the specification of causes is more comprehensive, including
all those forces mentioned in the two Pensées, and adding "precedents." The statement in L'Esprit des Lois also connects the causes
to the general spirit. "Mankind are influenced by various causes; by

the climate, by the religion, by the laws, by the maxims of government, by precedents, mores and manners; whence is formed a general spirit of nations." There may be some indications in this statement that Montesquieu is thinking about the whole of mankind but the context, particularly the next paragraph, clearly shows that he is thinking of the people of particular nations. While the specific formulation of doctrine of national spirit in *L'Esprit des Lois* refers to only seven general causes, other parts of the work identify what could be considered to be subspecies of various causes. For instance, maxims of government could well include the various rules on the structure and spirit of different kinds of government analyzed in Books II to X, and climate might embrace temperature, soil, and geography, which are considered along with climate in Books XIV to XVIII. There is less certainty about the scope of mores and manners, but these seem to be broad enough to cover commerce, occupations, domestic practices, class privileges, and even customs, each of which receive substantial attention in *L'Esprit des Lois*. The most elaborate subclassification is the nine-fold division of laws in Book XXVI, and each of these legal orders could be considered a contributing cause in the continuing evolvement of the national spirit.

The interrelationship of the general causes may be a key to the pattern of *L'Esprit des Lois* as well as to Montesquieu's theory of political system for another reason. The doctrine of a national spirit from general causes gives coherence to the books on various nonpolitical subjects, such as climate, mores, commerce, religion, and civil laws and also connects these to the books on government and political liberty. Thus, the doctrine is a way of joining or reconciling unity and diversity. However, the emphasis in *L'Esprit des Lois* is much more upon the relation of the several causes to each other than upon the spirit as a single entity or concept. Less than a fourth of Book XIX is given to explaining the general spirit while the remainder of that book, and most of many other books before and after Book XIX, analyzes at considerable length the relation of laws to the various causes and subcauses. Also, in presenting the doctrine, Montesquieu explains differences among national societies by reference to one or another of the general causes. The distinctive pattern of the causes in a nation is accentuated by the asserted effect of one upon the others. "In proportion as, in every country, any one of these causes acts with more force, the others in the same degree are weakened."[82] Thus, one cause may become more and more dominant. In fact, the general spirit of a number of ñations is described largely in terms of a single general cause. "Nature and the climate rule almost alone over the savages; manners govern the Chinese; the laws tyrannize in Japan; the mores had formerly all their influence at Sparta; maxims of government, and the ancient simplicity of mores, once prevailed at Rome." Undoubtedly, Montesquieu does not mean that only one cause is at work in a particular country; rather, he suggests that one may be stronger than the others among certain peoples.

The next chapter on "How far we should be attentive lest the general Spirit of a Nation be changed" contains some of Montesquieu's most sublime advice to legislators. He supposes a people, presumably the French, who are "of a social temper, open-hearted, cheerful, endowed with taste and a facility in communicating their thoughts," who are "sprightly and agreeable, sometimes imprudent, often indiscreet," and who also have "courage, generosity, frankness, and a certain notion of honor." With such a nation, he says, "no one ought to endeavor to restrain their manners by laws, unless he would lay a constraint on their virtues. If in general the character be good, the little foibles that may be found in it are of small importance." Perhaps, he adds, they "might lay a restraint upon women, enact laws to reform their mores and to reduce their luxury, but who knows but that by these means they might lose that peculiar taste which would be the source of the wealth of the nation." This reminder to legislators of the sublimity of the national spirit is similar to the remark in the Preface to *L'Esprit des Lois,* equally aimed at the French rulers. There Montesquieu says that the right to propose alterations to the maxims on which a nation is founded "belongs only to those who are so happy as to be born with a genius capable of penetrating the entire constitution of a state."[83] Montesquieu is not willing to assume that legislators generally were born so happily. Accordingly, he issues an admonition which reaches over the whole of *L'Esprit des Lois* and draws together many of the underlying meanings of natural government.

When Montesquieu tells the legislator "to follow the spirit of the nation, when it is not contrary to the principle of government," because "we do nothing so well as when we act with freedom, and follow the bent of our natural genius,"[84] he is giving what well may be his most fundamental piece of advice. The guide for the rulers is not as it was for Plato a transcendent idea of the good, but rather is an immanent sense of social relations. This need not be universal or eternal because it may vary from country to country, but it must be sociologically and psychologically relevant to the particular national society. Moreover, the legislator must also respect "the principle" of the respective government, that is, as he explains in Book III, the moving passion required for the success of the type of government. The warning on this matter need not mean that the principle is superior to the general spirit. The admonition may require no more than that there should be no legislation contrary to the principle. This prescription for the legislator also throws light upon Montesquieu's idea of liberty as the freedom of the group. If we can act freely when the legislator follows the spirit of the nation, then it would seem that liberty depends upon whether the laws are appropriate for the group rather than how they affect a particular person in his individual tendencies.

Montesquieu's equating of the national spirit with the natural genius of the people is further indication of his psychological approach to political theory, and it also provides some explanation of what he means by both "nature' and "spirit." His use of the two terms tends to assume that they are mutual in their force. The spirit is natural, and nature has spirit. For France, apparently, there would be no advantage, either at home or abroad, in trying to give "an air of pedantry . . . to a nation that is naturally gay." Montesquieu concludes: "Leave it to do the frivolous things in a serious manner and the serious things with gayety."

The idea that the national spirit would be moderate, if naturally opposing forces are allowed to act upon each other, is implicit in the warning "That Everything ought not to be corrected."[85] A gentleman of the nation described, presumably France, argues "leave us as we are . . . and nature will repair whatever is amiss." Nature, he says, "has given us a vivacity capable of offending, and hurrying us beyond the bounds of respect" but "this same vivacity is corrected by the politeness it procures, inspiring us with a taste of the world, and, above all, for the conversation of the fair sex." He explains further that "our indiscretions joined to our good nature would make the laws which should constrain our sociability not at all proper for us." This interplay of contrary forces may be basically similar, I suggest, to the countervailing powers of repulsion and attraction which Montesquieu sees in both government and the universe. In Book III, he found this pertinent to the idea that honor is the moving passion of nondespotic monarchy. "Honor sets all the parts of the body politic in motion, and by its very action connects them; thus each individual advances the public good, while he thinks only of promoting his own interest."[86] This may overstate slightly his general position, but he also found a self-correcting power in the three class structure of the Roman republic. "From its birth," he says, "abuses of power could always be corrected by its constitution, whether by means of the spirit of the people, the strength of the senate, or the authority of certain magistrates."[87] He may anticipate in some degree the harmony of interests later argued by the Physiocrats, Smith and Bentham,[88] but not all of it.

The implication in *Les Lettres Persanes*[89] and again in this portion of *L'Esprit des Lois* that the French are a rather gay and light-hearted people is fortified by references to classical Greece and the different modes of the people of Athens and Sparta. The disguised Frenchman remarks that the Athenians were a nation somewhat like ours. "They mingled gaiety with business; a stroke of raillery was as agreeable in the senate as in the theatre." This Athenian vivacity, he says, arose in the councils but went along with them in the execution of their resolves, while, on the other hand, the characteristics of the Spartans were "gravity, seriousness, severity, and silence." Montesquieu concludes that "it would have been as difficult to bring over an Athenian by teasing as it would a Spartan by diverting him."[90]

Montesquieu's interest in social communication is evident in the discussion that correlates a people's capacity for change to sociability and vanity but not pride. "The more communicative a people are the more easily they change their habits." This is because sociable people are much seen by each other and their peculiarities are mutually observed. Likewise, the climate which makes communication a pleasure also makes people delight in change. Vanity, but not pride, has similar consequences. "Vanity is as advantageous to a government as pride is dangerous." The numerous benefits which result from vanity he says include industry, the arts, fashion, politeness, and taste, while the many evils which spring from pride include laziness, poverty, neglect, and national decline. "Laziness is the effect of pride; labor, a consequence of vanity. The pride of a Spaniard leads him to decline labor; the vanity of a Frenchman to work better than others." By way of comment, the driving force which man gains from his interests and instincts seems to be an essential aspect of Montesquieu's view of human nature. True, there is more to man than the vanity inspired drive, but this is one of the forces which make up the contradiction and interaction within man, as Montesquieu sees him.[91] Thus, individual competition and social conflict are essential to a healthy political community; without such action and reaction the forces which give rise to the national spirit would not operate and the general causes would not be able to exert their capacity to correct what has become amiss.

The theory that a unique combination of forces may explain the particularity of national societies is implicit also in the chapters on virtues and vices. Montesquieu makes quite clear that national spirit is the consequence of a multiplicity of factors of varying strength and merit. "The character of the several nations," he says, "are formed of virtues and vices, of good and bad qualities." From the "happy mixture" of these forces, he asserts, "great advantages results"; but, on the other hand, "there are others whence great evils arise — evils which one would not suspect." Examples of unhappy mixtures are the Spaniards and the Chinese. The former, he notes, have been famous in all ages for their honesty but "this admirable quality" is joined to their indolence so that the result is "most pernicious," and the commerce of the Spanish monarchy is conducted by others in Europe. The Chinese character is formed of a mixture directly opposite to that of the Spaniards. The Chinese are inspired to a prodigious activity by the precariousness of their subsistence, but this excessive desire of gain has made them so unfaithful that no trading nation can confide in them. Montesquieu adds, upon reflection, that his mixing of virtues and vices, does not mean that there is no difference between the two. There is, he says, "an infinite distance" between the two and that he wishes to make "my readers comprehend that all politics are not all moral vices; and that all moral are not political vices; and that those who make laws which shock the general spirit of a nation ought not to be ignorant of this."[92] These comments make clear Montesquieu's differentiation of moral and political factors and provide further evidence of his interest in the secularization of political action and behavior.

The doctrine of general causes gives both unity and depth to the explication of the spirit of the laws. The books of *L'Esprit des Lois* which deal most peculiarly with the general causes, that is, the books on the influences of climate, mores, manners, and religion, include the deepest inquiries into the psychological and sociological behavior of the national society.[93] The depth of Montesquieu's inquiry into the life of man and society may account for the diversity of subject matter. The farther the search for generalization is carried the more varied are the objects encountered. What appears to be a series of digressions may be a monument to persistence in the quest for underlying principles. Likewise, the doctrine of a national spirit from general causes permits the national society to be considered a psychological and sociological system rather than a legal and theological one. The general causes bring all of man's social attitudes and behavior into relevant association with the political entity.[94] For instance, the comparative analysis of governments in the first portion of *L'Esprit des Lois* concerns not only institutions of authority but also the attitudes of different societies toward such matters as education, luxury, marriage, and the birth rate.[95]

Raymond Aron, in his recent study of historical trends in sociological thought, distinguishes Montesquieu's idea of a national spirit from the creative will of an individual or a group, that is, the existential choice of a Kant or a Sartre. This may be so, but Aron seems to place too much emphasis upon physical factors and too little upon moral and cultural ones when he describes the general spirit as "the way of living, behaving, thinking and feeling, of a particular collectivity as geography and history have produced it."[96] Religion, mores, manners, laws, and maxims of government as well as climate and precedents are included in the general causes and I believe that "history" has become too specific a discipline to stand for such a diverse number of nonphysical forces, if this is what Aron intends. Otherwise, he seems to ignore them.

The full importance of Montesquieu's theory of the general spirit and the companion doctrine of the spirit of the laws seems to have been recognized by Rousseau when he discussed systems of legislation in *Du Contrat Social*. Rousseau concludes that the constitution of a state "is rendered most solid and durable" when "the natural relations and the laws mutually agree on every point."[97] The laws, he adds, serve to assure, accompany and correct the former. If a legislator mistakes his object, and "acts on a principle different from that which arises from the nature of things," the laws will be insensibly weakened, the constitution altered and the state agitated until it is destroyed and "invincible nature has resumed her sway." The conflicts between legislative intent and natural relations are illustrated by Rousseau with alternatives of servitude vs. liberty, wealth vs. population, and conquest vs. peace. However, Rousseau's recognition of sociological forces seems to have been overridden by his theory of the general will, particularly when it is interpreted in a rationalistic manner, as it often is.

Does the doctrine of a national spirit from general causes, in seeking to avoid the prevailing theories of determinism, impose a new kind of determinism? This is considered by Werner Stark, whose work on Montesquieu's sociology of knowledge is probably the most intensive study of his epistemology. Stark says that the inevitability of imperceptible causes and the ineffectiveness of the arts of politics, which Montesquieu asserts in the essay *De la Politique,* are evidences of a "tendency toward sociological mechanism."[98] But the implication of these ideas, along with related tendencies toward rationalism and determinism, Stark asserts, belong to Montesquieu's younger period and are not applicable to his later writings. Stark regards Montesquieu to be considerably more of an empiricist than a rationalist and he asserts that any tendency toward determinism is countered by a direct rejection of fatalism in *Le Traité des Devoirs.*[99] However, the main point would seem to be who is being determined and by what. Stark endeavors to refute the full charge of determinism, but there would seem to be a key distinction between determinism of the society and that of the individual. In respect of a political society, there could be a determinism because of the general tendencies of the individuals who compose it. This would be an internal determinism, and it would not seem to have the evils of external determinism. I am willing to admit that Montesquieu may have recognized a "sociological mechanism" resulting from internal forces, that is, the individuals exercising their free will in a common way. National determinism resulting from inherent or internal forces of a sociological and psychological character would seem to be comparatively inoffensive, if offensive at all. Certainly, this is a long step from what France was experiencing in Montesquieu's day and what he was endeavoring to oppose.

While the doctrine of general causes may introduce elements of a social determinism, it does not exclude free choice in the individual. In fact, individuals exercising their free will in a common way produce the social determinism. There is a difference between the general tendencies of action and the individual capacity to act. A particular individual with freedom of will can act contrary to the general tendencies of the group, or even contrary to his own usual tendencies. Both *Les Lettres Persanes* and *L'Esprit des Lois* assume that man has the capacity to act with reason and justice even though he often acts in response to interest.[100] *L'Esprit des Lois* develops various ways of controlling self-interest, such as, inspiring attitudes of self-restraint, pitting interest against interest, and prescribing agencies detached from the competition of interests to preserve reason and justice.[101] But this extensive effort presupposes both a framework of objective reason in mankind generally and an individual free will among the particular members of the national society.

The Autonomy of National Mores and Manners

The most indefinite and probably the most inclusive of the general causes which give rise to the unique spirit of a national society are *les moeurs* and *les manières,* which, for reasons stated previously,[102] will be translated "the mores" and "the manners." Much of the time Montesquieu deals with them as if they were a single type of general cause and, on the several occasions when he speaks only of the mores, he may intend both. At one point he says that they concern interior and exterior conduct, respectively,[103] but this difference is not always apparent in the application.

More basic to a socially related political system than the distinction between the mores and the manners is the difference between this pair of general causes and what Montesquieu means by "the laws" in this analysis. In general, he seems to assume that the laws are positive enactments or decrees, while the mores and manners come close to being or including natural and customary law. For instance, he says that laws derive from "a particular institution" whereas mores are more attached to the general spirit; that laws are "established" while mores are "inspired."[104] This suggests that the laws result from acts of deliberate will expressly promulgated while the mores may accumulate, rather irregularly, from innumerable, spontaneous actions within the society. The statement that "the laws are the particular and precise institutions of a legislator and mores and manners are the institutions of a nation in general,"[105] may reflect the two basic ways of achieving social order, that is, through commands handed down by a political superior and by understandings or accomodations mutually developed by equal members of a society. One of Montesquieu's principal objectives throughout *L'Esprit des Lois,* I believe, is to focus attention upon the second method, which may be first in nature, both for what that ordering processes can accomplish in itself and for the limitations which it places upon the political-superior process of keeping order. He seems to assume that political law cannot and above all should not provide all of the rules for a national society. "Mores and manners are those habits," he says, "which are not established by legislators, either because they were not able or were not willing to establish them." The assumption that laws are mainly political while the mores and manners are ethical, social, or civil is evident also in the observation that "the laws are most adapted to regulate the actions of the citizens, and the mores to regulate the actions of the man." It is at this point that Montesquieu says that the mores relate to the interior conduct and manners to the exterior. If we accept Kant's distinction on ethics and jurisprudence, then manners would be closer to laws while mores would approach ethical habits. In one analysis of despotism, Montesquieu does say that manners take the place of laws. Likewise, there are observations that mores make better citizens than do the laws.[106]

While a good deal of indirect analysis of mores and manners appears in various books of *L'Esprit des Lois,* including those on luxury, terrain, commerce, money, and population (VII, XVIII, XX, XXI, XXII, and XXIII), the direct investigation of these two general causes is limited to Book XIX. It is largely an examination of how these causes are related to the laws of different kinds of nations. It is within the general framework of the relations of political decisions to sociological and psychological forces, and it specifically compares three general types of political systems: (1) the despotic state with China the most frequent example, (2) the classical republics of Athens and Rome, and (3) the mixed monarchy of contemporary England. This last is an extensive inquiry into the attitudes and political behavior of the English at the time. It is nearly as long as the famous chapter on the English constitution and it demonstrates that Montesquieu did go behind or beyond the constitutional laws and the formal structure of government in his investigation of England. This analysis of English politics has much bearing upon the general objective of this study, because I aim to show that Montesquieu was primarily interested in the psychology of social conflicts and that this, rather than the rational categorization of functions, is the basis of his theory of liberty-assuring government. But some preliminary consideration will be given to the discussions of mores and law in despotic and republican nations.

The study of laws, mores, and manners in a despotic state provides further proof that the essence of such a government amounts to the failure to respect the principles of "relational pluralism." This idea was evident in the earlier books of *L'Esprit des Lois* where the distinguishing characteristics of despotism were shown to be the disregard of law, the concentration of administration in a single vizier, the summary judicial methods, and the overrunning of class or group distinctions. In Book XIX despotism is portrayed again to be the confusing, confounding, or aribtrary combining of diverse forces. This time the unnatural intermingling concerns four of the general causes of the general national spirit, religion being added to laws, mores, and manners in several of the chapters.

The inquiry into the general spirit of a despotic state provides support for the broad proposition that laws should be revised with caution, particularly when the objective is a change in the mores and manners. "It is a capital maxim that the mores and manners of a despotic state ought never to be changed; for nothing would more speedily produce a revolution."[107] Here, Montesquieu may be telling his countrymen that the political style of the Bourbons is natural only in a despotism, and also reminding the king that social order rests more upon these general causes than upon the laws. He explains that in despotic states "there are no laws, that is, none that can be properly called so; there are only mores and manners," and he asserts that "if you overturn these you overturn all." He seems to be talking to the French monarch also when he says that the mores are inspired while the laws are established and that the former are attached more to the general spirit while the latter are associated more with a particular institution. Then, his assertion that there is more danger in subverting the general spirit than any particular institution shows again the extent to which Montesquieu considers the political system to be secondary to and even dependent upon the social system.

He also suggests a correspondence between the mores and manners, on the one hand, and the absence of communication, on the other hand. This suggests that these two general causes exert greater control where power is exercised arbitrarily than where liberty reigns, presumably because with less freedom and communication, there is less change of mores and manners. Also, Montesquieu explains, in despotisms, "the more established manners resemble the laws," and there is greater necessity than in any other country that the prince or legislator not oppose the mores and manners. All of these remarks, I believe, could be aimed at the contemporary French situation.

The pervasive character of these general causes is evident again when Montesquieu spells out "the natural means of changing the mores and manners of a nation."[108] Since laws are the particular institutions of the legislators and the mores and manners are the general institutions of the nation, "it follows that when these mores and manners are to be changed, it ought not to be done by laws" because "this would have too much the air of tyranny." Rather, "it would be better to change by introducing other mores and other manners." Thus, Montesquieu lays down the principle that when a prince wishes to make great alterations, "he should reform by laws what is established by laws, and change by manners what is settled by manners." He declares further that "it is very bad policy to change by law what ought to be changed by manners." The supporting example concerns Russian legislation and also throws light upon the supplemental influence of climate. Montesquieu observes that the laws which obliged the Muscovites to cut off their beards and shorten their cloaks and the rigor with which Peter I enforced these rules were "instances of tyranny." Then he says that the objective could be attained with milder methods because the mores of the Russians at the time "were foreign to the climate" and had been imposed upon them by conquest. "Peter I, in giving the mores and the manners of Europe to a European nation, found a facility which he did not himself expect. The empire of the climate is the first, the most powerful of all empires." The Tsar did not need laws to change the mores and the manners of his country; "it would have been sufficient to have introduced other mores and manners." This tells much of Montesquieu's ideas on the relation of physical and moral causes. Climate is but one factor, and it may be used to aid desired changes if the legislator is sufficiently circumspect to recognize and appreciate its influence. Likewise, the mores and manners are distinctive forces which should be respected for what they are, and dealing with them requires adherence to the natural principle of treating likes with likes.

The warning against unnatural changes applies to customs[109] as well as to mores and manners. Montesquieu asserts that nations generally hold tenaciously to their customs and that attempting to alter them by violence makes the people unhappy. He contends that, instead the people should be engaged to make the revisions themselves. Also, he indicates that there should be punishment only for what is necessary and that the law should not bother with things that are indifferent in their own nature. Thus, the legislators should respect the causes of the general spirit other than law and, when customs, mores, or manners are to be changed, this should be done without direct legislative enactment.

Rulers who do not respect the distinctions but confound the different orders, Montesquieu says, are likely to be classed as despotic. "Lycurgus made the same code for the laws, the mores and the manners; and the legislators of China have done the same."[110] It is not surprising, he adds, that the legislators of China and Sparta confounded these three causes because for them "the mores represent the laws and the manners represent the mores." However, Montesquieu explains that the objectives differed in the two countries. The legislators in China made their subjects live in peace by giving them rules of the most extensive civility. On the other hand, Lycurgus had no regard for civility and inspired the people with a warlike spirit so that they were in a continual state of disciplinary instruction, and their lives were marked by starkness and rigor rather than by complaisance.

The characterization of despotism to be the arbitrary commingling of naturally diverse social forces in both the input and the output channels of the political system becomes particularly striking when religion is brought into the analysis. Montesquieu superimposes this factor into an investigation of mores and manners, even though he regards religion as a distinct general cause and later takes two whole books to explain its natural relations to other general causes. This superimposition provides strong evidence of his deep antagonism to the mixing of religion with those forces, such as law and mores, which enforce the social order. Here again he implies that the coercive use of religion is the hallmark of despotism. While the attack upon religious intervention may be veiled to some degree, it is the sharpest thrust of *L'Esprit des Lois* and it brought him the bitterest criticism.[111] In Book XIX the attack is expressly against China, but it is done with such abandon that Montesquieu must have had in mind the government of France and the vizier-like ministry of Cardinal Richelieu.

With China at least the nominal target, what Montesquieu says about the commingling of religion with the laws, the mores, and the manners, is as sharp as it is comprehensive. On top of his previous contentions that the lawgivers of Sparta and China had imposed the same code for laws, mores, and manners, he asserts that the legislators of China "went further" and "confounded their religion, laws, mores and manners: all these were morality, all these were virtue."[112] The precepts relating to these four points were "rites" and the Chinese people spent their whole youth in learning them and their whole life in practicing them. The rites were taught by men of letters and inculcated by the magistrates. They included all the ordinary actions of life and when strictly observed, China was well governed. Two things facilitated the acceptance of these rites, Montesquieu explains. Both are connected with education. One is the difficulty of writing which took so much of the people's time and attention. The other was "that the ritual precepts, having nothing in them that is spiritual, but being merely rules of common practice, are more adapted to convince and strike the mind than things merely intellectual." Here is another implication that man generally acts more easily or more fully from the heart than from the mind. Montesquieu then asserts that princes who try to govern by punishments rather than by rites are trying to do what is beyond their power to produce, that is, to give mores. The infliction of punishment may put a stop to many consequences of the general evil, but it will not remove the evil. "Thus when the principles of the Chinese government were discarded, and morality was banished, the state fell into anarchy and revolutions succeeded." This, I believe, is another illustration of the danger of simple government and specifically of the tendency of unmixed monarchy to degenerate into either tyranny or anarchy. Montesquieu raises this problem in *Les Lettres Persanes,* and he implicitly devotes most of *L'Esprit des Lois* to finding a solution.

The commingling of general causes in China, he points out, is the reason that its laws are not changed by conquest. In other words, the effective revision of the laws may depend upon adjustments in the mores, manners, and religion. Hence, Montesquieu remarks, a conqueror could change himself more easily than he could change the vanquished people. This, of course, is what Henry IV did, and Montesquieu admires him almost as much as he does Charlemagne. The examples which he gives at this point expressly relate to religion in China. Montesquieu contends that Christianity could hardly be established in China because the mores and manners of that country would prevent the participation of women in the various Christian rites. The ceremonies of the Chinese call for a separation of the sexes and this separation goes with the spirit of despotism. For this reason, he contends, monarchies and all other moderate governments are more consistent with the Christian religion. This is supported by his explanation of how the Chinese legislators effected the union of religion, laws, mores, and manners. The object of the Chinese government was peace and tranquillity, and the government undertook to inspire a respect for parents. Rites and ceremonies were established for this purpose. The mutual respect of parents and children also appeared between the old and young, between the magistrates and those under their jurisdiction, and between emperor and his subjects. "This formed the rites, and these rites the general spirit of the nation."[113] The behavior within the family imprinted an idea, Montesquieu remarks, that forms the ruling spirit of the empire and to change the one would affect the other. There may be a further meaning to this illustration. The association of family authority with despotism could be an indirect attack upon one of the favorite theories of the absolute monarchy, that is, the analogy of kingship to paternal authority.

This analysis of mores and despotism shows that Montesquieu is concerned with more than legal processes and institutions in themselves. He recognizes the effects of behavioral and cultural forces upon a political system and he argues that despotism is not merely a disregard for the distinctive character of legal and political forces but may arise also from a lack of respect for the other forces that bear upon the formation of the national spirit, such as religion, mores, and manners. The opposite side of the coin appears when Montesquieu turns to the mixed republics of the classical period.

In contrast to the absolutism of despotic governments and their characteristic tendency to confound diverse general causes, Athens and Rome demonstrate the legislative wisdom of respecting the several general causes and their proper relationship. This consideration of how the laws ought to relate to the mores and the manners invokes the fundamental principle that things are both separate and related: "it is only singular institutions which thus confound laws, mores, and manners — things naturally distinct and separate; but though they are in themselves different, there is nevertheless a great relation among them."[114] By "singular institutions" he appears to mean governments like that attributed to China which is not mixed but despotic.

The next analysis of how the mores and the manners serve to

limit the imposition of laws is another example, I believe, of the related yet distinctive character of the general causes. Montesquieu refers to the comment of Solon upon the laws which he gave to the Athenians: "I have given them the best they were able to bear." This, Montesquieu remarks, is an attitude that ought to be understood fully by all legislators. Another example is the law of Moses, which was deemed by Divine Wisdom to be "not good" but to have "a relative goodness." Then he supports the proposition that "when a people have good mores, their laws become simple" by statements in Plato's *Laws* that in the administration of laws an oath should be required of people generally only when they are extremely religious.[115]

The several case-demonstrations of the proper relation of laws to mores and manners are additional evidence of Montesquieu's underlying interest in sociological and psychological factors. The first supporting example concerns the early history of Rome when the mores were "pure" and there was no law against embezzlement of public money. When this crime began to appear, it was thought so infamous that the mere order to restore what had been taken was considered a sufficient disgrace and no punishment was needed. Next, the Romans gave the right of tutelage to the next heir of an infant as long as the manners of the Romans raised no fear that the heir might take the life of the infant but later when the fear arose they gave the right of tutelage to the mother as a precaution. Third, the Romans forbade the giving of presents at a marriage because they were led to marriage only by frugality, simplicity, and modesty. The Spanish also limited gifts to a prospective wife but this was to curb ostentation. The Romans were moved by virtue and the Spaniards by beauty. Another example: the imperial laws on repudiation of marriage were drawn from the ancient manners and mores of the Romans, but these were later changed when the Eastern usages banished those of Europe.[116] These examples all support the basic proposition that the laws should be relevant to the natural activity of the people in the civil society.

The much more extensive chapter on how the laws contribute to form the mores, manners, and character of the English nation shows that Montesquieu did investigate and appraise the actual political life of England. In the famous chapter of Book XI on the three powers of the English government he expressly disavows consideration of actual practice, but here in Book XIX he clearly is working be-

hind the legal facade. He analyzes such matters as party attach-
ments, motives of colonization, preferences for civil rather than military service, trends in class identity, and freedom of discussion. He
is much concerned with the interaction of laws and the mores, manners, and character of a nation. The analysis deals with customs as
well; in fact, the opening sentence treats customs as an essential
part of the character of a nation. "The customs of an enslaved people are a part of their servitude and those of a free people a part of
their liberty."[117] He then makes clear that this inquiry is supplemental to the earlier analysis in Book XI on the English constitution. "I have spoken in the eleventh book of a free people, and have
given the principles of their constitution: let us now see the effects
which follow from this liberty, the character it is capable of forming, and the customs which naturally result from it."

There is at the start of the chapter an enlightening observation
that the influence of mores and manners as well as that of climate is
important in the guidance of legislation. "I do not deny that the
climate may have produced a great part of the laws, mores and
manners of this nation; but I maintain that its mores and manners
have a close connection with its laws." Here is further evidence that
the relations of laws and other general causes are mutual and that
the basic elements of Montesquieu's theory of natural government
are the interactions among sociological and psychological forces.

The first substantive observation about the political life of England concerns the much disputed relation of legislative and executive powers. Montesquieu sets down the premise that "there are in
this state two visible powers — the legislative and executive."[118] The
absence of the judicial power reflects the same attitude that is apparent in the chapter on the English constitution in Book XI where
a discussion of judicial power is cut short rather promptly and
where Montesquieu says that the judicial power is next to nothing.
He means that it does not concern the subject there, that is political liberty in respect of the constitution. Thus, Montesquieu twice
excludes the judiciary from the realm of government, politics, or
the constitution. His concentration on the legislative and the executive in the discussion of mores, manners, and laws, indicates that he
is talking about the political aspects of government. What follows
this identification of "two visible powers" is even more striking because the discussion is not about governmental operation but about
the political attachments of individual Englishmen. Montesquieu

asserts that since "every citizen has a will of his own and may at pleasure assert his independence, most men have a greater fondness for one of these powers than for the other." Thus, the distinctiveness of the legislative and executive powers lies in the fondness of particular citizens for one or the other, and he may be using "legislative" and "executive" to stand for factions or parties. The political character of this dichotomy appears also in the next observation that "the multitude have commonly neither equity nor sense enough to show an equal affection to both." This slightly cynical comment shows Montesquieu's awareness of the inclination of a person to identify himself with one or another of two political parties. Here is rather modern analysis and appraisal in social psychology.

The proposition in *L'Esprit des Lois* that most men have a "greater fondness" for either one or the other of the legislative or executive power, agrees, I believe with the observations of other commentators at the time that England had two political factions or parties and that these favored the commons or the crown. For instance, David Hume, in his essay on politics as a possible science, refers to a "country party" and a "court party."[119] These two parties appear to correspond to a proparliamentary group and a promonarchy one. This, also, supports the idea that the legislative and the executive were separate in a political party sense. Montesquieu's recognition of two factions and their association with the legislative and executive institutions shows his interest in the meta-legal aspects of the English political system. It also indicates that there was a separation or antagonism between the two political branches of the government in the political thought and behavior of the English citizenry, even though the members of the ministry may have been members of Parliament because of electoral intervention or corrupt practice.[120] Moreover, Montesquieu's comments here in Book XIX raise the possibility that, when he speaks about the legislative and executive powers in England, he is thinking about political inclinations of the people and not merely formal agencies or functions.

Montesquieu's understanding of practical politics is evident also when he talks about the disposition of employments by the executive power and the readiness of those who obtain favor to expose its cause, while those with nothing to hope from the executive power are liable to attack it.[121] Thus again he distinguishes the executive from the legislative and makes them politically separate powers. Montesquieu sometimes views the two as a pair, but he seems to assume that the executive is the driving force and the legislature the restraining power. This idea of their interrelationship has some similarity to Calhoun's analysis of the government and the constitution to be positive and negative forces acting upon each other.[122]

The examination of customs and mores penetrates even the cultural character of the people. Montesquieu pictures the English to have both an amibitous desire of riches or honors and an eventual tendency to moderate. Jealous passions, he says, are not a sign of weakness but rather one of strength. But he seems to assume that the passions in support of one group will be countered by those of the other group. Or he may even presuppose a common sense of balance or adjustment of forces. "These parties being composed of freemen, if the one becomes too powerful for the other, as a consequence of liberty this other is depressed; while the citizens take the weaker side, with the same readiness as the hands lend their assistance to remove the infirmities and disorders of the body."[123] Incidentally, this is one of the few instances in which *L'Esprit des Lois* uses the biological metaphor. But more important, is the recognition that man may have the capacity and inclination to shift his political attachment for reasons beyond particular interest. Montesquieu observes that "in this nation it frequently happens that the people forget the laws of friendship as well as those of hatred." Then, his remark that the "sovereign is here in the same case with a private person" suggests that the English king is confronted by political-party realignments. Both these comments show Montesquieu's insight into the extra-legal politics of the English.

Definitely, he considers representative government to be more stable than direct democracy. He assumes that the legislative body has the confidence of the people and is more enlightened than they so that it "may calm their uneasiness and make them recover from the bad impressions that they have entertained." This, he says, is the great advantage of the English government over those ancient democracies in which the people had an immediate power, because "when they were moved and agitated by the orators, these agitations always produced their effect."[124] Yet he does not deny all good to the passions of the people. He explains that only at those times when an "impression of terror has no certain object" does it produce clamor and abuse, and the popular passion, he says, does have "this good effect, that it puts all the springs of government into motion, and fixes the attention of every citizen."[125] This is similar to the remark in the study of the Romans that "a free government" is "a government constantly subject to agitation" and that it "cannot last if it is not capable of being corrected by its own laws."[126]

The exception which Montesquieu makes at this point for what he calls "a violation of fundamental laws" probably refers to a disregard of the laws of royal succession or to collusion with outside interests because he talks about the appearance of a foreign power. Also, he says that a revolution in such circumstances "would neither alter the constitution nor the form of government."[127] Incidentally, the inference that the form of government and the constitution are not the same suggests that by "constitution," Montesquieu means the political or social roots of authority, rather than simply the form of government. This has an important bearing upon his analysis of the English government in the book on political liberty in respect of the constitution. Likewise, fundamental law may not be the same as the constitution, because the first term was often used at that time for the rules of royal or dynastic succession.[128] The idea that the violation of the fundamental law involves the tyranny of a monarch is indicated also by the series of cryptic and epigrammatic assertions that "a revolution formed by liberty becomes a confirmation of liberty," that only a free nation can have a deliverer, and that "whoever is able to dethrone an absolute prince has a power sufficient to become absolute himself." Many aspects of the situation which Montesquieu describes here seem similar to the English Revolution of 1688 and to Locke's account of what happened. Moreover, Montesquieu's opinion that the representatives in the legislature have the ability and the authority to exercise independent discretion and even to guide the people away from impressions of terror that could cause clamor and abuse, may anticipate Edmund Burke's well known speech on the character of representation.

The theory that people generally act in political matters out of sense or passion rather than reason is reiterated here in respect of the English. "A people like this, being always in ferment, are more easily conducted by their passions than by reason, which never produces any great effect in the mind of man."[129] This is similar to the declaration in the study of the Romans that there is "nothing so powerful as a republic in which the laws are observed not through fear, not through reason, but through passion."[130] Here in *L'Esprit des Lois*, Montesquieu also observes that those who govern in Eng-

land could easily make the people undertake enterprises against
their true interests. He may be a bit more cynical than he was in
the study of the Romans because there he indicated that the republic is strengthened through the combination of the passion of the
people and the wisdom of the aristocracy. The same may be true in
respect of the English. I believe that Montesquieu is less anxious to
denounce the capability of the people than to suggest that strong
government comes from uniting the political passions of the populace with the reason or wisdom of the professional aristocracy and
that the combination not only imposes limitations upon each but
also utilizes the driving force of the popular motivations. This idea
is implicit in his further comments on the English. Montesquieu
says that that nation "is passionately fond of liberty, because this
liberty is real," that the nation can for its defense "sacrifice its
wealth, its ease, its interests" and that it can "support the burden of
the heaviest taxes, even such as a despotic prince durst not lay upon
his subjects." The English, he says, may hope that taxation will end
but even though the burden is heavy "they do not feel the weight."
Moreover, the nation must have a fixed and certain credit "because
it borrows of itself and pays itself." This adds another reason for
loyalty and service to the country. "To preserve its liberty, it
borrows of its subjects: and the subjects, seeing that its credit would
be lost if ever it were conquered, have a new motive to make fresh
efforts in defense of its liberty."[131] Thus, again liberty seems primarily collective and involves duties as well as rights.

The English would rather colonize than conquer, he says, to
avoid being "weakened by distant conquests." But this may be more
prescription for France. He argues that the soil of the country is
good and that the nation has no need to enrich itself by war. Also,
he observes that since "no citizen is subject to another, each sets a
greater value on his own liberty than on the glory of one or any
number of citizens." Here, there is promise of individual freedom.
Likewise, he points out that among the English "civil qualifications" are more esteemed than the military ones and that England
has become "a trading people" rather than a conqueror. It has utilized its raw materials, he explains, and, being a northern country,
trades extensively with the southern nations. This concern with
trade has affected its laws and its manners. The laws, "otherwise
mild and easy, may be so rigid in respect of the trade and navigation carried on with it, that it might seem to trade only with enemies."

The analysis of colonization is further evidence of Montesquieu's deep interest in the outer reaches of a political system. The English goals of extending its commerce rather than its dominion and of introducing elsewhere "what they have established among themselves" have given "the people of the colonies their own form of government" and have "raised great nations in the forests they were sent to inhabit." This obvious reference to the American settlers is followed by a contrasting picture of "a neighboring nation," presumably the Irish. While England "has given this nation its own laws, yet it holds it in great dependence," so that "the citizens there are free and the state itself is enslaved." Montesquieu concludes that this "conquered state has excellent civil government but it is oppressed by the law of nations."[132] These comments show again the distinctions which he assumes between civil and political orders and between the liberty of the citizen under law and the liberty of the society to participate in the making of law.

Montesquieu finds some correlation among the island habitat, the great trade, the sea power, and the continued liberty of the English. The empire of the sea inspires a natural pride so that the nation imagines its power to be as boundless as the ocean. England, he says, has great influence in the affairs of its neighbors and its friendship is courted even though its government is marked by inconstancy and domestic divisions. The English executive, he asserts, is almost always disturbed at home but is respected abroad. The contrast with the French executive is evident again when he remarks that the English ministers are forced to be comparatively honest in their diplomacy because they must justify their conduct before a popular council. The English nobility once had immoderate power, he says, but the monarch abased the nobles by raising the people, so that now England has the foundation of a free government and the form of an absolute monarchy. This is, of course, definite evidence that Montesquieu penetrated English political and social practices behind the legal pattern of its Constitution and also that he favors popular representation as well as aristocratic participation in government.

His study of the English mores and character includes some deeply interesting comments upon religion, and, since the attitude toward religion may be the most important aspect of French political theory, these comments are worthy of particular attention. The first observations indicate the impossibility of avoiding the religious factor. Montesquieu points out that in England each citizen has the free will to be guided by his own enlightenment or fancy, from which one of two results must follow: either that everyone must be indifferent to religions so that all would embrace the dominant religion or that everyone must be zealous for religion in general so that the number of sects will multiply. He recognizes that there may be men in England who have no religion, but he asserts that even they would prefer that there be freedom of choice.

One of the most fundamental aspects of *L'Esprit des Lois* is involved, I believe, in the next observation that the English clergy are not separate politically from the people.[133] Montesquieu's remarks that the clergy might have less credit than the other citizens, and that the clergy, "instead of a separation . . . have chosen rather to support the same burdens as the laity, and in this respect to make only one body with them," seem to refer to the inclusion of lords spiritual in the House of Lords and the admission of the less privileged clergy into the House of Commons, in contrast to the formation of a separate Estate in the parliamentary arrangement in French. These remarks, I believe, support the proposition that Montesquieu chose the English Parliament for his model legislature in order to exclude the separate order which the clergy had had in the French Estates General. Montesquieu goes on to praise the English clergy for their avoidance of a separate political role. He observes that they distinguished themselves "by a more retired life, a conduct more reserved, and a greater purity of manners." Also, he puts the clergy in the place of educators rather than political leaders. "The clergy not being able to protect religion, nor to be protected by it, only seek to persuade." He notes that they have produced "excellent works in proof of a revelation and of the providence of the supreme Being." This may be an inference that the French clergy have produced works which lack such merits. The suggestions that the clergy are better theologians when they are not a separate estate and that it is better to have imperfection in nonreligious matters than to have reform by the clergy, may well be relevant to the French political situation. These may be a prescription that the clergy stay with religion and keep clear of the government and the politics of the nation. There are many other suggestions of this idea throughout *L'Esprit des Lois,* and it may be one of the principal elements of Montesquieu's system of politics for France.

The inquiry into the character of English life includes comments upon the constitutional arrangement which suggest again Montes-

quieu's preferences for the class distribution of political authority
and the free activity of men in society. In respect of England, he
says that the "dignities which make a fundamental part of the constitution are more fixed than elsewhere; but, on the other hand, the
great in this country of liberty are nearer upon a level with the people; their ranks are more separated, and their persons more confounded."[134] He points out that in England men are less esteemed
for frivolous talents than for qualities which lead to riches and
personal merit. The English, he says, enjoy "a solid luxury" based
upon real wants rather than upon the refinements of vanity, they
seek only what nature has given, and they are occupied with their
own interests, leaving no time to develop politeness based upon indolence. Again, Montesquieu voices the case for activity in human
and social behavior. An absolute government, he says, produces indolence and this in turn gives rise to politeness, but what should
distinguish us from the barbarians is a politeness of mores rather
than a politeness of manners. In England, he points out, the circumstances are conducive to individual political activity, the climate may give the people a restless spirit, and there is much discussion of politics. "In a free nation it is very often a matter of indifference whether individuals reason well or ill; it is sufficient that
they do reason: hence springs that liberty which is a security from
the effects of these reasonings."[135] Thus, again, Montesquieu seems
to esteem mental activity among the citizens and prefer those governments which permit or even inspire it.

Montesquieu's study of the English mores draws upon literary
achievements for a final characterization. He argues that we should
look at literary performance to find the men of thought and deep
meditation. "Their satirical writings are sharp and severe, and we
find among them many Juvenals without discovering one Horace."
Likewise, he observes that the tendency to present the truth is
related to the type of government. Here, as in many other situations, he associates undesirable extremes with absolute monarchies
and unlimited freedom. "In monarchies extremely absolute, historians betray the truth, because they are not at liberty to speak it." On
the other hand, "in states remarkably free, they betray the truth because of their liberty itself." Liberty, he says, always produces division, and everyone becomes "as great a slave to the prejudices of his
faction as he could be in a despotic state." This is another indication that Montesquieu associates liberty with the society as well as
with the individual and that extreme democracy is as irrational, in

his opinion, as extreme monarchy. The concluding remarks in Book
XIX that the English poets are more likely to have "an original
rudeness of invention than that particular kind of delicacy which
springs from taste" and that they come nearer to the bold strength
of a Michaelangelo than to the softer graces of a Raphael, may be
Montesquieu's idea of the difference between the English and the
French. He may be fancying himself to be a Juvenal and a Raphael
but he is more likely trying to tell the French people to be moderate in both theory and practice.

Notes

1. *L'Esprit des Lois* (hereafter referred to as *Lois*) XIX, 5.

2. *Les Lettres Persanes* (hereafter referred to as *L.P.*) LXXX; Roger Caillois, *Oeuvres Completes de Montesquieu* (Paris, 1951), (hereafter referred to as Caillois, I or II), I, 110.

3. Montesquieu borrows from Gian Vincenzo Gravina, the Italian jurist and poet, who calls "the united strength of individuals" the body politic, and "the conjunction of all their wills," the civil state. *Lois*, I, 3.

4. The laws "should be in relation to the nature and principle of each government; whether they form it, as may be said of politic laws, or whether they support it, as in the case of civil institutions. "They should be in relation to the climate of each country, to the quality of its soil, to its situation and extent, to the principal occupation of the natives, whether husbandmen, huntsmen, or shepherds: they should have relation to the degree of liberty which the constitution will bear; to the religion of the inhabitants, to their inclinations, riches, numbers, commerce, mores and manners. In fine, they have relations to each other, as also to their origin, to the intent of the legislator, and to the order of things on which they are established; in all of which different lights they ought to be considered."

5. See the second section of this chapter, *infra*.

6. Ernst Cassirer, *The Philosophy of the Enlightenment* (Princeton, 1951), 3, 4, 8, 9, 11, 14, 20-21.

7. Robert Shackleton, *Montesquieu A Critical Biography* (Oxford 1961), 72.

8. *Lois*, X, 3; XV, 2, 6, 7, 11; XVI, 2, 12; XXVI, 3-6, 14.

9. William F. Church, *Constitutional Thought in Sixteenth-Century France* (Cambridge, Mass., 1941), 226-7.

10. *Lois*, XXVI, 5, 6, 15.

11. *Lois*, IX, 1; X, 2, 3.

12. *Ibid.*, IX, 3, 9; X, 4, 6, 8, 11-17.

13. *Ibid.*, XXVI, 1.

14. *L.P.*, XLVI.

15. *Lois*, II, 2, 5; VI, 5; XIX, 27.

16. *Ibid.*, VI, 5; II, 2.

17. *Ibid.*, IX, 9, 10.

18. Kingsley Martin, *The Rise of French Liberal Thought* (New York, 1956), 283-4; C. P. Courtney, *Montesquieu and Burke* (Blackwell, Oxford, 1963), 9, 10.

19. Peter Gay, *Voltaire's Politics, The Poet as Realist* (New York, 1965), 93, 115.

20. *Lois*, VIII, 2, 5.

21. *Ibid.*, VI, 15; XI, 15; XII, 13, 21; XXII, 22.

22. In the essay *De la Politique* Montesquieu speaks of the "universal soul" which is formed in every society and he calls a society only "a union of spirit." Caillois, I, 114.

23. *Lois*, XI, 5, 6; XII, 2, 3, 4; XVIII, 3, 4, 10, 11; V, 14, 4.

24. Callois, I, 110.

25. *Lois*, XIV, 10.

26. At one point Montesquieu admits that even despotisms may differ, *Lois*, XII, 29.

27. On the political thought of Hobbes, Locke and Rousseau, see Leo Strauss and Joseph Cropsey, *History of Political Philosophy*, (Chicago, 1963), 354-377, 433-468, 514-534; John Plamenatz *Man and Society* (New York, 1963), I, 116-154, 209-252, 365-442.

28. *L.P.* CII

29. Caillois, I, 767.

30. Caillois, I, 1099.

31. *Romains*, VI, Caillois, II, 107.

32. *Lois*, X, 13; XIV, 13.

33. *Romains*, VIII, Caillois, II, 115-6. (Authors translation).

34. Vaughan, *op. cit.*, I, 275.

35. Aristotle, *Politics*, VII, vii, 1327b; Jean Bodin, *Six Books on the Commonwealth* (Blackwell, Oxford, Abridged and translated by M. J. Tooley), 146. (Chapter I of Book V). There is some mention of climate in Plato's *Laws*.

36. J. B. Bury, *The Idea of Progress* (London, 1920), 146-7, which mentions as contemporary writers on the subject Fontenelle, the Abbé de Saint-Pierre, the Abbé du Bos, and Chardin. See also Robert Shackleton, *Montesquieu A Critical Biography* (Oxford, 1961), 302-19. Precursors of Montesquieu are given as John Arbuthnot, Francois-Ignace Espiard, John Chardin and Jean-Baptiste Dubos, *Ibid.*, 307, 303. Joseph Dedieu, *Montesquieu et la Tradition Politique Anglaise en France* (Paris, 1909), 209, says that the study of the influence of climate was the order of the day at 1740 and that Montesquieu is much a man of the times.

37. Dedieu, *op. cit.*, 212-225. Frederick J. Teggart, *Theory and Process of History*, 176-179, also states that Montesquieu's source was Arbuthnot's essay.

38. *Lois*, XIV, 1.

39. *Ibid.*, XIV, 13.

40. *Ibid.*, XIV, 7.

41. *Ibid.*, XIV, 5.

42. *Ibid.*, XIV, 6.

43. *Ibid.*, XIV, 9.

44. *Ibid.*, XVI, 12.

45. *Ibid.*, XVII, 2. *L'Esprit des Lois* lays greater emphasis upon the favorable effects of the northern climates than did the earlier work, *Essai sur les causes*. Stark, *op. cit.*, 120. Montesquieu sees in the northern atmosphere, Stark says, a "value-evoking influence in activity which lifts the head and the heart of man high." *Ibid.*, 121. This in a slight way foreruns Herder's esteem of northern races.

46. *Lois*, XVII, 3-5. See Stark, *op. cit.*, 111-2.

47. *Ibid.*, XVII, 6.

48. *Ibid.*

49. *Ibid.*, XVIII, 3.

50. *Ibid.*, XVIII, 4-7.

51. Shackleton, *op. cit.*, 69-76.

52. For an exhaustive bibliography of Montesquieu's works, see Shackleton, *op. cit.*, 400-408.

53. Shackleton, *op. cit.*, 69.

54. Caillois, I, 109-118; Shackleton, *op. cit.*, 74, 316.

55. Caillois, II, 69-209.

56. *Ibid.*, II, 19-38.

57. Shackleton, *op. cit.*, 149.

58. Caillois, II, 39-65; Shackleton, *op. cit.*, 314, 406.

59. Caillois, I, 974-1574; II, 1265-1438.

60. On the adoption of Bodin's theory of state sovereignty by the divine right theorists, see William F. Church, *Constitutional Thought in Sixteenth-Century France* (Cambridge, Mass., 1941), 243-5. On Bossuet's theory of divine right of kings, see Kingsley Martin, *The Rise of French Liberal Thought* (New York, 1956), 26-9; which suggests that Bossuet may have inadvertently undermined the theory by associating himself with Hobbes. See also, Vaughan, *op. cit.*, I, 130, 131, and A. J. Carlyle, *Political Liberty* (London, 1941), 41-4.

61. On the *thèse royal* and the *thèse nobiliaire* see Franklin L. Ford, *Robe and Sword, The Regrouping of the French Aristocracy After Louis XIV.* (Cambridge, Mass.. 1953), 222-245; see also Voltaire, "Commentaire sur Quelques Principal des Maximes De L'Esprit des Lois," *Oeuvres Completes de Voltaire* (Paris), XXX, 407-464, at 498-417, and Peter Gay, *Voltaire's Politics, The Poet as Realist* (New York, 1965), 87-116.

62. Caillois, I, 110.

63. *Ibid.*, I, 111.

64. *Ibid.*, I, 114.

65. *Ibid.*, II, 19-38.

66. *Lois*, IX, 7

67. Caillois, II, 20, 21.

68. For general discussions of Montesquieu's analysis of history, see C. E. Vaughan, *Studies in the History of Political Philosophy Before and After Rousseau* (Manchester, 1925), (New York, 1960), I, 253-302; R. Oake, "Montesquieu" *Journal of the History of Ideas*, XVI, 52, 53; Werner Stark, *Montesquieu Pioneer of the Sociology of Knowledge,* (London, 1960), 52-72, 122-142; R. G. Collingwood, *The Idea of History,* (Oxford, 1946), 78, 81, 82, 97, 200; and Frederick J. Teggart, *Theory and Processes of History* (Berkeley, California, 1960), 176, 177, 180, 183. Shackleton says that Montesquieu's distinction of cause and occasion solve for the historian the problem of determinism as it has been solved for the metaphysician by Malebrance, *op. cit.*, 168-9.

69. *Romains*, XXII, Caillois, II, 202-3. (Author's translation).

70. *Romains*, IX, Caillois, II, 119.

71. See Ernst Cassirer, *The Philosophy of the Enlightenment* (Princeton, 1951), 41. Cassirer quotes the statement of Giordano Bruno that it is worthy of God to be "the internal principle of motion."

72. See generally, Guido de Ruggiero, *The History of European Liberalism* (Oxford, 1927), 34-43, 47-50, 94-115. Montesquieu is not generally regarded as a forerunner of utilitarianism. Elie Halévy, *The Growth of Philosophic Radicalism* (London, 1949), 5, 19, 379. But see fn. 88, *infra*.

73. Caillois, I, 110, 114.

74. *Ibid.,* II, 58. The *Essai sur les Causes* declares that "there is, in each nation, a general character of which each individual charges himself more or less." It explains that the general character arises from "general education" as distinct from "particular education." The latter is received from our family and our masters and the other from the society and the people of the world. "It is necessary to receive both of these, because all things have two values: an intrinsic value, and a value of opinion." *Ibid.,* 57.

75. *Pensée* 645, Caillois, I, 1156-7. This was written during 1731-33, Shackleton, *op. cit.,* 316.

76. *Pensée* 1903, Caillois, I, 1458. This was written between 1733 and 1738. Shackleton, *op. cit.,* 316.

77. Caillois, II, 39.

78. *Pensée* 645, Caillois, I, 1156-7.

79. *Pensée* 1903, Caillois, I, 1458.

80. *Lois,* XXVIII, 11, 12, 37, 45; XIX, 27; V, 7.

81. *Ibid.,* XIX, 3.

82. *Ibid.,* XIX, 5. (Author's translation).

83. *Caillois,* II, 230.

84. *Lois,* XIX, 5.

85. *Ibid.,* XIX, 6. (Author's translation).

86. *Ibid.,* III, 7.

87. *Romains,* VIII; Caillois, II, 115-6. Lowenthal, *op. cit.,* 87.

88. Montesquieu is sometimes presented as a forerunner of utilitarianism, Julius Stone, *The Province and Function of Law* (Cambridge, Mass., 1950, 1961), 272, but is not usually regarded as a direct predecessor, see fn. 72, *supra.*

89. *L.P.,* XXVII, XXXIII, XLVIII.

90. *Lois,* XIX, 7.

91. *Ibid.,* XIX, 8-9.

92. *Ibid.,* XIX, 10-11.

93. A connection between the political and the nonpolitical portions of *L'Esprit des Lois* is suggested by Vaughan, *op. cit.,* I, 276..

94. On the extent to which Montesquieu dealt with the nature of society, see Emile Durkheim, *Montesquieu and Rousseau.,* 15-23. "Montesquieu's science is really social science." *Ibid.,* 17. Durkheim probably understates the extent to which Montesquieu considered psychological phenomena beyond the laws of nature, *ibid.,* 17, 19.

95. *Lois,* IV, VII, XVI, XXIII, XIV, XXIV, XXV.

96. Raymond Aron, *Main Currents in Sociological Thought* (New York, 1965), I, 43, 44.

97. Jean Jacques Rousseau, *Du Social Contrat,* II, 11. (Hafner edition, New York, 1947), 48.

98. Stark, *op. cit.,* 12, 16.

99. Caillois, I, 109. A similar statement appears in *Lois,* I, 1.

100. *L.P.,* CVI, LXXXIII, *Lois,* I, 1.

101. *Lois,* V, 2-8; XI, 4; II, 4; V, 7; XI, 6.

102. See fn. 80 and relevant text.

103. *Ibid.*, XIX, 16.

104. *Ibid.*, XIX, 12.

105. *Ibid.*, XIX, 14.

106. *Ibid.*, XIX, 16; X, 11.

107. *Ibid.*, XIX, 12.

108. *Ibid.*, XIX, 14.

109. *Ibid.* Here Montesquieu uses the word *"coutumes"* which has been translated as "customs" whereas in most of the previous discussions he spoke of *"les moeurs"* or *"les manières."*

110. *Lois,* XIX, 16.

111. See, for instance, M. Crevier, *Observations sur le Livre de L'Esprit des Lois* (Paris, 1764), 238-298.

112. "Les legislateurs de la Chine firent plus; ils confondirent la religion, les lois. les moeurs, et les manières: tout cela fut la morale, tout cela fut la vertu." *Lois,* XIX, 17. Caillois, II, 567.

113. *Lois,* XIX, 19.

114. *Ibid.*, XIX, 21.

115. *Ibid.*, XIX, 22. (Author's Translation). The reference is to Plato: *Laws,* XII, 948.

116. *Ibid.*, XIX, 23-26.

117. *Lois,* XIX, 27, par. 1. This chapter consists of 73 paragraphs and the discussion takes up the paragraphs in the order that they appear in *L'Esprit.*

118. *Lois,* XIX, 27, pars. 4, 5.

119. Henry D. Aiken (Ed.) *Hume's Moral and Political Philosophy* (New York, 1948), 305.

120. The French historian Paul Rapin-Thoyras published in 1717 a dissertation on the Whigs and the Tories which pointed out the abuses in election and patronagee that defeated the legal and formal separation of the ministry and the commons. The dissertation though written in French was accepted as authoritative even in England. See Shackleton, *op. cit.*, 292. It was included in the four-volume history of England by Rapin-Thoyras published in France in 1725. Vol. II., 796-807.

121. *Lois,* XIX, 27 (par. 5) .

122. John C. Calhoun, *A Disquisition on Government* (New York, 1953).

123. *Lois,* XIX, 27 (par. 8).

124. *Ibid.*, XIX, 27 (pars. 13, 14).

125. *Ibid.*, XIX, 27 (par. 15).

126. *Romains,* VIII, Lowenthal, *op. cit.*, 88, Caillois, II, 116.

127. *Lois,* XIX, 27 (par. 18).

128. William Farr Church, *Constitutional Thought in Sixteenth-Century France* (Cambridge, Mass., 1941) , 233, 235.

129. *Lois,* XIX, 27 (pars. 21, 22) .

130. Callois, II, 85.

131. *Lois,* XIX, 27 (pars. 23-26).

132. *Lois,* XIX, 27 (pars. 36-7). (Author's translation) .

133. *Ibid.*, XIX, 27 (pars. 50-52).

134. *Ibid.*, XIX, 27 (par. 53).

135. *Ibid.*, XIX, 27 (par. 64).

Chapter III

The Nonpolitical Orders of Social Action

Having examined Montesquieu's ideas about the nature of man and society, I will now begin the more specific explanation of his system of natural government. The most basic assumption in the development of his system is, I believe, his differentiation of political, economic, ecclesiastical, and civil government. This fourfold pattern of social and governmental action may receive formal expression only in the historical study of French civil laws,[1] but much of *L'Esprit des Lois* seems to be concerned with separating and ordering government along these lines. This differentiation is, I believe, more fundamental for Montesquieu than his more apparent typology of legal orders and his better known classification of governmental power.

In considering his system of government, I will deal first with the nonpolitical orders even though this will mean looking mostly at the last half of *L'Esprit des Lois* before analyzing the earlier books (II — XIII) which relate expressly to comparative government and political liberty. This approach, I hope, will provide greater perspective with which to view in subsequent chapters Montesquieu's theory of political structure and spirit. Accordingly, his inquiries into the economic, religious, and civil activity of national societies will be examined in the three sections of this chapter.

The New Economic Order

The large number of fragmentary sentences and paragraphs which Montesquieu wrote during the course of his life include one that declares that "each century has its own particular genius" and that "it is the spirit of commerce which dominates today."[2] This remark was not incorporated expressly into any of his works but it is

94

reflected in *L'Esprit des Lois*. There, nearly a fourth of the total pages deal with some aspect of economics and, in this field, commerce is the leading subject. Montesquieu does not seem to have regretted that commerce dominated his day. True, he does oppose the commingling of politics and commerce, and he expresses dislike of the growing practice of filling the civil offices with persons of large fortune.[3] Likewise, he would exclude those with special privilege from entering into commerce because those engaged in trade must be in a condition of equality.[4] Yet, the considerable attention which he gives to commerce and other aspects of economics throughout *L'Esprit des Lois* suggests that he enjoyed his association with the developments in those forces.

Montesquieu generally has not been classed as a pioneer in modern economic theory but one English commentator declares that no less a figure than Adam Smith "consciously or unconsciously followed the teaching of Montesquieu" on "such matters as money and interest, the identification of wealth with work, the democratic principle of sliding scale taxation," the inferiority of direct taxes, the method of tax-gathering, and the freedom of action in commerce and industry.[5] The foremost American commentator asserts that Montesquieu is "the first great political philosopher to consider commerce worthy of expansive empirical treatment within his major work."[6] The still more recent work of Raymond Aron agrees in general with these evaluations but maintains that Montesquieu shows fears of technological unemployment and hence lacks understanding of "the basic phenomenon of productivity." Yet such fears are almost too minor to be noticeable, and Aron does acknowledge that Montesquieu recognizes the need of consumption desires to motivate the productive efforts of the peasants.[7] Moreover, economic theories based upon consumption rather than production are a comparatively late development, later even than Marx.[8] Montesquieu does talk about commerce much more than about production, and he is concerned with agriculture more than with industry, but this was common for two or three more generations. Still Aron credits Montesquieu with a pioneer contribution in presenting "a picture of the factors which influence the growth of economies that is quite detailed and generally accurate."[9]

Futhermore, there is something historically logical in Montesquieu's greater attention to trade than to manufacture. Commercialization usually has preceded industrialization in the development of communities and nations. This is as true of the non-European world of today as of the western nations a century or more ago.[10] If the stress upon commerce in *L'Esprit des Lois* makes it less relevant to North Atlantic societies today, that emphasis makes the volume more relevant to the larger number of nations which today are striving to enlarge their commerce as suppliers in prelude to a hoped for industrialization. There is some discussion of economic matters in several books that are civil or political in character (such as Books VII, XIII, and XXIII), but the concentrated analysis is in the books of commerce and money (XX, XXI and XXII) which advance the cause of open trading relations more directly than industrialization proper.

The analysis of economic matters in *L'Esprit des Lois* makes important contributions to the sociological aspects of Montesquieu's concept of a political system. He recognizes the new commercial class groups and displays some sympathy for that class in contrast to the nobility. Also, he acknowledges the existence of a poverty class with observations on its causes and the need for special care. Moreover, he distinguishes business transactions from private ones, and he recognizes the beneficial effects of trade and communication upon cultural development.[11] His investigation of commerce concerns largely monarchies and republics, and this involves a geographical distinction as much as a functional one. The monarchical form is frequently associated with central government and a national capital city, while the republican form is associated with provincial government and outlying cities or regional capitals. Also, monarchy comes to stand for luxury and republic for frugality. These matters will be considered more specifically in the following discussions.

The economic contrast of monarchies and republics first appears in Book VII during a discussion of the legal control of luxury. This is a part of the general comparative analysis of the relation of laws to the principle or special spirit of four kinds of government, but there is little express mention of democracies or despotisms, and most of the inquiry deals with monarchies and republics. The analysis differs from previous books also because it develops an internal geographical contrast. Differences between capital cities and provincial towns or regions are implicit in the statements that the inhabitants of large cities are motivated by notions of vanity and by ambitions of distinguishing themselves through accumulations of masses of "trifles."[12] The remarks here are like some of those in *Les Lettres Persanes,* and they bring to mind Polybius's reference to

"purse-proud display" among the Romans and to Veblen's analysis
of "conspicuous consumption" among Americans.[13] Montesquieu
disagrees with those who argue that the great multitude in capital
cities is a hindrance to commerce. He asserts that "men have more
desires, more wants, more fancies, when they live together."[14] What
he is saying is relevant, of course, to France because of the striking
contrast then existing between the luxury of Paris and Versailles
and the poverty of many provincial areas, but I believe that Montesquieu is not trying to attack monarchical luxury so much as suggesting that the republican type of government is appropriate for
provincial regions and cities[15] and that there be more autonomy for
the provincial institutions and authorities.

Montesquieu's argument in Book VII that luxury is detrimental
to the spirit of equality and frugality needed by democratic republics concerns mostly his ideas about the special spirit required by
different kinds of government, to be discussed in Chapter V, but it
does bring out an incompatibility of luxury and republicanism.[16]
He declares that "equal distribution constitutes the excellence of a
republican government" and that "the less luxury there is in a republic, the more perfect it is." Here, he may assume that only a
few can have what he means by luxury. For verification of the de-
bilitating effect of luxury upon republics, he looks to the classical
cities. There was, he points out, no luxury among the Spartans and
the early Romans. He assumes also that the political character of a
republic requires that each citizen respect the general interest. "In
proportion as luxury gains ground in a republic, the minds of the
people are turned towards their particular interests." He observes
that as soon as the Romans were corrupted, their desires became immense. This leads to another dilemma of political arrangement. In
a "badly constituted aristocracy," by which he probably means an
oligarchy, the nobles have the wealth but are not allowed to spend
it, because this would be contrary to the necessary spirit of moderation. That form allows but two kinds of people, those who are extremely poor and cannot acquire and those who are very rich and
cannot spend.

In contrast, Montesquieu maintains that luxury is appropriate
and even necessary in monarchies. He finds support in a statement
by Tacitus that a German nation, the Suions, lived under a government of one because of their respect for luxury. "As riches, by the
very constitution of monarchies, are unequally divided," Montesquieu says, "there is an absolute necessity for luxury. Were the rich

not to be lavish, the poor would starve." Incidentally, here is another use of "constitution" to mean a pattern of social classes rather
than a plan of governmental arrangement. He finds in Roman history further support for the idea that monarchy needs luxury. The
shift from republic to empire, Montesquieu says, required a change
in attitude. He explains that during the reign of Augustus, senators
proposed to reform the mores and luxury of women and that
Augustus forbade this because he was founding a monarchy and dissolving a republic. Again, Tiberius opposed the revival of the ancient sumptuary laws because Rome had grown to consume the
riches of the whole world and he recognized that the ancient austerity was no longer appropriate. The economic contrast of the two
kinds of government is restated in a cryptic conclusion: "Hence
arises a very natural reflection. Republics end with luxury; monarchies with poverty."

In a republic, Montesquieu explains, the spirit of sumptuary laws
should be absolute frugality, whereas in a monarchy, such laws, if
any, should seek to promote a relative frugality, like the forbidding
of imports that are priced too high. This last is the character of the
Swedish laws, which he says are proper for a monarchy. "In general," he declares, "the poorer a state, the more it is ruined by relative luxury" and "the richer a state, the more it thrives by its relative luxury."[17]

The explanation of luxury in a despotism includes an indirect argument that despotic government is not warranted in France. Luxury may be needed in a despotism as it is in a monarchy, but, Montesquieu says, the objective differs quite sharply. In the one luxury
is the use of liberty, while in the other it is the abuse of servitude.
The circumstance that illustrates the need of sumptuary laws in
a despotism is a disproportionately large population, such as in
China. The people become so numerous that they have an uncer-
tain sense of subsistence, and all must apply themselves to agriculture. In such a situation, luxury would be dangerous, and severe
sumptuary laws are appropriate. But, Montesquieu points out, England and France are not in this condition because they have a sur-
plus production.[18]

Montesquieu's interest in the economic condition of provincial
areas is evident at other points in *L'Esprit des Lois*. The book on
the relation of taxes and liberty (XIII) includes the assertion that
"in some monarchies in Europe there are particular provinces

which from the very nature of their civil government are in a more flourishing condition than the rest." The different kind of civil government most likely would be republican. In fact, Montesquieu says that the nature and extent of taxes reasonably may vary with the kind of government as well as the degree of liberty. He contrasts republican and monarchical governments in this regard and equally moderate and despotic ones. The book on the relation of laws and the terrain (XVIII) also associates republican governments with a frugal economy and monarchies with a more fruitful condition.[19]

The idea that the analyses of economic matters have a somewhat different set of assumptions than the other parts of *L'Esprit des Lois,* while slightly evident in Book VII, seems much more definite in the books on commerce and money (XX, XXI, and XXII). In these, Montesquieu appears to favor laissez-faire principles and even to be a member of the commercial aristocracy. He is less a participating member than a learned, inquiring one, but nevertheless he is more concerned with economic matters than with political or legal theory. He was, of course, engaged in the export of wine so that he had at least some first hand knowledge of commercial pursuits and problems.[20] Yet his investigations and explanations go much beyond his own business relations and he gives considerable attention to commercial laws, export and import taxes, stimulation of manufacture and trade, investment banking, foreign exchange, the laws of money, the rise of the commercial classes, and the poverty classes and how to provide for their welfare. There is also a considerable historical inquiry into the development of commerce and finance. He may be a link between the mercantilist and the physiocrat theories of economics and, in fact, does anticipate to an appreciable degree the laissez-faire attitude toward commerce.[21]

There are a number of other indications that the book on commerce (XX) introduces a new approach. First of all, there is a lack of express connection with the doctrine of the general spirit explicated in the preceding book. The analysis of commerce contains some references to manners and the spirit of commerce, but it has no direct mention of either the general spirit or the two general causes (mores and manners) dealt with in Book XIX. Strangely commerce or economics is not one of the specified general causes, even though there is considerable analysis of commerce, and it comes in the midst of the books explaining the various general causes. Commerce could be subsumed under mores or manners, but it receives more express discussion than either or both of these.

Likewise, the book on the history of commerce seems to stand apart from the other historical books, even though they all reenforce the theory that civil laws and political practices develop indigenously. The history of commerce may have been written earlier than the others. It is included in the manuscript identified as the *"Premier Jet"* by the *Biblothèque Nationale*,[22] although with a somewhat different internal order than that of the final publication. But most of the other four historical books are not included in that manuscript, and there is evidence that they were written to offset the theories of renowned historians who differed with Montesquieu on the character of the early political arrangements in France.[23]

Unusual in another way, the books on commerce recognize only two general types of government, that is, monarchies and republics, whereas the comparative analysis of kinds of government in the first third or more of *L'Esprit des Lois* classifies political systems as fourfold, that is, democracy, aristocracy, monarchy, and despotism. In this respect, the books on commerce are similar to *Les Lettres Persanes*. Here is an additional bit of evidence that the commercial analysis was written at a comparatively early period.

Moreover, the limitation of governmental types to monarchies and republics in the analysis of commerce tends to give these forms a somewhat different meaning than they have elsewhere in *L'Esprit des Lois*. Monarchies seem to include those characteristics of absolute or arbitrary rule that the first ten books associate with despotic government. Perhaps an even greater difference pertains to the republics. In the discussion of economic matters they frequently seem to refer to provincial cities and regions with a high degree of autonomy. Little attention is given to whether they are democracies or aristocracies, but probably they are essentially aristocratic. More to the point is that they may be decentralized centers of political authority and economic activity. There are vague suggestions that the republics should be associated together in a loose confederation or commonwealth, with sufficient independence of the central monarchical rule that they can have a freer attitude than it toward external commerce. Montesquieu suggests in Book IX a confederate republic to provide security from external and internal dangers, but he makes no further application of such an arrangement until the

implicit ideas of a decentralized association in the books on commerce.

Nevertheless, despite the differences which may exist in the analysis of economic matters, the books on commerce, money, and population do provide further evidence of several of Montesquieu's underlying tendencies, such as his examination of sociological and psychological developments within the framework of traditional political theories, his differentiation of social forces, his implicit thesis
that France occupies a moderate position, his doctrine that sound
legislative policy reflects both historical trends and the immediate
environment, and his analysis of the interaction of diverse social
and cultural forces which give rise to the general spirit of a people.

The possibility that economics or trade could have been one
of the general causes of the national spirit is evident from the effects which commerce has upon the mores and manners or a people.
Montesquieu starts his analysis of commerce with the admission
that it should be dealt with more extensively than the work will
permit and then gives commerce a high place in the field of social
development. "Commerce is a cure for the most destructive prejudices," he asserts, and his remarks in the preface to *L'Esprit des
Lois* indicate that he aims to attack prejudices more than anything
else. He continues to credit commerce with a leading role in this endeavor, observing that "it is almost a general rule, that wherever we
find agreeable manners, there commerce flourishes; and that wherever there is commerce, there we meet with agreeable manners."
Montesquieu even recognizes historical progress at this point, noting that "if our mores are now less savage than formerly," commerce has brought about a diffusion of knowledge about mores and
"from this comparison arise the greatest advantages." His assumption that increased knowledge makes for improvement, of course,
accords with the general beliefs among intellectuals of his time and
country. But the progress may be a leveling process, because he adds
that commerce corrupts "the pure mores" while refining and polish-
ing the barbarous ones. He also asserts that commerce reduces the
conflicts of nation. "Peace is the natural effect of trade." Nations
which traffic with each other become reciprocally dependent because one has an interest in buying and the other in selling, and a
union is founded upon their mutual necessities.[24]

"But if the spirit of commerce unites nations, it does not in the
same manner unite individuals."[25] This acute observation on the

difference between relations of nations and that of individuals in the realm of economics is very interesting, because it is one explanation of the considerable extent to which a national society has been fragmentized into conflicting groups with each group representing a different shared interest. Montesquieu explains further that commerce tends to bring about an increase in social relations, particularly the less substantial ones, and also to bring about a large body of rather precise rules for the regulation of conduct. "We see that in countries where people move only by the spirit of commerce, they make a traffic of all the humane, all the moral virtues." There, the littlest things, which humanity demands, are done or given only for money. The spirit of commerce produces in men "a certain sense of exact justice," opposed on the one hand to brigandage and on the other to those virtues which forbid consideration of self-interest.

Another modern touch in the economic analysis is the specific identification of poverty classes. There are, it says, two sorts of poor people: those whose poverty is a part of their servitude and those whose poverty is a part of their liberty. The first are rendered poor by the severity of the government and they are incapable of almost any virtue, while the others are capable of performing great things but are poor because they are despised or do not know the conveniences of life.[26]

The classification of governments in the books on commerce first speaks of *le gouvernement d'un seul* and *le gouvernement de plusieurs,* which had also been mentioned briefly in Book XVII, but promptly these are referred to as monarchy and republic.[27] There is virtually no use of the terms democracy, aristocracy, and despotism which played so large a part of the earlier comparative analysis. Even more, the books on commerce and money tend to drop the use of general types and to speak about particular countries and cities. Many of these do have a common characteristic. There are numerous references to Tyre, Carthage, Athens, Marseilles, Florence, Venice, and Holland, all comparatively small societies heavily engaged in wide external trade.

Thus, in the analysis of commerce and money matters, Montesquieu seems especially interested in the republican aspects of the partially autonomous cities and provinces which have been commercially successful at various points of history. He may be suggesting for commercial development a confederation of republics, such as he proposed earlier for security purposes. Even more likely, is the possibility that he was recommending greater economic and political authority for the provinces and cities of the monarchy. He tends to associate monarchy with a highly centralized and perhaps absolute government and republics with fairly autonomous political systems. Here, monarchy is often a more absolute type than in the earlier classification which contrasted monarchy and despotism. Also, when the discussion of commerce speaks of republics, the emphasis is less upon the location of legislative power and more upon its being a small political society which depends much upon external trade. Whether it is democratic or aristocratic is not particularly relevant to the analysis. Montesquieu seems to be bringing in a new type of limitation upon the monarchical authority. This is the decentralization of control, at least in respect of commercial matters. Thus, Montesquieu may anticipate federal division as well as other distributions of political authority.

The association of monarchies with luxury and republics with frugality, which Montesquieu began in Book VII, is continued here. He acknowledges that he is dealing with general tendencies rather than absolute rules. Commerce in a monarchy, he says, may also be based upon real wants, yet its principal object is to procure for the nation everything that can serve its pride, its pleasures, and its fantasies. On the other hand, the merchants in a republic "have an eye to all nations of the earth" and "bring from one what is wanted by another."[28]

Montesquieu's tendency to associate the republican form of government with provincial regions or cities is seen in the considerable attention which he gives to Marseilles and its history. He describes it during the Roman period, acknowledging that its excellent harbor was particularly inviting to mariners but asserting that the sterility of the adjacent country determined its citizens to an economical commerce. "It was necessary that they should be laborious to supply what nature had refused;" that they should be just and moderate; and that they should be frugal in their mores in order to subsist by a trade that was "more certain as it was less advantageous."[29] I believe that these four traits attributed to Marseilles — labor, justice, moderation, and frugality — may well be Montesquieu's four cardinal virtues for republican societies.

The analysis of commerce is one of the several portions of *L'Esprit des Lois* which pays special attention to the social life of the English. Here, Montesquieu seems to regard England to be more of a republic than a monarchy. Thus, he finds that the English rely **upon legislative control more than upon executive action.** "Supremely jealous with respect to trade, they bind themselves but little by treaties, and depend only on their own laws." This seems to mean that parliament may make changes for internal reasons without hindrance from treaties that reflect external considerations.

The independence of the economic order is indicated by his declarations on the force of commercial interests to determine political ones. "Other nations have made the interests of commerce yield to those of politics; the English, on the contrary, have ever made their political interests give way to those of commerce."[30] Likewise, his observations at this point support not only the pluralistic character of the English society but also the related character of the various suborders. The English, he says "know better than any other people upon earth how to value, at the same time, these three great advantages — religion, commerce, and liberty." Whether or not this is true of the English, I believe that Montesquieu is trying to prescribe it for his own country. Here again he idealizes the harmonious relationship of seemingly antagonistic forces. Thus, the essence of proper order in society is not so much that there are separate or distinct orders but rather that they are combined in a way which permits each such force to contribute to the total spirit and life of the nation. Also, this is another indication that Montesquieu's analysis of the English went considerably beyond the formal legal structure of its government.

Whether Montesquieu favors republics to monarchies in respect of commerce because he is thinking of a confederation of republics or because he assumes that the republics are municipalities or provinces within a monarchical empire, he does criticize kingdoms which limit imports to goods from other parts of the realm. He says that such a kingdom would have to develop its own trade. This suggests a contemporary conflict between the central authority and constituent parts of the nation. He also points out that banks, trade associations, and free ports are more helpful in republics than in monarchies.[31] In the latter, they would add financial power to the political authority or would merely reduce luxury rather than stimulate trade. This also seems to assume that republics are smaller, less political, and perhaps members of a confederation or monarchical empire.

In his discussion of the relation of commerce to the form of government, Montesquieu, I believe, again shows his preference for republican government in trading regions or cities, and he throws light on his reasons for that preference. He indicates that, since economical commerce is more natural to a republican government, merchants there can start by gaining a little and thus will be encouraged to grow and gain much. Also, "the grand enterprises of merchants are always necessarily connected with the affairs of the public," while "in monarchies these public affairs give as much distrust to the merchants as in free states they appear to give safety."[32] A little later, he explains that an economical trade tends to be self-expanding, giving as examples the practices of the Dutch merchants to use French wines and oriental spices to attract other trade and the way that Dutch shipmasters needing ballast, carry low-profit materials as enticement for much wanted goods. Such commerce is, he says "a kind of lottery" but "mankind are generally fond of gaming."[33]

The inquiries into commercial practices give support to the differentiation of the economic order and the civil law realm. Montesquieu makes distinctions between regulation of commerce and of merchants and between commercial agreements and civil ones, but, while his examples concern several countries, France is in his mind because he argues for direct collection of taxes in contrast to the indirect, farming system used in France.[34] His answer to the severity of confiscatory laws is to suggest a distinction between "common civil contracts" and "conventions derived from commerce." Here, England is the good example while Spain furnishes the evil precedent.[35] The difference between private and commercial affairs in finance also appears in the comments upon Solon's law against the seizure of a person for civil debts. Merchants may need to borrow money for short periods, and they should be held to their engagements without delay. He says that strict rules are proper for public officials as well, and he approves a law of Geneva which bars public office to children who do not discharge the debts of a deceased father. He finds support for this view in Plato's *Laws*.[36]

The discussion of the limited role of the nobility in a monarchy, which appears in the midst of the book on commerce, is further evidence of Montesquieu's interest in class differentiation. His support of the proposition that the nobility in a monarchy should not participate in commerce would seem to be an effort to place both the commercial class and the nobility in a better position to perform

their respective roles in a national society. He argues that the exclusion of royalty and nobility from commerce is necessary to safeguard the welfare of the trading class. Examples are given of commercial ventures being seized by princes and of grants of privilege
being used to the detriment of the commercial class. One striking illustration concerns the emperor Theophilus who forbade his wife
to import merchandise, declaring: "By what means shall these poor
men gain a livelihood if we take their trade out of their hands?"
Montesquieu makes similar arguments for excluding the nobility
from commerce when the government is monarchical. To allow the
nobility to be merchants "would be pernicious to cities; and would
remove the facility of buying and selling between the merchants
and the plebians." He also asserts that it is contrary to the spirit of
monarchy to admit the nobility into commerce and he argues that
the custom of suffering the nobility of England to trade is one of
the things which mostly contributed to weaken the monarchical
government there.[37]

Thus, Montesquieu considers the merchants to form a distinct
group, the identity, respect, and well-being of which should be
maintained. He refutes contentions of the time that France should
enact laws that will allow the nobility to enter into commerce.
"These laws would be the means of destroying the nobility without
being of any advantage to trade." He adds that "merchants are not
nobles," but he recognizes that they may become nobles without
the "inconveniences" if they manage well their own profession and
attain "an affluent fortune." Montesquieu believes that a person
can and should be allowed to change his profession which, of
course, he did himself.[38] The possibility that a merchant may become a noble by "purchasing honor with gold," he says, "encourages many merchants to put themselves in circumstances by which
they may attain it." Thus, it would induce more and greater activity, and for Montesquieu this is desirable almost in itself. He
adds that he will not undertake "to examine the justice of thus bar-
tering for money the price of virtue," but he does say that there are
many governments where this may be "very useful."[39]

Montesquieu, in arguing that the nobility should not engage in
commerce, was probably also endeavoring to enhance the position
and dignity of "the nobility of the robe." He was a member of this
group and at crucial points throughout *L'Esprit des Lois* brings it
into his prescriptions. The role of the *Parlements,* of which he was

once a member at Bordeaux,[40] is a part of his idea of structured monarchy. The nobility of the robe might also contribute the intermediaries needed in monarchical administration. This matter will be discussed in the next chapter.

The analysis in Book XXI of the historical development of commerce provides several demonstrations of what this study calls "relational pluralism," because it describes in various situations the interaction of diverse forces, such as geographical, climatic, moral, and cultural aspects of social behavior. Likewise, it shows again, largely by indirection, that France is favorably situated for an active society and a moderate government. Not France, but India and Africa are the examples of how climate or terrain "may fix the nature of commerce forever." Trade with India, Montesquieu asserts, has been the same from Roman times to his own day. Every nation has brought in bullion and taken out merchandise. "It is nature itself which has produced this effect."[41] He explains that the African countries lack industry and arts but have gold in abundance so that every civilized nation is in an economic position to traffic with them. Whether these comments are accurate, then or now, seems to me a secondary matter. I believe that their purpose is to prepare for two distinctions which demonstrate the favorable situation of France. Montesquieu develops one contrast between the south and the north and another between the ancients and the moderns. The south of Europe, he declares, has few wants and many conveniences while the north has many wants and few conveniences. Thus, the geography of commerce in Europe "is a kind of balance between the southern and northern nations."[42] Nature gives much to the first group and demands much from the second. "The equilibrium is maintained by the laziness of the southern nations, and by the industry and activity which she has given to those in the north." Thus Montesquieu assumes that "equilibrium" is not a static condition but rather an active or dynamic one in which naturally diverse forces interact to provide mutual adjustment and accommodation. This, in part, supports the theories of the Physiocrats and the classical economists, but Montesquieu does not exclude the need for regulatory legislation. He believes that the political action should encourage rather than restrain activity within and among societies. He argues that the northern peoples have the most need for liberty, because the most effort is needed to satisfy their requirements. The contrast between ancient and modern commerce also supports the cause of wider trade relations. Ancient commerce was largely in the

Mediterranean where, he says, the similarity of climate reduced the need and effect of trade whereas the modern commerce of Europe involves excessive differences in climate and comparable diversity in needs or wants. Hence, there must be great trade and exchange.

Still more evidence of his insight into social psychology appears in the proposition that "the history of commerce is that of the communication of peoples."[43] By communication, he probably means all kinds of interrelationships because he adds that their various defeats and the flux of populations and devastations make up the great events of history.

Here, as in the work on the Romans, Montesquieu is interested in the principles behind crucial changes. The review begins with the ancients, extends through the Greek, Hellenistic, Roman, barbarian, and medieval periods, before considering the revival of commerce and the colonial expansions of the modern period.

Montesquieu's esteem of commercial forces is evident when he explicates the relation of trade and exchange to the cultural development of various peoples. Even among the ancients, for whom commerce was little more than a trail of pillage, with nations pillaging other nations and being pillaged in return, the commerce had beneficial consequences upon the arts and culture. "The effect of commerce is riches; the consequences of riches, luxury, and that of luxury the perfection of the arts."[44]

The arguments and explanations that Persia and Rome were poor trading countries also may be relevant to the situation in France. They suggest that too much political expansion is bad for commerce and that there should be economic freedom for the moderate sized provincial departments or cities. There are interesting contrasts between the Persians and Romans on one hand and the Athenians and the Jews on the other hand. The Persians did not develop substantial trade anywhere that they went. Montesquieu describes how Alexander changed the face of commerce by taking Tyre, Egypt, and India, by discovering the Indian Ocean, and by building ports and channels; and he also describes how Alexander did little to maintain trade once the ways were clear. While the Persians were not able to develop commerce during their occupation of Egypt, the Athenians, who settled there later, were able to command an extensive commerce and Egypt then became the center of the world.[45] Thus, while Montesquieu does not say so expressly, intangible factors outweigh the physical ones.

The Romans as well as the Persians were more interested in land than in the sea and Montesquieu emphasizes the commercial inferiority of Rome to Carthage and Marseilles.[46] He also says that "nature formed the Arabs for commerce and not for war," indicating again his belief that the expansionist wars of France were bad for its commerce. This historical account continues with the decline of commerce during the barbarian invasions and the revival under the influence of the Jews.[47] For Montesquieu, the Jews are the great example of uniform moral attitudes and cultural skills despite the variety of geographical conditions under which they have lived. This is mentioned in the *Essai sur les Causes*,[48] and it is implicit in his account of the history of commerce in *L'Esprit des Lois*. Likewise, he points out that the Jewish ingenuity in surpassing political restrictions developed many of the enduring aspects of commercial law and practice.[49]

The discussion of new world colonization is another demonstration of Montesquieu's antagonism to outside political expansion or exploitation and his preference for internal development of commerce and culture. The principal example of what not to do is found in the record of Spain. Montesquieu points out that in the colonization of America Spain treated the new countries as subjects of conquest whereas other countries "were more refined" and made the colonies the proper subjects of commerce.[50] The more enlightened objective of England, in preferring commerce to colonization, was described by Montesquieu in an earlier book, as noted in the preceding chapter of this study.

Montesquieu seems to be challenging the then prevailing mercantile colonial policy when he names three "fundamental laws of Europe."[51] The three are that all commerce with a foreign colony is a monopoly of the mother country, that an agreement to trade with the mother country is not permission to trade with her colonies, and that, when foreign commerce with a colony is prohibited, trade in the surrounding seas is presumptively barred. These would seem to be basic rules of the mercantile system being practiced at the time, and Montesquieu's comments upon them indicate an underlying dislike of the mercantilist accumulation of monetary metals. He acknowledges that the increased availability of silver enhanced trade with Africa and Asia and, perhaps satirically, that the needs for labor in the American mines and fields encourage trade in African slaves. But his principal target is the political focus upon money rather than trade and in this Spain is his prime example.[52] That country, he recounts, drew an unprecedented amount of gold and silver from the New World but from the height of its wealth it declined more rapidly than its rivals. Montesquieu's explanation of why this happened shows his insight into monetary theory and also the value which he places upon the cultural and social characteristics of even a conquered people. First he points out that the metals which Spain accumulated as money had a fictitious or representative value which declined as the quantity increased. Then Spain's narrow objective is contrasted with that of Germany and Hungary, which used their mineral discoveries to promote culture among their people whereas Spain used the Mexican and Peruvian mines to destroy the culture of the native people.

The Spanish record also shows the superiority of internal economic strength. Montesquieu remarks that it is a bad species of riches which derives from accident, and which does not depend upon the industry of the nation, the number of inhabitants, and the cultivation of the lands. If, he concludes, the king of Spain had received from the provinces of Castile a sum equal to that of the custom-house of Cadiz, his power would have been much greater. These comments echo assertions and implications found elsewhere in *L'Esprit des Lois*. Montesquieu no doubt has France in the back of his mind because in earlier books of his masterpiece he questioned the wisdom of Louis XIV's dream of being sovereign of Europe,[53] and many of the contrasts and interactions have France expressly or implicitly at the center.

A number of Montesquieu's favorite themes arise in the book (XXII) on monetary relations. His observation of the Roman operations in this field leads him to conclude that the Romans were never so superior as when they chose the circumstances for crucial ventures.[54] This reflects ideas expressed in the earlier study of the Romans. Likewise, some of Montesquieu's beliefs in respect of social class differentiations are evident in the comment that Russia never developed commerce because its laws allow only slaves and lords and "there is nobody left for the third estate, which ought to be composed of mechanics and merchants."[55] This shows again the importance which he attaches to the rising commercial and industrial classes.

The emphasis upon ambition and activity is evident also in the discussion of public debts. He questions the belief that a state benefits from being indebted to itself, principally on the ground that such financing may aid those who are indolent and passive. He asserts that the taxes raised to pay interest on the public debt are taken from those who are industrious, and then the money is conveyed to those who do not work. This is supported by his list of four classes of men who pay the debts of the state, that is, the proprietors of the land, those engaged in trade, the laborers and artificers, and, lastly, the lenders or investors who receive annuities. He concludes that the last class is the one which ought least to be spared in case of necessity because it is a class entirely passive while the state is supported by active vigor of the other three classes; but he acknowledges that the necessity of maintaining the confidence of that class, as well as of the others, obliges the state to give it protection.[56] Still his regard for the active workers and his remark that the passive recipient of annuities is least entitled to consideration would seem to place him on the side of the commercial and industrial classes.

That analysis is interesting from the viewpoint of present day developments in political science also because it differentiates four economic groups, that is, land owners, traders, artisans, and lenders, and because it recognizes that political relations and actions should not be the same for all types.

There is further group differentiation in the discussion of interest and usury.[57] Montesquieu distinguishes commercial from non-commercial transactions and divides the former between maritime ventures and land operations. At least loans for ventures at sea, he says, warrant high rates of interest. Also, he implies that religious objections to interest should not apply to commercial transactions. Montesquieu's method in attacking the dogmas against interest is, I believe, rather characteristic. He does not proceed by broad sweep but rather breaks down the problem into a number of issues and challenges the most vulnerable. His ultimate position is little more than that reasonable interest should be permitted on commercial loans. He builds the more theoretical aspects of his argument on a remark of Ulpian that the man who pays last pays least. This is interpreted to mean, in effect, that time has a money value. He attributes the religious confusion of usury and interest to the Mohammedans so that here again he condemns rules of Catholic theology by calling them laws of Mohammed. The general objective and tenor of the book on the relation of laws to the use of money is expressed in the final statements that "mankind are governed not by extremes, but by principles of moderation," and that whether interest be lawful is a question of whether the creditor can sell time and the debtor can buy it.[58] Thus, a moral issue is reduced to an economic choice.

The book (XXIII) on the relation of laws to population trends is another demonstration of Montesquieu's ideas on the interrelation of economics, religious, civil mores or laws, and political legislation. Most meaningful from the viewpoint of economics is the discussion of poverty and its effects. Montesquieu appears to have had a deep fear of a declining population in Europe, and he devoted eleven letters in *Les Lettres Persanes*[59] as well as one book of *L'Esprit des Lois* to the matter. The earlier work analyzes the effect upon propagation of the two types of poverty, which we noted in the later volume. One of *Les Lettres* says: "If a man is in bad circumstances and is sensible that his children would be poorer than himself, he will not marry, or if he does marry, he will be afraid of having too great a number of children." But this consideration will not affect "the rustic or peasant" because he has always a sure inheritance for his children, "which is a plough." Yet what purpose do such "miserable children answer in a state," Montesquieu asks. He replies that "almost all of them will perish as soon as they are born" and that those who survive are weak and feeble. So, if they reach manhood, they have no strength and languish for the remainder of their lives. Montesquieu seems to assume that this group reacts abnormally and retrogressively to the challenges of life. "Men are like plants that never flourish if they are not well cultivated," so that "among a miserable people, the species loses and even somtimes degenerates." France supplies an example. Young men, fearful of military draft, marry too young, are caught in "the bosom of poverty," and their children are "destroyed by misery, famine, and sickness."[60]

Social psychology rather than physical or economic influence underlies the argument that propagation increases, not with poverty, but with the youthfulness of a nation and the tolerance of their government. A newly-established people, Montesquieu asserts, increase rapidly because celibacy is inconvenient and a large family is not. The contrary is so when the nation is well established. However, those with absolutely nothing, such as beggars, he says, have many children always because they never support the burdens of society. Montesquieu again seems to be recognizing an economically substandard group which goes down still further before the hard-ships and problems of life. He describes a different reaction when the poverty is not inner-caused but is due to a severe government. Then, the poor have few children because, he says, they are moved by the lack of subsistence and the insufficient means to care for sickness. The doctrine that the heavier the taxes the more industri-ous the people will be, Montesquieu labels a sophism which arises from the facility of talking and the inability to examine the facts. His analysis tends to make severity of government the principal source of evil. The harshness of the government can be extended until the natural sentiments are destroyed by the natural sentiments themselves.[61] For example, the native women in certain areas of America have refused to bear children because of the cruelty of their masters. Other factors bearing upon the rate of propagation include the types of occupation. He also explains that different modes of agriculture require varying numbers of men. Pasture lands need little employment, corn-lands much, vineyards still more, and rice culture even more. Also, if land is not evenly distrib-uted, the arts must be developed to provide work for some and to provide a market for the land and the industry of others.[62] This classification of occupations and its relationships to other social fac-tors are definite steps toward the recognition of diverse attach-ments, groups, and shared interests, which subsequently has pro-duced the comparatively high degree of structural differentiation in the political systems of well developed countries.

In respect of his own day, Montesquieu declares that "the politics of this age call upon us to take the proper means of increasing our number." Moreover, the legislation should provide general rewards and penalties in contrast to the actions of Louis XIV which gave pensions to those with ten or twelve children. The remedial means suggested are the distribution of idle land to families and the en-couragement of trade and industry.[63]

Montesquieu's concluding discussion on poorhouses becomes a strong endorsement of human activity. "A man is not poor because he has nothing but because he does not work."[64] The man with only a trade is no poorer and may be richer than the man who owns ten acres of land which he must work for his subsistence. The mechanic who gives his skill to his children leaves them a wealth which is multiplied in proportion to their number, while the farmer with ten acres of land for his livelihood must divide it

among his children. This would seem to be a rather advanced idea
for a landed aristocrat of eighteenth century France. It goes beyond
the ideas of the Physiocrats but perhaps is less an understanding of
an industrial economy than a strong feeling that activity is vital to
man. Yet there are disadvantages for the mechanic and the artisan
in trading countries, and "the state is frequently obliged to supply
the necessities of the aged, the sick and the orphan." Montesquieu
even seems to recommend that the state should make work for the
idle. "A well regulated government draws this support from the arts
themselves." It gives employment to those capable of performing it
and teaches others to work, and "this teaching of itself becomes an
employment." His position brings him to the edges of the welfare
state. "The alms given to a naked man in the street do not fulfil the
obligations of the state, which owes to every citizen a certain subsistence, a proper nourishment, convenient clothing, and a kind of life
not incompatible with health." Montesquieu also argues that poorhouses go with rich empires. In a large country, he says, there are
inevitably some workmen who are in momentary necessity so that the
state is obliged to lend them a ready assistance to prevent either suffering or rebellion. He explains further that in such cases poorhouses or the like are needed to prevent misery but that, when a nation is poor, the individual poverty derives from the general misery
and in fact constitutes the general misery. Then, poorhouses could
not cure this condition but would actually inspire the spirit of indolence and thus increase the general and individual poverty. England again provides an example. Henry VIII in reforming the
Church put an end to the monks, "a lazy set of people, that encouraged laziness in others." He closed the poorhouses as well as the
monasteries, and "the spirit of trade and industry has been established in England."

A final bit of satire is thrown at Rome where the poorhouses
place everyone at his ease except those who work. Montesquieu
is less cynical in his final conclusion that wealthy nations need poorhouses because fortune subjects them to a thousand accidents, yet
he adds that for this purpose transient assistance would be better
than perpetual foundations. Because the evil is momentary and
particular, the succor should be of the same nature. Thus, Montesquieu's sense of perspective and proportion emerges at almost every
problem.

The Social Utility of Religion

The tendency of despotic rulers to use religion in support of political action may be Montesquieu's primary object of antagonism. One of his earliest essays was a dissertation on the policy of the Romans in respect of religion and this points out that the first kings of Rome established religion, not out of fear or piety or to improve customs or morals, but for matters of discipline and leadership.[65] Montesquieu remarks in that early work as well as in *L'Esprit des Lois* that every society and its ruler has need of religion, but repeatedly he opposes the close connection of religion and politics. The importance of keeping these two basic forces separate from each other is implicit in *Les Lettres Persanes,* as noted in the first chapter of this study. Then the work on the Romans expressly condemns the alliance of church and state. While speaking of the Greeks, i.e. the Eastern Empire, it declares that the "most vicious source of all misfortunes of the Greeks is that they never knew the nature or limits of ecclesiastical and secular power." This made them fall into "continual aberrations." Then it explains that the distinction between the two forces is the basis of the tranquillity of nations and "is founded not only on religion but also upon reason and nature, which ordain that really separate things — that can endure only by being separate — should never be confounded."[66] Here is a definite example of what is being called "relational pluralism."

The principle that reason and nature call for separation of religious and secular authority, despite their interrelationship, is implicit throughout much of *L'Esprit des Lois.* In fact the principal signs of despotism in various books of that work are the use of religion to enforce social or political order and the confounding of religion, laws, mores, and manners. The distinct character of these four causes is declared several times in the explanation of the general spirit of a nation, as noted in the preceding chapter of this study.

Religion is a matter which is particularly important to Montesquieu. He condemns the artificialities of organization and dogma and the misuse of religion in support of political action, but he considers that religion is necessary for man, society, and ruler. Much of his analysis of religion stresses the ethical aspects, and sometimes he seems to favor only a natural religion, but there is at least one statement that man needs a supernatural belief. In *Les Lettres Persanes* he is attracted by the factors that are common to various denominations and accordingly emphasizes the basic tenets of social ethics. One letter asserts that the principal parts of every religion are "obedience to the law, love of fellow man, and reverence for one's parents." Also, it asserts that the best way to please the Lord is "to live as a good citizen in the society where Thou has placed me, and to be a good father to the family Thou has given us." These remarks were the target of sharp criticism in 1751; Gautier declared that the first of all duties is to love God with all our heart and the second is to love our neighbor. He says that Montesquieu puts the second first and forgets the other. The criticism may have had more weight then than it does now, but it shows again that in relation to many of his contemporaries Montesquieu had little liking for religious wars and persecution. In fragmentary observations, Montesquieu asserts that "it is difficult to practice morality and very easy to dispute dogma." But he also says that natural religion is insufficient and that revealed truth is necessary to prevent men from falling into gross superstitions.[67]

Many of the ideas on religion expressed in the earlier works are assumed in *L'Esprit des Lois,* but the explicit treatment of religion varies considerably throughout the volume. At the start, Montesquieu abruptly rejects "blind fatality," flatly asserts that there is a prime reason, and identifies God to be both Creator and Preserver of the universe. This seems designed to forestall criticism of being an atheist or deist, but it did not spare him from being called a Spinozist or otherwise receiving sharp criticism from clerical commentators when the volume was published. After the opening remarks on legal relations and supreme reason, Book I explains that while there are divine laws and invariable principles of justice for guidance, man's freedom to deviate from these rules necessitates human laws in addition to the universal ones. The human laws are identified first to be the laws of religion, the laws of morality, and political and civil laws, but a second classification rather promptly omits the laws of religion and morality without any explanation. The brief analysis in Book I of the laws of nature includes a statement that the most important law to man is that which impresses on his mind the idea of a Creator, but this seems to be forced into a discussion of primitive psychological attitudes. Montesquieu adds that the law that is actually first, at least in time, is that of self-preservation. The idea that religion is one of many social forces is clearly assumed for the definition of the spirit of the laws, which declares that laws should relate to "the religion of the inhabitants" along with nearly a score of other objects. From Book I to Book XIX religion has only a minor, occasional role. The comparative analysis of governments in Books II — X give religion little more than the sinister function of supporting despotic rule.[68] There is only brief mention of religion in the books (XI — XIII) dealing with political liberty and those (XIV — XVIII) analyzing the relation of laws to physical influences.

Religion is recognized to be at least a major social force in Book XIX where it is one of the seven general causes which give rise to the national spirit, and thus is one of the co-ordinated forces that enter into this manifestation of what is being called "relational pluralism."

The fullest and most concentrated analysis of religion is presented in the two books (XXIV and XXV) which follow the books on commerce, money, and population. In Book XXIV the law-related object is expressly qualified to be "religion considered in itself and in its doctrine," while in Book XXV the law-related object is limited to "the establishment of religion and its external polity." These titles might suggest two sides of theological relations but actually the two books concern largely matters of sociology and psychology, respectively.

Montesquieu's social utility approach to religion is clear at the start of Book XXIV. There he declares that he is seeking knowledge of the relations among religious, civil, and political interests and particularly that to gain more light he is searching even "among false religions for those that are most conformable to the welfare of society." His test here is not whether a religion leads men to felicity in another life but rather whether it "may contribute most to their happiness in this." He professes to be not a divine concerned with the more sublime verities but a political writer dealing with human thought. His objective, he says, is to examine "the several religions of the world, in relation only to the good they produce in civil society." He asserts that his aim is not to make "the true religion" submit its interest to the political realm but to unite these. He assumes that they have common aims. "The Christian religion, which ordains that men should love each other, would, without doubt, have every nation blest with the best civil, the best political laws; because these, next to this religion, are the greatest good that men can give and receive."[69] This need not mean that the religious, political and civil orders are entirely one but is more likely to suggest that they are distinct even though interrelated orders.[70] The mutual interdependency of the religious and the civil realms is partly similar to ideas of the Anglican Bishop William Warburton.[71] His work of 1736 on the alliance of church and state asserts that while civil and religious societies have different ends and means,[72] they should act conjointly and that this involves mutual communication, support and concession.[73] But Montesquieu's ideas on the interdependence of civil and religious forces may be of a more subtle character, as subsequent discussions will indicate.

The conclusion of Bishop Warburton's book seems to be similar to some of the propositions in Book XXIV of *L'Esprit des Lois*. The Englishman concludes "that one true end for which religion is established is, not to provide for the true Faith, but for civil utility."[74] Similarly, Montesquieu declares "that it is not so much the truth or falsity of a doctrine which renders it useful or pernicious to man in civil government as the use or abuse of it."[75] He argues that true doctrines may have bad effects if they are not connected with the principles of society, while false doctrines may have excellent consequences when united with these principles. He illustrates this with the attitudes toward the immortality of the soul. Confucius and Zeno did not believe in it, but these two sects had admirable influence on the society. On the other hand, the religions of Tao and Foe who believed in the immortality of the soul, drew from this sacred doctrine the most frightful consequences. The confusion of the immortality of the soul with the resurrection of the body, he says, often caused women, slaves, subjects, and friends to kill themselves upon the decease of an honored one. Thus, Montesquieu suggests again that a thing should be viewed not merely for its intrinsic character but also for its relations in society. "It is not enough for religion to establish a doctrine; it must also direct its influence." Examples of false doctrines that are "extremely useful" are the beliefs of the ancient Persians that only those with children could pass at the day of judgment and that all the good actions of the children will be imputed to them.[76] In all of these analyses, Montesquieu seems to be testing religion by its utility to an active society and to be asserting that the function of religion in the civil and political society he assumes should be based upon its natural rather than its supernatural aspects.

Yet Montesquieu recognizes that there is an individual personal need for a supernatural element in religion. This seems to be the import of his criticism of Pierre Bayle in the midst of the sociological analysis of religion. Even a bad religion, he says, is better than none, and he condemns Bayle's statement that "it is better to be an atheist than an idolator." Bayle had argued from the idea that it is preferable to be unknown than to be regarded as a villain. Montesquieu calls this a sophism; "it is of no importance to the human race to believe that a certain man exists whereas it is extremely useful for them to believe the existence of God."[77] The thought of God's nonexistence, he adds, would lead to independence or disobedience.

Even here he applies the pragmatic test, appraising the restraining power of religion by relative rather than absolute criteria. He argues that, while religion may not always restrain, the same may be said of the civil laws. Incidentally, this is further evidence of his assumption that religion and civil laws are distinct orders. He compares the restraining power of religion also with monarchical and republican government and points out that they, as well as civil laws and religion, have produced evils and "frightful things."

In *L'Esprit des Lois,* as well as in *Les Lettres Persanes,* Montesquieu insists that a political ruler should have a religious character. I believe that Montesquieu has in mind that this restraint upon a king or emperor is necessary for moderate, nondespotic government. In *L'Esprit* his argument with Pierre Bayle turns to the religion of a ruler, and Montesquieu asserts that, even if religion were of no advantage to the subjects, it would be to the prince. The idea that religion may be "the only rein which can restrain those who fear not human laws" is supported by some of Montesquieu's most colorful language. "A prince who loves and fears religions is a lion who stoops to the hand that strokes or to the voice that appeases him," Montesquieu declares, adding that he "who fears and hates religion is like the savage beast that growls and bites the chain which prevents his flying on those who come near him." The person "who has no religion at all is that terrible animal who perceives his liberty only when he tears in pieces and when he devours."

The assertions in this analysis of a correspondence between kinds of religion and types of government provide another instance in which Montesquieu seems to assume that moral forces have greater influence than physical ones. In explaining that a moderate government is most agreeable to the Christian religion and a despotic government to the Mohammedan one, he declares that Christianity hindered the establishment of despotism in Ethiopia despite the contrary influence of the climate.[78] This comment may be aimed at France and the tendency of clerical ministers to increase the authoritarianism of the French monarchy. Montesquieu goes on to connect the Mohammedan religion with conquerors and the sword and there may be indirection in this as well. He may be reminding his readers of the religious wars in Europe and the plight of the Huguenots in France itself. Earlier in *Les Lettres Persanes* he did express himself against the Massacre of St. Bartholomew and the revocation of the Edict of Nantes.[79]

Possibly, Montesquieu believes that the ethical aspects of religion are more agreeable to moderate governments while theological dogmas are more appropriate for despotism. A manuscript originally planned for *L'Esprit des Lois* contains a statement that in moderate governments men are more attached to morals and less to religion while in despotic countries they are more attached to religion and less to morals.[80] Some weight is added to such a possibility by the statements in *L'Esprit des Lois* that make depotisms depend upon religion.[81] The argument that different kinds of religion tend to go with different species of government might also be a suggestion that a tolerant attitude is more likely under a socially mixed government.

The comparative analyses of religions also brings out relationships between organizational structure, social spirit, and human activity. In arguing that Catholicism is most agreeable to monarchy and Protestantism to a republic, Montesquieu asserts that, when a religion is introduced in a country, it usually conforms to the existing form of government.[82] He points out that both monarchy and Catholicism have a visible head, and, implicitly, the reverse is true of republics and Protestantism. He also says that the people of the north embraced the new religions because they have a spirit of independence and liberty that the peoples of the south do not have and because a religion which does not have a visible head is more agreeable to the independence of climate. This proposition is demonstrated by observations on Lutheranism and Calvinism. Luther had to appeal to great princes and could hardly succeed with "an ecclesiastical authority that had no exterior preeminence" while

Calvin, who dealt with people under republican government or in the minority of a monarchy, could well avoid dignities and preferments. Each religion, Montesquieu asserts, was believed to be perfect for its situation: the Lutheranist looking to what the Apostles had practiced and the Calvinist to what Christ had said. This would seem to suggest that monarchy is appropriate for France in its entirety but that republicanism is more fitting for provincial regions if they are Calvinist or otherwise dissident.

The social consequences of the two religions are asserted in *Les Lettres Persanes,* when the decline of population in Europe is considered. Montesquieu charges that the decrease is due to Christian restrictions on divorce, which he says make for unproductive marriages whereas the easy divorce policy of pagan Rome actually increased mutual attachment. He declares that Protestant countries have more populace than Catholic nations because the one supports commerce which gives life to everything while the other supports monasticism which spreads inaction. These comments at least show that he dislikes Catholic high policy and favors commerce and social activity.

The criticism of Pierre Bayle at this point[83] is probably Montesquieu's most sustained defense of Christianity, but it supports general principles of Christian ethics more than the creeds and the organization of the Catholic church or any other denomination. Throughout *L'Esprit des Lois* and other works, Montesquieu repeatedly places more emphasis upon civil ethics and the social utility of religion than upon the truth of theological creeds. *Les Lettres Persanes* lampoons the casuistry and cant of theological disputes and sets forth basic tenets of a natural religion.[84] *L'Esprit des Lois* is less satirical but still shows a preference for the more social aspects of religion. It declares that where the religion is not given by God, that is, is non-Christian and nonrevealed, it should always accord with the morality because the religion, even if it is false, is the best guarantee of the probity of men. Examples are the religions of the inhabitants of Pegu in Burma, the Essenes, and the Stoics. The principle points in the beliefs of the Peguians "are not to commit murder, not to steal, to avoid uncleanliness, not to give the least uneasiness to their neighbor, but to do him, on the contrary all the good in their power." With these rules they think they should be saved in any religion whatsoever. The Essenes vow to observe justice to mankind, to do no ill to any person, to keep faith with all the world, to hate injustice, to command with modesty, always to side with truth, and to fly from all unlawful gain.[85] Stoicism receives high praise. "Never were any principles more worthy of man nor more proper to form good men than the ideas of the Stoics" but Montesquieu adds, perhaps for safety, that it is second to Christianity. The Stoics, he says, carried to excess only those things in which there is true greatness, that is, "the contempt of pleasure and of pain." Stoicism alone, he continues, knew how to make citizens great men and great emperors. While the Stoics looked upon grandeur and disquietude as vanity, they were "entirely employed in laboring for the happiness of mankind and in exercising the duties of society."[86] Thus, again, there is emphasis upon the natural duties of the citizens and the governors with the implication that natural rights involve social duties.

The preference for social activity and utility is apparent also in the criticisms of "too contemplative a life." Here the express target is Mohammedanism but the real target is the ascetic and monastic aspects of the Catholic church. The Mohammedans are said to become speculative by habit. They pray five times a day, and each time they are obliged to cast behind them everything which has any concern with this world. In addition, there is the indifference which comes from the doctrine of unalterable fate. This leaves the Mohammedans in a weakened position when faced with adverse circumstances. He also blames the downfall of Persia upon that religion. But he may be less concerned with the elements of religion than with certain social traits. This is indicated by his injection of a one sentence chapter that tersely reiterates a number of his favorite social values: "It is better that repentances be joined with the idea of work, not with the idea of idleness; with the idea of good, not with that of supereminence; with the idea of frugality, not with the idea of avarice."[87] So again he shows his emphasis upon activity and moderation.

The differentiation of the political and the religious realms is indicated here by the analysis of human laws and religion. This arises out of his argument with Pierre Bayle and the assertion that Bayle does not understand the difference between "the orders for the establishment of Christianity and Christianity itself." This, presumably, is the distinction between church organization and the essence of religion. Montesquieu distinguishes "counsels" from "precepts," and these seem to mean advisory opinions and enforceable laws, respectively. He urges that the legislators give counsels when the use of legislation would be contrary to the spirit of the laws. Thus, the legislators should not place secular coercion behind religious principles. Then he makes an express distinction between human law and religion, asserting that laws are made "to direct the will" and "ought to give precepts and not counsels" while religion is made "to influence the heart" and "should give many counsels and few precepts." Montesquieu's idea that political and religious procedures and punishment should not be confounded is expressed also in Book XII on political liberty in respect of the citizen. There, also, he seems to be saying that executive and judicial action should not be based on rules purporting to state perfection in matters of faith. He points out specifically that the enforcement of celibacy has made new laws necessary again and again in order to oblige men to observe the existing rules.[88]

The proposition of this study that Montesquieu uses the theory of climatic influence to moderate or even undermine sacred dogmas of religion and politics is supported by the explanation at this point of the difficulties of transplanting a religion from one country to another. I think that here as elsewhere in *L'Esprit des Lois* Montesquieu assumes that his readers, or at least many of them, accept the theory of climatic influence and that he is using this to loosen the hold of those sacred practices which are ritualistic but have little bearing upon the maintenance of civil order. Specifically, a religious rule which Montesquieu considers to have resulted from geographical conditions and which accordingly may have only relative worth is the taboo of the Arabs against eating pork. He emphasizes the nonreligious character of the rule with the remark that eating pork in certain areas may cause skin disorders. A similar attitude is disclosed about other supposedly sacred ways. He finds that there is social value in the religious rule that prayer be conducted in a running stream because there is usefulness in frequent bathing with seemingly no regard for the symbolism of cleansing the soul by cleansing the skin. These examples may suggest that climate is a primary determinant,[89] but the fundamental objective would seem to be that climatic origin makes for moderation. The physical origin excludes religious absolutism, removing from the rule its assumed moral or theological force and rendering it more relative than absolute, more circumstantial than substantial. As a guide for legislators and others, the important lesson seems to be that many rites are not really religious after all.

While Book XXV is entitled "The Relation of Laws to the Establishment of Religion and its External Polity," the discussion deals largely with two subjects: religious attachment and religious toleration. Throughout the book, there may be, as Joseph Dedieu has pointed out, a considerable similarity to the ideas expressed earlier in the century by Bernard Mandeville.[90] Montesquieu's emphasis upon psychology in the analysis of the external aspects of religion is touched off by a simple characterization of the pious man and the atheist. Both always talk about religion but "the one speaks of what he loves and the other of what he fears." Pursuing this approach Montesquieu observes the diversity of religious sentiments and describes seven different motives of attachment. These, incidentally, may help to explain the diversity of societies in the universe.

The first motive of attachment is "the satisfaction that we find in ourselves at having been so intelligent as to choose a religion which raises the deity from that baseness in which he had been placed by others." While we are much addicted to idolatry, we are most attached to those religions which teach us to adore a spiritual being. "We look upon idolatry as the religion of an ignorant people and upon a religion which has a spiritual being for its object as that of the most enlightened nations."[91] The second motive of attachment arises from our sensible nature. When the worship adds items of a sensible type to the idea of a spiritual being, there is an even greater attachment to the religion because it combines our pride in spiritual ideas with "our natural inclinations for the objects of sense." This reflects Montesquieu's concept of human nature as a combination of intellectual reflection and instinctive tendencies.

The motives of religious attachment also include the pride of being a member of what we believe is God's choice of a select group; the propensity to things in which we are continually participant, such as, the numerous ceremonies; the strong inclination to passions of hope and fear; and the love of morality. This last he makes a definite requirement of a religion. "In order to raise an attachment to religion it is necessary that it should inculcate pure morals. Men who are knaves by retail are extremely honest in the gross; they love morality."[92] This suggests a theory of immoral men and moral society.

The final motive of attachment to religion is the appeal of great magnificence in the temples and the clergy. The development of temples is attributed to the fact that almost all civilized nations dwell in houses. Naturally, people wish to build a house for God and "nothing is more comfortable to mankind than a place in which they may find the deity peculiarly present and where they may assemble together to confess their weaknesses and tell their griefs." Those who do not cultivate the land but are nomads and have no houses, he says, are never known to build temples for their gods. Thus, ecological influence enters the nature of religious worship in another way.

Social psychology also explains how ministers of religion came to be. This analysis like many others in *L'Esprit des Lois* tends to lessen the sanctity and absolute character attached to the clergy. At first, Montesquieu points out, men sacrificed vegetables and the worship was so simple that everyone might be a priest. The natural desire of pleasing the deity multiplied the ceremonies and then those engaged in agriculture could not perform all of the rites. Also, particular places came to be consecrated to the gods and ministers were necessary to take care of them. Since personal purity was deemed appropriate for those who approached the gods, the ministers were men of honor, and, when the worship of the gods became a continual application, the clergy were treated as a separate body. Ecclesiastics were estranged from business, and in some religions separated from the embarrassments of a family. Here, Montesquieu says he will not treat of the consequences of celibacy but nevertheless does comment upon it. First, he suggests that man prefers the difficult and the severe, as if struggle was the natural desire. "By the nature of the human understanding we love in religion everything which carries the idea of difficulty; as in point of morality we have a speculative fondness for everything which bears the character of severity." Celibacy, he says, would seem to be the least adaptable to the southern countries of Europe but is accepted there and banished from the northern countries where it would seem more adaptable.[93] Hence, he finds the practice contrary to the influences of the climate, which either lessens the determinism of climate or renders celibacy the more unnatural.

Montesquieu's recurring attacks upon celibacy and monasticism are further evidence of his esteem for natural activity in a dynamic society, and of his antagonism to any force that hinders man's ambition for productive accomplishment.

At this point in the examination of the external polity of religion Montesquieu tends to leave the psychological analysis of religion and take up again his dislikes about the clergy as a social class and about the relation of spiritual and secular affairs in Western Europe at the time. In the remainder of Book XXV, he urges laws to limit the riches of the clergy, questions religious extravagances, and pleads for greater tolerance.

His criticism of the clergy as a separate class, which Montesquieu began in *Les Lettres Persanes,* supplies another bit of evidence for the proposition of this study that he favors the English Parliament over the French Estates General because the latter recognized the clergy to be an estate of their own with a potential veto upon the others. Here, Montesquieu directs his attack against their riches, as a group. He acknowledges that the clergy cannot be eliminated but asks that its wealth be fixed. He would allow individual members to increase their participation and their wealth but asserts that "the clergy is a family which ought not to enlarge itself," and its goods should be limited. His view of the clergy as "a family" suggests that he sees and fears them as a distinct class. He proposes a number of means for restricting their riches. "Instead of prohibiting the acquisitions of the clergy we should seek to give them a distaste for such things; to leave them the right and take away the deed." In respect of the "luxury of superstition" he draws upon Plato, who condemned as impious and pernicious three types of persons: those who deny the existence of the gods, those who treat gods with indifference, and those who think that the gods can be easily appeased by sacrifices.[94]

Like Bernard Mandeville, Montesquieu combats intolerance. But this attitude can be seen in *Les Lettres Persanes* which he wrote as a young man when Mandeville's *Fable* was not much known in France.[95] Even more Montesquieu hardly had to get the message from an Englishman. Religious conflict was long standing in France and the persecution of the Huguenots was too striking to be missed. Montesquieu had special attachments to the religious opposition.[96] The Parlements were often the spokesman of the Jansenist viewpoint and Montesquieu usually sided with the Parlements.[97]

The criticism in *Les Lettres Persanes* may be directed at proselytizing even more than at mere intolerance. At one point, a priest acknowledges that "a strong desire to draw others to our opinion, perpetually torments us" and is "fixed to our profession." This, he adds, "is as ridiculous as it would be for the Europeans to labor, for the honor of human nature, to wash the Africans white."[98] The priest puts the whole attitude quite succinctly. "We trouble the state, we torment even ourselves to make men receive the non-essential points of religion." Thus, again he suggests that we may lessen conflicts by not pressing what is merely circumstantial.

Another one of *Les Lettres Persanes* is particularly relevant to the issue of religious toleration in France.[99] The letter attacks an order of a Persian Shah that all Armenians become Mohammedans or leave the country. This means that all traders and most artificers would be exiled and the nation would lose its most industrious subjects. There is a similiarity to the banning of the Huguenots from France. Montesquieu interposes a general observation "that the members of tolerated religions commonly make themselves more useful to their country than those of the established religions because being excluded from all honors, they can only render themselves considerable by their opulence." He adds that "they are led to acquire it by their industry and to embrace the most toilsome employments in the society." Montesquieu would recognize all religions which exist within a nation. Since "all religions contain precepts useful to society," they should be observed with zeal and the multiplicity "animates this zeal." Presumably, he is thinking of the restraining forces of a religion. He acknowledges that "histories are full of religious wars" but asserts that "it was not the diversity of religions that occasioned these wars; it was the untolerating spirit which animated those who believed they were dominant." The proselytizing spirit, he explains, passed from the Egyptians to the Jews and then to the Mohammedans and Christians and he calls it "the spirit of enthusiasm which in its progress can be looked upon as nothing else but a total eclipse of human reason." The man who "would have me change my religion," he concludes "does it, no doubt, because he would not change his own if he were forced to it."

The opposition to proselytizing is evident also in *L'Esprit des Lois.* Montesquieu argues that the people as well as the officials should be tolerant of other religions and that when the legislators allow a number of religions they should enforce toleration among them. "It is a principle that every religion which is persecuted becomes itself persecuting; for as soon as by some accidental turn it arises from persecution, it attacks the religion which persecuted it; not as religion, but as tyranny."[100] This suggests that religion could disturb a social order based upon mutual regard and moderation.

Montesquieu seems to assume that social harmony involves horizontal duties as well as vertical ones. "A citizen does not fulfil the laws by not disturbing the government; it is requisite that he should not trouble any citizen whomsoever." The portion of social order which derives from the mutual regard of individuals for each other may be considered, I believe, to be inner directed without commands of a superior. It is spontaneous and a matter of multiple adjustments. It may be more fragile than an enforced order and it may lack strength in face of outside pressures. What Montesquieu seems to be concerned about is the possibility of religious mandates overpowering our natural propensity for spontaneous civil order. If and when this occurs, he implies that the legislator as the maker of political laws should redress the balance between the religious and civil forces. Thus, in the interplay of religious, political, and civil realms, Montesquieu gives the civil order his highest blessing and calls upon the political forces to protect the civil order from the disturbances of religious persecution and proselytization.

His antagonism to religious zeal would seem to explain Montesquieu's rather peculiar combination of tolerance toward all religions existing within a nation and, at the same time, opposition to allowing other religions to enter. The idea that religions are inherently over-reaching seems to be at the bottom of his warning to keep out other creeds. He argues that religions which have a great zeal to establish themselves elsewhere are usually persecuting religions "because a religion that can tolerate others seldom thinks of its own propagation." Accordingly, "a very good civil law" would provide that when the state is already satisfied with the established religion, it would not suffer the establishment of another. He declares further that "a fundamental principle of the political laws in regard to religion" is that "when the state is at liberty to receive or to reject a new religion it ought to be rejected; when it is received it ought to be tolerated."[101]

Montesquieu explains further that the prince who undertakes to destroy or change the established religion of his kingdom exposes himself to great danger. Even if his government is despotic, he runs a greater risk of revolution from the disturbance to religion than from political tyranny itself. "The reason of this is that a state cannot change its religion, its mores and its manners in an instant and with the same rapidity as the prince publishes the ordinance which establishes a new religion." The ancient religion is connected with the constitution of the kingdom and the new one is not. Also, the former may favor the climate and the new one is likely to be opposed. The citizens may become disgusted with their laws and view the government with contempt; they may conceive a jealousy against the two religions instead of a firm belief in one and for some time at least they become "both bad citizens and bad believers." Montesquieu's explanation of these statements in his *Defense de L'Esprit des Lois* makes a distinction between "the religion of the sky" and "the religion of the earth" and asserts that the Christian religion will triumph over the climate and that unknown decrees of God determine the limits of religion.[102]

The strong stand against criminal penalty for religious nonconformity, suggested earlier in Books VI and XII, is reiterated here. Penal laws in respect of religion should be avoided, he declares, because religion has its own coercive laws which also inspire fear, and with the different fears, "the mind becomes hardened."[103] The threats of religion, he says, are so terrible and its promise so great that the magistrate "leaves us nothing when he deprives us of the exercise of our religion."

Montesquieu's condemnation, at this point, of a striking instance of religious persecution has been called his most impassioned piece of writing.[104] He quotes from the purported letter of an eighteen year old Jewess just before she was burned at an *auto-da-fé* at Lisbon. The letter is addressed to the inquisitors of Spain and Portugal, who tried her. "You would have us become Christians," the girl writes, "and you will not be so yourselves." She tells the inquisitors that they are behaving not like Christ, but like Diocletian, and she implores them that "if you will not be Christians, be at least men." Thus, again social ethics is put above theology and mankind above denomination.

The analysis of religion concludes with another illustration of its sociological character. The aspects of religion which depend upon the climate, laws, mores, and manners, are deemed to work against the success of transplanting religions. Montesquieu presents the most favorable situation — a despotic government and a people willing to tolerate any religion. He finds such nations in Asia. "All the people of the East, except the Mohammedans, believe all religions in themselves indifferent," but it does not follow from this, he says, "that a religion brought from a far distant country, and quite different in climate, laws, mores and manners, will have all the success to which its holiness might entitle it." He indicates that even in the most favorable situation the transferred religion may not succeed. It might be accepted at the start because strangers are tolerated, but as soon as the visitor has any success and disputes arise, the people will proscribe both the religion and those who preach it.[105] Thus again, the interdependence of the general causes of the national spirit is demonstrated, and religion is treated as mutually related to the other forces of the national society.

The Priority of Civil Laws

Respect for the civic culture is one of the fundamental principles of Montesquieu's theory of natural government. The degree of autonomy which he gives to the civil mores of a national society was discussed in the preceding chapter and there is throughout *L'Esprit des Lois* an even more express recognition of the civil legal order. Montesquieu assumes that the civil laws of a nation constitute a social ordering process which is so natural and humanistic in its character that it could provide the standard for much of the national political action. In fact, one basic question to consider is whether he makes the civil mores and laws of a nation the equivalent of a natural law for that society. If this is so, each national society would have a higher legal standard that is substantially unique to the particular nation even though it may have much in common with the comparable legal order of other nations, particularly those in a similar situation.

Clearly, civil laws receive more direct and express attention than any other legal order. This results in part[106] from the controversy which Montesquieu had with contemporary legal theorists and historians about the source of the French civil law. The major issue was whether it was Roman or Gallic in its origin, and Montesquieu strongly sides with the latter. In *Les Lettres Persanes* the willingness of some Frenchmen to accept the civil laws of other nations is contrasted rather sarcastically with the French pride in their own hairstyles.[107] His insistence upon the French origin is a part of his general theory of government because a theory of Roman origin for the French political law and practices supports absolutism in opposition to limited monarchy.

Montesquieu's theory of the priority of civil laws to political ones, both in time and value, presupposes that the two legal orders are distinct as well as related. A few discussions in *L'Esprit des Lois* may seem to place civil and political laws in the same category, but this is usually to contrast them with some other kind of legal realm, particularly the laws of religion and the law of nature. Most of the time he assumes a fundamental difference between the civil and the political laws, and this is particularly noticeable because he formulates the distinction in a number of ways.

The initial effort to distinguish civil and political laws appears in the first book of *L'Esprit des Lois*. These two and the law of nations are called the three kinds of positive law, and they are defined with particular attention to the flow of relations. The political law involves the relationship of superior and inferior, the law of nations involves the interactions among peoples or nations, and the civil law the relations among citizen themselves. These three types of positive law may be Montesquieu's most asserted basis for classifying secular authority in a national society. We will see in Chapter VII that this trichotomy may be his first approach to the division of governmental power. Then, such a threefold classification of community action also seems implicit in a discussion in Book XXI of the Roman attitude toward commerce. Montesquieu undertakes to prove that the Romans are averse to commerce and he bases his argument upon the character of their actions in three areas which seem comparable to the political law, the law of nations, and the civil law. While examining the foreign policies of the Romans, he declares that they attacked Carthage as a rival nation and not as a commercial power and that they feared barbarians but not trading people. "Their genius, their glory, their military education and the very form of their government," he says, "estranged them from commerce."[108] These factors presumably are what Montesquieu considers to be political matters because his next remark is that "their political constitution was not more opposed to trade than their law of nations." In respect of this second legal order, he then explains that the Roman aversion to commerce in foreign affairs is shown by the fact that, except for allies or friends, they did not respect the property of other nations nor expect other nations to respect their property. Then he asserts that "their civil law was not less oppressive" to commerce. This is supported by remarks that the women who retail merchandise are in the same class with slaves, tavern mistresses, daughters of public housekeepers, and those condemned to fight in the amphitheater. Accordingly, his method of proving that the Romans disliked commerce is to find that it is not favored in the three areas of law, which presumably exhaust their community life.

The three kinds of positive law provide a general pattern for most of *L'Esprit des Lois*. Books II — VIII concern the civil law much more than any other common type of legal order while Books IX and X quite clearly deal with the law of nations. Then Book XI turns to the political law in expressly considering political liberty with respect to the constitution. Political liberty and law are the subjects of Book XII, which expressly concerns political liberty in respect of the citizen and deals with the crime of treason more than any other one subject. Book XIII may also be in this category. Then, civil law is the most consistent subject throughout the last half of *L'Esprit des Lois,* that is, Books XIV — XXXI. The books on the influence of climate include analyses of civil, domestic and political slavery while the book on the relation of laws to terrain (XVIII) includes an extended argument that the French Salic law of royal succession has a civil law origin. The books on commerce and money introduce such distinctions as that between ordinary civil arrangements and commercial ones. The book on population trends gives express consideration to civil laws and the books on religion (XXIV and XXV) include an analysis of the relation of religion and civil laws. Book XXVI investigates the relations of diverse legal orders to each other and gives most attention to the civil law. Books XXVII and XXVIII expressly concern the origin of Roman and French civil laws. Then the final two books which purport to be inquiries into the French "feudal laws" actually deal with the relation of civil and political laws prior to the year 1000, when the feudal period is generally considered to start. Many of the discussions of civil law have been considered in previous sections and chapters. In the remainder of this chapter particular attention will be given to the relation of civil laws to population trends, religion, and other types of law, which Montesquieu examines in Books XXIII, XXIV, XXV, and XXVI of *L'Esprit des Lois.*

The analysis in *L'Esprit des Lois* of population trends emphasizes the importance of civil laws. It asserts that among well ordered nations, the propagation of the race is encouraged by the civil law institutions of marriage and the family. Illicit conjunctions are deemed to contribute little to the growth of the species because the father, who has the natural obligation to nourish and raise the children, is not fixed and because the mother, to whom the obligation remains, finds a thousand obstacles from shame, remorse, constraint

of her sex, the rigor of the laws, and the lack of means.[109] Montesquieu then observes that "laws and religion sometimes establish
many kinds of civil conjunctions." He points out that among the
Mohammedans there are several orders of wives, "the children of
whom are distinguished by being born in the house, by civil contracts, or even by the slavery of the mother, and the subsequent acknowledgement of the father." In certain countries, only children
of the first order inherit; and in some of these countries, the children of concubines are deemed to belong to the first or principal
wife. By this fiction, there are no illegitimates. Montesquieu says
that bastardy is a by-product of the laws of monogamy since there
must be a stamp of infamy upon concubinage. The attitude may
vary with the nature of government. "In republics, where it is necessary that there should be the purest morals, bastards ought to be
more degraded than in monarchies." The laws of Rome may have
been too severe in this regard, but there was a duty to marry and divorce was easy. The effect of laws regulating marriage may depend
upon the circumstances. The requirement of the father's consent
tends to be disregarded in England where monastic celibacy is not
established whereas in France "young women always have the re-
source of celibacy." Yet in Spain and Italy, convents are established
and still women marry without paternal consent. Generally, it is the
young men that need to be encouraged. What determines marriage
is the force of natural tendencies over the problem of subsistence.
"Wherever a place is found where two people can live commodi-
ously, they enter into marriage. Nature has a sufficient propensity
to it when unrestrained by the difficulty of subsistence."[110] Thus,
what appears to be moral choices, are decided by economic and
civil conditions.

One of the ways in which Montesquieu raises the standing of the
civil laws is to insist upon a distinction between that order and religion. Under the circumstances in which he wrote, the effort to separate the two provides a way of broadening the scope and raising the
standing of the civil law. His argument in the first book on religion, that both religion and the civil laws should tend principally
to render men good citizens, gives religion a social utility purpose
and allows the civil laws to be on an equality with it. The consequence is to raise the status of civil law and this is strengthened by
the supporting illustrations, which tend to place religion in an unpleasant position. Montesquieu points out that the reigning religion of Japan proposes neither future rewards nor future punish-

ments and thus requires that laws supply what is lacking. Further, he expresses a distinction between a religion with a dogma of necessity and one with a dogma of liberty. An example of the former is predestination, which he condemns for causing inactivity in the soul and repose in the citizen. "In a case like this the magistrate ought to waken by the laws those who are lulled asleep by religion."[111] This is further evidence of the high value that Montesquieu attaches to active man and an active society and also of how he calls upon civil authority to overcome the effects of religion.

The assertion that civil laws and religion have the same goal of developing good citizens is followed by a more rigid differentiation of the two in which Montesquieu declares that religion should not encroach upon the realm of the civil laws. "When religion condemns things which the civil laws ought to permit, there is danger lest the civil laws, on the other hand, should permit what religion ought to condemn."[112] Thus each has its realm and disregard of the other may result in a counteracting intervention. Montesquieu is urging a working deference and a combination of mutual autonomy and constraint. Either of these invasions, he says, is "a constant proof of a want of the true ideas of that harmony and proportion which ought to subsist between both." This is another indication of the logic of social structure and operation which this study calls relational pluralism or diversity. The relationship of religion and civil laws is demonstrated also by the case of a false religion and a disordered state. The supporting examples draw upon pre-Christian Greece and Rome. The first illustration of how civil laws may correct distortion in religious practice deals with ceremonies that may be detrimental to children and Montesquieu calls upon Aristotle's observation that when traditional ceremonies are shocking to modesty, the laws permit the fathers to celebrate these mysteries for their wives and children. Another illustration is the rule of Augustus excluding unaccompanied children at any nocturnal ceremony. On the other hand, "religion may support a state when the laws themselves are incapable of doing it." For instance, Montesquieu explains that in kingdoms where wars are not entered into by general consent and there are no legal means of terminating or preventing them, "religion establishes times of peace or cessation from hostilities," so that the people may perform those labors that are necessary for the subsistence of the state. Religion may also assist peaceful order by invoking a horror of murder, proscribing other crimes and, where a state has many causes of hatred, providing ways of reconciliation.[113]

The most inclusive single list of legal orders in *L'Esprit des Lois* appears at the start of Book XXVI. This identifies nine kinds of law which govern mankind: natural, divine, ecclesiastical, general political, particular political, civil, and domestic laws and the law of conquest as well as the law of nations. There is no express mention of either physical or moral law. Book XXVI is largely concerned with demonstrating how these diverse legal realms are distinct from and related to each other. It is a fairly coherent display of "relational pluralism" and may be the only place where Montesquieu gives any formula for determining which kind of law is to govern a particular situation. "There are therefore different orders of laws," he says, "and the sublimity of human reason consists in knowing perfectly to which of these orders the things that are to be determined ought to have a principal relation, and not to throw into confusion those principles which should govern mankind." The chapters of Book XXVI which compare and contrast various types of law would seem to be a case analysis of "the sublimity of human reason." What the examples involve is a combination of circumspect observation and deliberate accommodation so that the desired faculty might be called trained empirical judgment. No doubt, "sublimity of reason" was a more appealing designation in eighteenth century France. Nevertheless, the formula may serve for more than a selection of appropriate legal realms. It could apply also to the determination of which general cause or which law-related object a legislator or other decision maker should prefer in case of a conflict among the several diverse forces and objects which influence political action.

The case explanations in Book XXVI of the interrelationships of various legal orders are of two general types. One concerns the relations of the civil laws to what might be called the higher species of law, that is, the divine law, the law of nature, and the ecclesiastical laws. The other explanations concern the three kinds of positive law which govern or directly affect most of the governmental activities, that is, the political law, the law of nations and the civil law.

The first guide to "the sublimity of human reason" by which the various legal orders are distinguished is the admonition that "we ought not to decide by divine laws what should be decided by human laws; nor determine by human laws what should be determined by divine laws." This statement soon brought Montesquieu criticism for placing divine and human laws on a basis of equality[114] but the critic was probably hypersensitive about existing ecclesiastical doctrine. Montesquieu, I believe, is aiming primarily at separation. He seeks to confine the prestige and force of divine law to its own peculiar realm and to exclude its absolutism in support of law made by human authority. He does not use the term "human laws" with any regularity but rather speaks of specific types of positive law. Throughout his writings he is critical of efforts to give conditional laws, whether canon or political, the sanctity of divine law. In these analyses, I believe that he is assuming the supernatural character of religion rather than its natural or civil aspects.

Montesquieu expressly contrasts divine and human laws with respect to their character, their origin, their objects, and their effects. He declares that human laws are by nature subject to all the accidents that can happen and that they vary with the will of man, whereas the laws of religion, by their very nature, never vary. This may be intended to suggest that the awesome term religious should be applied only to those rules that never do vary, that is, that the term should be used sparingly. With respect to the origin of laws, he explains that we have a firmer belief in the laws of religion because they are associated with antiquity. "Human laws, on the contrary receive advantage from their novelty, which implies the actual and particular attention of the legislator to put them in execution." He remarks that the laws of some kingdoms, most likely referring to France, depend only on the capricious and fickle humor of the sovereign, while the laws of religion have value because of their stability. He also indicates differences with respect to goals. "Human laws appoint for some good; those of religion for the best." Good, he explains, "may have another object because there are many kinds of good; but the best is only one," and therefore it cannot change. Finally, there is a difference in the force or effectiveness of laws. The influence of religion, he says, derives from its being believed, whereas the influence of human laws springs from their being feared.[115] The import of this analysis, I believe, is that human laws are more changeable than religious laws and that human laws should be sociologically or psychologically relevant.

The boundary between civil laws and the laws of nature is demonstrated by two types of cases, one in which the law of nature limits the civil law and the other in which the reverse obtains. In the first type of situation the law of nature is deemed to render void a law denying a slave the right to defend himself against a freeman and also a law denying an accused the right to confront witnesses. Incidentally, these are criminal matters, suggesting that civil law includes penal rules. The other instances of civil laws being voided by the law of nature concern the regulations of women in their domestic affairs, such as the law requiring a woman who is carrying on a criminal commerce to declare it to the king before her marriage, a law condemning to death a woman who lost her child if she had not made her pregnancy known to the magistrate, a law permitting girls of seven to choose a husband, and finally a law leaving divorce to the power of a third person, without the consent of either spouse.[116]

More striking is the second set of situations in which the civil law is deemed to curtail the principles of the law of nature. This is extraordinary because natural law is commonly regarded as superior in moral content and authority. But Montesquieu asserts that civil law principles limit the natural law obligation of children to support an indigent father, because the obligation is suspended where the father did not provide the child with the means of earning a livelihood or where the father prostituted his daughter.[117] These exceptions might seem to be natural law principles themselves, but Montesquieu calls them civil laws and the result is to enhance the standing of that realm of order.

The tendency to broaden the scope of civil law and narrow that of natural law appears also in the cases on the succession or inheritance of property. Here, Montesquieu may extend civil law to some aspects of what had once been customary law and which Bodin sought to make a part of the natural law.[118] Montesquieu points out that the law of nature requires fathers to support their children, but he says that this does not obligate them to leave inheritances. The division and succession of property, he says, "can be regulated only by the community; and consequently by the political or civil laws."[119] Such laws often demand that children succeed to their fathers but, he asserts, this is not necessary. The argument adds support to the general premise of *L'Esprit des Lois* that man-made laws are not absolute but rather circumstantial. In fact, Montesquieu concludes that his analysis is one explanation for the varying laws in different countries on the right of a bastard to succeed to the property of the father.

An assertion that could account for some of the criticism which Montesquieu received from church officials is the statement that civil laws might override the "precepts of religion." Yet the case illustration does not go to the essence of religion. The supporting example concerns the fifty days of fasting among the Abyssinians, which makes them incapable of conducting business or defending themselves. This goes against Montesquieu's ideal of the active man but his specific argument reflects the law of preservation. "Religion ought, in favor of the natural right of self-defense, to set bounds to these customs." Likewise, he questions the rule against resisting attack or seige on the sabbath. "Who does not see that self-defense is a duty superior to every precept."[120] The effect of this, of course, is to narrow the absolute character of religious laws and to support the doctrine of sociological relevance.

The way in which the civil law and the law of religion are differentiated also tends to broaden the scope of the civil law by making it the basis of morality and welfare in particular societies. Montesquieu lays down the general proposition that "things which ought to be regulated by the Principles of civil laws can seldom be regulated by the Laws of Religion," and he identifies the characteristics of the two types of laws. "The laws of religion have a greater sublimity; the civil laws a greater extent." Montesquieu explains further that in contrast to the laws of religion which concern the goodness of the person more than of the society, the civil laws, "have more in view the moral goodness of men in general than that of individuals." For this reason, he says, religion "ought not always to serve as a first principle to the civil laws; because they have another, the general welfare of society."[121] A number of illustrations are presented in support of these ideas. The first concerns the law on the morality of women during three stages of Roman government. The Roman republic adopted political regulations to preserve the morals of women; and in the Roman monarchy civil laws were made for this purpose. When the Christian religion became predominant, the laws concerned the holiness of marriage more than the general rectitude of morals and made marriage more of a spiritual than a civil condition. Montesquieu sharply attacks the religious tribunal, expressly referring to the inquisition. "In monarchies it only makes informers and traitors; in republics, it only forms dishonest men; in a despotic state, it is as destructive as the government itself." If two persons are accused of a capital crime in the religious court, the one who denies is condemned to die while the one who confesses avoids the punishment. For religious purposes, he explains, the one is in a state of impenitence and damnation while the other is in a state of repentance and salvation. But such a distinction cannot concern the human tribunals, Montesquieu explains, because human justice, which sees only the actions, has but one compact with men, that is, innocence, whereas divine justice, which sees the thoughts of men, has two compacts with men, that of innocence and repentance.[122]

The role of civil laws in matters often associated with religious or natural law is demonstrated further by reference to certain rules of marriage. Montesquieu again seems to limit religious law to what is invariable. He explains that while some ceremonies are religious, other ceremonies, like the consent of the father, are civil. This, of course, lessens the area of rigid control and broadens the area of flexibility and moderation. He says that dissolution is determined only by the religious laws, noting that this avoids contradictions and uncertainties about the status of a marriage. Hence, the object of civil law controls would seem to be the process of entering marriage relations and not their termination. He adds in this same vein that, while civil violations of the marriage bond may result in penalties, they do not or should not void the arrangement. "The civil law determines according to the circumstances; sometimes it is most attentive to repair the evil, other times to prevent it."[123] Thus, the civil law must be sociologically relevant.

Likewise, he limits the scope of the law of nature by treating the rules on the marriage of close relatives to be civil laws. This endeavor involves considerable analysis of various types of marriages and the closeness of relatives in the early history of the household customs. He declares that it is an extremely delicate thing to set exactly the point at which the laws of nature stops and the civil laws commence in these matters, but still he undertakes to establish some principles. He asserts that the marriage of son to mother and of father to daughter are both contrary to nature. However, he sees two added obstacles to the first type. There is a conflict between the unlimited respect of a son for his mother and the unlimited respect which a wife owes a husband. In contrast, presumably, the daughter-wife would owe unlimited respect in both capacities. Then, the difference in ages would mean a period of unproductivity in the case of the mother but not for the father. Montesquieu points out that this is the reason that a Tartar is allowed to marry his daughter but not his mother. However, Montesquieu opposes father-daughter unions because of the natural duty of the father to watch over the modesty of his children and to bring them up and preserve their bodies and minds from corruption.[124]

Another example of the civil character of what might seem to be a moral dictate concerns the differing rules of a marriage between those of the same generation. Such marriages, Montesquieu explains, have been permitted or prohibited on the basis of whether the particular kind of relatives lived within the same household during the early history of the nation. Brothers and sisters were raised in the same house and, accordingly, the natural duty of maintaining the morals of the family made brother-sister marriages "contrary to nature." Cousins-german were raised in the same household in some regions and not in others, Montesquieu points out, and argues that in the first type of area their marriage "ought to be regarded as contrary to nature" but, where they do not live in the same house, natural law itself would not forbid their marriage. But this is a sociological view of nature because Montesquieu promptly declares that "the laws of nature cannot be local" and that a law for or against such marriages, accordingly, is a civil law.[125] Thus again he excludes from the law of nature and brings within the civil law what earlier legal theorists had regarded as either customary or natural law.[126] The designation of this rule to be civil law rather than a law of nature removes it from the realm of the invariable and puts it in the realm of accommodation and moderation. It becomes more open to change by judge or legislator and less appropriate for moral and religious penalties. This is somewhat similar to the developments in England two or three generations later, when there was a shift in emphasis from natural law to positive law jurisprudence in the work of the utilitarian and legal reformer, Jeremy Bentham.[127]

Book XXVI identifies a number of ways for distinguishing civil and political laws with some mixing of criteria. To begin, it recognizes both a general and particular political law, defining the one to concern "that human wisdom whence all societies derive their origin" and the other to have only one society as its object. The subdivision of political law is not utilized expressly in any discussion before or after its identification. Moreover, the examples of political law go much beyond the mere origin and establishment of political society or authority. The definition of civil law at this point is that "by which a citizen may defend his possessions and his life against the attacks of any other citizens."[128] Like the other definitions of civil law, this is broad enough to cover many types of criminal law. In general, Montesquieu seems to assume in much of Book XXVI that the political law concerns the superior executive and the society while the civil law relates to the interest of the individual, the latter embracing protection of property as well as person. Still another articulation of the difference between political and civil law appears in the midst of Book XXVI, where Montesquieu takes up the specific analysis of these two types of legal order. He starts this discussion with the titular proposition in Chapter 15 that "we should not regulate by the Principles of political laws those Things which depend on the Principles of civil law." There is some attention to the way positive law communities originate when he declares that "As men have given up their natural independence to live under political laws, they have given up the natural community of goods to live under civil laws." But if this has similarities to Locke, Montesquieu seems more intent upon distinguishing two kinds of positive law than explaining how they arose. He goes on to assert that the people acquire liberty by the political laws and proprietorship by the civil ones. He identifies another factor in the difference between the two kinds of laws while asserting that "We should not decide by the laws of liberty, which, as we have already said, is only the government of the community, what ought to be decided by the laws concerning property."[129] There are a number of interesting ideas embodied in these statements. For one thing, they suggest that there is both a political community and a personal community, both by nature and by law. The political laws concern one community, and the civil laws the other. Then the association of the political laws with liberty reflects the earlier portion of *L'Esprit des Lois* which distinguishes two kinds of political liberty.[130] These I will discuss in Chapter VI.

A modern, libertarian point of view is evident in the discussion of the limitations upon governmental seizure of private property. Montesquieu draws upon the better aspects of the civil property law in developing a procedure that reflects the now familiar constitutional principle that private property should be taken only for a public purpose and then with fair compensation. He uses his concept of the public good to limit the occasions for acquisition but applies his concept of the civil law to require consideration or indemnification for the seizure. In the course of the argument he says that individual wealth should give way to the public good only when it operates for the authority of the community, that is to say, "the liberty of the citizen," because the public good always aims to preserve for everyone the property given him by the civil laws. Next, he declares as a maxim that "it is not for the advantage of the public to deprive an individual of his property, or even to retrench the least part of it, by a law or a political regulation." Such cases should follow "the rigor of the civil law, which is the palladium of property." His arguments throw new light on the character of the civil law. When the public has need of the estate of an individual, he says that "it ought never act by the rigor of the political law" but should proceed according to the "civil law which, with the eyes of a mother, regards every individual as the whole community."[131] Thus, he seems to assume that the civil law is the law of the community in a nonpolitical capacity.

The proposition here that the civil law rather than the political law should control governmental taking of private property seems designed to assure compensation or indemnification. Montesquieu declares that if the political magistrate wishes to erect a public edifice or build a new road, he should indemnify those who are injured. "The public is in this respect like an individual who treats with an individual." It is enough, he says, that the public can force the citizen to give up his property. A precedent is found among the nations which destroyed Rome. After they had abused their conquests, "the spirit of liberty called them back to that of equity." They exercised the most barbarous laws with moderation, he points out, as Beaumanoir attests in his admirable twelfth century work on jurisprudence. Montesquieu concludes that the conquering nations determined at that time by the civil law what is determined in his day by the political law. Presumably, a taking under the political law involves no indemnification. A present day parallel would seem to be the Supreme Court decision that wartime rent ceilings do not amount to a governmental taking under the fair compensation principle.[132] The condemnation of land for a building or road today follows the general pattern which Montesquieu presents. The state may take the land in its political capacity, but the process of indemnification is much like a damage suit between private individuals, the injured party being entitled to fair compensation. The absence of compensation under the political law may be one reason for Montesquieu's subsequent contention that the termination of a line of royal succession should be determined by the political law and not the civil law.

The distinction between political laws and civil laws is modified again when the idea that the former concerns liberty while the other deals with property is subordinated to the principle that one concerns public matters and the other private ones. This occurs with the assertion that the political law governs the succession of royal authority. The order of royal succession, Montesquieu asserts, is not for the sake of the reigning family but in order that the state should have a reigning family. "The law which regulates the succession of individuals is a civil law, whose view is the interest of the individuals," while the regulation of succession to monarchy "is a political law, which has in view the welfare and preservation of the kingdom." Here, Montesquieu is determining the character of a law by its objective as well as by its content. The distinction between public and private purposes is strengthened and even extended by the assertion that when the political law has established an order of succession and that order comes to an end, it would be absurd to claim succession according to the civil law of some nation. This presumably refers to the attempt of Louis XIV to inject a rule of land succession into the selection of a Spanish king, which led to the War of Devolution. Montesquieu asserts his belief that laws are indigenous and peculiar to each nation. "One particular society does not make laws for another society. The civil laws of the Romans are no more applicable than any other civil laws." This principle would seem to explain the purpose of the next two books which inquire into the origin of the laws of succession at Rome and into the development of the French civil laws. The distinction between civil and political law is further elaborated with the remark that restitutions provided by the civil law "may be good against those who live in the law but they are not good for those who have been established for the law and who live for the law". The analysis ends with a bit of cynicism: "It is ridiculous to pretend to decide the rights of kingdoms, of nations, and of the whole globe by the same maxims on which we decide the right of a gutter between individuals, to use an expression of Cicero."[133]

A number of case analyses at this point seem designed to give the civil law a moral and sensible tone by excluding certain rules from the scope of that legal order and placing them elsewhere. First, there is the statement that ostracism is political rather than civil. "Ostracism ought to be examined by the rules of politics and not by

those of the civil law."[134] Moreover, Montesquieu argues that banishment should be distinguished from punishment, and he makes
reference to Aristotle's assertions that ostracism from a city is universally recognized to be both humane and popular. Another apparent effort to disassociate harsh rules from the civil law concerns
the custom that a Roman could lend his wife to another man. This
is deemed to be a law of politics designed to give the republic children of a good species. Montesquieu says that the rule does not contradict the civil law for the preservation of morals, by which penalties were imposed upon a husband who suffered his wife to be debauched without either bringing her to justice or taking her back
again. Likewise, the rule that a slave should inform upon an unfaithful wife is deemed to be proper only in those Eastern countries
where women are under constant guard. There it concerns the
household and not the community. It "may be, in certain cases at
the most, a particular domestic regulation but never a civil law."[135]
This is similar to the contention in the discussion of slavery that
the power of the master over the slave is a matter of domestic law
rather than the civil.[136]

Montesquieu makes the civil law a model or standard for the law
of nations, as well as for the political law. In the discussion of the
civil law and the law of nations,[137] he tends to view the civil law for
its principles of justice and liberty more than for its protection of
property. In fact, when the civil law is contrasted with the law of
nations, it seems to stand for the whole internal legal order of the
society. In the preceding analysis, the civil law was associated with
property and the political law with liberty, but now, in the confron-
tation with the law of nations, the civil law is declared to be the
basis of liberty. This is a shift of perspective rather than a fundamental change in the definition of civil law, I believe, because
property rights concern civil liberty among individuals, such as the
freedom from trespass. This kind of liberty is now relevant because
the law of nations concerns the order of various societies as particular entities on a basis of equality and mutuality, analogous to the
individual citizens within a national society.

Montesquieu's approach here is similar to that in *Les Lettres Persanes* where he recognizes only two kinds of positive law, that is, *Le
droit public*, which seems to be the law of nations, and *le droit
civil*. In that earlier work he is critical of the law of nations and argues that it should adopt the higher standards of justice found in

the civil law. He asserts that *le droit public* is better understood in Europe than in Asia but that all of its principles have been corrupted by "the passions of princes, the patience of nations, the flattery of authors." It has become, he notes, "a science which teaches princes to what degree they may violate justice, without hurting their own interest."[138] With the two kinds of law, he observes, "there are two kinds of justice entirely different, one which regulates the affairs of private persons, which reigns in the civil law; another which regulates the differences that arise between people and people, which tyrannizes in *le droit public*." His remark that the latter might be a civil law of the world may concern its form more than its standards.

His attitude becomes more constructive in the next letter. "The magistrates ought to administer justice between citizen and citizen," he says, and "Every nation ought to do the same between themselves and another nation."[139] He asserts that the maxims of the first should be applied in the second and even argues that there is less excuse for injustice among nations because there is little need for a third party judge. "The interests of the two nations are generally so separate, that nothing more is necessary but a love of justice to find it out," he notes. In contrast, individuals have interests so mixed, so confounded and so numerous "that it is necessary for a third person to clear up what the covetousness of the parties endeavors to obscure." This more optimistic turn of Montesquieu's attitude toward foreign relations appears also in *le Traitè des Devoirs* of 1725. There he declares that the duty of the citizen is a crime when it overrides the duty of the man. He elaborates that the impossibility of putting the universe under one society has rendered men strangers to each other but this does not prescribe against the first duties. Man, above all reasonable, is neither Roman nor barbarian.[140] The idea of a world humanity and the proposition that justice among nations should be the same as justice in the civil order would seem to be some anticipation of Kant's ideas on Perpetual Peace.[141]

In *L'Esprit des Lois* the contrast of the civil law and the law of nations is asserted in relation to liberty rather than justice. It is still a matter of living under laws but now liberty is the preferred value which the civil laws are deemed to assure. "Liberty consists principally in not being forced to do a thing, where the laws do not oblige: people are in this state only as they are governed by civil

laws; and because they live under those civil laws, they are free."
The consequence is, he says, that "princes who live not among
themselves under civil laws, are not free; they are governed by
force; they may continually force or be forced."[142] Thus, treaties
made by force are obligatory even though persons living under civil
laws are not bound by a contract entered into under force. A
prince, being always in the situation of either forcing or being
forced, cannot complain of a treaty which he has been compelled to
sign. "This would be to complain of his natural state" and "would
be contrary to the nature of things." Here, Montesquieu is describing the law of nations as it is whereas previously he was concerned
with what it ought to be.

Political law comes back into the analysis but largely for the
purpose of arguing the uniqueness of the laws of each nation. Montesquieu devotes a good deal of *L'Esprit des Lois* to the argument
that national laws and particularly the civil law are or should be
largely peculiar to each nation. Books XXVII and XXVIII deal exclusively with the indigenous character of the Roman and French
civil laws. This argument is part of Montesquieu's conflict with
contemporary historians over the effect of Roman law and legal
and political theory upon the character of the French monarchy.
He claims that the French monarchy was limited and the extended
historical inquiries in the final portion of *L'Esprit des Lois* are designed to refute those contemporary historians who asserted that
the French king was modeled after the absolute Roman emperors.
Here, in Book XXVI, the discussion of the law of nations turns to
the question of what laws control the conduct of a foreigner. Montesquieu takes the side of the national law and in general takes a
modern stand in deciding which nation it is. He asserts that "Political laws demand that every man be subject to the criminal and civil
courts of the country where he is, and to the censure of the sovereign." But he suggests exception for ambassadors. They should
not be subject to the political laws of the country to which they are
sent. They are the voice of the prince who sends them and this
voice ought to be free. They should be judged by the law of nations
and not the political law. If they misuse their representative character, they may be recalled and judged by the prince. Montesquieu re-
capitulates his ideas here by reference to the "unfortunate lot of the
Ynca Athualpa," presumably meaning Atahualpa, the last emperor
of the Incas. The principle of respecting the distinctive character of
different legal orders, Montesquieu declares, was "cruelly violated

by the Spaniards" when they tried this Peruvian leader, not by the law of nations, nor by the political or civil laws of his own country, but by the political and civil laws of their own country.[143]

In the same general view, Montesquieu reiterates the principle expressed a number of times previously that the political laws of a nation should not be borrowed or transported from another people. Particularly, he asserts that the rule of royal succession should serve the society because "the safety of the people is the supreme law," and that when a law of political succession becomes destructive of the state, another rule should be made to change the order. This most likely concerns the dynastic politics of Europe, especially the rule that brought the Bourbons into the Spanish succession. He adds the companion idea, also expressed on several previous occasions, that a great state weakens itself when it becomes accessory to another state. The interest of the nation requires that it "have the supreme magistrate within itself, that the public revenues be well administered, and that its specie be not sent abroad to enrich another country." Again he stresses the unique character of national political laws. "It is of importance that he who is to govern has not imbibed foreign maxims; these are less agreeable than those already established." Moreover, he adds, "men have an extravagant fondness for their own laws and customs: these constitute the happiness of every community." Montesquieu invokes the lessons of history on the deep affection of people for their own law and customs. He declares that the histories of all nations teach us that these national heritages "are rarely changed without violent commotions and a great effusion of blood."[144] The supporting examples or illustrations concern rules of royal succession. Montesquieu approves of the law of Russia which excluded from the crown any heir who possessed another monarchy and the law of Portugal which disqualified the foreign claimants who asserted succession by right of blood. Moreover, Montesquieu declares that a people may oblige a prince to renounce a marriage that would rob the nation of its independence or integrity.

The several arguments and illustrations about the national uniqueness of rules of succession and other political laws are relevant to both previous and subsequent discussions in *L'Esprit de Lois*. In earlier books, Montesquieu criticized the foreign venture of Louis XIV and also argued that civil and political laws develop peculiarly within particular societies. Hence, there is nothing fundamentally new in his implied objections to the attempt of the French monarch to capitalize on a local custom of land succession. Moreover, the emphasis upon the national uniqueness of positive laws anticipates subsequent books of the volume. In fact, the principle being argued here would seem to be further explanation for the inclusion of the two ensuing books, the one on the Roman law of civil succession and the other on the development of French civil laws. These historical inquiries undertake to prove that civil laws are indigenous and, indirectly, that the French monarch was not as absolute as the Roman emperors.

Book XXVI concludes with further examples of "the sublimity of human reason." The civil law is distinguished from police regulations of a recurring and trifling character. In this discussion, incidentally, there is another implication that the civil law include the more common criminal laws. Also, the final case in the book provides further support of Montesquieu's insistence that the laws have a sociological relevance. It argues that civil obligations incurred by sailors during a voyage should not be subjected to the general provisions of the civil legal order because they were not contracted to support the civil society.[145]

The various discussions of civil law in Book XXVI seem to have the common object of raising the standing of that legal realm to the highest level of all man made law and even the natural law. This purpose is served both by excluding from the civil law any rule that would bring it no moral or humane value and by including within its scope subjects often reserved for the laws of religion and the law of nature.

Notes

1. *L'Esprit des Lois* (hereafter referred to as *Lois*) XXVIII, 10.
2. *Pensée* 1228, Roger Caillois, *Oeuvres Complètes de Montesquieu* (hereafter referred to as Caillois I or II) (Paris 1951), I, 1306.
3. *Pensée* 1227, Caillois I, 1306.
4. *L'Esprit des Lois* (hereafter referred to as *Lois*), XX, 19-22.
5. Frank T. H. Fletcher, *Montesquieu and English Politics, 1750-1800.* (London, 1939), 46-67. Fletcher also points out the similarity of Montesquieu's ideas to such later writers as Adam Ferguson and James Steuart.
6. David Lowenthal, "Montesquieu," in Leo Strauss and Joseph Cropsey, *History of Political Philosophy* (Chicago, 1963), 485.
7. Raymond Aron, *Main Currents in Sociological Thought* (New York, 1965) I, 42, 39.
8. Robert Tucker, *Philosophy and Myth in Karl Marx*, (Cambridge, 1961) 130-5; Erich Fromm, *Marx's Concept of Man*, (New York, 1961) 26-43.
9. Aron, *op. cit.*, 42.
10. David E. Apter, *The Politics of Modernization* (Chicago, 1965) 43. Apter observes that in many non-Western areas "modernization has been a result of commercialization and, rather than industrialization, bureaucracy." See also Jason L. Finkle and Richard W. Gable, *Political Development and Social Change* (New York, 1966) 230, 235, 244.
11. *Lois*, XX, 1, 3; XXI, 5, 6.
12. *Ibid.*, VII, 1.
13. Polybius, *Histories*, VI, 57 (Loeb Classical Edition) III, 399; Thorsten Veblen, *The Theory of the Leisure Class* (New York, 1926) 68-101.
14. *Lois*, VII, 1.
15. See, for instance, "The Marquis d'Argenson on the Condition of France in 1739," in George Rudé (Ed.) *The Eighteenth Century, 1715-1815* (New York, 1965) 70-74.
16. *Lois*, VII, 2,3.
17. *Ibid.*, VII, 4, 5. (Author's translation).
18. *Ibid.*, VII, 6.
19. *Ibid.*, XIII, 12-15; XVIII, 1.
20. Robert Shackleton, *Montesquieu A Critical Biography* (Oxford, 1961), 204, 206.
21. Raymond Aron states that Montesquieu "was not particularly systematic" as an economist, that he belonged neither to the mercantilist nor to the physiocrat school, and that he may be regarded "a sociologist who anticipated the modern analysis of economic development, precisely because he took into consideration the multiple factors involved." Aron, *op. cit.* 42.
22. The manuscript pages for Book XXI are the final portion of the fourth of five volumes, *Bibliothèque Nationale*, n.a.f. 12835. 186-358. Several chapters differ from the published work, a number of chapters are absent, and what became Chapters 10 and 14 are in a substantially different location.
23. See Shackleton, *op. cit.*, 320.
24. *Lois*, XX, 1, 2.
25. *Ibid.*, XX, 2.
26. *Ibid.*, XX, 3.

27. *Lois*, XX, 4; Caillois, II, 587. Nugent translates these terms as monarchy and republic rather than government by one and government by several.

28. *Lois*, XX, 4.

29. *Ibid.*, XX, 5.

30. *Ibid.*, XX, 7.

31. *Ibid.*, XX, 8-11.

32. *Ibid.*, XX, 4.

33. *Ibid.*, XX, 6.

34. *Ibid.*, XX, 15, 12, 13.

35. *Ibid.*, XX, 14. In the war with England, he says Spain punished with death importation from or exportation to the enemy. This "shocks our mores, the spirit of commerce and the harmony which ought to exist in the proportion of penalties; it confounds all our ideas, making a crime against the state of what is only a violation of good order." (Author's translation). Thus, even in analyzing commerce, Montesquieu applies familiar principles, such as the propriety of established mores, the view of social activity for its spirit, the relevance of punishment to the offense, and the distinct character of the political and civil realms of order.

36. *Lois*, XX. 15-18. He agrees with Plato's statement that in a city where there is no maritime commerce there ought to be about half the number of civil laws, Plato: *Laws*, VIII, 842.

37. *Lois*, XX, 19-21.

38. Shackleton, *op. cit.*, 14-19, 27-39, 83-4. Montesquieu in *L'Esprit des Lois* attacks laws which "oblige every one to continue in his profession, and to devolve it upon his children." Such laws are of no use except in despotic kingdoms. "Let none say that every one will succeed better in his profession when he cannot change it for another: I say that a person will succeed best when those who have excelled hope to rise to another." *Lois*, XX, 22.

39. *Lois*, XX, 22.

40. For Montesquieu's views on the Parlements see Shackleton, *op. cit.*, 279-281.

41. *Lois*, XXI, 1.

42. *Ibid.*, XXI, 3. Montesquieu describes various expeditions with considerable attention to details of travel and navigation. Among the ancients, land expeditions were the more important. "Today, we discover the lands by the sea voyages; in other times they discovered the seas by the land conquests." For instance, the Indian Ocean was discovered by land exploration. The many voyages to and around Africa at a later period are analyzed in detail for proof that the early mariners had no compass. *Lois*, XXI, 10. Montesquieu seems to have an intense interest in every kind of operation. He carries into the eighteenth century curiosity of nature all of the intellectual avidity of the Renaissance man.

43. *Ibid.*, XXI, 5.

44. *Ibid.*, XXI, 6.

45. *Ibid.*, XXI, 9. Montesquieu is much taken by Hanno's account of his voyage to the west coast of Africa. "Great commanders write their actions with simplicity: because they receive more glory from the facts than from words." *Ibid.* XXI, 11.

46. *Ibid.*, XXI, 11, 14.

47. *Ibid.*, XXI, 17-18.

48. Caillois, *op. cit.*, II, 60.

49. *Lois,* XXI, 20.

50. *Ibid.,* XXI, 21 (par. 9).

51. *Ibid.,* XXI, 21 (pars. 12-15).

52. *Ibid.,* XXI, 22.

53. *Ibid.,* IX, 7.

54. *Ibid.,* XXII, 12.

55. *Ibid.,* XXII, 14.

56. *Ibid.,* XXII, 17-18.

57. *Ibid.,* XXII, 19-22.

58. *Ibid.,* XXII, 22.

59. *Les Lettres Persanes* (hereafter referred to as *L.P.*). CXII-CXXII. He says that calculation shows the population of the earth to be one-tenth of what it was in ancient times and that this depopulation goes on daily. *L.P.* CXII. The discussion in *L'Esprit des Lois* seems not to assume such a drastic decline.

60. *L.P.* CXXII; *Lois,* XXIII, 2-4. "The public continence is naturally connected with the propagation of the race." It is a dictate of reason that in a marriage the children follow the status of the father; if no marriage, they can only belong to the mother. Almost everywhere it is the custom for the wife to pass into the family of the husband. At Formosa the reverse is the case. A law that fixes the family in a succession of persons of the same sex, greatly contributes to propagation because, "the family is a kind of property" and a man is not satisfied until he has children of the sex which can perpetuate the family. The name of a family may also inspire every member with a desire to extend its duration. *Lois,* XVIII, 4.

61. *Ibid.,* XXIII, 11.

62. *Ibid.,* XXIII, 12-15.

63. *Ibid.,* XXIII, 28.

64. *Ibid.,* XXIII, 29.

65. *Dissertation sur la Politique des Romains dans la Religion,* Caillois, I, 81-92.

66. *Considérations sur Les Causes de la Grandeur Des Romains et de Leur Décadence,* XXI, XXII, Caillois, II, 192, 194, 196-203. Lowenthal, *op. cit.* 210.

67. Jean-Baptiste Gautier, *Les Lettres Persanes convaincus d'impiété,* (1751) 64; *Pensées,* 2112, 2110, Caillois, 1, 1550.

68. *Lois,* II, 4; III, 10; IV, 3; V, 14; XII, 29; XIX, 17-19.

69. *Lois,* XXIV, 1.

70. The separate character of religious and secular authority is stressed in the final chapters of the work on the Romans. But that work also indicates that religion in best guaranteed when it accords with the mores of the people. The idea that *L'Esprit des Lois* is relevant to the French situation in this matter is advanced by Joseph Dedieu. For one thing, he says that, after a long period of bitter conflict, the church and the state were viewed by many Frenchmen as rival forces the union of which could only be bad. But unlike this study, he argues that Montesquieu believed that their interests were identical. Dedieu seeks to show that the inspiration was English, particularly Bishop Warburton. Joseph Dedieu, *Montesquieu et la tradition politique anglais en France,* (Paris, 1909), 239, 246-253.

71. William Warburton, *The Alliance between Church and State, or, the Necessity and Equity of an Established Religion and a Test-Law Demonstrated from the Essence and End of Civil Society, upon the Fundamental Principles of the Law of Nature and Nations*. (London, 1736; a French translation under the title *Dissertations sur L'Union de la Religion, de la Morale et de la Religion, de la Morale et de la Politique*, was published in London in 1742).

72. "The ultimate end of one being the care of souls, and that of the other, of bodies." The means of one is by internal actions and of the other by external. Warburton, *op. cit.*, 40. The religious society is deemed to have no "coactive power" such as is possessed by the civil society.

73. " . . . the great Preliminary or fundamental article of Alliance is this, that the church shall apply all its influence in the service of the state; and that the state shall support and protect the church." Warburton, *op. cit.*, 68. Each society is said to be "naturally distinct and different" and they can act conjointly only by a "mutual concession." But, where Warburton bases the alliance upon convention, Montesquieu seems to consider it a natural relationship, less formal and more social in character.

74. Warburton, *op. cit.*, 158.

75. *Lois*, XXIV, 19.

76. Montesquieu interposes that the Christian religion has done this in an admirable manner, by making us hope for the object of our faith and not that of our experience so that even the article on the resurrection of the body leads us to spiritual ideas. *Lois*, XXIV, 19. The doctrine of immortality of the soul is described as having three branches, that of pure immortality, that of a simple change of habitation, and that of a metempsychosis. The latter doctrine of the Indians has had both good and bad effects: there are few murders even without the death penalty but women burn themselves at the death of their husbands. *Lois*, XXIV, 21.

77. *Lois*, XXIV, 2.

78. *Ibid.*, XXIV, 3, 4.

79. *L.P.*, XXIV, LXXXV, CI.

80. Shackleton, *op. cit.*, 343.

81. See fn. 68.

82. *Lois*, XXIV, 5.

83. *Ibid.*, XXIV, 6.

84. For letters on casuistry, see *L.P.*, XXIX, LVII, LXXV, and CXXXIV. The principles common to all religions are "observance of the laws, love of fellow man, and piety toward one's parents," *L.P.* XLVI. The biographer Shackleton says that Montesquieu believed a revealed religion to be more assailable than a natural one because the former is based upon facts and the latter upon the internal sentiment of man. Shackleton compares Montesquieu to Alexander Pope for being a Catholic at birth and death, while during his life being more concerned with morality and the rational principles of natural religion than with dogma, Shackleton, *op. cit.*, 353-4.

85. *Lois*, XXIV, 8, 9.

86. *Ibid.*, XXIV, 10.

87. *Ibid.*, XXIV, 12, 13. A pagan religion which is aimed at the hand and not at the heart and which forbids only grosser crimes might have expiable crimes, Montesquieu says, while a religion which bridles all the passions and establishes a new kind of justice leads us to

both love and repentance and mediates between criminal and judge. *Lois*, XXIV, 13.

88. *Lois*, XXIV, 7.

89. "It seems to all appearances as if the climate has prescribed the bounds of the Christian and Mohammedan religions," *Lois*, XXIV, 26.

90. Joseph Dedieu says that "Mandeville was an important source of religious doctrines" for *L'Esprit des Lois*, Dedieu, *op. cit.*, 256, and Mandeville is cited *Lois*, VII, 1, but a commentary upon Mandeville says that it is probable that "Montesquieu did not read the *Fable* until his opinions were pretty well formed." F. B. Kaye, *The Fable of the Bees* (Oxford, 1924, 1957), I, cxxxii, fn. 1.

91. *Lois*, XXV, 2.

92. *Ibid.*, XXV, 2 (par. 8).

93. *Ibid.*, XXV, 4.

94. *Ibid.*, XXV, 5-8. The reference is to Book X of Plato's *Laws*.

95. The work of Mandeville appears not to have been well known in France until 1723 which was some two years after the publication of *Les Lettres Persanes*. See Kaye, *op. cit.*, in fn. 90. Letters on toleration include LX, and LXXXV.

96. On Montesquieu's interest in Jansenism, see Shackleton, *op. cit.*, 344-7.

97. *L.P.*, XXIV, CXI.

98. *Ibid.*, LXI.

99. *Ibid.*, LXXXV.

100. *Lois*, XXV, 9.

101. *Lois*, XXV, 10.

102. Caillois, II, 1147.

103. *Lois*, XXV, 12.

104. Shackleton, *op. cit.*, 354.

105. *Lois*, XXV, 15.

106. Civil law and liberty received more attention in the eighteenth century than it does now. See Kingsley Martin, *The Rise of French Liberal Thought* (New York, 1956), 140; J. Walter Jones, *Historical Introduction to the Theory of Law* (Oxford, 1956), 63, 152, 176; Elie Halevy, *The Growth of Philosophic Radicalism* (Boston, 1955), 37.

107. *L.P.*, C.

108. *Lois*, XXI, 14.

109. *Ibid.*, XXIII, 2-4.

110. *Ibid.*, XXIII, 5-10.

111. *Ibid.*, XXIV, 14.

112. *Ibid.*

113. *Ibid.*, XXIV, 15-17.

114. Jean-Baptist Louis Crevier, *Observations sur le Livre de L'Esprit des Lois* (Paris, 1764), 256-260.

115. *Lois*, XXVI, 2.

116. *Ibid.*, XXVI, 3, 4.

117. *Ibid.*, XXVI, 5.

118. William Farr Church, *Constitutional Thought in Sixteenth Century France*, (Cambridge, Mass., 1941), 254-255, 281-282.

119. *Lois*, XXVI, 6.

120. *Ibid.*, XXVI, 7.

121. *Ibid.*, XXVI, 9.

122. *Ibid.*, XXVI, 11, 12.

123. *Ibid.*, XXVI, 13.

124. *Ibid.*
125. *Ibid.*, XXVI, 14.
126. See fn. 118, *supra.*
127. See generally, Carl J. Friedrich, *The Philosophy of Law in Historical Perspective* (Chicago, 1957), 95-99; Elie Halevy, *The Growth of Philosophic Radicalism* (London, 1928), 37-42.
128. *Lois,* XXVI, 1.
129. *Ibid.*, XXVI, 15.
130. *Ibid.*, XI, XII.
131. *Ibid.*, XXVI, 15.
132. *Woods v. Miller,* 333 U.S. 138 (1948).
133. *Lois,* XXVI, 16. (Author's translation).
134. *Ibid.*, XXVI, 17.
135. *Ibid.*, XXVI, 18, 19.
136. *Ibid.*, XV, 2.
137. Ibid., XXVI, 20-23.
138. *L.P.,* XCIV.
139. *Ibid.*, XCV.
140. Roger Caillois, *Montesquieu Oeuvres Completes* (Paris, 1951) (hereafter referred to as Caillois, I or II), I, 110.
141. See generally, Carl J. Friedrich, *Inevitable Peace* (1948).
142. *Lois,* XXVI, 20. The contrast of internal order under civil law and external order under the law of nations appears also in the discussions of England's supervision of Ireland, *Lois,* XIX, 27.
143. *Ibid.*, XXVI, 21, 22.
144. *Ibid.*, XXVI, 23.
145. *Ibid.*, XXVI, 24, 25.

Chapter IV

The Political Capabilities
of the Three Classes

The first substantive portion of *L'Esprit des Lois,* that is, Books
II — X, appears to be a comparative study of traditional forms of
government, but I believe that it is more fundamentally a comparison of the three main classes of a national society and that the analysis is less an end in itself than a means of suggesting the need for
mixed government. Montesquieu's examination of democracy, aristocracy, monarchy, and despotism tends to bring out the differing
roles of the many, the few, and the one. The unexplained lack of
symmetry in the typology of governments seems to serve this objective. There is a frequent shift from simple to mixed government
with an interrelationship of political classes. Moreover, Montesquieu appears to presuppose a basic division between the control
and the action of government. His studies of democracies and aristocracies relate mostly to control by election and legislation while
the inquiries into monarchies and despotisms deal largely with administrative and adjudicative actions.

For a closer examination of these implicit factors, the three sections of this chapter will analyze Montesquieu's pattern of comparative analyses, his examination of political control, and his investigation of political action, each with particular attention to the potential contribution to Montesquieu's system of a natural government by mixed classes.

The Patterns of Comparative Analysis

The classification of governments which appears in Books II
through X of *L'Esprit des Lois* is substantially more complex than
that found in *Les Lettres Persanes.* In the earlier work, Montesquieu speaks only of monarchies and republics. The first type tends
to be despotic and the other moderate. Both presumably are un-

mixed or simple types which contrast sharply with each other. The difference is portrayed graphically in the observation, previously mentioned, that European monarchies tend to degenerate into either tyranny or popular anarchy. The contrast of these two forms of government brings to mind the remark by Plato in the *Laws* that there are two mother forms of government, monarchy and democracy, and that any good form of government must include parts of both.[1] In *L'Esprit des Lois,* Montesquieu endeavors to develop a combination that is relevant to the structure and spirit of the French national society.

The two kinds of government recognized in *Les Lettres Persanes* constitute the takeoff point in the comparative analysis which begins with Book II of *L'Esprit des Lois.* Promptly Montesquieu divides republics into democracies and aristocracies and in effect divides monarchies into another two types by adopting the term despotism for the absolute rule by one and leaving monarchy to stand for limited government. In making these distinctions, he assumes that political functions are divided between control and action but he does not say this in so many words. He uses the social location of control to categorize republics, explaining that for democracies the supreme power is in the whole people, while for aristocracies it is in a part of the people. Then the distinction between the two kinds of rule by one is the mode of action. He defines monarchy to be rule under law with administration in part by more or less independent intermediaries and despotism to be rule without law with administration by an all-powerful vizier.[2] Likewise, he makes a distinction between the nature or structure of a kind of government and the principle or special spirit of the respective type. There are as many kinds of special spirit as there are structures of government and the peculiarities of classification are much the same for both nature and principle.

The categorization of governments in Books II — X has both definite and indefinite aspects. We cannot be sure whether the basic typology consists of three, four, or five, or even more kinds. Montesquieu begins with three, that is, republics, monarchies, and despotisms; then there are four when he divides republics into democracies and aristocracies. But this may also result in five types because he sometimes combines democratic and aristocratic elements. Still more types may be present because monarchy often stands for some kind of mixed government. It is rarely a pure or simple type and usually includes one or more political, administrative, or judicial elites as well as a social nobility. Consequently, despotism is the only pure type and it is consistently a bad form. Montesquieu often seems most certain about what he dislikes.

Still further variation arises from the ways in which Montesquieu uses the general types. The classification may differ with the subject matter. In general, a fourfold pattern of democracy, aristocracy, monarchy, and despotism is fairly common in Books II, III, and V while a threefold scheme of republic, monarchy, and despotism is more usual in Books IV and VI through X. Then, the discussions of economics, like *Les Lettres Persanes,* tend to assume only republics and monarchies. In other books, the comparative analysis of government is less frequent and the typologies still less specific.

Likewise, Montesquieu gives the traditional terms differing applications. Republics are sometimes ideal, other times actual, and they may be democratic, aristocratic, or mixed. Democracy is at first direct and later becomes representative, and sometimes it assumes an exclusively popular sovereignty while on other occasions it stands for shared sovereignty. Aristocracy alternates between two forms. In one, a small elite is all-powerful and hence despotic while in the other, the nobility is large and divided, with one elite serving another. Also, monarchy may vary in form according to the number and character of implementing organs. Moreover, in all types there is an uneven mixture of generalization and particularization. The general terms sometimes stand for particular governments. For instance, republic frequently means one of the classical cities of Athens, Sparta, or Rome, and monarchy usually stands for France, either past or present. The reverse is also true. Frequent references are made to China but often a China that has been abstracted into a pure type of despotism.[3] What is meant in a given situation must be determined by close attention to the context. Also, Montesquieu sometimes identifies governments by the terms "moderate" and "free," and these probably mean either a republic or a monarchy that is responsive to law and social interests.[4] Finally, there is an implicit distinction that cuts across the whole presentation, that is, that government is good or bad according to whether it is socially mixed or not. The extent to which Montesquieu asserts and supports this proposition is one of the principal considerations of this study.

The classifications of government in *L'Esprit des Lois* have some

of the marks of the traditional typologies found in the works of
well-known Greek, Roman, and early modern theorists, but there
are also some peculiarities not found in the prior systems. The
source of these differences is a matter for speculation and inquiry.
The unusual features in Montesquieu's classification may be original, or he may have adapted them from the works of theorists who
have received little attention in present day surveys. There are a
number of similarities to the classification presented by Xenophon
in his recollections of Socrates. Like Montesquieu, Xenophon identifies two rules by one and at least the foremost American translation uses the same terms that Montesquieu does.[5] Xenophon calls
one kingship and says that this is based upon consent or law, and he
calls the other despotism for lack of such a basis. Also, Xenophon
defines three other types of government by reference to the qualifications for sharing power, partly in the way Montesquieu first divides the general type of republics. Xenophon says that in aristocracy officials must meet legal requirements, in a plutocracy that there
is a property qualification, and that in a democracy all are eligible.
Xenophon's typology has received comparatively little attention in
the history of political thought, but it is one of the closest to the pattern with which Montesquieu begins his comparative analysis in
Book II.

The way in which Montesquieu divides and adapts the republican form of government may have been inspired in part by the
work of the Italian poet-jurist, GianVincenzo Gravina, whose definition of a state is noted twice in Book I of *L'Esprit des Lois*.
Gravina's work on the origin and spirit of Roman laws, published
in 1708, includes a rather unusual classification of governments.[6]
He begins with two kinds of empire, pure and mixed. The one is a
rigorous rule by an absolute prince while the other is limited rule
by magistrates. These have general comparability to Montesquieu's
categories of despotism and monarchy. But most of Gravina's classification concerns three types of republic: pure, mixed, and
confused. In the first all the people have virtuous political motives.
This ideal may embody the virtue which Montesquieu later says is
necessary for a democratic republic. In Gravina's mixed republic,
the persons holding political authority act with reason and the
others act out of sense. This may be similar to the distinction between Plato's guardian and economic classes and also to the difference between two of the classes in Aristotle's mixed aristocracy
and in Montesquieu's mixed monarchy. Gravina's "confused repub-

lic" assumes that the ruling element acts out of sense and interest rather than by reason and duty. Gravina then divides these republics among those governed by one, by few, and by many. Finally, he falls back upon the classical doctrine that the three good forms degenerate into three bad types, which he calls tyranny, oligarchy, and mob-rule.

There are some parallel aspects in the classifications of Gravina and Montesquieu. Both attach importance to psychological attitudes; both acknowledge that men are more likely to act politically out of their sense than their reason; and both recognize that republics need reason in the ruling element. Yet, while this may make republics preferable to Gravina, I believe that it makes pure democracies unattractive if not unattainable for Montesquieu. The fable of the Troglodytes in *Les Lettres Persanes,* as noted in Chapter I, presents the underlying belief that people prefer to live under the laws of a rational authority rather than under their own restraint. To explain how Montesquieu would obtain and assure government that is both rational and responsive to the natural dispositions of the people, is one of the principal objects of this study.

Still other lesser known theorists of his own age or the preceding generation may have also inspired Montesquieu in his choice of terminology and arrangement. These include Paolo-Mattia Doria, and Chevalier St. George (otherwise known as Saint-Hyacinthe) and Jean Domat. Abbé Joseph Dedieu, the leading French biographer of Montesquieu, has emphasized the influence of Doria's *La Vita Civile,* which, among other things, explicates three ways of life: the military, the economic, and the pretentious.[7] But Robert Shackleton, the leading English biographer, tends to question the extent of Doria's influence[8] and calls attention to the fact that both Montesquieu and Saint-Hyacinthe use the terms monarchy and despotism for the two types of rule by one.[9] This terminology is perhaps unique but there is much in Saint-Hyacinthe which Montesquieu does not duplicate, such as the description of the English government as a combination of despotism, oligarchy, and democracy.[10] Oudin, the French commentator, sees more likelihood of influence by Jean Domat,"[11] whose analysis of French law may have been the foremost available in Montesquieu's day. But Domat's influence would seem to be more in respect of the interrelationship of natural law, civil laws, and the activity of society, rather than in regard to forms of governments on which he presents little that is new.

The two kinds of government by one which Montesquieu calls monarchy and despotism have a general similarity to the good and bad forms of rule by one described by Plato, Aristotle, Polybius, and Cicero, but there are precedents that seem to be closer in both terminology and substance. Xenophon's division of rule by one was mentioned previously. There is also the differentiation made during the late middle ages when much critical thought was directed as distinguishing two aspects of kingship.[12] Contrasts were made between reasonable and arbitrary decision making, between the office and the person of the king, between the political authority and the regal, and between law and prerogative. These distinctions mark the early development of constitutional and limited monarchy, and traces of them can be found in Montesquieu's comparative analysis.

A more likely source is the political theory of Jean Bodin who adapted traditional terms to early modern developments. His analysis of government is in a number of respects a point of departure for Montesquieu. Bodin, after reviewing some of the past typologies, says that there are three kinds of monarchy: royal, despotic, and tyrannical.[13] In a royal monarchy the prince obeys the laws of God, and the subjects obey the laws of the prince with the result that "natural liberty and the natural right of property is secured to all." The despotic monarchy arises from the right of conquest in a just war. "Tyrannical monarchy is one in which the laws of nature are set at naught, free subjects oppressed as if they were slaves, and their property treated as if it belonged to the tyrant." Bodin asserts that the same diversity can be found in aristocracies and popular states because each can be legitimate, despotic, or tyrannical in the way described. What Bodin calls royal and tyrannical monarchy are similar to the first descriptions of monarchy and despotism in *L'Esprit des Lois*. Montesquieu does recognize what Bodin calls a despotic monarch, that is, one holding authority by right of conquest[14] but Montesquieu does not give it a special label. Another similarity between the typologies of Bodin and Montesquieu is that the distinguishing feature among the types of monarchy is the mode of operation.

There may be a temptation to say that Montesquieu's typology of governments is derived from this or that theorist because of a similarity in name or content. But, if there are some points of agreement between his classification and that of one of the Greeks or Romans, or that of Machiavelli, Saint-Hyacinthe, or Gravina, there are other aspects of each which Montesquieu clearly does not adopt. If he developed a pattern of categories by taking a bit from each of several theorists but not taking much from any one, he was about as original as a political thinker can be. Even if he did borrow some things, his own standards and objectives determined what he took and what he rejected. The chances are that he deliberately took very little in a direct manner. He was widely read in his field and he clearly had imagination and a capacity for adaptation. The construction of his own pattern from the vast array of material was definitely within his abilities. The appropriateness of his typology to his general objectives, that is, as preparatory to the development of a type of mixed government, is further evidence of uniqueness. His originality is not denied by the few similarities between his pattern and that of some others, and, in fact, his creativeness is virtually proven by the considerable extent to which he differed from other political theorists.

What is most original about Montesquieu's comparative analysis in Books II — X seems to be his explanation of the special spirit required by each of the traditional types of government. This is an elaboration of the first portion of his definition of the spirit of the laws at the end of Book I. There he declares that law, meaning presumably the positive law, "should be in relation to the nature and principle of government of each government: whether they form it, as may be said of politic law or whether they support it, as in the case of civil institutions." In saying that he will examine first the relations which laws bear to "the nature and principle" of each government, he adds that "this principle has a strong influence on laws," and that he will seek to understand it thoroughly, because "if I can but once establish it, the laws will soon appear to flow thence as from their source," and then he can proceed to "more particular relations." He does give considerably more attention to the principle than to the nature of the governments. At least six books deal expressly with the relation of laws to the principle of different systems. Montesquieu does not define nature and principle or explain their difference until the start of Book III. There he says that the nature of a government "is that by which it is constituted" and that the principle is "that by which it is made to act." He amplifies this and explains that one is the "particular structure" of a government "and the other the human passions which set it in motion." I will call the principle a "special spirit" to distinguish it from the general spirit of a nation, previously discussed. Later explanations will show that Montesquieu usually assumes the nature of a government to be its existing structure while the principle tends to be the moving spirit which the people or a political class ought to have for the perfection of the particular kind of government. Unlike the general spirit, the principle sometimes concerns only a class of the national society.

Montesquieu uses the word "principle" in not the usual sense of a general rule or truth, but as the beginning, source, or cause of a phenomenon. This has some precedent. Aristotle and perhaps the Ionian naturalists employed the term in that way.[15] However, for Montesquieu the relevant causative or motivating force is limited in scope and circumstances. This chapter will show that it is the collective attitude that is needed for the success of the respective type of government, that it may not apply to all the people, and that for some types of government it is a restraining attitude or force while for the other forms it serves to activate a class to a certain kind of participation.

The classification of the different kinds of principle has many of the peculiarities previously noted in typology of the nature or structure of government. There is a special spirit for each species, and democracy and aristocracy have both the common quality of a republic and their own distinct qualities. The types of governments and their respective principles are:

Republic	Virtue
Democracy	Equality and Frugality
Aristocracy	Moderation
Monarchy	Honor
Despotism	Fear

At first, virtue is deemed to be the principle of republics generally, and then in Book V the principle of democracy is more specifically described to be the love of equality and frugality while that of aristocracy is designated to be moderation. In this matter the four types of government tend to pair off in much the same manner as was shown previously in respect of the nature of government. The principles of the republican types will be shown to concern the attitude of the class of persons who hold the supreme power of controlling the government through election and legislation, while the special spirit of monarchy and despotism will be shown to pertain to the administration or other operation of government.

The principle of a species of government, as explained in *L'Esprit des Lois*, differs in at least one way from what Plato describes in Book VIII of the Republic as the individual character of man in the different types of government.[16] The spirit of what Plato calls the timocratic man, the oligarchic man, the democratic man, and the despotic man is the passion or motivation which leads the respective type of government into excess and degeneration. On the other hand, Montesquieu considers the special spirit of the respective species of government to be a disposition which would prevent the respective type of government from leading itself into excess and degeneration. Plato describes the respective evil instincts whereas Montesquieu identifies what is necessary for effective government.

This leads to the basic and somewhat perplexing problem of whether the nature of government determines the principle or the principle determines the nature. The close and perhaps vital relation of the two is emphasized by Montesquieu at the start of his comparative analysis of principle in Book III when he says that the nature of a government enables him to discover the principle and that the latter is naturally derived from the nature of the political system. However, I believe that this does not mean that the special spirit of government was derived by deduction or that principle is secondary in character to the nature of government. Werner Stark, in his study of Montesquieu as a pioneer in the sociology of knowledge, rejects any such conclusion and, in fact, suggests that Montesquieu found the life-principles of the three forms of government in reality: that is, through the study of facts and by inductive reasoning rather than by deductive logic.[17] Stark in general regards Montesquieu as an empiricist and says that any evidence of simple rationalism is limited to a younger period which Montesquieu outgrew.

The concluding paragraph of Book III throws much light on the relation of the principle to the nature of a kind of government. Here, Montesquieu says that his discussion of principle does not mean that in a particular republic the people are actually virtuous but that they ought to be virtuous. Likewise, in a monarchy or a despotism the people "ought to be directed by these principles, otherwise the government is imperfect." These assertions indicate that the principles are something to be sought and not what necessarily or even usually occurs. Montesquieu is designating the most important attitude or moving spirit when the respective government is at its theoretical best. The statement that a deficiency of principle makes the government imperfect suggests that the principle is a force needed to complement the nature of the government and that it would offset the characteristic weakness of respective structure. For instance, a pure democracy is regarded generally as having an inherent defect because the people are likely to abuse their authority through too much self-interest. The principle of democracy would counteract such a tendency because the principle is a love of equality and frugality. Similarly, in an aristocracy there is an inherent danger that the nobility will use its power too much to its own ends and the special spirit of moderation would serve to counteract that tendency. In a monarchy, there is the common danger pictured in *Les Lettres Persanes* of degeneration into despotic tyranny or popular anarchy. The principle of honor is designed to lessen this danger by stimulating professional aristocrats to mediate on an interest-free basis between the king and the people. Likewise, with respect to despotism, the inherent weakness of this type of government is that the despot will rule with arbitrary and capricious will. The only kind of response from the people that could allow such a government to maintain order and cohesion is one of fear. Thus, the principle of each kind of government is that particular attitude among a certain group of people that would tend to perfect the operation of the government by overcoming what Montesquieu regards as the inherent weakness of the respective type. In this sense, there is a logical connection between the nature and the principle and this may be what he had in mind when he stated at the beginning of Book III that the principle "is naturally derived" from his knowledge of the nature of a government.

The identity of the principle or special spirit may be deducible from the nature or structure of the government, but it seems to me that the principle is more difficult to establish than the structure. Likewise, the structure of a government may be more readily apparent than the principle so that an observer is more likely to begin with the former and then say what the principle ought to be. Yet the principle is the more fundamental matter because the structure of a government is more easily changed than the psychological quality of a society. A legislature attempting to bring nature and principle into harmony with each other would usually find less difficulty in adjusting the structure to fit the existing spirit than in trying to make the psychological attitude conform to the needs of the structure. In other words, creating and changing formal institutions would seem to be easier than establishing or altering the collective attitudes of a people. While Montesquieu says that he derived the principle from the nature, still the import of the whole of *L'Esprit des Lois* is that the government should conform to the psychology of the national society. For him, society is naturally mixed or differentiated and government should be likewise. Also, it is easier to alter the attitude of a comparative small class, like the professional aristocracy, than the attitude of a whole citizenry. Mixed monarchy may be effective and tolerant if the professional aristocracy is honorable, but a democratic republic needs the far more difficult and less attractive achievement of self-imposed restraint by the whole citizenry as holders of the supreme power. The people potentially may be capable of such a degree of political self-denial, but it is burdensome and it interferes with their economic and cultural well-being. Sooner or later, I think, the structure of a government would be determined by the kind of special spirit that the people can provide. If the people could have no motivation other than fear, then the nature of the government ought to be despotic. Or, if the people have a strong sense of virtue, that is, they have such a love of equality and frugality that they will restrain themselves in the exercise of supreme political power, then the government may be a democratic one. One of the principal questions that arises in the interpretation of this portion of *L'Esprit des Lois* is whether Montesquieu believes that the French people would not accept the restraint, equality, and frugality that is necessary for the popular sovereignty of a full democracy. This question will be considered in the next chapter after further analysis of Montesquieu's classification of political structures, functions, and capabilities.

Montesquieu's recognition of the principle or special spirit of government is further evidence of his interest in the behavior of social classes. In most of his analyses of the different kinds of government, the focus is less upon institutional arrangement or the legal allocation of authority than upon the ways in which the attitudes and behavior of the different classes of people affect the policy of the governmental system. The principle or special spirit specifies what is deemed necessary for effective operation rather than what actually exists, but it involves the inclinations and actions of men in society more fundamentally than the structure of legal institutions. It may deal with only a part of the present discipline of social psychology, and its application may lack the clinical methods known today, but it does bring to the study of politics and government a deep regard for collective attitudes and group behavior. The extended treatment of the principle or special spirit of different kinds of governments, which even Hegel commends for depth of insight,[18] would seem to place Montesquieu among the pioneers of modern collective psychology.

The Social Allocation of Political Control

The most fundamental assumption of Montesquieu's typology of governments in the first portion of *L'Esprit des Lois* (Books II — X) is probably his tendency to associate certain forms with the realm of control and others with the realm of action. He uses democracies and aristocracies to explain the distribution of legislative and electoral authority while he employs monarchies and despotisms to illustrate different modes of administration. In both situations, I believe that he is laying the groundwork for the system of mixed monarchy and moderate government which he articulates in later books. This section will consider the ways in which political control is allocated among social classes in the different types of republics while the next section will deal with the assignment of political action in moderate and despotic governments.

Montesquieu's peculiar adaptation of traditional terms is evident first of all in his characterization of republics. They are defined, not by contrast to the other principal types, that is, monarchies and despotisms, but rather by differentiating the subtypes of republics, that is, democracies and aristocracies. Montesquieu discloses his emphasis upon the social class location of political power when he says that a republic is called a democracy if the body of the people possesses the supreme power and is called an aristocracy if the supreme power is lodged in the hands of a part of the people. Then, using the French term *le monarque* to mean sovereignty, he observes that "in a democracy, the people are in some respects the sovereign and in others the subject."[19]

The specification of sovereign power gives further indication of Montesquieu's allocation of political control. He asserts that the people can be sovereign only if the suffrages are their own will. This is so because "the sovereign's will is the sovereign himself." In calling the laws which establish the right of suffrage "fundamental" in this government, he indicates that fundamental laws refer to the social roots of authority, that is, who rightfully has power. This idea is amplified a few sentences later when Montesquieu remarks that "It is an essential point to fix the number of citizens who are to form the public assemblies."

Then, Montesquieu begins to show quite definitely how he assumes that the nature and scope of political authority should be made to conform to the governing capabilities of the particular classes. "The people in whom the supreme power resides," he says "ought to have the management of everything within their reach" and "that which exceeds their abilities must be conducted by their ministers." Their power rests in their control of the identity of the ministers. "But they cannot properly be said to have their ministers, without the power of nominating them" and accordingly it is "a fundamental maxim" in democracy that "the people should choose their ministers." Likewise, the people have occasion, he says, to be directed by a council or senate and, to have "a proper confidence" in the council or senate, they should be able to choose its members. For support of this idea, Montesquieu turns, as he often does in such circumstances, to the classical republics. In Athens, he points out, the election was by the people themselves and at Rome it was by a magistrate deputed for that purpose. Yet, while the people may have limitations in political activity, there are roles for which they are peculiarly adept. "The people are extremely well qualified," Montesquieu says, "for choosing those whom they are to intrust with part of their authority." Thus, in the division of governmental functions there are some processes that are appropriate to the few and others proper for the many. The functions allocated to the people generally are of a control type while those reserved for the few are more directly concerned with governmental action. To some extent the distinction between control and action corresponds to that between legislative and executive, but the realm of control also includes the election of magistrates and the realm of action must be broader than merely executing laws.

For the purposes of the class distribution of political functions Montesquieu seems to assume that the people act out of sense much more than out of reason. He remarks that the people's choice of magistrates can "be determined by things to which they cannot be strangers and by facts that are obvious to sense."[20] The people can tell, for instance, when a person has fought many battles with success and so they are capable of selecting a general. "They can tell when a judge is assiduous in his office, gives general satisfaction, and has never been charged with bribery; this is sufficient for choosing a praetor." Also, they know the wealth of citizens and that is enough to select an edile. "These are facts of which they can have better information in a public forum than a monarch in his palace." Proof of "the people's natural capacity" in this matter appears in two cases: the report that the Roman people never exerted their assumed right of raising plebians to public office and Xenophon's account that the common people of Athens never petitioned for employments which could endanger their security or glory. Most citizens, Montesquieu explains, have the ability to choose administrators and to call them to account even though the citizens themselves cannot administer. The people's capacity seems to be associated with the impulsive action or inaction which goes with sense motivation rather than with deliberation or rational calculation. "The public business," he observes, "must be carried on with a certain motion, neither too quick nor too slow." But the motion of the people "is always either too remiss or too violent. Sometimes with a hundred thousand arms they overturn all before them; and sometimes with a hundred thousand feet they creep like insects."[21]

What may be rather disturbing to present day ideas of democracy is the way in which Montesquieu takes for granted that political classes exist in a democracy and in fact may be necessary in that kind of government. He asserts that "in a popular state the inhabitants are divided into certain classes,"[22] even though a stratified society and class qualifications may seem contrary to the very essence of democracy. He elaborates that "great legislators" have distinguished themselves by the manner in which they made or utilized the divisions of society. The duration and prosperity of democracy, he declares, rests upon this division of society. Verification is found in Rome and Athens. Servius Tullius followed the spirit of aristocracy in the distribution of classes, dividing the people of Rome into 93 "centuries" which formed six classes. Montesquieu describes only three: the small number of rich were in the first group; those in middling circumstances were in the next, and the indigent multitude were in the last. Each "century" had one vote so that elections reflected property interests as well as the numbers of persons. Such a scheme has some similarity to Aristotle's combination of oligarchy and democracy in that each seeks to combine both an equality of property and an equality of persons.[23]

The example of class structure in the Athens of Solon is even more indicative of the varying capacity of people to participate in government.[24] Montesquieu, in commenting about the way in which the people of Athens were divided into four classes, says that Solon was directed by the spirit of democracy. The objective was not to determine who are to choose but rather those who are eligible for office. Every citizen was given the right of election and the right to be judges, but only those in the three classes with the greatest fortunes were eligible for the positions of magistrates. The exclusion from executive office of those in the lower class may reflect, I believe, their necessity of devoting their time to gainful occupations, probably more than the insufficiency of education or native capacity. Solon's acceptance of them for judicial functions accords with the general Athenian practice of trials before popular assemblies, such as the jury of 501 that heard Socrates. The participation of the people in such judicial assemblies as well as the law making ones is intermittent and in conjunction with a sizeable number of other citizens.

A more express contrast of political class action appears in the methods of filling offices. Selection by lot is "natural" to democracy while selection by choice is "natural" to aristocracy. The former, he says, offends no one and gives each citizen "the pleasing hope of serving his country." Yet, selection by lot has inherent defects which warrant its qualification. Montesquieu explains how Solon provided that persons elected should be examined by judges and that everyone had a right to question whether the nominee was worthy of the office. Even more, Solon prescribed that military positions be filled by choice even though senators and judges were selected by lot. Here we see an early distinction between political positions and professional ones.

The differentiation of political classes also appears in the fundamental laws on the manner of voting. The immediate problem is whether voting should be public or secret. Montesquieu notes that Cicero attributed the decline of the Roman republic to laws requiring secret vote, and he in turn concludes that the "people's suffrages ought doubtless to be public." This should be "a fundamental law of democracy. The lower class ought to be directed by those of higher rank, and restrained within bounds by the gravity of eminent personages." But while democratic voting should be public, aristocratic voting ought to be closed. Montesquieu explains that when the body of nobles have the suffrages, either directly in an ar-

istocracy, or as the senate in a democracy, the voting should be secret because the business then is only to prevent intrigue. He makes
a striking distinction on this practice. "Intriguing in a senate is
dangerous; it is dangerous also in a body of nobles; but not so
among the people, whose nature is to act through passion." In fact,
Montesquieu argues quite sharply that the misfortune of a republic
is when intrigues are at an end. By intrigues he probably means the
interplay of factional interests. When such intrigues cease, he says,
the people are held by bribery and corruption. They grow indifferent to public affairs, avarice becomes their predominant passion,
and they quietly wait for their hire. Thus, Montesquieu seems to
prefer the individual driven to competitive action by self-interest in
contrast to the self-effacing figure who accepts his economic situation in a passive manner. With this would seem to go the idea implicit in a number of other discussions, that the deliberative process
of thinking out specific rules of social order should be left primarily
to the rational calculation of a political elite, not because the people lack reason but because they are occupied with economic and
cultural matters to such an extent that they can exercise only general control of political affairs.

Though the people in a democracy are deemed to have the supreme legislative power, even this description of more or less simple
democracy suggests that an elite be given some law making authority. Montesquieu refers approvingly to the power of the Athenian
and Roman senates to issue decrees which had the force of law for
one year without action of the people and permanently if ratified
by the people. But Montesquieu never denies completely the sover-
ign right of the people in the legislative field. Even when, in Book
XI, he discusses the constitutional requirements of political liberty,
he leaves legislative initiative with the representative assembly and
allows the senate of nobles and the monarch merely protective ve-
toes. There, he says, the people must act through representatives
rather than directly, but their representatives are considered the
primary legislative body.

Montesquieu seems to want aristocracy as well as democracy to be
a combination of classes, but he is less explicit about the divisions
of the former. Clearly, he is as unhappy with simple aristocracy as
he is with simple democracy. His assumptions about the structure
of aristocracy seem to differ, the range of possibilities being from a
small, unified nobility, to an extensive aristocracy, which divides

into several groups, socially and politically. At first, he says that the few persons who hold the sovereign power in an aristocracy both make and execute the laws and that the other people are like the subjects in a monarchy. Presumably he must feel that this is not desirable, because he argues that officials in an aristocracy should not be selected by lot. One chosen by lot, he says, would still be an aristocrat, and the people would be no more satisfied because "it is the nobleman they envy and not the magistrate." Likewise, Montesquieu warns against a self-centered aristocracy. A senate should not be self-perpetuating, and for an example of outside selection, he cites the early Roman practice of having the senators nominated by the censors.

In addition, Montesquieu cautions against the private citizen who suddenly rises to great power. Such a ruler is worse than a monarch because, in a monarchy, the constitution and the principle of government check the monarch, whereas in a republic the laws do not provide against the abuse of power by one-man rulers. Still more, Montesquieu finds virtue in short terms. "In all magistracies, the greatness of the power must be compensated by the brevity of the duration." The commonest term for legislators is a year; "a longer time would be dangerous and a shorter contrary to the nature of the thing."[25]

The idea of different classes of aristocracy seems to involve a strange kind of mixed government. Montesquieu explains that "When the nobility are numerous, there must be a senate to regulate the affairs which the body of the nobles are incapable of deciding, and to prepare others for their decision." Presumably, the less capable nobles would be represented in some kind of larger assembly. He elaborates that "In this case it may be said that the aristocracy is in some measure in the senate, the democracy in the body of nobles, and the people are a cipher." Moreover, he suggests here as well as elsewhere that the nobility should have a more tolerate attitude. "It would be a very happy thing in an aristocracy if the people, in some measure, could be raised from their state of annihilation." He mentions the situation at Genoa where the people are given a certain influence in the government by their administration of the bank of St. George.

The meanings of the three or more kinds of principle or special spirit also reflect differences in the capabilities of the social classes. This is evident most of all in the unusual way in which Montesquieu applies the word "virtue." He gives this term a peculiar meaning in about four ways, and the inclination of many readers and commentators to take the term in its more usual sense has caused considerable misunderstanding and criticism. The term "virtue" has had, of course, a variety of meanings throughout the history of political thought, but none of these seem to be what Montesquieu has in mind. He does not mean moral in an ethical sense nor does he refer to the idea of excellence associated with the Greek work *arête*. It may be closer to the Greek idea of not too much or the virtue of temperance.[26]

The special meaning of "virtue" and particularly the statement that it is not the principle of monarchy drew immediate criticism[27] and Montesquieu inserted an explanatory note in the second edition of *L'Esprit des Lois* which underscores the peculiar use of the term.[28] The note brings out the distinction between the general meaning of virtue as a condition or value of conduct and its special meaning as a spring of governmental control or operation. Montesquieu says that what he calls virtue in a republic is the love of country or the love of equality. "It is not a moral, nor a Christian, but a political virtue; and it is the spring which sets the republican government in motion." He compares this to the way that "honor is the spring which gives motion to monarchy." He admits that he is giving new meanings to old terms, and he explains, probably to those who are disturbed at the remark, that virtue is not the principle of monarchy, that there may be even political as well as moral or Christian virtue in a monarchy but it is not the spring of that government. This explanation means, I believe, that virtue, like the other principles, is not a general attitude of the governing authorities or the citizens but rather a certain disposition among a certain group of people, which differ among the several kinds of government. Even the designation of virtue as a "spring" of government may be a bit misleading because virtue refers to a pressure of restraint more than one of positive action.

The idea that virtue is necessary in a republic but not in a monarchy is explained in the initial discussions of the special spirit of a democracy at the beginning of Book III. Montesquieu declares that while the force of laws in a monarchy and the prince's arms in a despotic country are sufficient to maintain those forms of government, "in a popular state, one spring more is necessary, namely, virtue." This, he says, is confirmed by the unanimous testimony of historians and is extremely agreeable to the nature of things.[29] His comments throw light upon his method. Montesquieu seeks verification in the observations of others and himself. Specifically, proof is based upon the uniformities in the views of historians and upon the general character of surrounding circumstances. This is a search for objectivity, given the limited data available.

But the substantive point here is why laws and force can maintain monarchies and despotisms, respectively, but are insufficient in a democracy. The reason must lie with something peculiar to democracies. Thus, the principle in such forms of government cannot relate to the people as subject to laws and force because these last elements are present in other types of government as well. What is peculiar to the people in a democracy is their possession of supreme political power and, accordingly, virtue as the special spirit of that kind of system must relate to the possession of political power by the people rather than to their role as obedient citizens. This interpretation is fortified by Montesquieu's further remarks. He points out that the need of virtue in a democracy also concerns the control of the executive as well as the legislative. Both of these controls were described in the preceding book as coming within the supreme political power of the people in a democracy. He assumes that democratic government has an elected or delegated executive and this is given as a further reason for the need of virtue in a democracy. Whereas, in a monarchy the chief executive would consider himself under other limitations, in a democracy he is likely to regard himself subject to only the direction of the people and as a consequence in that form of government "the person intrusted with the execution of the laws is sensible of his being subject to their direction."[30] Moreover, "a monarch who, through bad advice or indolence, ceases to enforce the execution of the laws, may easily repair the evil." He has only to take advice or to change his attitude. "But when, in a popular government, there is a suspension of the law, the state is certainly undone, because the suspension can proceed only from the corruption of the republic."

These statements indicate that the democracy being assumed at this point is a simple system of popular control, and Montesquieu seems to make it unattractive, if not unattainable. The difficulty of maintaining a republican system and its principle of virtue is evident in the case histories which he presents in this analysis. He refers to "the impotent efforts of the English towards the establishment of democracy" and points out that their government was repeatedly changed, that the English vainly attempted a commonwealth, and that after "the most violent shocks, they were obliged to have recourse to the very government which they had so wantonly proscribed." Rome also furnishes examples. "When Sylla thought of restoring Rome to her liberty, this unhappy city was incapable of receiving that blessing. She had only the feeble remains of virtue, which were continually diminishing." Things were better in classical Athens, which is contrasted sharply with its present day involvement in commercial interests that presumably leave little aptitude or time for self-restraint. "The politic Greeks, who lived under a popular government, knew no other support than virtue. The modern inhabitants of that country are entirely taken up with manufacture, commerce, finances, opulence, and luxury." What happens when the attitude of the people changes is described quite strikingly.[31] When virtue is banished, Montesquieu says, "ambition invades the minds of those who are disposed to receive it and avarice possesses the whole community." The objects of their desires change. Where "they were free while under the restraint of laws," they "would fain now be free to act against law." As a consequence, "each citizen is like a slave who has run away from his master." What was a maxim of equity they now call rigor, what was a rule of action is now called constraint, and precaution is given the name of fear. This is doubly significant in understanding Montesquieu's theory of natural government. He is indicating again that virtue is a matter of self-restraint and also that freedom is a matter of living under social laws. The statement also reflects the idea implicit in *L'Esprit des Lois* that the success of democratic self-government depends upon a high degree of self-imposed restraint. His picture of what happened to the Greeks when their preoccupation with industry, trade, and finance led to a banishment of virtue, raises the question of whether the virtue necessary to a democracy is possible in a society which is deeply and widely absorbed in the interest conflicts of commerce and industry.

Thus, Raymond Aron might be challenged on his suggestion that Montesquieu did not anticipate the modern preoccupation with economic activity.[32] Whether or not he foresaw the future industrial development, Montesquieu does seem to say that a people busily engaged in commercial activity should not be burdened with the task of thinking out the restraining rules of social order, not because they lack the capacity, but because they are occupied with other matters which are also important to the community.

When *L'Esprit des Lois* turns to the principle or special spirit of aristocracy, there is still a problem of self-restraint by holders of political control. Virtue is declared to be necessary in an aristocracy as it is in a democracy but "it is not so absolutely requisite." Montesquieu asserts that the people in an aristocracy are restrained by the laws and that "there is less need of virtue" than in respect of the people in a democracy. In other words, self-limitation among the controlling class is less necessary than in a democracy because there are fewer holders of supreme political power in an aristocracy. He points out that the inherent difficulty in a pure or simple aristocracy is how to limit the few when they hold all of the governing authority. Montesquieu asks rhetorically: "how are the nobility to be restrained? They who are to execute the laws against their colleagues will perceive immediately that they are acting against themselves." Given his assumptions of human nature, a pure aristocracy might be self-defeating,[33] because its success would depend upon its tendencies toward democracy. This should be kept in mind in considering the various suggestions that the nobility, particularly, the nobility of the robe should play an intermediary role in moderate or mixed monarchy. Montesquieu explains that an aristocratic government has "an inherent vigor, unknown to democracy," and also that the nobles form a body which restrains the people and which inevitably executes the laws. The source of the problem is the difficulty of the nobles restraining themselves. The aristocratic constitution by its nature "seems to subject the very same persons to the power of the laws, and at the same time to exempt them." Montesquieu goes on to say that a body of nobles can restrain itself in only two ways: either by "a very eminent virtue, which puts the nobility in some measure on a level with the people," or by "an inferior virtue, which puts them at least upon a level with one another." But in prescribing the first, he supersedes "virtue." He states that "the very soul" of aristocratic government is "moderation," and he hastens to add that he means a moderation founded upon virtue and not upon "indolence and pusillanimity." Thus, it appears that, while the structure of republics, both democratic and aristocratic, provides means of controlling those who have been delegated executive authority, the special spirit of republics is designed to meet the problem of controlling the holders of supreme power themselves. Montesquieu may regard the problem as beyond solution; at least, he does not solve it within the confines of the aristocratic form. In general, he does not believe, as some classical theorists did, that moderate and stable government can be achieved by an attitude of self-restraint or general interest among a single governing class.[34] Later portions of *L'Esprit des Lois* develop the idea of moderating political power by distributing authority among conflicting classes, as well as by making the combination respond to the general socio- logical and psychological character of the nation.[35]

Hegel declares that moderation as the principle of aristocracy im- plies the start of "a divorce between public authority and private interest."[36] Both he and Montesquieu seek to disassociate political decision from economic action but they may differ on how much the aristocracy can contribute to this objective. Hegel adds a re- mark that public authority and private interest touch each other so closely that the aristocratic constitution stands on the verge of laps- ing into tyranny or anarchy. This is the danger that Montesquieu is striving to avoid through various means and particularly by the mediating and moderating role of the aristocracy. He may assume an aristocracy that has professional competence and responsibility to a greater degree than does Hegel. Moreover, the latter regards government more as authority and less as arbitration than does Montesquieu. Hegel's uneasy recognition of the problem may indi- cate that the accommodated pluralism which Montesquieu seeks does not fit well into Hegel's scheme of ideas. He emphasizes the whole in relation to the parts.[37] In Montesquieu the tendency is the other way.

The Professional Allocation of Political Action

The distinction between political control and action which is im- plicit in Montesquieu's comparative analysis of government has a double consequence upon the distribution of political authority and responsibility. While political control is allocated to the classes of a national society, the operating authority to deal with specific applications is assigned to various elements of the professional aris- tocracy of the nation. This makes possible a separation of functions among elites and the place of such a phenomenon in Montesquieu's theory of natural government will receive increasing consideration throughout this study. Montesquieu does not use the term "profes- sional" but I believe that it is appropriate and helpful.

The special application of traditional terms in *L'Esprit des Lois* is evident also in the characterizations of monarchy and despotism. These are not defined, as were republics, by the location of the supreme legislative power, but rather they are identified and distinguished by the quality of executive action.[38] They concern not the manner of allocating general control but the ways of exercising the power to apply and administer. The mode of such operation in monarchy is essentially complex and rational whereas in despotism it is essentially simple and arbitrary. The two modes of operation are first distinguished by their contrasting attitudes toward customary law and then by their differing institutional arrangements but finally the contrast is based upon their divergent regard for the rights and privileges of social classes.

Montesquieu's initial definitions of monarchy and despotism, which stress the legal approach, are somewhat like those by Xenophon and Bodin. Xenophon describes kingship as "government of men with their consent in accordance with the laws of the state" and despotism as "government of unwilling subjects and not controlled by laws, but imposed by the will of rulers." For Bodin royal monarchy is government under law with natural rights of property while tyrannical monarchy is rule without the laws of nature or property rights. In turn, Montesquieu first declares that in monarchy "a single person governs by fixed and established laws" whereas in despotic government "a single person directs everything by his own will and caprice."[39]

The distinction between monarch and despotism to which most attention is given in Book II is the social basis of the institutions found in a true monarchy and absent in a true despotism. Montesquieu declares that "The intermediate, subordinate and dependent powers constitute the nature of monarchical government." His explanation that by monarchical government he means one in which "a single person governs by fundamental laws," indicates that government under law requires or is tantamount to the proper institutional arrangement. In fact, he asserts that "These fundamental laws necessarily suppose the intermediate channels through which the power flows," because if there is "only the momentary and capricious will of a single person to govern the state, nothing can be fixed, and, of course, there is no fundamental law."[40] This is another use of the term "fundamental laws" to stand for the rules by which authority is rightfully established. That term seems to mean in France the rule of royal succession, and the sanctity of the royal demesne rather than basic principles of right or wrong for people

generally.[41] Here Montesquieu is extending it to require the establishment of intermediate channels through which monarchical
power must flow. This amounts to a distribution of executive
power and it could be called a constitution for executive authority.

The quoted statements may be an illustration of how Montesquieu revised his text in order to circumvent the censors. Shackleton, the biographer, reports that the original draft used only the
term "intermediate powers" and that modifications were made to
avoid possible censorship.[42] The adjective "subordinate" was
added first and then at the last minute there were inserted the word
"dependent" and the entire second sentence to the effect that all
power derives from the prince. The force of the original language is
that government by fundamental law means administration
through intermediaries largely independent of the monarach.

The use of class conflict to limit government is evident in this
choice of aristocrats for administrative positions. The monarch and
the nobility are deemed to be essential to each other. Montesquieu
declares that the fundamental maxim of this governmental type is
"no monarch, no nobility; no nobility, no monarch."[43] Since the
nobility is to provide the principal restraint upon the executive
actions of the monarch, what Montesquieu has in mind would seem
to be not the great nobles nor the *intendants* of Louis XIV and
XV,[44] but rather a comparative independent and professional
nobility.

Still more reliance upon professional elites comes with the proposition that monarchy should include a despositary of law. Like the
Bordeaux *Parlement,* of which Montesquieu was once a leading
member,[45] this is to be staffed by the nobility of the robe, rather
than by nobles generally.[46] "It is not enough to have intermediate
powers in a monarchy, there must be also a depositary of the laws."
Montesquieu explains that this institution can be only "the judges
of the supreme courts of justice who promulgate the new laws, and
revive the obsolete." What he is talking about for these administrative or judicial offices is I believe a specific professional group because he expressly excludes "the nobility" referring to their "natural ignorance, indolence and contempt of civil government." For
this reason "there should be a body invested with the power of re-
viving and executing the laws, which would otherwise be buried in
oblivion." This is, of course, much like the function of the *Parlement de Paris.* While Montesquieu at this point does not expressly

class the judges as members of the nobility, he clearly does so in Book XX. There he refers to "the dignity of the long robe, which places those who wear it between the great nobility and the people." The great nobility probably refers to those of idle prestige whom Louis XIV had installed at Versailles. The nobility of the robe, Montesquieu says, does not have "such shining honors" as the great nobility, but it does have all their privileges and these include a dignity which encircles the depositary of laws, with glory even if it leaves the members in a mediocrity of fortune. These nobles have, he says, "no other means of distinction but by a superior capacity and virtue."[47] The depositary is a further basis for distinguishing monarchy from despotism because the latter has no fundamental law and "no such kind of depositary." In despotic countries, he notes, religion or custom may form a kind of depositary. Montesquieu tends to treat the use of religion in lieu of laws as one of the principal criterion of a despotism,[48] and this became one of the prime sources of criticism when *L'Esprit* was published.[49]

The importance of autonomous groups is further demonstrated by the argument that the king or prince cannot serve properly as a depositary of laws. In so doing Montesquieu implies that laws are something more than the will of the sovereign ruler. A prince's council cannot undertake the function of a depositary of laws, he explains, because such a council is "naturally the depositary of the momentary will of the prince and not of the fundamental laws." The prince's council is continually changing so that it is "neither permanent nor numerous." Moreover, it lacks a sufficient share of the confidence of the people and, consequently, "is incapable of setting them right in difficult conjunctures or of reducing them to proper obedience."[50] Montesquieu seems to visualize courts having experienced, professional judges, and occupying a mediating position between the king and the people. This is another indication that he may consider the king to represent will, the people sense, and the professional elites reason in political affairs.

His characterization of despotism reflects Montesquieu's tendency to be sharply conceptualistic and even dogmatic in his expressions of dislike for concentrations of political authority. Despotism is portrayed to be arbitrary and capricious action through a simple institutional structure. There is no dividing of power. For a supporting illustration, Montesquieu calls attention to the report of the historian John Chardin that Persia had no council of state. In a despotism, all power is committed for execution to a single person. Montesquieu explains that the exercise of power must be delegated because the prince is so happy that he would neglect the management of public affairs. "A man whom his senses continually inform him that he himself is everything and that his subjects are nothing is naturally lazy, voluptuous, and ignorant."[51] The more extensive the empire the less he attends to the cares of government; the more important his affairs the larger his seraglio must be and the less he deliberates on his affairs. This is not wholly irrelevant to the Bourbon kings. Moreover, the commitment of power in a despotism must be to a single person because if the prince delegated administration to a number, there would be continual disputes and intrigues which he would be obliged to settle. "It is, therefore, more natural for him to resign it to a vizier, and to invest him with the same power as himself. The creation of a vizier is a fundamental law of this government." Perhaps Montesquieu intends the French readers of his day to visualize their king's chief minister to be the vizier of a despot.

Much of the second half of Book V is concerned with explaining the different modes of action in monarchy and despotism.[52] At the start of the discussion, monarchy is pictured in a middle position between republics and despotisms in respect of the manner of operation. Montesquieu asserts that monarchical government has a great advantage over a republic because it is conducted by a single person and can act with greater expedition. But he is quick to add that expedition can degenerate into rapidity so that laws are needed to slacken the pace. Laws, he says, "ought not only to favor the nature of each constitution, but likewise to remedy the abuses that might result from this very nature." Yet the main point of the analysis is the contrast of monarchy and despotism, and the comparison with republic serves to show that monarchy is a moderate rather than an extreme form of government. In comparison to despotism, monarchy avoids the danger of too rapid action.

Class differentiations become a central factor in the explanation of "the excellence of monarchical government" in contrast to despotism. Monarchy "naturally requires there should be several orders or ranks of subjects," Montesquieu points out, and for this reason, "the state is more permanent, the constitution more steady, and the person of him who governs more secure."[53] Thus, the class society in a monarchy makes for stability and security. Support is

drawn from the history of Rome. Cicero asserted "that the establishing of the tribunes preserved the republic," and Montesquieu adds
that the people in a despotic country are without tribunes, while in
a monarchy "the people have some sort of tribunes." Again he
views monarchy as mixed government.

The association of despotism with extremism appears also in
Montesquieu's explanation of how a despot's methods are conta-
gious among the society. He observes that the precipitancy of despotism may infect the people until they are hurried away by their
passions and push things too far. "The disorders they commit are all extreme" whereas "in monarchies matters are seldom carried to excess." In a monarchy the chiefs are restrained by
the fear of being abandoned, and the intermediate dependent powers do not allow the populace to have the upper hand. The estates
of the kingdom are rarely corrupted in their entirety. The seditious
have neither the power nor the will to dethrone the prince. "In
these circumstances men of prudence and authority interfere; moderate measures are first proposed, then complied with, and things at
length are redressed; the laws resume their vigor and command submission." Countries with moderate governments, Montesquieu says,
have civil wars without revolutions whereas despotic governments
have revolutions without civil wars.

Accordingly, the difference between monarchy and despotism can
be reduced to contrasting attitudes toward the order of a society.
Monarchy embodies an acceptance of the diversity of social forces
and a recognition of the basic idea that things are distinct as well as
related. On the other hand, despotism is basically a failure to recognize this doctrine of "relational pluralism." The extended analysis
of despotism in Book V emphasizes its disregard of the diversity of
forces which naturally arise in a national society.

As a basis for distinguishing monarchy and despotism, the respect
for law extends to the prince as well as to the other officials and
members of the society. The idea that the despot suffers as much or
more than his subjects from his own want of religion, morality, or
legal responsibility, appears at a number of points throughout *L'Esprit des Lois*. Here, in the analysis of the special spirit of despotism,
the thought is expressed quite sharply. Just as "people who live
under a good government are happier than those who without rule
or leaders wander about the forests," Montesquieu declares, "so
monarchs who live under the fundamental laws of their country are
far happier than despotic princes who have nothing to regulate,

neither their own passions nor those of their subjects."[54] This contrast is one of the most profound criticisms of despotic government, and it is followed by sharp attacks upon the attitude of the despot. "Let us not look for magnanimity in despotic government; the prince cannot impart a greatness which he has not himself; with him there is no such thing as glory." Despotic government makes slight use of laws. The principle of such a government being fear, an ignorant and faint-spirited people have no occasion for a greater number of laws. Everything here depends upon two or three ideas, he says, and there is no need for new additions. The tone of Montesquieu's comments and the implied reference to the Bourbon Kings in this analysis brings to mind the light cynicism of *Les Lettres Persanes*. Montesquieu portrays the plight of a prince who is shut up in his seraglio and who cannot leave his voluptuous abode without alarming those who keep him confined. He seldom wages war in person and hardly dares to instruct his generals. A despot is captive to his own extremes. He is "generally governed by wrath or vengenance" and has "no notion of true glory." Such a prince has so many imperfections that he is held in his palace to keep the people ignorant of the situation.[55]

Despotism also may mean a lack of distinction between the prince and other aspects of government. "Politics, with its several springs and laws, must here be very limited; the political government is as simple as the civil."[56] There is also a commingling with domestic administration as well. The whole effort in a despotism "is reduced to reconciling the political and civil administration to the domestic government, the officers of state to those of the seraglio." Such a nation is happiest, Montesquieu says, when it can look upon itself as the only one in the world; for example, when it is separated by deserts from any foreigners. With fear as the special spirit, the goal of the government is tranquillity, but it is the tranquillity of a town about to be invaded. Its strength lies with the army, and the preservation of the state means the preservation of the army. Civilian and military government are one and the same.

The use of religion to do the work of laws is made a mark of despotic government here as it is at other places throughout *L'Esprit des Lois*. In such states, "religion has more influence than anywhere else; it is fear added to fear." The veneration of the prince in Mohammedan countries is due in part to the religion. Likewise, religion reinforces the Turkish constitution. "The subjects who have no attachment to honor or to the glory and grandeur of the state, are connected with it by the force and principle of religion."

Despotism is marked also by a disregard for legal differentiations. If a prince fails to respect private ownership and declares himself to be proprietor of all lands, agriculture is neglected and nothing is repaired or improved. Also, despotism has no respect for the fundamental laws of royal or political succession, and the new despot is named by the prince himself (as Louis XIV tried to do) or by civil war. The remark that the reigning family in such countries as Morocco and Russia resembles a state, which is too weak in itself and has a head that is too powerful, seems relevant to France under the Bourbons. Even the suggestion that the despot places himself above his family, as Artaxerxes did in putting his children to death for conspiring against him, might be aimed at a French sovereign. Clearly, the whole discussion of royal succession shows again Montesquieu's insistence upon rules and limits for the monarch.

The acknowledgement at this point that despotisms have been much more common in history than limited monarchies includes comments that are particularly pertinent to the issue of how political power should be distributed. Montesquieu admits that his explanation of despotism would make one imagine that human nature should perpetually rise up against despotism, and he recognizes that, despite man's natural love of liberty and innate hatred of force or violence, most nations are subject to despotic rule. The reason for this, he declares, is the difficulty of forming a mixed or moderate system. "To form a moderate government, it is necessary to combine the several powers; to regulate, temper and set them in motion; to give, as it were, ballast to one, in order to enable it to counterpoise the other." The accomplishment of this, he adds, "is a masterpiece of legislation, rarely produced by hazard and seldom attained by prudence." On the other hand a despotic government "offers itself, as it were, at first sight; it is uniform throughout; and as passions only are requisite to establish it, this is what every capacity may reach."[57] The final remark suggests that political reason is a comparatively scarce commodity. I believe that this is one of the assumptions of *L'Esprit des Lois,* and that the scarcity is due to preoccupation with economic and other interests rather than to lack of natural ability. But what may be equally, if not more important in this study, is that these statements raise interesting questions about the theory of separate powers. Montesquieu says that for a moderate government it is necessary to combine the powers. Combination can be reconciled with separation if both are taken to mean distribution. More will be said later about whether this is what Montesquieu means by separation. But, the doctrine must require something more than the mere division of functions into three categories and their assignment to three organs on a one to one basis. That would be a relatively simple operation whereas Montesquieu talks about the difficulty of attaining a "counterpoise" of powers. Presumably, the doctrine involves consideration of deep lying forces and not merely a surface division of functions as functions.

The comparative analysis of various types of public employment in the final chapters of Book V makes further contributions to the contrast of monarchy and despotism.[58] Incidentally, Montesquieu here is inquiring into arrangements of output functions and into the way communication is channeled in various political systems. He points out that in a monarchy power is dispersed or distributed, with even the king retaining some authority, while in a despotism the entire power is delegated to a vizier, who thereby becomes a despot himself. A division of authority would cause disputes and the need of an arbiter which are inconsistent with the idea of despotism. Likewise, Montesquieu calls attention to the division of civil and military authority in a monarchy and its absence in a despotism. Moreover, a despot cannot establish a judicial magistracy because here law is merely the arbitrary will of the despot. The final chapter on the comparison of public employment in republics, monarchies, and despotisms seems designed to make monarchies appear more attractive to Frenchmen than either of the other forms of government. Montesquieu points out most of all the burdens of popular democracy. He asserts that in a republic public employment must be accepted and that even an inferior army post must not be refused, "because virtue in a republic requires continual sacrifice of our persons and of our repugnances for the good of the state."[59] This is not so in monarchies, where honor supplies the standard. The final crowning of monarchy is that it needs no censors while they are necessary in a republic.

The principle or special spirit of monarchy as well as that of despotism is further evidence that these species of government, as conceived by Montesquieu, are centered upon administrative methods in contrast to the focus upon electoral and legislative control which characterizes his idea of republican types of government. In respect of each monarchy and despotism, the special spirit seems designed to maximize the effectiveness of executive action. In the one case, honor is proposed as a means of enlisting and reforming the aristocracy as intermediaries between the king and the people, and in the other fear is frankly acknowledged as the way in which a despot or vizier may seek absolute obedience.

An understanding of honor as the principle or special spirit of monarchy requires an appreciation of the limited and specialized relationship which Montesquieu has in mind in this matter. He is concerned with the attitude of neither the whole governing system nor the whole body politic of a monarchy. Rather, honor as the motivating spirit pertains to the ideas put forth in the preceding book (II) on the structure of monarchy, that there be intermediaries between the king and the people and that the nobility are best situated for this role. Honor is designed to be a stimulant to recruitment and a standard for participation. It pertains to the aristocracy, not as holders of supreme political power, as de Ruggiero seems to think,[60] but as mediating administrators and judges, whose role is to prevent monarchy from falling into some kind of simple absolutism, whether of one, few, or many.[61]

Montesquieu's distinction between the role of aristocrats as intermediaries and as holders of supreme political power is recognized by Franklin L. Ford in his scholarly study of the pre-revolutionary French nobility. "It is an elementary point, no doubt, but an essential one," he points out, "to have clearly in mind, that when Montesquieu talked of the French nobility's proper role he was not applying his definition of aristocracy as a pure form of government." Ford explains that Montesquieu associates the pure form of aristocratic government with Sparta, Rome and Venice, and that *L'Esprit des Lois* views France as a monarchy to be improved by "proper utilization of a privileged aristocracy."[62] Some application of the idea that the French nobility should serve as intermediaries between the king and the people may have been attempted to a small degree during the third quarter of the eighteenth century,[63] but the circumstances were not those assumed by Montesquieu. There was no representative assembly of the people to put the aristocracy in a middle position, and the monarch did not recognize autonomy in the professional nobility. Even more, there was little reform among the aristocracy in the way Montesquieu suggests a number of times.[64] The nobility acted much more for their own interests than as intermediaries and they lacked the tolerant, moderate attitude that Montesquieu considered necessary. The requisite tolerance probably would arise only if the aristocracy is flanked by a representative assembly and a strong chief executive. The attitude of the nobility is important but it is not assured unless there are institutional guarantees and much of *L'Esprit des Lois* is devoted to the explanation of the appropriate institutions.

While *L'Esprit des Lois* concentrates upon the mediating role of the aristocracy in monarchical government, this is not the whole story of that system of government. There is also the duty or willingness of the people to respect authority, obey laws, serve in the army, and engage in the occupations that will make for economic well-being and national security. The stimulation of popular participation, or at least attachment and loyalty, seems to have been explained in *Les Lettres Persanes,* where monarchy is assumed to be largely the prince and the people without intermediaries.[65] In the earlier work, Montesquieu indicates that the people are inspired by the glory which monarchy engenders. One letter, which includes an express comparison of the French and the Persians,[66] begins with an analysis of the feeling for glory. The letter asserts that every man has a passion for glory just as every animal has an instinct for self-preservation. Man desires to enlarge his existence by projecting it into another's memory and thus acquiring "a new life" as precious as the one received from heaven. But just as men are not equally attached to life, so they are not equally sensitive to glory. "This noble passion is always well engraved in their hearts, but imagination and education changes it in a thousand ways." This remark gives an insight into Montesquieu's epistemology. He seems to say that we may not have innate ideas but that we do have innate feelings, which the inner and outer influences on the mind bring forth in various ways. This combination of factors would indicate that there may be some common qualities in human nature, but that there are also factors of individual free will, observation, and thought, which cause the attitude toward glory, and logically other matters as well, to differ among various individuals and, as Montesquieu says, to differ even more among nations. He also introduces a quantitative variable, observing that the desire for glory rises and falls with "the liberty of the subjects." But he adds that it never accompanies servitude. This may indicate again that monarchy is moderate while despotism is absolute in character.

In fact, *Les Lettres Persanes* seems to make the appeal of glory a social affection which makes for obedience without coercion. The same letter pictures the French to be more free than the Persians and thus more in love with glory and in turn willing to do things with pleasure and taste which a sultan could obtain only by ceaseless pleas and rewards. When the letter looks at the classical republics, there is a strong tendency to speak of "honor" rather than "glory." It also emphasizes the attachment to mere honor, observing that at Rome, at Athens and at Sparta, "a crown of oak or laurel, a statue, a eulogy" were deemed to be immense recompense for "a battle won or a city taken." *Les Lettres Persanes,* at times, speaks of honor as well as glory among the French nobility but in line with the general attitude of that work, the nobility means the social aristocracy and it is subjected to ridicule and satire. The passion of the French nobility for dueling is portrayed to be exaggerated and artificial. It is also used to show the force of mores against the law. The noble man, caught between state laws against dueling and the laws of honor for it, is pictured in the dilemma of either dying or being unworthy of life.[67]

The discussion in *L'Esprit des Lois* of the nature and principle of monarchy, with the emphasis upon the honor-inspired roles of aristocratic mediators, is not, I believe, a denial of glory or other motive of obedience and loyalty among the people generally. Honor in monarchy like virtue in a democracy pertains only to certain roles; in one it concerns the citizens as holders of supreme control power while in the other it is the professional aristocracy as the administrators and judges of the political laws. In both, the principle concerns the spirit of only a portion of the political system, and other psychological factors, such as the attitudes of officials and the general loyalty or habit of obedience of the citizens, are assumed to make their contribution to the maintenance and effectiveness of the government.

The difference in the political capabilities of the social classes is implicit also in the contrast of virtue and honor. In the way that Montesquieu uses these terms throughout this analysis, virtue concerns the holders of supreme political power and pertains in large measure to the higher levels of policy making. Moreover, it is a matter of self-imposed restraint by the general class of citizens in a popular government. On the other hand, honor concerns political intermediaries, which are a comparatively small class of professional aristocrats. Also, it relates to service in the output functions of rule-application and rule-adjudication. Finally, it is to motivate voluntary activity rather than to enhance self-restraint.

The idea that virtue means self-restraint is indicated again in the observation at this point that in monarchies "policy effects great things with as little virtue as possible" just as "in the nicest machines art has reduced the number of movements, springs and wheels." Here, monarchy is assumed to permit freedom of activity in contrast to the restraint needed in a democratic system. Monarchy, he says, does not need those "heroic virtues" of the ancients which we know only by tradition. The statement that "The laws supply here the place of those virtues" also assumes that laws do not restrain the people in a democracy because they make the laws. There, virtue must impose that restraint while in a monarchy the laws supply "the place of those virtues." They are not wanted "and the state dispenses with them."[68] An implicit identity of public good and private interests in republics may be behind the remarks that "in republics private crimes are more public" while "in monarchies, public crimes are more private." In one they attack the constitution more and in the other the individuals more. Montesquieu says here that "in a monarchy it is extremely difficult for the people to be virtuous" but he explains in a footnote that he is speaking of political virtue, "which is also moral virtue as it is directed to the public good," rather than of private moral virtue or the virtue of revealed truths. He defends monarchies further by recognizing that there may be virtuous princes and that moral virtue is not excluded from a monarchy.[69] It is simply that virtue is not the spring of this type of government.

The propositions that Montesquieu favors human activity and that class conflicts give rise to essential social activity are evident also in the analysis of the special spirit of monarchy. He calls honor "the prejudice of every person and rank" and says that "here it is capable of inspiring the most glorious actions."[70] The psychological character of this analysis appears also in the contrast of good subjects and good men. There are traces of Aristotle and perhaps Plato in the comment that "in well-regulated monarchies, they are almost all good subjects, and very few good men; for to be a good man, a good intention is necessary, and we should love our country, not so much on our own account, as out of regard to the community." This may anticipate some aspects of Kant's theory of morals and his distinctions between ethics and jurisprudence.[71]

The idea that honor is the special spirit of monarchy tends to reenforce Montesquieu's previous association of monarchy with social class differentiations. "A monarchical government supposes," he says, "preeminences and ranks, as likewise a noble descent." Honor is properly the principle of this kind of government because "it is the nature of honor to aspire to preferments and titles." The desire in monarchy for higher status makes for a more active and competitive society, and this is in accord with Montesquieu's esteem of the active man and the active society. The superiority of monarchy in this respect is clearly evident in the next paragraph: "Ambition is pernicious in a republic. But in a monarchy it has some good effects; it gives life to the government, and is attended with this advantage, that it is in no way dangerous, because it may be continually checked."[72] The fundamental character of this interest in social activity comes out in the next explanation. Monarchy is compared to the system of the universe in which there is a power that constantly repels all bodies from the center and a power of gravitation that attracts them to it. "Honor sets all the parts of the body politic in motion, and by its very action connects them; thus each individual advances the public good, while he thinks only of promoting his own interest." This is probably not a full acceptance of the laissez-faire doctrine because Montesquieu still believes that some laws are necessary in a monarchy for purposes of restraint. But it does show that he considers monarchy conducive to the essential, natural activity of man in society. The statement that ambition is pernicious in a republic would seem to concern only aristocracies because in the explanation of democracy Montesquieu points out that intrigue is not dangerous among the people generally or their representatives.[73] If ambition has good effects in a monarchy and not in republics, it is, I believe, because the latter are being viewed as simple types of aristocracy whereas monarchy is conceived as mixed government with the aristocratic intermediaries restrained by the king and inferentially by the people or their representatives.

Hegel comments that honor as the principle of a monarchy can apply only to a feudal monarchy where, he says, relationships are crystallized into rights of private property and privileges of individuals and corporations.[74] But he may give to these rights and privileges a much greater degree of independence from the sovereign than Montesquieu seems to contemplate. L'Esprit des Lois assumes a rather non-feudal legal and economic system, which Hegel may not recognize. Also, Hegel seems to assume that the principle of honor relates to those who hold supreme political power rather than to those who serve as intermediaries. This may account for his belief that Montesquieu is concerned with only a feudal type monarchy. Montesquieu's realization that the growing commercial class is an important element of modern society is evident in the several books of *L'Esprit des Lois* which deal with such subjects as luxury, commerce, money, occupation, and population trends, as discussed in Chapter III. In fact, the increasing complexity of the modern commercial society is one reason why intermediaries and impartial professionals are needed in the political system.

The idea that Montesquieu is using the terms monarchy and despotism to mean ways of governing more than kinds of structure becomes quite clear in Book VIII when he discusses the corruption of the principles of the different kinds of government. When talking about the corruption of the principle of aristocracy, he says that "if the reigning families observe the laws, it is a monarchy with several monarchs" and that "when they do not observe them, it is a despotic state swayed by a great many despotic princes." Thus, monarchy and despotism are not so much government by one but rather systems that are reasonable or arbitrary, respectively. The principle of despotic government "is even in its nature corrupt," and other forms of government become corrupt when any one political class, whether democratic, aristocratic, or monarchical, usurp all of the power. "As democracies are subverted when the people despoil the senate, the magistrates, the judge of their functions," he argues, "so monarchies are corrupted when the prince insensibly deprives societies or cities of their privileges."[75] This is another indication that the basic difference between moderate and despotic government is whether it is mixed or unmixed, that is, whether authority is distributed or concentrated.

Notes

1. Plato, *Laws,* III, 693.

2. *L'Esprit des Lois* (hereafter referred to as Lois), II, 4, 5.

3. This tendency of Montesquieu seems to be overstated in Lucien Levy-Bruhl, *History of Modern Philosophy in France* (Chicago, 1899), at 152: "Despotism is Persia or Turkey, and occasionally also France under Louis XIV. His republic is the ancient city, Sparta, Athens or Rome. His monarchy means ordinarily the French monarchy, but sometimes the English, and last, his oligarchy is nearly always Venice." I believe that China is even more the example of despotism and Spain sometimes plays the role. Montesquieu's "ideal type" of oligarchy is probably the Decemvirs of Rome.

4. *Lois,* III, 10; V, 14; VI, 9; XI, 4; XIII, 12, 15. There is an observation upon moderate government in *Pensée* 1795: "All moderate government, that is to say where one power is limited by another power, has need of much wisdom in order to be able to establish itself and much wisdom to conserve it." Caillois, I, 1429. A definition is given by the leading biographer: "A moderate government means any government other than a despotism, that is, a republic or monarchy, inspired by the principle, respectively of virtue, or of honor." Robert Shackleton, *Montesquieu A Critical Biography* (Oxford, 1951), 272-3.

5. Xenophon, *Memorabilia,* IV, vi, 12. "Kingship and despotism, in his [Socrates] judgement, were both forms of government, but he held that they differed. For government of men with their consent and in accordance with the laws of the state was kingship; while government of unwilling subjects and not controlled by laws, but imposed by the will of the ruler, was despotism. And where the officials are chosen among those who fulfill the requirements of the laws, the constitution is an aristocracy: where rateable property is the qualification for the office, you have plutocracy: where all are eligible a democracy." Montesquieu makes three references to Xenophon on other matters, *Lois* IV, 8; XX, 18; XXI, 7.

6. Jean-Vincent de Gravina, *Esprit des Lois Romaines,* (Paris, 1821), 142-177.

7. Joseph Dedieu, *Montesquieu et la tradition politique anglais en France,* (Paris, 1909), 132 note. See fn. 8, *infra.*

8. Robert Shackleton, "Montesquieu et Doria", *Revue de Litterature Comparee,* (Paris, 1955), 173-183.

9. Robert Shackleton, *Montesquieu a Critical Biography,* (Oxford, 1961), 267.

10. Chevalier de S. George, Saint-Hyacinthe, *Entretiens dans lesquels on traité des enterprises de l'Espagne.* (The Hague, 1719), 215.

11. Charles Oudin, *De l'Unite de L'Esprit des Lois de Montesquieu* (Paris, 1910), 67, referring to Jean Domat's work on *The Civil Law in its Natural Order.*

12. The categories of monarchy, aristocracy, and democracy appear in the works of Marsilius, *Defensor Pacis,* I, 8 and Calvin, *On Civil Government,* IV, 20. On the two phases of kingship, see Bryce Lyon, *A Constitutional and Legal History of Medieval England* (New York, 1960), 588-9, 496-9, Francis D. Wormuth, *The Origins of Modern Constitutionalism* (New York, 1949), 30-40.

13.   Bodin begins with the basic idea that there are only three types of state or commonwealth, that is, monarchy, aristocracy, and democracy, to be distinguished by whether rule is by one, few, or many. But he acknowledges that Plato added a fourth for the rule of the wise, and that Aristotle introduced a fifth for the mixed state. Then he says that Polybius distinguished seven types, and Cicero four, each including one composed of a mixture of three good ones. However, Bodin himself seems to be more interested in three types of monarchy, as explained in the text. Jean Bodin, *Six Books of the Commonwealth,* (Blackwell, Oxford), 51-2, 56-7.

14.   *Lois,* X, 3-17

15.   Aristotle, *Physics* I, iv, v, 188a, 19, 20; II, i, 192b — 15.

16.   Plato, *Republic,* VIII, 543 a — 576 b.

17.   Werner Stark, *Montesquieu, Pioneer in the Sociology of Knowledge,* (London, 1960) , 162, 6-12.

18.   Hegel, *Grundlinien des Philosophie des Rechts,* translated by T. M. Knox, *Hegel's Philosophy of Right* (Oxford, 1942), 177-178.

19.   *Lois,* II, 2.

20.   *Ibid.* Incidentally, this remark throws some light upon Montesquieu's epistemology.

21.   See also, *Lois,* V, 10, on the expedition peculiar to the executive power in monarchies.

22.   *Lois,* II, 2.

23.   Aristotle, *Politics,* III, ix, 1280 a.

24.   *Lois,* II, 2.

25.   *Ibid.,* II, 3.

26.   The variety of meanings is indicated in Carl J. Friedrich, *The Philosophy of Law in Historical Perspective* (Chicago, 1957), 21, 39, 113. On the meaning of *arête* see, T. A. Sinclair, *A History of Greek Political Thought,* (London, 1951) , 46, 55, 211.

27.   Abbé Joseph de la Porte, *Observations sur L'Esprit des Lois, ou l'art de lire ce livre, de l'entendre et d'en juger* (Amsterdam, 1751) , 126-7.

28.   Roger Caillois, *Oeuvres Complètes de Montesquieu* (Paris, 1951), II, 227-8.

29.   *Lois,* III, 3 (Par. 2).

30.   *Ibid.* (Par. 3).

31.   *Ibid.* (Par. 7)

32.   Raymond Aron, *Main Currents in Sociological Thought,* (New York, 1965) , I, 33.

33.   *Lois,* III, 4 (Pars. 3, 4).

34.   *Ibid.,* XI, 9.

35.   For instance, *Lois* XI, XIX; see chapters VII and VIII of this study.

36.   T. M. Knox, *Hegel's Philosophy of Right* (Oxford, 1942), 178.

37.   W. T. Stace, *The Philosophy of Hegel* (New York, 1955), 203-5.

38.   This dual criteria is noted by Aron, *op. cit.,* I, 19.

39.   *Lois,* II, 4. Later, at one point, Montesquieu makes the attitude

toward law more telling than the number of persons holding power, declaring that, when the reigning families do not observe the law, "it is a despotic state swayed by a great many despotic princes." *Lois*, VIII, 5.

40. *Lois*, II, 4.

41. See William F. Church, *Constitutional Thought in Sixteenth-Century France* (Cambridge, Mass., 1941) 233, 235.

42. Shackleton, *op. cit.*, 278-9. On censorship generally, see F. C. Green, *Eighteenth-Centruy France* (London, 1929), 194-221.

43. *Lois*, II, 4.

44. On the role of the nobility, see generally, Franklin L. Ford, *Robe and Sword, The Regrouping of the French Aristocracy after Louis XIV* (Cambridge, Mass., 1962), 246-252; Shackleton, *op. cit.*, 279.

45. The *Parlement* had several judicial and administrative duties, both at Paris with respect to the national government and at fourteen provincial centers, including Bordeaux. Montesquieu from 1716 to 1726 was *Président à Mortier* of the *Parlement de Bordeaux*. The *Parlement de Paris* was the despository of the national laws. Royal edicts and decrees were not in force until they had been registered with that body. The judges could suspend registration until the monarch made a special request in person, and, thus, they had a restraining power at the heart of lawful government. In fact, in Montesquieu's time, the various *Parlements* and other "sovereign courts" were the principal hope of any independent action against the king. The offices were held largely by members of comparatively able noble families. See Shackleton, *op. cit.*, 278-81; Ford, *op. cit.*, 37, 129, 134-5; Kingsley Martin, *The Rise of French Liberal Thought* (New York, 1956), 80-88, 151-2.

46. *Lois*, II, 4.

47. *Ibid.*, XX, 22, See Chapter III, of this study.

48. *Lois*, II, 4. One analysis of *L'Esprit des Lois* makes this attribute of despotism quite conclusive. "The one and only check on the caprice of the despot is religion." C. E. Vaughan, *Studies in the History of Political Philosophy Before and After Rousseau* (New York, 1960), I, 265.

49. Abbé Joseph de la Porte, *Observations sur L'Esprit des Lois, ou l'art de lire ce livre, de l'entendre, et d'en juger* (Amsterdam, 1751), 15-16, attacks the idea that religion enforces despotism more than monarchy.

50. *Lois*, II, 4.

51. *Ibid.*, II, 5.

52. *Ibid.*, V, 10-19.

53. *Ibid.*, V, 11.

54. *Ibid.*,

55. In contrast, Montesquieu pictures the subjects in monarchies as "encircling the throne and being cheered by the irradiancy of the sovereign." Each person is deemed to be capable of exercising those virtues which adorn the soul, with equal independence, and true dignity and greatness. Then Montesquieu presents the most extreme portrait of despotism. "When the savages of Louisiana are desirous of fruit, they

cut the tree to the root, and gather the fruit. This is an emblem of despotic government." *Lois*, V, 12, 13.

56. *Ibid.*, V, 14. "The preservation of the state is only the preservation of the prince, or rather of the palace where he is confined."

57. *Lois*, V, 14.

58. *Lois*, V, 16-19. Throughout Book V there are several discussions of laws relating to commerce. The positions expressed are mostly similar to those later set forth in Books XX and XXI.

59. *Lois*, V, 19. The comparative analysis of administrative behavior includes practices of making presents and rewards. *Ibid.*, V, 17, 18.

60. Guido de Ruggiero, *The History of European Liberalism*, (Boston, 1959), 59. De Ruggiero's remark that mixed monarchy is a mere facade for aristocratic rule seems to overlook the other elements of mixed monarchy prescribed by Montesquieu, such as the reform of the nobility, the presence of a spirited monarch, and the representation of the people in at least one chamber of the legislative department.

61. *Lois*, II, 4; XI, 6.

62. Franklin L. Ford, *Robe and Sword, The Regrouping of the French Nobility after Louis XIV* (Cambridge, Mass., 1962), 240.

63. *Ibid.*, 251.

64. *Lois*, II, 3 (Par. 10); III, 4; IV, 2 (education in monarchies deals with training of the aristocracy). *Lois,* V, 8; and VIII, 5.

65. *L.P.* CII.

66. *Ibid.*, LXXXIX.

67. *Ibid.*, XC

68. *Lois*, III, 5.

69. *Lois*, III, 5; see also Preface, Caillois, II, 227.

70. *Lois*, III, 6.

71. Aristotle, *Politics*, III, iv, 1276 b 11-1277 b 24. Immanuel Kant, *The Metaphysics of Morals* (Translated by John Ladd), (Indianapolis, 1965).

72. *Lois*, III, 7.

73. *Lois*, II, 2 (Par. 26).

74. Hegel, *op. cit.*, 178.

75. *Lois*, VIII, 5, 6.

Chapter V

The Political Responsibilities
of the Three Classes

The manner in which the comparative study of government in Books II — X of *L'Esprit des Lois* prepares for the explanation of mixed government is most distinctive when Montesquieu deals with the political attitudes of the democratic and aristocratic classes. He is opposed to unmixed government whatever the superior class, and this is most evident when he talks about despotisms. He illustrates absolute monarchy, which he consistently calls despotism, by portraying an Oriental vizier sustained by a pervading sense of fear among the subjects. His condemnation of simple, closed aristocracy is almost as clear when he refers to the Roman Decemvirs, but it is less certain when he comments on Venice or other commercial republics. He is still more indirect in bringing out the difficulties of what I call monolithic democracy, that is, unlimited and unshared popular sovereignty.

In the first section of this chapter I will explicate the various ways in which he indicates that the general sense of restraint needed by simple democracy is both unnatural and unattractive for national France. Then, the second section will review Montesquieu's ideas on educating and reforming the political nobility so that they will respect both the king and the people. Finally, the third section will summarise and appraise those discussions in the first portion of *L'Esprit des Lois* (Books II — X) that concern the political reponsibilities of the three classes and which thereby bear upon Montesquieu's theory of a natural system of mixed government.

The Psychological Burden of
Monolithic Democracy

One of the most fundamental aspects of *L'Esprit des Lois* is the way Montesquieu uses the comparative analysis of traditional forms

195

of government to make unlimited popular sovereignty appear unattractive to the French people. This objective becomes increasingly evident when the explanations of the structure and spirit of democracy throughout the first portion of the work (Books II — X) are examined in relation to the possibility of a mixed or competitive government. Montesquieu is deeply antagonistic to absolutism and this includes democratic as well as aristocratic and monarchical absolutism. He is quite definitely opposed to any kind of monistic or monolithic sovereignty, and the possession by the people as a single collective class of the supreme political power would be one form of that kind of sovereignty. The present day counterpart of monolithic democracy would be a state with unlimited sovereignty in a one-party unicameral legislature. Political parties are not present expressly in *L'Esprit des Lois* but the basis for partisan division exists in such phenomena as the conflicts of traditional estates and the competition of the newly arising commercial classes. Some of the complexity of *L'Esprit des Lois* derives from the fact that Montesquieu was writing at a time when the counteracting forces of political control were shifting in various, undefined ways from the traditional conflict of the nobility and the commonalty to the political party rivalry of conservative and liberal economic interests. Montesquieu speaks more directly of the former, but there is much evidence in his discussions of France and England that he was well aware of the latter.[1] His analyses may not seem patently applicable to present day conditions, but they are implicitly relevant because they are based in substance upon the political sociology of group interaction, whether the conflict be conceived to be between traditional classes, legislative chambers, political parties, or interest associations.

The imperfections of monolithic democracy appear at various points throughout the comparative analysis of governments in the first portion of *L'Esprit des Lois*. The more express limitations appear in the analysis of structure, which quickly turns to the limited political capabilities of the commonalty. At the beginning of Book II, Montesquieu asserts that the people cannot engage directly in executive and administrative functions. He recognizes the ability of the people to select those who will govern them, but he is equally clear about their limited capabilities. He even suggests that, when the people have authority to make law or policy, they need the guidance of a senate or similar body. Likewise, he recommends that voting be public so that the common people may have the examples of the more eminent personages.

The difficulties of popular sovereignty also concern the principle or special spirit needed for that kind of government, but the explanation is considerably more complex than that of the structure. Montesquieu seems to be struggling with deep thoughts about the psychological burdens of monolithic democracy. He changes at least three times his definition of the "virtue" needed by popular republics. He gives the term rather peculiar meanings which have been disputed since *L'Esprit des Lois* appeared.[2] The definitions in Book III and in the explanatory note to the second edition of the work were discussed in the preceding chapter. There the conclusion was expressed that the "virtue" required to make democracies effective is a general self-imposed restraint by the people in the collective exercise of their sovereign political authority. Still more explanations and specifications of the meaning of "virtue" appear in Books IV and V, which deal with the educational methods, the laws, and the institutions that might be used to develop and maintain the special spirit needed by particular types of government.

The treatment of education in Book IV of *L'Esprit des Lois* on the relation of educational methods to the principle of different kinds of government may have some resemblance to the ideas of Plato and Aristotle on the education in the spirit of the constitution.[3] Montesquieu may seem to be arguing for some kind of thought control for political conformity.[4] In this light, education would have a more limited purpose than it had in classical Greece where service to the *polis* was the moral fulfillment of the individual. Montesquieu unlike Plato or Aristotle, considers religion, morals, and civil behavior to be distinct from political relations. Moreover, what Montesquieu proposes in Book IV does not concern education in its entirety. It deals only with the political education in particular types of special spirit and the proposals may vary in scope and effect. Training a few in honor or moderation may have substance but there seems to be something artificial or even cynical in trying to teach everyone fear for despotism or virtue for absolute democracy. In any case, this education is special and limited.

Montesquieu's ideas about education in general are more fully represented by what he says in the *Essai sur les Causes*.[5] There he discusses not political education but rather two kinds of what I would call civil education. The analysis there starts with the basic

proposition that "all things have two values: an intrinsic value and
a value from opinion." Correspondingly, Montesquieu posits two
kinds of education: a particular education which forms each character and a general education that is received in the society where
one lives. He says that we receive particular education from our
masters and the general education from the people of the world.
Both the particular and the general education can be distinguished
from the special education in the principle of a government, which
is the subject of Book IV of *L'Esprit des Lois*. Here, Montesquieu
indicates that education in the moving spirit of the government
would be partly the product of family life, but this would not seem
to preclude a particular education aimed at developing individual
capacity and behavior. The openness of Montesquieu's views on individual education is demonstrated by his assertion that persons
should be permitted to change their occupations or professions,[6] as,
of course, he did himself.

The limited objective of the educational analysis in Book IV
should be kept in mind when Montesquieu remarks that "every private family ought to be governed by the plan of that great household which comprehends them all" and that "if the people in general have a principle, their constituent part, that is, the several families, will have one also." The laws or methods of this special education are keyed to the respective type of principle and the emphasis
here is not that all conform but rather that there be an area of conformity relevant to the particular species of government. Montesquieu declares quite promptly that the laws will be different for
each kind of political system: "in monarchies they will have honor
for their object; in republics, virtue; in despotic governments,
fear."[7]

The special meaning of "virtue" developed in Book III of *L'Esprit des Lois* receives further elaboration in Book IV, where Montesquieu takes up education in republics. Now he says that education is important in republics, and he seems to be thinking of monolithic democracies. He asserts that "in a republic government the
whole power of education is required" because "virtue is a self-re-
nunciation, which is ever arduous and painful." Thus, he assumes
that the principle of democratic government is difficult of attainment. He then defines this virtue to be "the love of the laws and of
our country" and points out that it demands "a constant preference
of public to private interest." Here we may have the distinction
which Rousseau later makes between the general will and the par-

ticular wills of all. This seems implicit in the express assertion that such a virtue is the principle of only popular government. "This love is peculiar to democracies. In these alone the government is intrusted to private citizens. Now a government is like everything else; to preserve it we must love it."[8]

These statements bring out a number of basic ideas about the processes of a republic. For one thing, the remark that virtue is a love of the laws as well as of the country would seem to refer to the laws which should guide the people as legislators rather than the laws which they produce as holders of the supreme political power. Virtue is hardly the love of one's own creation. These laws are not the same as those which bind the citizens individually. The virtue which he is identifying is peculiar to democracies because in other types of government the citizens do not possess supreme political power. Likewise, the virtue which Montesquieu is talking about is a self-restraint, which does not come easy and which may be burdensome. When he says that virtue is the principle of republics and not of monarchies, he is not showing preference for the republican form but rather portraying the inherent burden of democratic republics upon the individuals and the society.

What Montesquieu has to say at this point about the love of country reveals his emphasis upon sense rather than reason and upon psychology rather than logic. Everything in a republic, he says, depends upon establishing this love "and to inspire it ought to be the principal business of education, but the surest way of instilling it into children is for parents to set them an example." Parents generally have power to communicate their ideas to their children, but they are even better able to transfuse their passions. "It is not the young people that degenerate; they are not spoiled till those of mature age are already sunk into corruption."[9] These remarks also show Montesquieu's awareness of the psychology of socialization and the role of the family, the school, and other institutions in carrying on the belief system of a people. He inquires into the educational methods which would develop or fortify the respective special spirit. In democracies this is a matter of encouraging self-restraint and a love of equality and frugality. In aristocracies, the objective is increased tolerance and moderation. In monarchies, it is the enhancement of a sense of honor that will motivate the professional aristocracy to serve as mediators, and in despotisms it is the development of a widespread sense of fear. With this many-sided emphasis upon attitudes and motives, Montesquieu is more engaged in observing the psychology of man in society than in speculating about the traditional concepts and ideals of government. Education and legislation in these matters concern hypothetical attitudes, and there is repeated reference to sensations, passions, the heart, types of love, happiness, and the desires for prestige and superiority.[10]

The discussion of classical republics in the final chapters of Book IV provides more instances in which Montesquieu assumes that self-government requires a high degree of austerity. The Greek cities are portrayed to have stern policies and to require many of the aspects of Plato's republic, such as the community of goods, the high respect for the gods, the separation from strangers, and an extensive commerce carried on by the community rather than by private citizens. To prevent corruption of morals, a magistrate needs to make all contracts and sales in the name of the city. These requirements of virtue are contrasted with the free, active life of monarchies,[11] Montesquieu declaring that it is more troublesome to inspire virtue than honor or fear. Also, he adds that the requirements of virtue can take place only in a small community where a general education is possible, and the whole people can be trained like a single family. Then he makes a quite interesting comment, asserting in effect that a classical democracy is not appropriate to a commercial people. He draws upon Polybius and Xenophon as well as Plato and Aristotle in explaining a paradox in the manners of the ancients. The Greek republics would not have the citizens apply themselves to trade, agriculture, or the arts but yet would not have them idle. They were allowed only gymnic and military exercises with the appropriate music. Music did not inspire virtue but prevented savage effects and enabled the soul to share in education despite the want of harmony. These descriptions could mean that democracy is not conducive to economic development, except perhaps in small states. Montesquieu also may be suggesting that government in economically advanced countries must utilize representative and professional elites.

The explanation in Book V of the ways in which the special spirit of different kinds of government may be established and maintained through political laws and institutions provides a more intensive analysis of the "virtue" needed by a democratic republic than is presented in the preceding books.

A psychological approach is evident from the start of the inquiry into the meaning of democratic virtue. Montesquieu assumes that this moving spirit must arise from common sense more than by reason, declaring that "Virtue in a republic is a most simple thing; it is a love of the republic, it is a sensation, and not a consequence of acquired knowledge; a sensation that may be felt by the meanest as well as the highest person in the state."[12] This may give a new, lofty role to his idea in the work on the Romans that "there is nothing so powerful as a republic in which the laws are observed, not from fear, not from reason, but from passion."[13] Likewise, it is in line with the statement in Book I of *L'Esprit des Lois* that the most natural government is that which best agrees with the humor and the dispositions of the people. The fact that virtue is a sensation makes it especially appropriate to the populace generally. "When the common people adopt good maxims, they adhere to them more steadily than those whom we call gentlemen." Corruption rarely commences with the common people, and actually, Montesquieu says, their mediocre vision often gives them a strong attachment to what is established.

The idea that the desired virtue in a democracy is a matter of sensation or passion does not mean that it is necessarily inner-directed. It is a particular type of sensation: it is a love and judging by the objects of the love, it is basically a regard for the community. Montesquieu identifies it successively as the love of the republic, the love of our country, and the love of democracy. Characteristically, he sees cause and result in mutual support of each other. "The love of our country is conducive to a purity of mores, and the latter is again conducive to the former."[14] Moreover, he expressly suggests that the individual passions may be satisfied ultimately by service to the public rather than in self interest. "The less we are able to satisfy our private passions, the more we abandon ourselves to those of a general nature." Thus, the roles of an individual as a good citizen and as a moral man interact for their mutual benefit and strength. Individual sentiment and common good are brought even closer together when the democratic principle is identified as the love of both equality and frugality. Everyone here has a right to the "same hopes, which can be expected only from a general frugality." The idea that equality involves a common frugality rather than a common abundance may reflect the difference between the economy of the eighteenth century and that of today, but it also indicates a frankness on the part of Montesquieu which is not found among libertarians of the present day.

The definition of virtue in a republic to be the "love of country,"

with the implication that this is not necessary in a monarchy, was
the object of criticism by the contemporary assailants of *L'Esprit
des Lois*. The commentary of the Abbé de la Porte, which appeared
in 1751 and which was probably the soundest of the critical tracts at
that time, argues that "if virtue in a republic is the love of the republic, the virtue in a monarchy is similarly the love of the monarchy."[15] What the Abbé does not take into account is that this love
of a republic concerns the people as holders of supreme political
power and not as the subjects of the law and order of a political society. Montesquieu is not talking about the need of people being law-
abiding or obedient to the decisions of the political authority. He is
giving principle and virtue rather peculiar meanings. Virtue, as he
is using the term, could not apply to the contemporary French
monarchy because the people did not hold even a coordinate political power. This virtue applies to a citizenry holding high political
power and, when Montesquieu says that only democratic republics
need it, he seems to be making that form of government unattractive to the French. Specifically, he says that a love of equality in a
democracy "limits ambition to the sole desire and the sole happiness of doing greater service to our country than the rest of our fellow-citizens." For the less capable, the duty is to serve with "equal
alacrity." Montesquieu makes pure or unlimited democracy a matter of duties and detriments rather than rights and benefits, and he
assumes that the root of political obligation in simple democracies
is not consent but the feeeling of denial and service. Here is another indication that Montesquieu associates democratic government with self-restraint more than with free action.

The further elaboration of the austerity inherent in pure democracy becomes slightly cynical. It points out that the love of frugality limits the desires of individuals to necessaries for the family
and superfluities for the country. Riches give a power which a citizen cannot use for himself because he would no longer be equal.
Well-regulated democracies by establishing domestic frugality make
way for public expenses. In Athens and Rome, "magnificence and
profusion arose from the very fund of frugality." The laws required
a frugality of life so the gods could be liberal to the country. The
restraint extends to the whole of man's actions in society. "The
good sense and happiness of individuals depend greatly upon the
mediocrity of their abilities and fortunes."[16] These various indications that democracy is not an attractive type of government would
seem to be directed against monolithic democracy and not against

the inclusion of democratic elements in a mixed political system.

Montesquieu's interest in social psychology is evident in his remark that the "love of equality and of a frugal economy is greatly excited by equality and frugality themselves, in societies where these virtues are established by law." Thus, the habits of the people are deemed to generate their passions. For frugality as well as equality Montesquieu remarks, "To love it, we must practice and enjoy it."[17] But he does say that the virtues of equality and frugality must be established by law if these virtues are to be loved in a republic. This suggests that the people in a democracy must establish the necessary virtue by laws which would seem to be imposing it upon themselves or at least upon many of their number. Again, Montesquieu may be indicating that monolithic democracy might necessitate a general repression of natural activity. In this same discussion he points out that in monarchies and despotic governments there is no thought of equality and "all inspire to superiority." This kind of competitive activity, I believe, appeals to Montesquieu, and this is one of his reasons for favoring a mixed monarchy for the central government of a national society. His stress upon the need for equality and frugality in a democracy, even to the point of making people feel inferior, indicates again that he is endeavoring to make popular sovereignty appear unattractive to the French. The statement that both monarchies and despotisms arouse a desire for superiority and that even the lowest individual may under those governments indulge the hope of emerging from obscurity, shows that Montesquieu is motivated here primarily by opposition to democratic republics because elsewhere he says that despotic government imposes an equality of serfdom.

The first suggestion on how laws may establish the equality needed in a democracy is a traditional one. Montesquieu refers to the equal divisions of land made by Lycurgus and Romulus. Settlements of this kind, he acknowledges, can take place only upon the foundation of a new republic or when an old republic is so corrupt that the poor think themselves obliged to demand and the rich consider it wise to consent to such a remedy. Also, such diversions of land must be followed by what are now statutory enactments. "If the legislator, in making a division of this kind, does not enact laws at the same time to support it, he forms only a temporary constitution; inequality will break in where the laws have not precluded it, and the republic will be utterly undone."[18] Thus the legal system must be developed at more than one level to be effective. Also, there may be need for exceptions. Montesquieu recognizes that a division of lands may not be absolutely equal. "Though real equality be the very soul of a democracy, it is so difficult to establish, that an extreme exactness in this respect would not be always convenient." It is enough to reduce the differences to a certain point. But inequalities should be consistent with the type of government. "All inequality in democracies ought to be derived from the nature of the government, and even from the principle of equality." For example, he explains that a person who is obliged to live by his labor should not be considered for public employment if this would impoverish him and cause him to neglect his duties for other work. This shows the importance which Montesquieu attaches to the economic classes and is evidence of an idea that their political participation should not interfere with their primary contributions to the society.

The idea that the love of frugality is not natural seems to be implicit in the assertion that legislation is necessary to establish a love of frugality. In his further explanation of virtue, Montesquieu declares that "it is not sufficient in a well-regulated democracy that the divisions of land be equal; they ought also to be small, as was customary among the Romans."[19] He adds, perhaps cynically, that a citizen should be satisfied with a piece of land that is sufficient to maintain him. He also argues that frugality and equality are mutually enforcing. "As equality of fortunes supports frugality, so the latter maintains the former." Here is another illustration of the interdependence of distinct forces. Montesquieu makes this clear: "These things, though in themselves different, are of such a nature as to be unable to subsist separately." He explains further that "they reciprocally act upon each other; if one withdraws itself from a democracy, the other surely follows it." On the immediate subject of the unattractiveness of popular sovereignty, Montesquieu is arguing that it is frugality and impliedly not liberty, that naturally goes with equality. Earlier, L'Esprit des Lois had emphasized that general self-restraint is necessary to the success of a democracy and now this is made more specific by arguing that frugality as well is required. In both instances, Montesquieu is saying, I believe, that democracy entails a common spirit of self-control and even of self-denial by the people in the exercise of their supreme political power.

The idea that virtue in a democracy is a restraint which interferes with the free activity of man and thus makes that form of government unattractive, appears not only in *L'Esprit des Lois* but also in *Les Lettres Persanes*.[20] There, in the fable of the Troglodytes, the two families who endeavored to live by their own virtue without government, taught their children that individual interest is always in the common interest, that to separate these interests is to invite ruin, and that virtue is not costly to achieve nor painful to exercise. But the time came when they found that it was too costly and too painful. Then they sought a king to rule over them. The leader they selected tells them what is happening: "Your virtue begins to be heavy for you. In the state you are, without a head, you are constrained to be virtuous, in spite of yourselves, or you cannot subsist, but must sink into the miseries of your ancestors." He tells them that the yoke of their own virtue is too hard and that they prefer to be subject to a king and to obey his laws, which are "less rigid than your mores." This is implicit in *L'Esprit des Lois*. That work says in effect that the self-government of a democratic republic would require a degree of self-imposed restraint that the people would find burdensome and that it would be less exacting to live under the laws of a rational monarchy than to try to impose rules upon themselves. This is relevant to France and seems to be a development of the admonitions to the French in *Les Lettres Persanes* that they should respond to the spirit of their natural sense more than to the artificial restraints of calculated reason.[21]

While Montesquieu explains that this virtue is more particular than general and more political than ethical, he does not make too clear another peculiarity of meaning, that is, that virtue concerns the people in their collective capacity of supreme power-holders in a monolithic democracy. It does not relate to their capacity of political inferiors. The virtue of democracy is a matter of restraint, but I believe that the essential factor is that it pertains to the people as law-makers or policy-makers rather than as law-recipients or subjects. Such a virtue logically could not apply to the monarchical situation because there the people are not political superiors. When the people have the supreme law-making power they, in a collective capacity, are not restrained by their own legislation. Each particular person might be restrained by the laws even though he was a member of the body politic but the society in its collective status would not be bound. This would seem to be a necessary assumption for Montesquieu's remark that the people in a democracy are not bound by the laws. It also helps to explain his assertion that virtue is not the principle of a monarchy as well as the statements at various points that in a democracy virtue takes the place of laws and that in a monarchy the laws take the place of virtue. When Montesquieu makes such assertions, I believe that he is assuming democracy to be simple and complete. Or perhaps more specifically he is thinking about the simple, democratic process by which the people are supposed to have the supreme political power. The presupposition of such an abstract form of democratic process seems necessary to support Montesquieu's conclusion that the people are not restrained by the laws because they made them and can change them. In this analysis, he is not talking about the individual citizen who may be restrained in fact by laws even though the citizen is a member of the body politic or the possible majority which made the laws. Here he seems not to distinguish the people from the majority which approves a particular law nor from their representatives. This may be a common characteristic of democratic theorists in that age,[22] and it seems to be particularly present in Rousseau's explanation of a general will. But the idea that a people have a single collective purpose and the assumption of a community will like an individual will are not characteristic generally of Montesquieu's writings even though they seem to be present in the analysis of democratic virtue. With these assumptions, democracy requires a high degree of collective self-restraint and it becomes unattractive if not unattainable.

This may be an indirect argument against popular rule for France. The French would not seem to be anxious to undertake a kind of government which could succeed only if the people generally exercised a high degree of self-imposed frugality as well as a deep love of equality. The peculiar association of "virtue" with republics and not with monarchies may give the immediate impression that Montesquieu prefers republics to monarchies. But the reverse may actually be the case, particularly in respect of national government. The virtue in question is a special type of political inclination. It is a restraint in exercising supreme political power and in effect requires the democratic class to subordinate its natural desires to those of other classes or groups. This amounts to saying, I believe, that absolute democracy will not succeed because of its one-class tendency and that popular sovereignty when not qualified by countervailing power in other classes is as inherently destructive as absolute monocracy or aristocracy.

Books VI and VII dealing with civil laws and socio-economic matters seem to be attacks on despotism and to cast some favor upon monarchies and republics that are responsive to the social structure and its mores. They do not appear to concern popular sovereignty and monolithic democracy.

The crowning evidence that the necessary virtue of full democracy is unattainable comes in the Book VIII when Montesquieu discusses the corruption of the principle or special spirit of different kinds of government. In fact, he makes egalitarian zeal and extreme participation in governmental functions corruptive forces in themselves. He asserts, "The principle of democracy is corrupted not only when the spirit of equality is extinct, but likewise when they fall into a spirit of extreme equality, and when each citizen would fain be upon a level with those whom he has chosen to command him."[23] Thus, the love of equality, which he said earlier is necessary for the effective operation of democratic sovereignty, now becomes a force which could corrupt the spirit of such government. This point arises when the people desire to be equal to those who they have selected to govern them. "Then the people, incapable of bearing the very power they have delegated, want to manage everything themselves, to debate for the senate, to execute for the magistrate and to decide for the judges." When this comes about, "virtue can not longer subsist in the republic." Here, Montesquieu is using the term republic to mean a government of popular sovereignty, and virtue in a democracy is again portrayed to be self-restraint. He asserts that, if the people desire the authority of the magistrates and the senate, those institutions cease to be revered. In this mood of antagonism to a usurped concentration of authority, Montesquieu over-paints the picture. He portrays disrespect and license spreading to family relations until he concludes that there will be "no more of mores, love of order, or virtue." After a reference to the abuse of equality at Xenophon's Banquet, he reviews the degenerative forces which cause democracy to fall into anarchy and then become prey to tyranny. He describes how officials conceal their own avarice by flattering the people and extolling the grandeur of the state. Public monies then are divided with the people who blend their poverty with the amusements of luxury. Next, he explains, the people give their suffrages for money and they seem to be deriving the most from their liberty but are actually approaching the loss of freedom. Petty tyrants arise with all the vices of a despot and the people are soon stripped of everything, even the profits of their corruption.

The idea that extreme equality tends to corrupt democracy is, of course, not new but its introduction here is a further indication that the principle of democracy, previously defined to be a love of equality and frugality, may not be attainable and that ideal democracy is either undesirable or ineffective for such reasons. It is also an indirect suggestion that the spirit of successful government is moderation. Montesquieu again stresses the evils of extremes, asserting that democracy has two excesses to avoid: "the spirit of inequality which leads to aristocracy or to the government of one; and the spirit of extreme equality, which leads to the despotism of one, as the despotism of one itself ends in conquest."[24] For supporting instances, Montesquieu observes that in the Greek cities corruption may not always have led to tyranny because the Greeks had a greater passion for eloquence than military art, but at Syracuse the people ever faced the cruel choice of having a tyrant govern them or of acting the tyrant themselves. Other historical illustrations attribute corruption to the intoxication of success. Athens was corrupted by the victory at Salamis and Syracuse by its defeat of the Athenians. In contrast, Marseilles never experienced such transitions from lowness to grandeur and always preserved her principles.

The argument at this point on the difference between "the true spirit of equality" and "the spirit of extreme equality" seems to indicate that having equality is a matter of being equally under law. Montesquieu says that the true spirit of equality means "not that everybody command, or that nobody command, but rather that we obey and command our equals." This idea is supported by an observation on the state of nature and the origin of positive laws. "In the state of nature, all men are born equal but they cannot remain in this condition. Society makes them lose it and they recover equality only by the laws."[25] This also suggests that equality requires living in a society under law. Montesquieu explains further that in "a well-regulated democracy" men are "equal only as citizens" and not as magistrates, senators, judges, fathers, husbands, or masters. This says in effect that equality in a democracy includes many duties but only a few political rights. A citizen, Montesquieu seems to assume here, may participate in the representative assembly or in the selection of legislators and magistrates but equality does not extend to other positions of authority.

At this point there is also another indication that the special spirit of government should be moderation. This is the remark that "the natural place of virtue is near to liberty, but it is not nearer to excessive liberty than to servitude."[26] In fact, there seems to be an underlying assumption that equality and liberty may conflict and that the two ideals of equality and liberty must both be limited in a democracy. Impliedly, Montesquieu infuses moderation into democracies as well as into aristocracies and monarchies. The idea that every legislator should be guided by the spirit of moderation is not stated expressly until Book XXIX, but even the discussion in Book VIII on the corruptive effect of an attitude of extreme equality in a democracy seems to anticipate what *L'Esprit des Lois* finally sets forth as the highest standard for a legislator.

Political Socialization of the Aristocracy

The most persistent feature of the comparative analysis in the first portion of *L'Esprit des Lois* is the relation of the aristocracy to the other classes of a national society. In the discussions of both the structure and the spirit of all four kinds of government, Montesquieu develops in various ways the idea that the contribution of the nobility is not to rule but to mediate and moderate between the monarch and the people. Increasingly throughout Books II — VIII the answer to the dilemma presented by *Les Lettres Persanes* is that professional aristocracies should occupy mediating positions in the government in order to avoid the tyranny of either the one or the many. Montesquieu gives more and more attention to the political recruitment and socialization of elites with the objective of making the political system responsive to the society and the natural inclinations of the people. He recognizes quite definitely that a political aristocracy must have a moderate attitude and a public spirited motive, and he also assumes that to fill such a role the French nobility needs substantial education and considerable reform.

The first suggestion that the aristocracy should play an elite political role appears in the structural analysis of democratic republics at the start of Book II. Here Montesquieu says that a people with the supreme political power need aristocrats for magistrates, a senate for guidance in law making, and eminent persons to provide public examples of voting prudence.

Then the explanation in the same book of the aristocratic type of republics soon becomes an argument for broadening the noble class and improving its attitude toward the popular class. Montesquieu prefers a nobility that is large and perhaps even divided in some ways. He seems to inject a bicameral legislature into aristocratic government when he states that where the nobility is large "there must be a senate to regulate the affairs which the body of the nobles are incapable of deciding and to prepare others for their decision."

In that case, he says, the aristocracy is in the senate and democracy in the body of nobles, and the people are naught. This last he finds unfortunate and wishes it were overcome. "It would be a very happy thing in an aristocracy if the people, in some measure, could be raised from their state of annihilation." Moreover, he asserts that aristocracy improves as it tends toward democracy. "The best aristocracy is that in which those who have no share in the legislature are so few and inconsiderable that the governing party have no interest in oppressing them."[27] In support of this, he refers to a law by Antipater at Athens that limited the power to vote to those worth two thousand drachmas. This, he says, excluded only a few persons. The conclusion seems a bit exaggerated and has been challenged,[28] but it shows that he prefers a broad political base that might assure tolerance in the elite. Aristocratic families ought, he says, "to level themselves in appearance with the people." Here Montesquieu gives the relations of the nobility to the people a higher value than those with the king. "The more an aristocracy borders on democracy, the nearer it approaches perfection and, in proportion as it draws toward monarchy, the more is it imperfect."[29] The most imperfect situation of all, he adds, is that in which the people are in a state of civil servitude to those who command. His illustration of this is Poland where the peasants are slaves to the nobility. Montesquieu's insistence that the aristocracy be tolerant of the poorer class is much like that expressed by Aristotle.[30] Both seem to be seeking a working stability between the two principal classes of the society.

Montesquieu's preoccupation with the roles of what I call the professional aristocracy in mixed government is quite obvious when he undertakes in Book II to describe the structure of monarchy.[31] The very first paragraph declares that there must be intermediaries with such independence of the monarch that Montesquieu chose to qualify their autonomy for the sake of the censor.[32] Immediately monarchy stands for a mixed political system, and he goes on to explain that this also means a class differentiated society. Montesquieu's remark that where there is no nobility there is no monarch and where there is no monarchy, no nobility, shows the degree to which he regards the two classes to be interdependent. The need for elites to temper the operation of monarchy is evident also in the insistence upon a depositary of laws. This, of course, is support for the *Parlement de Paris* and the limitations upon divine right monarchy for which it has come to stand in France.

The vital importance of mediating aristocracies to Montesquieu's concept of monarchy is accentuated by the structural analysis of despotism. That form of government is marked by the lack of even comparatively independent intermediaries and by the absence of a professional depositary of laws. Still more, despotism is associated with the suppression of social aristocracies or elite groups.[33]

The need for interclass tolerance is implicit throughout the discussions in Book III of the principle or special spirit needed for the different kinds of governments. The virtue required by republics is a self-restraint by those who hold supreme political power. In a democracy this would mean, among other things, respect for the upper classes. The special spirit of aristocratic republics is first said to be virtue on a smaller scale than democracy. This is a self-restraint by the few power holders, and inferentially it is a respect for the lower classes of the society. Later, in Book V, Montesquieu becomes more specific and says that the principle of aristocracy is moderation. He explains that this is a kind of "eminent virtue" and not something proceeding from indolence or pusillanimity.[34] The idea that moderation is the special spirit of aristocratic republics takes on added importance in later portions of *L'Esprit des Lois*. In Book XXIX, Montesquieu makes the spirit of moderation the final standard for any legislator. Thus, the special spirit of aristocracies becomes the spirit of mixed or natural government. This would seem to indicate, I believe, that in the early books of *L'Esprit de Lois* Montesquieu is anticipating the role of the elites in mixed government. These concern not only the administrative intermediaries and depositors of the laws, but also the mediating position of a senate in the tripartite legislature which in Book XI he calls the fundamental constitution for the assurance of political liberty by right.

The recruitment of mediating aristocrats takes the spotlight in the discussions of the principle of monarchy. The special spirit of that type of government is not the attitude of the king, nor is it that of the people generally, as it is in democracy or despotism. Rather, it is the spirit of the professional nobility. The principle of monarchy is honor and it is designed to enlist the aristocracy for mediating roles. When in this part of Book III Montesquieu finishes the preliminary explanation of why virtue is not the special spirit of monarchy and starts to explain positively what the principle is, he asserts that monarchical government presupposes a social stratification and that the strata include those of noble descent.[35] Then he connects this requirement with the need for natural motion. He says that ambition, although pernicious in a republic, has good effects in a monarchy. He draws an analogy to the motion of the universe and explains that "honor sets all the parts of the body politic in motion."[36] The importance of honor-motivated elites to monarchical government is reflected in the discussion of the principle of despotic government. Montesquieu argues that honor cannot be the principle of despotism and that, in fact, honor would be extremely dangerous there.[37] He also emphasizes the absence of value differentiation in a despotic country. Much of the analysis of both monarchy and despotism seems to be directed at the corruption of the nobility in France and the tyrannical ways of the Bourbon dynasty.

The political socialization of the aristocracy for mediating roles in mixed government seems to be the principal theme of Book IV which expressly concerns the relations that the laws of education ought to have to the principles or special spirits of the different kinds of government.

What is most striking about the book on education in *L'Esprit des Lois* is the preponderant attention given to monarchies and to the fact that even here Montesquieu does not undertake to train a monarch or a prince, as did Fortescue, More, Machiavelli, Bossuet and Fenelon. Rather, he is concerned almost exclusively with the education of the aristocracy. In this respect, *L'Esprit des Lois* may have some similarities to Plato's *Republic* and its plan for the education of a guardian class. Montesquieu is concerned here with the training and recruitment of a limited class, that is, the professional aristocracy, and he too would have them supply the rational calculation needed for political order while the people furnish the social and economic sense. But there is this difference. Montesquieu would not train the aristocracy to be rulers. Rather, he would have them prepared and reformed to be intermediaries between the king and the people. His belief that the existing French nobility could be a mediating and moderating force in government may make *L'Esprit des Lois* something of a Utopia. He recognizes that most of the nobility is not qualified and that even the professional aristocracy requires a more tolerant dedication. Of course, the French nobility did little to reform, and there was no representative assembly that might make them more tolerant or even provide them an opportunity for mediation. Yet viewed as a model, Utopian or otherwise, Montesquieu's system of mixed monarchy, with a democratic assembly and a mediating role for the aristocracy, has considerable basic similarity to those present day governments that feature a prominent chief executive, an elected bicameral legislature, and a professional bureaucracy. Montesquieu did conceive an important role for a reformed nobility but above all this was to be a mediating and moderating role. He was strongly opposed to the aristocracy ruling alone without being flanked by democratic and monarchical institutions.

The ideas presented on the training and recruitment of the nobility may explain the kind of honor needed to motivate professional elites for service in the roles of mediators and moderators. Montesquieu's ideas on the education that will develop such honor may be in part like those of Aristotle for training citizens because he aims at a practical virtue more than an intellectual one. He calls for an education that is not limited to the offerings of formal institutions. Morover, there is a deep regard here for the interrelationship of political attitudes and the character of the society. "In monarchies the principal branch of education is not taught in colleges or academies." Rather, it commences, "at our setting out in the world" because "this is the school of what we call honor, that universal preceptor which ought everywhere to be our guide." The training calls for constant emphasis upon three rules or maxims, that is, "that we should have a certain nobleness in our virtues, a kind of frankness in our morals, and a particular politeness in our behavior."[38] Montesquieu seems to be thinking of his own limited class because he remarks that these virtues "are less what we owe to others than to ourselves," and that "they are not so much what draws us toward society, as what distinguishes us from our fellow-citizens."

There are some grounds here for saying that Montesquieu resembles Machiavelli. This is evident in his unusual stress at this point upon actions that are grand and extraordinary rather than merely just and reasonable. Both tend to see politics as a noble art in which excellence of performance is a primary objective. And they are comparable in other respects. Both Montesquieu and Machiavelli tend to be humanists and both emphasize action and honor rather than subservience to established dogma. But there are also general differences. Montesquieu considers socially mixed monarchy under law to be more appropriate to France than either the meta-legal prince of Machiavelli's famous work or the republic under virtue esteemed in his *Discourses*.

The emphasis in *L'Esprit des Lois* upon nobleness, frankness, and politeness in the education of the man of honor, is another demonstration of Montesquieu's interest in political recruitment and socialization. The analysis has several modern touches even though it reflects some of the cynicism of *Les Lettres Persanes* or that of Machiavelli's *Prince*. The center of attention is the social psychology of political dynamics and the specific objective is the conditioning of the political aristocracy for the crucial role of class mediation. Montesquieu admits that honor "allows of gallantry when united with the idea of sensible affection, or with that of conquest" and admits that for this reason "we never meet with so strict a purity of morals in monarchies as in republican governments." Yet he is clear that education in monarchies should develop frankness and open carriage. "Truth is requisite only because a person habituated to veracity has an air of boldness and freedom." The aim is also politeness of behavior. "Man is a social animal formed to please in society." A person who would break the rules of decency would lose the public esteem. This mildly Machiavellian tone continues. "It is pride that renders us polite." In monarchies politeness is "naturalized" at court because of the eminence of the king. "A courtly air consists in quitting a real greatness for a borrowed one." The education is to form "a man of honor" and the "prince never ought to command a dishonorable action because this would render us incapable of serving him." Montesquieu cites particular events in verification of that proposition. For instance, "Crillon refused to assassinate the Duke of Guise but offered to fight him." Also, he refers to the case of Viscount Dorte, governor at Bayonne, who would not execute the Huguenots even though ordered by Charles IX to do so.

Montesquieu likewise calls upon the nobility to enter the military service and he has high praise for such a career. "There is nothing that honor more strongly recommends to the nobility than to serve their prince in a military capacity." It is the favorite profession of the nobility, he says, because its dangers, its success, and even its miscarriages are the road to grandeur. He remarks that "we should be at liberty either to seek or to reject employments" and that the nobility prefers this liberty even to an ample fortune. Montesquieu concludes that education must respect the three supreme laws of honor. These are "that we are permitted to set a value upon our fortune but are absolutely forbidden to set any upon our lives;" that when we are raised to a post we should never look upon ourselves as inferior to the rank we hold; and that the things which honor forbids or commands are more rigorous when there are no laws forbidding or commanding them. This emphasis upon a military career coincides with the tendency at the time of the nobility of the robe to enter the nobility of the sword.[39] In summation, the whole treatment of education in monarchies seems to be aimed at making the nobility more eager and better qualified to serve for prestige and renown rather than for gain or interest. Thus, Montesquieu would have the aristocracy provide the political rather than the economic elites for the nation.

The sharp contrast which marks the concepts of monarchy and despotism in *L'Esprit des Lois* appears also in the analysis of political education. Whereas the objective in monarchies is to raise and enoble the mind, particularly that of the aristocracy, the aim of education in despotic countries is to debase the mind. Montesquieu reiterates the thesis that even the despot needs a depraved attitude. A servile mind, he says, is appropriate for even those in power because every tyrant is at the same time a slave. "Excessive obedience supposes ignorance in the person that obeys;" and also "in him that commands, for he has no occasion to deliberate, to doubt, to reason; he has only to will." When a government is despotic, the family has an increased role, and "each home is a separate government." Education in a despotism consists chiefly in social converse and it must be very much limited; "all it does is to strike the heart with fear, and to imprint on the understanding a very simple notion of a few principles of religion." This last remark is another instance in which Montesquieu suggests that despotism uses religion to enforce its rule, and the next chapter amplifies the theme in a contrast of ancient and modern education. It points out that most ancients lived under governments that had virtue for their "principle" and that, when this was in full vigor, they performed actions which astonish "our narrow minds." Montesquieu attributes that to the absence of "contrary impressions" which could have undone their education. "In our days," he remarks, "we receive three different or contrary educations, that is, of our parents, of our master and of the world." The last reverses the ideas of the others, and, in part, this "arises from the contrast we experience between our religious and worldly engagements, a thing unknown to the ancients."[40] Here we can see his attachment to natural religion and the reasons for the bitter criticism which *L'Esprit des Lois* received from clerical writers when it was published.

The need for aristocratic elites in every kind of liberal government seems implicit in Book V when Montesquieu discusses the laws and institutions that might assure a proper political spirit. He

analyzes the relation of legislation to the special spirit of democracy, aristocracy, monarchy and despotism, but the central portion
of the book tends to have a single theme, that is, the inevitable role
of a political elite to maintain the principle of any nondespotic government. The elite is of different kinds: a senate of distinguished
elders in a democracy, the governing nobility in an aristocracy, and
professional administrators or arbiters in a monarchy. Thus, in
each of the nondespotic forms of government Montesquieu assigns
an essential function to an elite group.

With respect to democracies, he recognizes that the ideal condition of equality and frugality may not always be attainable through
his first proposal, that is, a division of lands. He makes the alternative suggestion that the established mores be preserved by a senate
of eminent, elderly men. This is saying that an aristocratic institution is necessary in a democracy to assure the proper attitude
among the people. As an observation, we can see again that the
twin ideas of supporting laws with institutions and of using one
class to limit the self-interest motives of another class are underlying themes of *L'Esprit des Lois*.

Montesquieu may be a bit vague about the identity of the senate
for preserving social virtues. He does not say expressly that the
members belong to the nobility, but he lays down qualifications
that limit them to the nobility or a comparable class. Their selection should be based upon "years, virtue, gravity and eminent services." The senators, by being exposed to public view like the statues of the gods, "must naturally inspire every family with sentiments of virtue." Yet he adds an admonishment to the senators.
"Above all, this senate must steadily adhere to the ancient institutions, and mind that the people and the magistrates never swerve
from them."[41]

The stress upon maintenance of traditional beliefs may seem to
be a change of position from previous analysis of democratic government. Before, the love of equality and frugality was considered
necessary for popular sovereignty, but now the democratic virtue
appears to be what the past has established rather than what the future might bring. "The preservation of the ancient customs is a
very considerable point in respect of mores." Montesquieu argues
that, since a corrupt people seldom perform any memorable actions
or enact laws and since most institutions are derived from those
whose mores are simple and austere, "to remind men of the ancient
customs, ordinarily brings them back to their virtue." In addition,

he says that "if by some revolution the state has happened to assume a new form, this seldom can be effected without infinite pains and labor, and hardly ever by idle and debauched persons." Even a successful revolution needs good laws, he says, reiterating that the ancient institutions ordinarily tend to reform the people's behavior, while new institutions corrupt them. "In the course of a long administration, the descent to vice is insensible; but there is no reascending to well-being without a struggle."[42] Hence, all this is evidence that Montesquieu is intent upon showing that monolithic democracy is a difficult means for the maintenance of social order and growth.

The idea of separate or distinct elites seems implicit in Montesquieu's explanation of the differences between "a senate designed to be a rule" and "the depository, as it were, of manners." The members of a legislative senate may be subject to frequent change, but the members of the senate for preserving the mores ought to be chosen for life. Such a practice, Montesquieu says, would enhance the respect for age and, inferentially, this would strengthen the respect for law and authority in general. "Nothing gives a greater force to the laws than a perfect subordination between the citizens and the magistrate." Montesquieu refers to Xenophon's distinction of Sparta and Athens on this ground, the Spartans being the more willing to obey the laws and depend upon the magistrates. Parental authority is likewise of great use in the preservation of the mores. A republic which has less coercive force in the government, he says, must supply this defect by parental authority. At Rome, the father had the power of life and death over his children, and at Sparta every father had a right to correct another man's child. "Parental authority ended at Rome with the republic. In monarchies, where such a purity of mores is not needed, they are controlled only by authority of the magistrates."[43] Accordingly, republics call for a long minority, not to extend youthful freedom but to continue duty and obligation to the parent. Moreover, parental authority may project itself beyond the immediate family to the society generally with every father over every child. Thus again Montesquieu associates republican democracy with a degree of austerity that the French would not be happy to accept.

When Montesquieu turns to laws and principle in an aristocracy, the discussion is still concerned with the relationship of the nobility and the people. In fact he assumes a mixture of aristocracy and democracy and urges that the laws reflect a spirit of moderation.

His first suggestion for aristocracy in Book V is the reduction of social inequalities, and he makes this objective the general criterion
of excellence in an aristocracy. "If the people are virtuous in an aristocracy, they enjoy very nearly the same happiness as in a popular
government, and the state grows powerful."[44] However, such a
sharing of virtue is rare when men's fortunes are unequal, so that
"the laws must tend as much as possible to infuse a spirit of moderation and endeavor to re-establish that equality which was necessarily removed by the constitution." Thus, he seems to say that the
spirit of moderation is an attitude of restraint upon the elite just as
in a democracy the love of equality and frugality are restraints
upon the people. In the earlier explanations of aristocracy and its
principle, Montesquieu indicated that the laws limit the people and
that the principle of moderation is needed to restrain the nobility.[45] Now he argues for tolerance on the part of the nobility. This,
I think, suggests that he is thinking of the qualities of that aristocracy which would serve in intermediary positions.

At this point, as well as at other times, Montesquieu seems anxious to reform the nobility in their relations with the government.
He admonishes the nobles to avoid the ostentations of a monarch.
"As the pomp and splendor with which kings are surrounded forms
a part of their power, so modesty and simplicity of manners constitute the strength of an aristocratic nobility." He asserts that when
the nobles effect no distinction, when they mix with the people,
dress like them, and share their pleasures, the people are apt to forget their subjection and weakness. Moreover, he suggests that the
nobility should assume no more privileges than those of the senate.
Montesquieu's statements here that every government has its nature
and principle and that aristocracy must not assume the qualities of
monarchy, have been interpreted to mean that the form of government is unchangeable.[46] But such a meaning is not necessary or, I
believe, even appropriate. What he is saying here is that the aristocracy should not act like kings, as some of the French nobles may
wish to do. He is telling the aristocracy to stay within its place and
not assume privileges to which they are not entitled. He argues that
"privileges ought to be for the senate, and simple respect for the
senators." Thus, even the upper house of a legislature is a collective
body, and individual nobles should restrain from adopting lofty
pretences. This is in line with his previous remarks that a monarch
is necessary for a nobility, and he implies that the presence of the
king serves to keep the aristocracy in its place.

The increasing stress upon moderation is evident also in his sharp warning against excessive inequality. The two principal sources of disorder in aristocratic governments, he says, are "excessive inequality between the governors and the governed; and the same inequality between the different members of the body that governs."[47] Hatred and jealousies arise from these two inequalities and laws ought to prevent or repress them. This again shows Montesquieu's antipathy to extremes, and it also indicates the potential role of positive laws in seeking to overcome extremes in passions and instincts. Presumably, the force of laws may alter the power of natural affections as well as be altered by such feelings. Examples of inequality between the governors and the governed in an aristocracy are the nonpayment of taxes by the nobles, fraudulent exemptions, taking public moneys, and subjecting the common people to tribute. He calls the Roman republic the ideal situation. There the magistrates received no emoluments from their office; the chief men of the republic paid taxes equally if not more heavily than the others, and they did not share in the public funds but rather bestowed freely on the people. Montesquieu asserts that the people should be convinced at least that public revenues are being well administered. He declares quite forcefully that it is "a very essential point in an aristocracy that the nobles themselves should not levy the taxes." The first order of the state in Rome left this to the second order. If the nobles themselves levied the taxes, there "would be no such thing as a superior tribunal to check their power." Thus, even aristocracy must be a mixed government. These remarks anticipate in some degree the model constitution which Montesquieu prescribes when he discusses the governments of England, ancient Germany, and Rome in Book XI. There, we will see, he places the aristocracy between the king and the people in the joint possession of legislative power.

The aim of raising the professional attitude of the nobility is evident in the way that Montesquieu lays down definite limits and duties for the aristocracy. He asserts that laws should forbid the nobles of all kinds to engage in commerce and, while this has been interpreted to mean that commerce is beneath the dignity of the nobles, Montesquieu here as elsewhere in *L'Esprit des Lois* explains that the privileges of the nobility would give them an unfair advantage over other merchants. They would have "unbounded credit" and would monopolize the trade. "Commerce is a profession of people who are upon an equality." The most miserable despotisms are those in which the prince applies himself to commerce, Montesquieu declares, pointing out that the laws of Venice debar the nobles from commerce, "by which they might even innocently acquire exorbitant wealth." Montesquieu's insistence upon a democratic attitude among the aristocracy is quite evident in this analysis. "The laws ought to employ the most effectual means for making the nobles do justice to the people." Clearly, Montesquieu seems determined that the nobility should reserve themselves for roles as professional administrators or magistrates and that they should perform such offices with tolerance and deep regard for the people generally and particularly for those engaged in economic pursuits.

Likewise, flagrant inequality among the nobles themselves may be damaging to an aristocracy. The nobility should be neither too poor nor too wealthy,[48] and they should pay their debts on time to avoid poverty. Prudent regulations may be needed to moderate the excess of wealth, but there should be no confiscations, no agrarian laws, no expunging of debts because these are productive of infinite mischief. Also, the laws should abolish the right of primogeniture among the nobles so that by the continual division of inheritance fortunes will seek a level. In general, the laws should preserve a proper harmony or union among the nobles and quarrels should be decided quickly so they do not spread into family feuds. Thus, in a variety of ways Montesquieu suggests that the aristocracy make itself more responsive to the character and responsibilities of modern society.

The discussion in Book V of the relation of laws to the principle of monarchy is still another demonstration of Montesquieu's concern with the public service of the aristocracy in mixed government. He declares that the laws "should endeavor to support the nobility in respect to whom honor may be, in some measure, deemed both child and parent." Specifically, the laws should render the nobility hereditary, "not as a boundary between the power of the prince and the weakness of the people but as the links which connect them both."[49] Presumably, the hereditary status would provide the aristocracy with the independence that they need in order to be the unifying bond of the social fabric. They require position and stability of office in order to serve as intermediaries between the king and the people, and for this there must be protection of their privileges, in respect of both person and land. "All these privileges must be peculiar to the nobility, and incommunicable to the people, unless we intend to act contrary to the principle of government, and to di-

minish the power of the nobles together with that of the people."
The function of the nobility as an intermediary between the king
and the people shows how Montesquieu conceives the interacting
relationships of the parts of the political society. It also indicates
that he has the French situation in mind.

Montesquieu, in arguing that the nobility should not engage in
commerce, was probably also endeavoring to enhance the position
and dignity of "the nobility of the robe." He was a member of this
group and at crucial points throughout *L'Esprit des Lois* brings it
into his prescriptions. The role of the Parlements, of which he was
once a member at Bordeaux,[50] is a part of his idea of structured
monarchy. The nobility of the robe might also contribute the intermediaries called for in monarchical administration.

The position of the French nobility, and particularly their civil
and military roles, during 1715 to 1748, is the subject of Franklin L.
Ford's scholarly work on *The Robe and Sword*.[51] The nobility of
the robe, he reports, were about one percent of the total nobility of
roughly two hundred thousand.[52] I would say that they were probably the best educated professional group in France and, after the
death of Louis XIV in 1715, they gradually gained the leadership of
the French nobility. Their principal opposition was from the
peerage, but by midcentury their leadership generally was recognized by the monarchy.[53] The absence of the Estates General accentuated their power but also narrowed their outlook, and they did
more to preserve the feudal-like privileges of the nobility[54] than to
mediate between the king and the people as Montesquieu prescribes
at several points throughout *L'Esprit des Lois*. The sovereign courts
which they occupied had administrative as well as judicial functions, and Montesquieu may have intended that the nobility of the
robe would be the administrative or executive intermediaries which
he considers vital to a proper monarchy. Undoubtedly, he did not
have in mind the *Intendants* which Louis XIV had developed as his
special executors of authority. What Montesquieu wanted was a
body of capable nobles who had independence of the king. The last
two books of *L'Esprit des Lois* argue that the French nobility had a
right to be independent of the monarch.

Clearly, Montesquieu was not thinking of all of the nobility, nor
the peerage, nor the indolent nobility of prestige who clustered
around the king at Versailles. He was thinking of a highly
educated, professionally experienced nobility who could hold judicial and administrative positions in the central and provincial gov-

ernments. This is evident, as noted in Chapter III, from his remarks in Book XX on the exclusion of the nobility from commerce. There he says that in France, the dignity of the long robe places those who wear it between "the great nobility and the people." Their service as the depositary of the laws, he says, gives them glory while privately they are "in a mediocrity of fortune."[55] Here, he does not say that they have hereditary privileges but rather describes their dignity to be "but by a superior capacity and virtue." Montesquieu's idea that the nobility should eschew commerce would seem to mean that the aristocracy of the robe should concentrate upon judicial and administrative functions for the state and thus increase its distinction and excellence in those professional activities. Their hereditary and propertied independence would enable them to be a better qualified and a more stable group than officials otherwise selected. The condition of education at the time was such that only among the nobility was there any assurance of finding an educated group of sufficient numbers to fill the professional ranks of the government. The nobility of the robe was the professional elite of his day, and Montesquieu suggests that this group should be inspired by honor and intellectual distinction to devote itself to the judicial and administrative functions of the state. He does recognize that there is another career by which they might obtain honor and distinction. This is the nobility of the sword or, as he says, "the warlike nobility." Many in the ranks of the robe had entered that of the sword during Montesquieu's time.[56] The roles of these elite groups, he points out, "have necessarily contributed to augment the grandeur of this kingdom."

An understanding of Montesquieu's ideas on the political role of the aristocracy requires at least two basic distinctions. One is the difference between the nobility generally and the professional nobility, and the other is the difference between the actual performance of the French nobility of the robe and the function envisioned by Montesquieu for a professional nobility. His solution to the old problem of government degenerating into either tyranny or anarchy, noted by Pascal and others and by himself in *Les Lettres Persanes*, is a three class government with mediation by a comparatively independent professional aristocracy. In the France of his time, only the nobility of the robe could have furnished such an elite, but for this role they would need to have greater dedication and tolerance as well as restraint by the democratic influence of a representative assembly. These developments did not come to

France in the decades ahead and the nobility became even less inclined to think of other classes. But Montesquieu is not simply a spokesman for a feudal minded aristocracy, as Ford seems to imply.[57] What Montesquieu drew out of French history were the elements of modern constitutional government. Clearly, France would have fared much better if the pre-revolutionary decades had brought into being a national assembly and a reformed nobility, which Montesquieu prescribes, to limit and moderate the monarchical rule.

The Approaches To Mixed Monarchy

Why I believe that the analyses of governmental types in the first portion of *L'Esprit des Lois* (Books II–X) is fundamentally a study of social classes and the foundation for mixed government, will be summarized in this section.

In Book II Montesquieu starts with a few types of government and his definitions of republics, monarchies, despotisms, democracies, and aristocracies, look like a familiar exercise of classical political thought. But his typology of political systems is neither as symmetrical nor as complete as those presented by many other theorists. Moreover, the way that he develops special meanings and hybrid applications suggests that he has something else in mind than the mere categorization of different kinds of government. True, he uses traditional names, and to some degree these terms control the substance of the explanation as well as the form of presentation. Nevertheless, the peculiarity of his definitions and the diversity of the meta-political areas to which he applies the method of comparative analysis make me think that he is intent upon building up ideas and propositions other than the mere classification of governmental types.

Whether we consider that he starts with three, four, or five basic types — and this choice in itself shows that there is something hidden at work — there is no simple classificatory symmetry to the presentation. In the initial three types, monarchy and despotism appear to be good and bad types of the rule by one. But this leaves republics to stand for all other kinds of government, which clearly is an unbalance if not an inaccuracy. When republics are divided into democracies and aristocracies, there is some recognition of the traditional division of the few and many, but still the only distinction between good and bad applies to merely the rule by one. Eventually, I believe, monarchy and despotism stand for all kinds of good and bad government, respectively. In the process, as I will try to explain, democracy and aristocracy become elements of mixed monarchy, and despotisms stand for any single-class government. The factors that lead me to such conclusions will be discussed in the following paragraphs.

First, let us look at the fourfold typology of democracy, aristocracy, monarchy, and despotism, which is probably the closest that Montesquieu comes to the classical pattern of three good and three bad types. Here, he clearly is not concerned with merely the rule by one, few, or many, nor merely with the simple test, evident in Plato's *Statesman* as well as in Aristotle, Polybius and Cicero, of whether the rulers are motivated by the common good or by their own interest. There is no single criterion or even any single set of criteria which he uses to differentiate the four types of government. The inquiries into democratic and aristocratic republics deal with one set of problems while the investigation of monarchy and despotism involves another set of issues. Then other unique lines appear. Despotism is the only type of bad government, and its deficiencies are not only a disregard for the common good and the customary law but also a lack of institutional diversity and the failure to respect the privileges and interests of social classes. The typology of governments in *L'Esprit des Lois* is unusual also for the way in which the aristocracy becomes involved in the description of every category. Democracy needs aristocrats for magistrates and senators. Monarchy needs qualified nobles to be administrative intermediaries and the depositary of laws. But simple aristocracy is frowned upon. When the nobility disregard the laws or, like the Decemvirs of Rome, seize all power, there is a despotism despite the numbers holding the power.[58]

Another peculiar feature of the descriptions of governmental structure in *L'Esprit des Lois* is the unbalanced character of the analyses of the particular types. The explanation of democracy and aristocracy concerns mostly the means of control through legislative and electoral power while that of monarchy relates to modes of action. Specifically, the scope of democratic processes is much limited; the people must leave administrative functions to elite magistrates and even the legislative power may be exercised in part by a senate. For aristocracy, Montesquieu abhors a compact, all-powerful small group, which other theorists often call oligarchy, and he prefers such size in the aristocratic class that a separate political elite will emerge. Also in monarchy, administration is to be through an independent and capable nobility and the door seems to be left open for democratic and aristocratic participation in the legislative process. One of the striking things of Montesquieu's classification of governments is the promptness with which he defines monarchy to be a class structured operation.

The intermixture of the nondespotic forms of government in L'Esprit des Lois raises a number of possibilities about Montesquieu's objectives in his description of the kinds of government. Cassirer has suggested that Montesquieu was describing ideal types.[59] This would seem to be true only of despotism. Occasionally, it might be true of democracy or aristocracy. Montesquieu tends to be conceptualistic of what he dislikes. He disfavors despotism consistently because it is virtually always simple, unmixed government. Democracy and aristocracy are simple forms only at certain times. His monarchy rarely is. The explanations of the structure of democracy, aristocracy, and monarchy rather quickly turn from any possibility of ideal types to qualified, mixed patterns. Democracy is first defined to mean legislative supremacy in the people but it is quickly limited by placing the executive authority beyond the reach of the common people and by imposing a senate with at least short run authority. Aristocracy rather quickly calls for a division of authority between two levels of nobility. Monarchy is characterized by the limitations upon the actions of the king and the distribution of authority to the nobility. There may be a few occasions when democracy or aristocracy are unmixed, but in those instances Montesquieu considers it to be an undesirable extreme. Ideal types would seem to mean simple forms and the whole of L'Esprit des Lois is an argument for government that combines a multiplicity of forces and attitudes.

Above all, the classification of different kinds of government is not an end in itself. Its objective is not simply to categorize political systems. Rather, I believe that it shows the undesirable character of any simple form of government in which a single class is supreme. Indirectly, it suggests the advantage of a mixed form of government which takes into account the various forces at work in a national society. Montesquieu seems impelled by a gnawing desire to be done with the simple matter of defining and explaining particular types of government and to get on with the portrayal of the challenging interrelationships of diverse forces of a sociological and psychological character.

The underlying interest in mixed government is evident in a number of ways. For one thing each one of democracy, aristocracy, or monarchy is explained to need some element of a contrasting type. This development is accentuated by the persistence with which despotism remains a pure type of unmixed rule. Both monarchy and despotism are first defined to be rule by one, but shortly monarchy loses this character while despotism persistently retains its one-man, one-view posture. Monarchy is soon held to require more or less independent intermediaries between the king and the people while despotism is characterized by the indivisibility of authority and the grant of complete power to a tyrannical vizier.[60] Even more, monarchy must have privileged classes while despotism concentrates right as well as power in one person. In *Les Lettres Persanes* the only types of government are monarchy and republics, and the descriptions of the former often stress its despotic potentials.[61] But *L'Esprit des Lois* divides rule by one into monarchy and despotism, and all or most of the undesirable aspects of royalty are associated with despotism, thus leaving to monarchy the more glorious and noble ways of doing things. In addition, monarchy is made to share executive and administrative power with certain autonomous nobles and to leave judicial functions largely to aristocratic professionals. Moreover, the system leaves place for a joint legislative institution including the nobles and the people. Such a tripartite arrangement is proposed expressly in Book XI.

The explanations of aristocratic and democratic republics also involve a distinction between pure types and mixed ones even though the differentiations are much less clear. In fact, each term is used for both a simple and a complex pattern. The discussions of republics most frequently concern the classical ones of Athens, Sparta, and Rome, but sometimes they refer to the contemporary ones of Europe. Most of these have both aristocratic and democratic features and a few include chief magistracies. Occasionally aristocracy is conceived to be simply government by the few. The extreme example is the Decemvirs of Rome, which Montesquieu repeatedly condemns. The explanations of democracy may also assume a mixed form. In the examples of that form the executive authority usually is exercised by one or a few, and at times there is acknowledgement of a senate of aristocrats. In fact, democracy is generally mixed and the only time it is conceived in an unqualified condition is during the discussion of the special spirit needed by democracies. Then, he assumes that the people possess a single collective will and all other forces are excluded. A political system in which the people arrogate all power unto themselves is described in Book VIII to be a corruption of the democratic principle. Thus, even in the analysis of republics, Montesquieu condemns the concentration of authority. He says in effect that any single class government, that is, where only one class possesses political power, is a despotism, whether that class is the one, the few, or the many.

The idea that each kind of government requires a particular psychological attitude among the people or a certain group is another demonstration of the limitations of single-class political systems. What Montesquieu calls principle is not the spirit or attitude which actually exists in the respective kind of government but rather is that disposition which is needed if the type of political system is to be effective and successful. There is a special spirit required for each type of government, and even the general attributes of the various principles differ from situation to situation. With respect to one form of government, it may concern some of the people while for others it affects all; again, it may be a restraining attitude or an activating one; it may come at the top, at the middle, or at the bottom of the political system, depending upon the kind of government involved. In republics, virtue means a self-imposed restraint by the people or the class holding the supreme political power. This is further identified in democracies to be the love of equality and frugality and in aristocracies to be moderation. The required special spirit in monarchies, i.e. honor, I believe, is designed to inspire professional aristocrats to perform patriotic service in maintaining the social structure and spirit. For despotisms, the principle is fear and this is needed to keep the subjects obedient to arbitrary rule. These are the attitudes which must exist for the particular type of government to be effective. Or we may say that success is proportionate to the existence of the respective attitude.

Books IV and V provide further evidence that the comparative analysis prepares the way for mixed government. The book on education is concerned with the political socialization of the different classes, particularly the aristocracy, in its roles of mediator and moderator. Then Book V does much to make any kind of single-class government appear unattractive. It portrays the unpleasant austerity which simple democracy would need for successful operation, and it dramatizes from a number of approaches, the fear needed to make despotism effective. In contrast, it casts favorable light upon governments that embody some appreciable degree of class tolerance, suggesting that democracy should not remove all in-

equality and that aristocracy should undertake some measures to reduce social inequality.

The dangers of simple political systems are particularly evident
in several parts of the book (VI) on civil laws, criminal judge-
ments, and penal methods. Here Montesquieu clearly shows his antagonism to the summary, arbitrary way of judging that is often associated with despotic government, and he expresses his sympathy
for the deliberate, regularized procedures which tend to accompany
multi-class societies and mixed political systems. He defends at some
length the complex and even slow-moving processes of a judicial
system that respects class privileges and established rules of procedure. His emphasis upon the judiciary in this book may reflect the
attitude in one of his notes on his travels in England. He remarks
that, when he goes to a country, "I do not examine whether there
are good laws, but whether there is execution of those that exist, because there are good laws everywhere."[62] This may explain the considerable attention which he gives to the mode of operation
through the many-faceted contrast of monarchy and despotism. It
also suggests that mere separation of executive or judicial power is
not sufficient to assure liberty or justice. There must be laws to
guide these powers, but there must also be controls to assure that
the laws are being applied. When Montesquieu proposes a tripartite legislature in Book XI he prescribes also that the representative
assembly should have authority to review the executive branch in
order to assure that the laws are being administered as they should
be.[63] Thus, he does not assume, as some commentators suggest,
that legislation in itself controls execution and adjudication.[64]

The limitations of single-class government appear also in the
books (VII, VIII) on the relations of political laws and spirit to
economic, domestic, and geographic factors. Economically, republics are associated with frugality and monarchies with luxury. The
frugality here may concern trading more than consuming and thus
relate to commercial aristocracies more than to popular sovereignty.
Then, on the condition of women, monarchies allow moderate freedom, republics necessitate moral restrictions while despotisms make
a commodity of women. Finally, in the matter of geographical size,
Montesquieu lays down the familiar proposition that republics
need to be small, monarchies medium-sized, and despotisms may be
large. The division of governmental functions between the central
authority and the provincial societies would be a logical consequence of the confederate republic proposed in Book IX, and it

may also be implicit in the analysis of economic forces in Book VII. In the second idea Montesquieu seems to indicate that the constituent cities and provinces should be republics with a substantial degree of autonomy while the central authority is monarchical. This may mean a rather loose relationship characteristic of a commonwealth of nations or a confederation of republics. The discussion in Book IX frowns upon a mixture of monarchies and republics for the constituent states, but it does not exclude the idea of a central monarchy along with constituent republics. The geographical distribution of political authority could be another approach to the recognition of class differentiation because municipal and regional institutions are likely to have interests and viewpoints which differ from those of a central authority, particularly when the latter is monarchical.

The various explanations in this portion of *L'Esprit des Lois* of the natural relations of laws to the structure and spirit of government in the differing legal, cultural, economic, and geographical situations, provide further evidence that the underlying logic of Montesquieu's theory of government is what this study calls "relational pluralism." The full scope of this doctrine covers the whole of *L'Esprit des Lois,* but even the limited subject matter of the first portion of the volume demonstrates the ways in which legislation should take into account the dynamic interrelationship of political law and the sociological and psychological forces which affect the internal and external character of a national society.

Montesquieu's characterization of various kinds of government is noteworthy also for the value placed upon social class differentiation. Democracy and aristocracy are distinguished by the class location of the supreme power. The concept of monarchy clearly goes to the heart of class conflict. Montesquieu much prefers the *thèse nobiliare* to the *thèse royale* but not in an absolute sense, and he actually combines the two. For him, monarchy as well as democracy should allocate certain executive functions to the aristocracy. The distribution of authority among classes tends to make these types of government good and acceptable. Despotism comes when there is no political power in the few and the many. The despot and his vizier are in a class by themselves, and all others are subject to political servitude. On the basis of these analyses, the general conclusion seems to be that any good form of government in Montesquieu's scheme of things necessarily recognizes and supports a substantial degree of power in each of the three classes.

In fact, Montesquieu tends to make democracy, aristocracy, and
monarchy stand for political classes even more than types of government. The analysis of democracy is an explanation of the participation of the commonalty, that of aristocracy describes the role of
the nobility, and that of monarchy explains the limited contribution of the king. Each class has a partial and an interdependent
role. There may be times when Montesquieu portrays the different
types as if they were whole governments, but more frequently he describes them to be potential parts of a mixed government. He is arguing that France by its nature is not meant for despotism and that
it should have the socially based institutions which go with its natural situation. Clearly Montesquieu is never really satisfied with
pure and simple types of government, and his evaluations of governmental form come down to the simple issue of whether a government is well mixed or not. What are to be mixed include certain elements of monarchy, aristocracy, and democracy. Each of these
types is acceptable insofar as it can become a part of a government
which embraces all three. Despotism is bad because it is the complete absence of mixed government with no distribution of power
among autonomous social classes or their representatives. When
Montesquieu speaks of monarchy, aristocracy, and democracy, he
has in mind not so much the rule by one, few, or many, but rather
the role of the one, the few, and the many, in modern government.

Accordingly, the comparative analysis in the first portion of *L'Esprit des Lois* serves less to define particular kinds of government
than to identify the capabilities and responsibilities of different political classes. The explanation of democracy, aristocracy, and monarchy indicates the kind of political activity which lies within the capacity and inclination of the many, the few, and the one, respectively. The discussions of democratic and aristocratic republics
focus upon the role of the people or a part of the people in the control of government by legislation and election of magistrates, while
the discussion of monarchy and despotisms concentrates upon executive, judicial, and administrative modes of application. The explication of different kinds of government turns promptly to the assignment of political functions and roles according to class identity.
The opening statement that a democracy exists when the people
possess the supreme power immediately acknowledges that while
the people are sovereign in some respects they are the subject in
other matters. Later, this is amplified by the declaration that the
things which exceed the abilities of the people must be conducted

by the ministers. The people are said to be well qualified to choose the magistrates and call them to account, but they are incapable of conducting the administration themselves. Montesquieu is speaking about the people in a collective arrangement. He observes that the people act either too slowly or too abruptly. This would seem to concern a public assembly and could not be true of every individual in the general class of citizens. The most striking observation in this analysis is that "in a popular state the inhabitants are divided into certain classes."[65] Montesquieu then refers to the division of Rome into six classes of varying wealth, among which votes were allocated on such basis that "it was property rather than numbers that decided the election." Even clearer is the reference to Solon's segregation of the Athenians into four classes and the exclusion of the poorest class from the magistracies.

A recurring theme in *L'Esprit des Lois* is the effort to cast the aristocracy in an ameliorating role. The analysis of democracy recognizes the need of aristocrats in a senate and in many administrative and judicial positions. The description of monarchy promptly calls for administrative intermediaries drawn from the nobility so that there is virtually a joint holding of executive authority. Then the recommendations that judges have professional training and moderate attitudes tends to limit judicial positions to the nobility of the robe. Thus, qualified elites are given a key position in every area of government. This is done not merely to permit them to safeguard their own privileges but even more because they more likely to have the necessary professional training and the semi-independence needed to impose operating limitations upon the monarch and to arbitrate or adjust rationally between the king and the people. Even when discussing aristocracies, Montesquieu urges the nobility to take a tolerant attitude toward the people generally and above all not to act like kings. Moreover, he prefers a large nobility and one which governs through representatives or selected officials so that there is within the nobility a conflict of the governing elite and the social elite. All of these suggestions tend toward a more restrained and tolerant attitude, away from the despotisms of the much condemned Roman Decemvirs.

While the aristocracy is given central roles in both democracy and monarchy, it is placed under restrictions in both forms of government. One implicit limitation is its responsibility to established professional standards. This is most evident in respect of the judiciary, but it has some application to their role as administrative intermediaries. The elites are to act in accordance with established laws and procedure and to consider the sociological consequences upon the community and the psychological situations of the individuals under trial. The role of the aristocracy is restrained also by its division into legislative, executive, administrative, and judicial areas. The specific discussion of separation of powers comes with Book XI but it is assumed throughout much of the earlier portion of the volume. Yet it is meaningful only with respect to the aristocracy and has little applicability to the king or the general populace. The king is necesasrily a unity and officially the people act only in a collective manner, such as voting in an election.

On the face of things Montesquieu may seem to make aristocratic participation a limitation upon monarchy but more fundamentally and more thoroughly he makes monarchical participation a limitation upon the professional aristocracy. The immediate exercise of governmental authority rests primarily and largely with the aristocracy. To prevent aristocracy from becoming despotic it is limited in a number of general ways. For one thing, it is to be flanked by the king and the people, both in the general scheme of things and in the legislative institution. This last is prescribed later, particularly in Book XI, but the general idea that the aristocracy should occupy some kind of mediating position between the monarch and the populace is evident throughout the early portion of the volume and continues to the end. The nobility is admonished to be more democratic and to seek less inequality among its own ranks. On the other side, Montesquieu insists that there must be a monarch to keep the aristocracy from acting like kings. Also, the monarch may provide a sense of unity and a symbol of national purpose. With these conditions, Montesquieu brings the aristocracy into his scheme of government to act as mediators between the king and the people and thus avoid the irreconcilable conflict portrayed in *Les Lettres Persanes*.

The foregoing discussions have indicated that the comparative analysis of the different kinds of governmental structure in Books II — X becomes increasingly meaningful when it is considered to be preparatory to the subsequent analysis of mixed government. Likewise, the comparative analysis of the principle or special spirit of different kinds of government investigates indirectly the underlying correspondence between the pattern of political classes and the set of psychological attitudes which enter into a system of natural government. Montesquieu attempts to solve the problem raised in *Les Lettres Persanes* on the irreconcilability of prince and people but he does not propose any simple psychological solution. He is scornful of Aristotle's idea that the rule of one is good or bad according to the attitude of the monarch toward the general interest. Likewise, he does not rest all upon an attitude of benevolence or enlightenment in the manner of Voltaire and certain other contemporary *philosophes*. Rather, Montesquieu assumes that neither the prince nor the people can be counted upon to limit and restrain themselves in the manner necessary for a pure form of either government by one or government by many. Thus, psychologically, government must be something more than princely authority or popular will. Montesquieu suggests at a number of points the use of reformed aristocrats in the administrative, executive, judicial, and legislative areas of government, not to rule but to mediate. Likewise, his definitions of both the spirit of the laws and the general spirit of a nation bring home to the legislators and other political decision makers that government should be relevant to a whole host of sociological forces and their net total psychological impact.

The class differentials presupposed throughout *L'Esprit des Lois* may provide a means of dealing with the conflict of sense and reason in the field of political behavior. Montesquieu considers the great merits of the individual to be his natural inclination for productive activity and his overriding moral sense. Likewise, Montesquieu assumes that the principal interest of most people is economic and cultural rather than political. The time and effort required by these primary endeavors would seem to leave the ordinary man little opportunity for thinking out the regulations needed for political order. This last function Montesquieu makes the immediate responsibility of a comparative few, implicitly within the moral sense limitations imposed by the people through elections or representation. Thus, the bulk of society is free most of the time for cultural and economic pursuits. Their collective moral sense is an appropriate control for the few engaged in political reason because, for another matter, sense is generally broader than reason.

By and large, *L'Esprit des Lois* as well as *Les Lettres Persanes* assumes that the people may prefer to live, like the latter-day Troglodytes, under reasonable laws handed down by a king than to take time and effort to formulate and impose restrictions upon themselves. Much of the first portion of *L'Esprit des Lois* seems to say that, while the people have the capacity for political reason, they prefer to use their reason elsewhere. The political faculty which best fits the people generally seems to be the expression of sense and interest while they are applying deliberate reason in economic and cultural activity. Appropriately, then, the function of laying down political restraints, regulations, and accommodations is for another group or class. Clearly, for Montesquieu this is the responsibility of the professional aristocracy and he imposes greater limitations upon that class than upon the people generally. The arrangement may be what Montesquieu had in mind when he remarked that the people generally may act appropriately out of interest and may form factious groups. These remarks also indicate that political example is the special responsibility of an aristocratic group. Montesquieu asserts that it should be a fundamental law of democracy that, when the people give their suffrages, they ought to be public. "The lower class," he says, "ought to be directed by those of higher rank, and restrained within bounds by the gravity of eminent personages." For historical support, he claims that "by rendering the suffrages secret in the Roman republic, all was lost." However, when the nobles vote in an aristocracy, or in the senate of a democracy, "the suffrages cannot be too secret." His argument for this involves a distinction between political relations among the aristocrats and those among the people generally. "Intrigue in a senate is dangerous; it is dangerous also in a body of nobles, but not so among the people, whose nature is to act through passion."[66] The misfortune of a republic, he declares, is when intrigues are at an end. This happens when the people are corrupted by bribery because, he says, they grow indifferent to public affairs, and avarice becomes their predominant passion. Thus, the people generally are to be reconciled in their conflicts of interest by the detached action of the aristocracy, acting in the capacity of administrative and judicial mediators with a spirit of moderation.[67]

The emphasis upon noble activity within the society is evident in the analysis of the principle or moving spirit of monarchy. The honor which Montesquieu considers necessary to the effectiveness of that form of government is primarily a means of inspiring the nobility to provide meritorious public service. He asserts that honor in a monarchy "is capable of inspiring the most glorious actions and, joined with the force of laws, may lead us to the end of government as well as virtue itself."[68] Montesquieu also says that a monarch gains followers by the favors that he grants. These ambitions for riches and honors are the passions of the strong, and they are a necessary part of the life of the community; otherwise, "the state would be in the condition of a man weakened by sickness, who is without passions because he is without strength."[69] Passions are essential to the life of a free people — this is an assertion of Montesquieu for which there is a parallel in Madison's analysis of the nature of factions in the tenth essay of *The Federalist*.[70]

The most fundamental differentiation among psychological attitudes throughout *L'Esprit des Lois* is probably that which makes the three general political classes of one, few, and many, stand for political will, political reason, and political sense, respectively. These distinctions are more implicit than express. Yet there are instances in which Montesquieu associates reason with the few and sense with the many and this would seem to be a general assumption in much of his work. In other words, the few are to supply rational deliberation in the ordering of a competitive society while the many are to supply the spontaneous and interest driven activity of an economically progressing society. This does not mean that the king or the people lack reason but rather that in the operation of the political society the peculiar faculty of the monarch is his expression of the will of the state, while the people provide the interest drive and the common sense. The people furnish most of the economic activity, and they exercise reason in these occupational endeavors and in respect of their family. In political affairs, their moral sense provides the general lines of control, but the deliberate and specific operations rest with aristocratic classes. This view assumes that reason is a detailed, calculative process and that the natural sense of the people generally is sufficiently moral so that it keeps collective conduct within reasonable limits. The limited role of the people in direct political activity is not because they lacked the potential talent but rather because of their preoccupation with economic matters and because of the primary importance of economic activity.[71]

In summation, there seem to be several underlying principles in *L'Esprit des Lois*: that economics is for the many and politics for the few; that the many have little time for direct, individual participation in political action; that the many should participate largely by collective and indirect means; that the people generally have sufficient natural moral sense to provide a sound general direction to the political system; and that sense, being more comprehensive than reason, is more appropriate than reason for the general direction of government. Accordingly, the natural and effective relationship of the people and the aristocracy is for the former to control by use of their sense and for the latter to administer by use of their reason.

With this allocation of political faculties between the few and the many, the role of the one is primarily that of being the political will. Montesquieu does not reduce the monarch to the role of ceremonial will, but he considerably limits royal functions in that direction. The insistence upon a monarch for the expression of political will serves strongly to limit the aristocracy and to prevent them from acting as kings. Finally, the central, single will furnishes an object of attachment which strengthens the image of a single purpose and a single object of achievement for the political society.

Notes

1. *L'Esprit des Lois* (hereafter referred to as *Lois*) XIX, 27; XX, 7, 12, 14, 21, 22; XXII, 10. See discussion in Chapter III, third section of this study.

2. See for instance, Abbé Joseph de la Porte, *Observations sur L'Esprit des Loix, ou l'art de lire ce livre, de l'entendre et d'en juger* (Amsterdam, 1751), 47, 53, 121-7.

3. Plato, *Republic*, VIII; Aristotle: *Politics;* V, ix, 1310 a, VII, vii, 1328 a.

4. The objectives of education in Plato's theory have been stated as first, state unity, and then virtue or civil efficiency, Frederick Eby and C. F. Arrowood, *The History and Philosophy of Education Ancient and Medieval* (Englewood Cliffs, N. J., 1940), 367, 369.

5. Roger Caillois, *Oeuvres Complètes de Montesquieu*, (hereafter referred to as Caillois, I or II) (Paris, 1951), II, 57, 58,. The *Essai sur les Causes qui Peuvent Affect les Esprits et les Caractères* was written between 1736 and 1744 but not published until 1892; see Robert Shackleton, *Montesquieu A Critical Biography* (Oxford, 1961), 314, 315, 406.

6. "Let none say that every one will succeed better in his profession when he cannot change it for another. I say that a person will succeed best when those who have excelled hope to rise to another." *Lois,* XX, 22.

7. *Lois,* IV, 1.
8. *Ibid.,* IV, 5.
9. *Ibid.*
10. *Ibid.,* III, 3; IV, 2, 4, 5, 6; V, 2 − 5, 7, 9; XIV, 1.
11. *Ibid.,* IV, 7.
12. *Ibid.,* V, 2.
13. *Considerations sur les Causes de la Grandeur des Romans et de leur Decadence,* IV; Caillois, II, 85.
14. *Lois,* V, 2.
15. Abbé de la Porte, *op. cit.,* 53.
16. *Lois,* V, 3.
17. *Ibid.,* V, 4.
18. *Ibid.,* V, 5. Bodin also refers to the use by classical legislators of the equal division of lands as a means of avoiding revolutionary conflict between the rich and the poor. However, Bodin rejects the device as too disturbing to the established order, Jean Bodin, *Six Books on the Commonwealth,* abridged and translated by M. J. Tooley (Oxford, Blackwell) 158-161.
19. *Lois,* V, 6.
20. *Les Lettres Persanes* (hereafter referred to as L.P., (X − XIV)
21. *L.P.,* XI, XVII, XXXIII, LII, LXXXIII.
22. The tendency to look upon the self-governing privileges of democracy as those of the group with little distinction between the individual and the society seems to have been fairly common among theorists of the seventeenth and eighteenth centuries; see generally, A. J. Carlyle, *Political Liberty,* (Oxford, 1941), Rousseau's "general will" likewise would seem to involve the identity of the individual and the community. This tendency probably arose from the attention focused upon the distinction between state and society rather than upon that between society and the individual. The theorists favoring a free society may have identified the individual and the society to such an extent

that they assumed an individual would not be restrained or coerced by what is done by the collective of which he is a member.

23.   *Lois,* VIII, 2 (Par. 1).

24.   *Ibid.,* VIII, 2 (Par. 7), (Author's translation).

25.   *Ibid.,* VIII, 3. (Author's translation).

26.   *Ibid.*

27.   *Ibid.,* II, 3.

28.   A letter published by the *Journal de Trévoux* during the month of April 1749 asserts that only 9,000 qualified under the 2,000 drachma rule, and that 22,000 did not. Montesquieu's response appended to the *Defense de L'Esprit des Lois* is that the 22,000 persons mentioned by Diodorus were those sent to Thrace. Perhaps most important is Montesquieu's final remark that the words *grand* and *petit* are relative and that 9,000 *souverains* is an immense number while 22,000 *sujets* is an infinitely small one. Caillois, II, 1170-1.

29.   *Lois,* II, 3 (Par. 10).

30.   Aristotle, *Politics,* V, vi, 1305a, b; V, viii, 1308a.

31.   *Lois,* II, 4.

32.   See Robert Shackleton, *Montesquieu A Critical Biography* (Oxford, 1961), 278-9; see discussion in Chapter IV of this study.

33.   *Lois,* II, 5; III, 9; IV, 3; VI, 1, 2.

34.   *Ibid.,* III, 4.

35.   *Ibid.,* III, 5.

36.   *Ibid.,* III, 7, 8.

37.   *Ibid.,* III, 9.

38.   *Ibid.,* IV, 2.

39.   *Ibid.,* IV, 4; XX, 22.

40.   *Ibid.,* IV, 3, 4.

41.   *Ibid.,* V, 7.

42.   *Ibid.,* V, 7 (Author's translation).

43.   *Ibid.,* (Author's translation).

44.   *Ibid.,* V, 8.

45.   *Ibid.,* III, 4.

46.   *Lois,* V, 8. One commentator interprets the cited statements to mean that Montesquieu seeks the continued preservation of the particular existing form of government, C. E. Vaughan, *Studies in the History of Political Philosophy Before and After Rousseau* (New York, 1960), I, 266. This conclusion is difficult to reconcile with other statements, such as the one in the work on the Romans, that, when Rome reached a high point in expansion, there was necessity of changing the form of government if Rome was to meet its new and enlarged responsibilities. *Romains.* XVIII; Caillois, II, 173. The assertion in the cited paragraph that an aristocracy should not assume the nature and principle of monarchy seems to be either a truism or an admission that nature and principle do not determine the species of government. If the nature and principle do determine the form of goveernment, then it would be impossible logically for aristocracy to have the nature and principle of monarchy. On the other hand, if aristocracy could possibly have the nature and principle of monarchy, then something other than nature and principle, such as the non-political causes of national spirit, logically must be the determinants of the form of government. Montesquieu probably does not think in so rigidly logical a manner. What he probably intends to say is that the nature and principle of a government should harmonize with the social forces and vice versa, and that in the situation under discussion the nobility

should act like senators and not like kings. The idea that nature and principle should be socially relevant seems more likely to be Montesquieu's intention than the idea that nature and principle should never be changed.

47. *Lois,* V, 8.

48. "There are two very pernicious things in an aristocracy — excess either of poverty or of wealth in the nobility. To moderate the excess of wealth, prudent and gradual regulations should be made." *Lois,* V, 8.

49. *Lois,* V, 9.

50. For Montesquieu's views on the *Parlements,* see Shackleton, *op. cit.,* 279-281.

51. Franklin L. Ford, *Robe and Sword The Regrouping of the French Aristocracy After Louis XIV* (Cambridge, Mass., 1962).

52. *Ibid.,* 27, 247.

53. *Ibid.,* 248.

54 *Ibid.,* 251.

55. *Lois,* XX, 22.

56. Ford, *op. cit.,* 68, 138.

57. *Ibid.,* 251. Ford indicates that Montesquieu was more influenced by feudal influences than by the parliamentary ones.

58. *Lois,* VI, 15; VIII, 5; XII, 13, 21.

59. Ernst Cassirer, *The Philosophy of the Enlightenment,* (Princeton, 1951) 210. But there is strong comment to the contrary. "It would be an illicit exaggeration to say that M. de la Brede has anticipated Weber's concept of ideal type." Werner Stark, *Montesquieu, Pioneer of the Sociology of Knowledge* (London, 1960), 69.

60. *Lois,* II, 4, 5.

61. *L.P.,* XIX, XXIV, XXXVII, LI, LXXX, CII, CIV, CXLVI.

62. Caillois, I 879.

63. *Lois,* XI, 6.

64. Montesquieu's emphasis upon the need for consistent enforcement and his concern for established judicial procedure, *Lois,* VI, XII, would seem to refute the remark of Justice Holmes that "Montesquieu had a possibly exaggerated belief in the power of legislation, and an equally strong conviction of the reality of abstract justice." Max Lerner (Ed.) *The Mind and Faith of Justice Holmes* (New York, 1954) 381. Montesquieu as well as Justice Holmes favored the empirical law building of the courts and he is equally if not more sympathetic to the civil law which is primarily the product of the judiciary.

65. *Lois,* II, 2.

66. *Ibid.,* II, 2 (Par. 26, 27).

67. Repeatedly Montesquieu pictures the nobility to be the potential agency of moderation, *Lois,* III, 4; V, 8; VIII, 5.

68. *Lois,* III, 6.

69. *Ibid.,* III, 7.

70. A case could be built for the proposition that Montesquieu recognized the controlling force of a diversity of factions. This would seem to be a logical derivative from his basic ideas of social interaction, his admonition that legislation agree with the inclinations of the people, and his explanation of the diverse forces which enter into the general spirit of a nation.

71. See *Lois,* VI, XX, XXI; see also Chapter III, third section, of this study.

Chapter VI

The Liberty of the Citizen

The underlying continuity of *L'Esprit des Lois* in explaining the elements of a natural political system takes on a new facade at the start of Book XI. The previous books concern the nature and principle of government while the next three (XI — XIII) deal expressly with liberty. There still is the search for the structure and spirit of a governmental arrangement that is sociologically and psychologically appropriate to France; there still are the implicit distinctions between society and the state, between civil and political, and between control and action; and there is even more emphasis upon the separate character of politics, economics, and religion. But henceforth the approach to multi-class government is more positive than previously. Montesquieu, I believe, is here more certain that class representation is essential to a political system if it is to reflect and protect the natural inclinations of man in a differentiated society. As a consequence, he begins to prescribe more definitely the elements that will assure liberty to the people of a national society.

Montesquieu's study of the relations of liberty is part of his explanation of the spirit of the laws. The Book I definition of that concept says in part that the laws "should have relation to the degree of liberty which the constitution will bear." This is a rather limited approach to liberty but it helps to understand Book XI, which is entitled "the laws that form political liberty with regard to the constitution" and which contains the analysis of the English three-class Parliament. The limited scope of that discussion is accentuated by the subject of the next book (XII) which deals with the laws that form political liberty in respect of the citizen. These kinds of political liberty are only two of several types of liberty which are assumed at various points throughout *L'Esprit des Lois*. Before considering the book on constitutional liberty, we will endeavor to identify and classify the various kinds of liberty. The first section will explain the typology of liberty, and the other two sections of

240

this chapter will review Montesquieu's ideas about civil and political liberty in relation to the citizen. The next chapter will then take up political liberty in respect of the constitution and what it develops in the way of a mixed legislature.

The Typology of Liberty

Definitions and illustrations of liberty appear at the start of both Books XI and XII and, in this section, I will draw upon both of these sources as well as other works of Montesquieu. My aim will be to bring together the various meanings and applications in the hope of developing a coherent as well as a composite typology of liberty.

Montesquieu says near the beginning of Book XI that "there is no word that admits of more various significations, and has made more varied impressions on the human mind, than that of liberty."[1] This is more appropriate than even he may realize. He proceeds to identify several different meanings but there are other and more fundamental phases of the matter which he does not recognize expressly until subsequent books and still others which he never does bring to the surface.

The most controlling assumption in this portion of *L'Esprit des Lois* is the idea that liberty is living under law rather than living above or outside law. Here, Montesquieu seems to assume that law means a predictable social order based upon custom and mores as well as upon written rules, and I believe that he considers an individual to have liberty when the individual is able and willing to participate in a community which has standards of social behavior that are commonly accepted and enforced. Likewise, there are indications here that society and order refer to the civil realm even more than to the political one. *L'Esprit des Lois* presupposes a distinction between the civil society and the political apparatus, and I contend that for Montesquieu liberty involves first of all the freedom of the civil order from political despotism. On this basis, the freedom of the individual within a society is dependent upon the freedom of the society from arbitrary rule. In other words, the right kind of political structure and spirit allows the society to maintain a rational pattern of activity, to which each man may will his own actions. Thus, free living under law involves an obligation by both superiors and inferiors to act with reason or sense; that is, there must be reasonable laws and there must be general acceptance of the laws. The combined or synthesized effect is an interaction which I believe Montesquieu assumes to be essential to liberty.

The idea that political liberty is general as well as particular is evident when Montesquieu undertakes to explain the meaning of liberty by identifying the varying beliefs of peoples or nations. He points out that some people (meaning, I believe, some nations) take liberty to be the right to depose a person with tyrannical power while others consider it to be the opportunity of electing the superior whom they are obliged to obey. Then, some deem it to be a right to bear arms; still others the privilege of being governed by a fellow national, or by their own laws. The Muscovites, he notes, for "a long time thought liberty consisted in the privilege of wearing a long beard." Montesquieu has the same approach when he sets forth illustrations of how freedom or liberty relates to a form of government. Some people, he says, "have annexed this name to one form of government exclusive of others; those who had a republican taste applied it to this species of polity; those who liked a monarchical state gave it to monarchy. Thus they have all applied the name of liberty to the government most suitable to their own customs and inclinations." This reflects the definition in Book I of the government most conformable to nature and it connects liberty with what is natural for the particular society.

These approaches to the meaning of liberty are more sociological and psychological than legal and political. Also, what constitutes liberty is not universal nor absolute but national and conditional. Its meaning varies with the time, the place and the people. The important matter, I believe, is not that it is relative, but that it is relative to some customary or national community. Montesquieu assumes that liberty pertains first of all to the society, in contradistinction to both the state and the individual. This is one of the more subtle ways in which he seeks to avoid the conflict of the ruler and the people which *Les Lettres Persanes* presented but did not answer.[2]

His explanation of what is meant by liberty also seems to carry forward the implicit theme of several preceding books, that is, that a general restraint is needed in democracies, particularly those inclined to be monolithic. The previous books on the principle or special spirit required by the different kinds of government explain in various ways that a political system in which the people have the supreme controlling power cannot succeed unless there is a high degree of restraint and a love of frugality among the people generally.[3] Now, in the discussions of the different meanings of liberty, the rather deceptive character of this type of government is approached from another angle. Montesquieu says here, that in republics, and clearly he is thinking of democracies, the people do not have a constant and immediate view of the instruments of evil of which they complain. This is, he says, because the laws seem to speak more than the magistrates. He looks at the common belief that liberty resides in republics and not in monarchies and finds that the belief arises from a confusion. He explains that because "in democracies the people seem to act almost as they please, this sort of government has been deemed the most free, and the power of the people has been confounded with their liberty."[4]

It is from this assertion that in democracies the power of the people is confused with their liberty that Montesquieu proceeds to require the checking of power with power to prevent the abuse of liberty. What he says is often quoted to mean a doctrine of checks and balances, but I believe that these statements are part of the continuing exposure of democratic republics and their rather deceptive appearances. The definitions and explanations of liberty which follow are a bit confusing, but there seems to be less difficulty if they are interpreted in light of the previous arguments that the success of monolithic democracy depends upon a common denial of self-interest and a general love of frugality.

The idea that democratic government should involve general restraint more than individual freedom is seen in the further explanations of liberty. "It is true that in democracies the people seem to act as they please," Montesquieu recognizes, but he asserts that "political liberty does not consist in an unlimited freedom." He declares that in a state or government, "that is, in societies directed by laws, liberty can consist only in the power of doing what we ought to will, and in not being constrained to do what we ought not to will." Hence, there is a moral burden inherent in any political role. There is here a limitation upon popular sovereignty which previously Montesquieu tried to explain by the requirement of a common love of equality and frugality in democracies. Now he suggests the restraint by pointing to a basic distinction. "We must have continually present to our minds the difference between independence and liberty." This difference is the key to the idea that liberty is a matter of living under a social legal order. "Liberty is a right of doing whatever the laws permit," Montesquieu declares, explaining that if a citizen could do what the laws forbid he would be no longer possessed of liberty because all his fellow-citizens would have the same power.[5]

The proposition that liberty is a matter of living under a social legal order would seem to mean that liberty is the opportunity to act or not to act according to a normative standard, and this norm would seem to be what is meant by the laws. Hence, liberty is not a matter of living under just any positive laws but living under laws that meet some standard, moral or social. Independence, presumably meaning freedom from laws, is not liberty because if all citizens possessed that power none would have liberty. This suggests that individual liberty entails a general duty as well as a specific right to live according to the legal order. Yet, there must also be an assumption that the laws are morally or socially relevant; otherwise, living by the laws would be servitude and not liberty. Thus there would seem to be a double obligation: a duty of the political law giver to enact laws that are rational and empirically relevant and a duty upon the citizens to abide by such laws. This is similar to the twofold prescription set forth by Bodin: if the subjects obey the laws of the king and the king the laws of nature, then there will be a rule of law.[6] Montesquieu does not identify the political lawgiver, nor the higher law, nor the ideal value. In fact, the duty of the legislator at this point is left unexpressed but the essentials of the prescription are much the same as those of Bodin, except that Montesquieu would probably prefer the civil laws rather than the natural law to be the guide for political decisions. Likewise, while he does not say so here, Montesquieu may well assume that the laws which permit liberty are those which conform to the spirit of the laws and the general spirit of the nation. These, as discussed previously, are two concepts which seek to relate political legislation to the sociological and psychological character of the national people.

The idea that the people must live under some standard of restraint continues to be present as Montesquieu moves from one portion of *L'Esprit des Lois* to the next. The preceding books (II — X) held that a democracy required general self-limitation. Now, in the books on liberty, the restraint upon the people may be external to them, such as a legislature in which they are only one joint holder of authority.

If democracy must have external limitations, it is in fact a qualified or mixed democracy. This is implicit in the additional explanations of the meaning of liberty. These are indirect criticisms of single-class government, similar to several of the arguments developed in the previous books on the comparative analysis of kinds of government. Montesquieu is clear that neither kind of republic is a guarantee of liberty. "Democratic and aristocratic states are not in their own nature free," but both need the moderation which ultimately *L'Esprit des Lois* makes the prime standard for legislation. "Political liberty is to be found only in moderate governments," Montesquieu declares, and he adds that even in these systems it is not always found. "It is there only when there is no abuse of power."[7] This is the point at which Montesquieu takes the pessimistic view about the effects of power, and it comes not in a discussion of government by one, but rather in the consideration of democracies and aristocracies. He seems to be thinking about legislatures representing the few and the many when he asserts that "constant experience shows us that every man invested with power is apt to abuse it and to carry his authority as far as it will go." He asks rhetorically: "Is it not strange, though true, to say that virtue has need of limits?" The idea that liberty will not result from virtue alone and that limitations are necessary would seem to be directed at the theory of benevolent despotism held by Voltaire and others, which Montesquieu clearly opposes. In other words, a good attitude by a ruler is little assurance of liberty without countervailing institutions. He is not willing to risk social liberty with a single class, however virtuous it may seem.

The fact that Montesquieu is talking about democracies and aristocracies in this analysis should be remembered when considering his suggestions on how to avoid abuse of power. "To prevent this abuse, it is necessary from the very nature of things that power should be a check to power." The remedy involves respect for law, not the disregard of it. "A government may be constituted, as no man shall be compelled to do things to which the law does not oblige him, nor forced to abstain from things which the law permits."[8] The idea of checking power with power could be an invitation to mixed government and particularly to a mixed legislature. Montesquieu associates democracies and aristocracies with political control and especially with representative law-making bodies. The continuing power of democracy is largely in the legislative function, and the check of that power would seem to call for a multi-class legislature in which popular sovereignty is qualified by the aristocratic and monocratic elements of the political society. We must see whether the formula for preventing abuse of power is distribution in such a manner that the classes or social groups would have a mu-

246 Montesquieu's System of Natural Government

tual veto upon each other. What Montesquieu prescribes later in Book XI will be discussed in the next chapter.

The assumptions that liberty applies to society as well as to an individual and that liberty depends upon an established social order may differ from mid-twentieth century beliefs. Today the emphasis is upon individual liberty with little conscious recognition that this depends upon the freedom of society. The latter is now taken for granted. But Montesquieu was engaged in pioneer work to attain or regain the freedom of society from tyrannical politics. In the seventeenth and eighteenth centuries, liberty was more a goal of the society than of the individual because the whole society was oppressed by the Bourbon monarchical apparatus. Throughout history, the search for liberty has been a matter of release from the prevailing source of oppression, and in those centuries the principal struggle was against monarchical absolutism. This is the reverse of the struggle of the last one hundred years or so, perhaps best expressed by John Stuart Mill.[9] Now the struggle is that of the individual or the minority to gain freedom from the society or the majority of it.

The social approach to liberty does not mean that Montesquieu abandons his belief in the free will of man, which he defended with such persistence in *Les Lettres Persanes*.[10] The doctrine of free will is not negatived in *L'Esprit des Lois*. Montesquieu makes an express distinction at the start of Book XII between philosophic liberty and political liberty. The one consists in the exercise of the will and the other consists in security. Montesquieu assumes, I believe, that a man must have reasonable security within his society or his freedom of will would be meaningless. Without security, he would be at the mercy of the will of others.

Montesquieu also makes a distinction between actual liberty and imagined liberty, the one resting in reality and the other in opinion. When he distinguishes philosophic liberty from political liberty, he says the first consists of the free exercise of the will "or at least, if we must speak agreeably to all systems, in an opinion that we have the free exercise of our will." He makes similar comments about political liberty saying that it consists in security, "or, at least, in the opinion that we enjoy security." In a later book, he identifies two corresponding sorts of tyranny. One kind of tyranny is real and arises from oppression while "the other is seated in opinion, and is sure to be left whenever those who govern establish things shocking to the existing ideas of a nation."[11] The idea that liberty is belief in one's security makes it tantamount to freedom from fear and thus the opposite of the moving spirit of despotic government.[12] The antithesis of the free state and the despotic state is thus identified by contrasting attitudes. In fact, all of Montesquieu's observations upon liberty, tyranny, and the spirit of government show his awareness of the social psychology at work in a political system.

One of the most important steps in the development of Montesquieu's theory of natural government is the distinction between two types of political liberty. As noted previously, Book XI concerns laws which establish political liberty with respect to the constitution while Book XII deals expressly with laws that form political liberty with respect to the citizen. One type may exist without the other, or at least is distinct for purposes of analysis. "The constitution may happen to be free and the citizen not," Montesquieu explains. Or then, the citizen may be free and not the constitution. "In those cases, the constitution will be free by right, and not in fact; the citizen will be free in fact, and not by right."[13] Thus the two types may be called political liberty by right and political liberty in fact. The famous chapter on the constitution of England appears in the book on political liberty by right and not in the book on political liberty in fact. This distinction is probably accentuated by the idea that liberty may involve a belief or opinion as well as an actuality. The analysis of the English government seems to combine the concept of political liberty by right with the idea of liberty as a belief, thus making the political liberty in respect of the constitution still more remote from actual enjoyment of liberty. Montesquieu is quite consistent with this analysis of political liberty when he says in respect of the English constitution, that he is concerned with the liberty implicit in its legal structure and not what is actually enjoyed by the English people.

The distinction between liberty by right and liberty in fact is not explained specifically until Book XII when one is said to arise from "a certain distribution of the three powers" and the other to consist "in security or in the opinion people have of their security."[14] Much of the preliminary discussion in Book XI uses simply the term "liberty" without qualification and seems to mean some kind of collective liberty. Strangely, the only definition of political liberty in Book XI is "political liberty in a citizen." This is said to be "a tranquillity of mind arising from the opinion that each person has of his safety," and to require a government so constituted that "one citizen need not fear another."[15] What Montesquieu intends to emphasize here, I believe, is the psychological aspect of political liberty generally rather than one type. What he discusses thereafter in Book XI, once he passes a brief inquiry of judicial processes, is the distribution of political control among the different classes or their representatives.

Emile Faguet seems to have interpreted correctly the distinction between liberty by right and in fact when he says that the difference is between a free people and a free man.[16] He explains that, when a people have no government, they are free but the man is not. He assumes, I believe, that, unless the society is ordered in some way, man cannot count upon a predictable relation and hence cannot live according to any rational pattern. There is one aspect of Faguet's analysis which might be qualified. He assumes that a constitution is free when it is not imposed from without. But I believe that Montesquieu would not consider it free if it were imposed by a single class for its own benefit without means of protection in the other classes. Faguet might presuppose that a constitution adopted by a society would have such an element of multiple representation. In such a case, his analysis appears to agree with that of Montesquieu.

Professor Plamenatz, in his scholarly study of Montesquieu's social and political theory, asserts that the distinction between a free constitution and a free citizen is a misleading paradox.[17] The problem arises, I believe, from Montesquieu's use here of the terms "constitution" and "citizen" to identify two general aspects of the political law process, that is, the place of the society in the control of legislation and the status of the individual in the application of law. Accordingly, one type of political liberty relates to the constitution of the legislature and depends in effect upon the participation or representation of the three political power classes in legislative and related functions while the other type of political liberty concerns the character of executive and judicial procedures in the enforcement of political laws, such as those dealing with treason, sedition, and taxes, against particular citizens. Professor Plamenatz says that this last, which Montesquieu calls political liberty in fact, is what "is usually meant by the phrase *the rule of law*."[18] This is probably the commonest meaning where representative legislatures have been well established. In Britain and America it is the area in which lawyers most often act as lawyers, but its standards of legality, fairness, and particular liberty may be lost without the presence of a legislature which is responsive to judicial standards and social customs. The rule of law has had at various times other meanings, such as rational decision, respect for custom, and mixed government.[19] If we assume that it has the same scope as political liberty, then I believe that "the rule of law" concerns the legislative process as well as the executive/judicial one. This is probably not disputed because we have come to take representative legislatures for granted in the North Atlantic community. However, in eightenth century France there was a court system but no representative parliament; the one needed to be reformed while the other needed to be established. This, I believe, is the principal reason why Montesquieu dichotomizes political liberty and deals in one kind with the constitution of the legislature and in the other with the procedure of enforcement institutions. He seeks to reform the latter but he gives most attention to the structure and spirit of the legislature. Hence, the division of political liberty seems appropriate as well as useful in his undertaking.

Also, there is a specific meaning of "constitution" involved in this matter. Montesquieu's statement in the definition of the spirit of laws about "the degree of liberty which the constitution can withstand" suggests that liberty may be limited by the constitution and that constitutions may vary in the amount of liberty which they can withstand. What Montesquieu means by "constitution" may be more limited and more relative than the present day signification of the term, at least in the United States. Actually, the term "constitution" did have a variety of uses in eighteenth century France and some of these were quite narrow and special. At one time it stood merely for the Bull Unigenitus which the Pope had issued in 1713. Montesquieu uses it in this sense in a memoire and in one of *Les Lettres Persanes*.[20] However, in *L'Esprit des Lois* he uses the word to mean some kind of basic political arrangement. This is not synonymous with "fundamental law" as then used. The latter prescribed the line of royal succession and prohibited the alienation of the royal demesne,[21] while Montesquieu seems generally to use "constitution" to mean an allocation of political power among the social classes or groups of the nation.

His limited meaning of constitution, as well as of the terms political, state, and government, arises in part from his special emphasis upon the civil society and its mores and upon the civil judiciary and its laws. He seems often to assume that political laws are made

by the legislature and civil laws by the judiciary. When he talks of
the constitution in Book XI, he appears to mean the allocation of
legislative power so that one might say that it is the legislative constitution. Similarly, the ideas expressed in Books II — V about the
allocation of administrative powers, might be termed an executive
constitution, and what is said about who should be judges could be
called the judicial constitution. But Montesquieu uses the term
"constitution" mostly when speaking about the distribution of legislative powers. Thus, in general, political liberty with respect to
the constitution concerns legislative arrangements while political
liberty with respect to the citizen deals with administrative and judicial matters.

Other varieties of liberty may be implicit in the analyses of different kinds of servitude in *L'Esprit des Lois*. When Montesquieu
discusses the traditional type of slavery in Book XV, he calls it civil
slavery but then says that it is based upon domestic law.[22] The
book on domestic servitude (XVI) is principally about the conditions of women. These are rare instances in which he treats the domestic realm expressly apart from the civil one. He lists both domestic law and civil law at the start of Book XXVI, when naming
the types of legal order which govern mankind but usually he includes domestic relations within the civil ones.

The three kinds of servitude are analyzed in relation to climatic
influences. The total import of the discussions seems to be that
France should have moderate government just as it has moderate
climate. Montesquieu posits three climatic regions, the hot, the
cold, and the temperate. He says that liberty is more likely to be
found in northern countries than in southern ones, and he stresses
the correspondence of despotic governments with hot climates but
he seems more concerned with temperate situations than with
the northern countries.[23] This may be part of his ideas about
government for his native land. France is clearly in a center
position from the viewpoint of climate as well as other physical
qualities so that there is a not too subtle implication that whatever
influence climate may have, it provides no justification for despotism in France. Rousseau claims that Montesquieu's ideas on climate
can be stated in a single sentence: "Liberty not being a fruit that
every climate will produce, it is not within the abilities of all peoples."[24] There is no indication that Rousseau thinks that France is
excluded from enjoyment of liberty by its physical situation.

A few additional comments on the meaning of liberty appear in

Book XVIII. This deals with the relation of laws, climate and terrain, and the effect of soil conditions upon types of occupations and upon the scope of civil laws.

Montesquieu begins with a remark that probably would have been challenged on the American frontier. "The goodness of the land, in any country, naturally establishes subjection and dependence. The husbandmen, who compose the principal part of the people, are not very jealous of their liberty; they are too busy and too intent on their own private affairs." The rub is in the comprehension of liberty. For Montesquieu, it means active participation in government rather than freedom from interference. A wealthy country, he suggests, wants tranquillity. Monarchy requires less involvement than a democracy and it is found more frequently in fruitful countries than in unproductive ones. Examples of this maxim are noted in ancient Greece where the barrenness of the Attic soil established a democracy at Athens while the fertility of the soil at Sparta resulted in an aristocratic constitution, which Montesquieu suggests is as close as the classical Greeks came to monarchy. Thus, the more difficult the soil to cultivate, the more time devoted to political activity, whereas the wealth and leisure of a fertile country tends to breed only more leisure. Montesquieu may have France and Switzerland in mind when he asserts that a people inhabitating a level surface have need for a stronger government than those living in a mountainous and rugged area because the former are less able to contest a strong outside power.[25]

The idea that liberty is relative to the custom of the particular society appears also in Book XIX where Montesquieu argues that the minds of a people should be prepared for the reception of the laws, regardless of how good the laws may be. He refers to institutions which the Romans admired and which would be unacceptable to other peoples. "Liberty itself has appeared intolerable to those nations who have not been accustomed to enjoy it," he explains, adding that "pure air is sometimes disagreeable to such as have lived in a fenny country."[26] This is generalized when he defines two kinds of tyranny, with one seated in opinion while the others rests upon fact. He remarks that the one based upon opinion "is sure to be left whenever those who govern establish things shocking to the existing ideas of a nation." Thus, beliefs may be as forceful as facts, we may conclude. In support of this suggestion, Montesquieu recalls the manner in which Caesar, the Triumvirs, and Augustus, even though they were invested with regal power, each respected the Roman dislike of kings and preserved all the outward appearance of equality. He explains that the Roman resolve to have no king meant merely that they retained their manners. Another example of the importance of public psychology concerns Augustus and an actor. The laws of Augustus exasperated the Romans but when he recalled the banished comedian Pylades, the discontent ceased. Montesquieu's conclusion about this incident, that "a people of this stamp have a more lively sense of tyranny when a player is banished than when they are deprived of their laws,"[27] bears out an earlier remark that a society loves its mores even above its laws.[28] It also shows his insight into the social psychology of political behavior.

Since liberty is living under law, logically there could be as many kinds of liberty as there are types of law, but Montesquieu usually limits his analysis to two or three sorts of legal order. In *Les Lettres Persanes* he speaks only of civil law and public law and he discusses two corresponding types of justice.[29] These could be two forms of liberty, but he does not say so expressly. The public law is much like a law of nations, and the corresponding justice is inferior to civil justice. In fact, he argues that the latter should be the model for justice among nations. In *L'Esprit des Lois,* law is much more differentiated at some points, but the bulk of the work pays more attention to civil and political law than to the other kinds of legal order. The final quarter of the work has more to say about civil laws than any other single subject. Montesquieu rarely uses the term "civil liberty," but the word "liberty," when unqualified, might mean civil liberty. This seems to have been the attitude of writers in eighteenth century France. Kingsley Martin points out that by "liberty the *philosophes* mean civil liberty."[30] One of the aims of *L'Esprit des Lois* is, I believe, to raise the status of civil liberty by strengthening the force of civil laws. The emphasis upon such laws in contrast to royal sovereignty is evident throughout the whole of the work from the first book to the last. The express treatment of "political liberty" in Books XI — XIII complements his general interest in civil liberty. Political liberty may have become essential to civil liberty, but the higher objective is civil liberty and its protection from political despotism.

Montesquieu's omission of criminal law from the list of nine types of law which govern mankind and his implicit division of crimes between the civil and political legal orders,[31] is another demonstration of the importance which he attaches to the distinction between these two types of law. Their separate character is pronounced in Book I, assumed in Books VI, XI, and XII, expressed in the titles of Books XV and XVII, and is the principal subject matter of Books XXVI, XXVII and XXVIII. Destutt de Tracy, in his 1819 commentary upon *L'Esprit des Lois*, asserts that in Book VI Montesquieu "does not distinguish with sufficient care civil justice and criminal justice."[32] This would seem to indicate that Montesquieu is more concerned about the distinction between civil and political than with the more technical differences between criminal and civil matters recognized in Anglo-American law and apparently even in the continental legal analysis. The contrast of the civil legal order with the political one is an essential element of Montesquieu's theory of natural government.[33] It corresponds in part to the difference between civil and political liberty and between private and public law. At least twice *L'Esprit des Lois* expressly distinguishes private and public crimes.[34] The contrast of civil and political also corresponds to the still more implicit distinction between law-making by the judiciary and by the legislature. *L'Esprit des Lois* seems to treat the judiciary as the primary source of the civil law while the legislature is associated most with the enactment of political laws, whether we call them statutory or constitutional.[35]

L'Esprit des Lois may assume a civil liberty by right and a civil liberty in fact, just as it expresses two kinds of political liberty, but neither of the types of civil liberty is identified explicitly. The civil liberty by right would consist of the civil mores and customary laws, and Montesquieu would consider it more natural in development and higher in social value than the political liberty by right. This is seen in the considerable attention which Montesquieu gives to the civil mores and civil laws, as discussed in Chapters II, section three and III, section three of this study. The civil liberty in fact, I believe, is what is described in Book VI on the relation of the principle of governments to the civil and criminal laws, forms of judgment and methods of punishment. This book is the civil counterpart of Book XII, which is concerned with what Montesquieu calls political liberty in fact. The desire to preserve civil liberty, in both its collective and its individual application, is surely one of the principal objectives of *L'Esprit des Lois*.

A recognition that Montesquieu does assume these four general types of liberty is essential to an understanding of his analysis of the English constitution in Book XI because that concerns only one of the four. Before reviewing the analysis of political liberty by right (Book XI) in the next chapter of this study, consideration will be

given in the second and third sections of this chapter, to civil liberty
in fact (Book VI) and political liberty in fact (Book XII).

Civil Liberty in Fact

Montesquieu assumes that the civil order of a nation has priority
in time and value to the political arrangement, as explained in previous discussions, and he devotes considerable effort to assuring the
institutional means for preserving civil liberty in both its collective
and its individual application. His deep interest in protecting the
personal and property rights of the citizens is quite evident in Book
VI of *L'Esprit des Lois*. This is entitled "the consequences of the
principles of different governments with respect to the simplicity of
civil and criminal laws, the form of judgments and the inflicting of
punishments." Under this multiple title, he examines the judicial
systems appropriate to monarchies, republics, and despotisms and
gives particular attention to the relation of procedural laws to the
character of the society and the psychology of the people involved.
Montesquieu's efforts in these matters has earned him high praise
as a pioneer in the development of sociological jurisprudence.[36]
Book VI deals with five subjects that are relevant to the present
study: the importance of the civil judiciary, the defense of legal
complexity in class structured systems, the distribution of judicial
authority, the comparative psychology of punishment in different
types of societies, and the proportionment of punishment to the
crime. Each of these will be considered in this section.

This is one of several places in *L'Esprit des Lois* where Montesquieu stresses the importance of the civil judiciary in contradistinction to both the political judiciary and the political legislature. He assumes in general that the civil judiciary is law-making in
itself and that the civil law develops primarily out of the social
mores and private conflicts. For him, the civil law is both national
and natural. Several of the ways in which he raises the position of
the civil law at the expense of not only the political law but also
the natural law and perhaps even the ecclesiastical law, were
discussed in Chapters II, section three, and III, section three,
of this study. In Book VI, he devotes special attention to the
relation of civil laws to the social structure and to the procedure by
which coercive laws may be applied with respect for the sociological
and psychological situation of the citizens involved.

Montesquieu's concept of the judicial function differs from that prevalent in present day American political thought, and there are two general reasons for this. One, the courts of today are considerably more involved in public law and political controversy. The administrative law field has grown immensely, and the doctrine of judicial review of legislation for constitutionality is distinctly new. The latter may have some resemblance to the power of the *Parlement de Paris* to delay the registering of royal edicts,[37] but the French practice lacked the substance and judicial character of the American doctrine. The other difference in judicial functions then and now is the strong tendency of both lay and professional political observers in the United States to associate the judiciary with its newer functions rather than with its more traditional function of settling disputes between private litigants. The civil controversies involving private property, contract rights, domestic relations, and so on, still constitute the major part of the work of the courts.[38] But only practicing lawyers give much attention to that phase of the judicial function. Political scientists and any others who observe the judiciary stress the symbolic, policy decisions of the Supreme Court on issues of broad constitutional values, such as equality and freedom. These actions are often uncharacteristic of the judicial function, but they are what the judiciary means to much of the public and the political science profession.

In constrast, Montesquieu looked at the work of the courts from the position of the law student and the judge and even that of the lawyer involved in civil controversies. He apparently disliked the procedural side of the law, probably never practiced, and was pleased to give up his judicial robes.[39] But he does show a broad, continuing interest in the issues of private law, such as the inheritance of property, marriage, and other problems encountered in legal practice. Throughout his writings, there is much attention to the type of controversy to which political scientists generally give little attention, like the person to person conflicts over commercial contracts and the laws of sucession. These, apparently, were the principal subjects for the practicing lawyer. The comprehensive analysis of Civil Laws by Jean Domat,[40] which was probably the outstanding work on French law in Montesquieu's time, is largely a digest of the law in which practioneers become engaged and the work, after an introductory analysis, is divided between contracts and the law of succession.

The scope and intensity of Montesquieu's early interest in matters of private law is shown by the summary analysis which he made, probably during his period as a law student, of the Justinian Code. His endeavor fills six notebooks, totaling 700 to 800 pages. The set of volumes is now called the *Collectio Juris* by the *Bibliothèque Nationale* where it reposes.[41] Five notebooks are filled with a methodical review of most of the digest portion of the Corpus Juris Civilis and the sixth summarizes much of the Novella. Montesquieu was somewhat selective in his analysis. Certain subjects appear to have attracted him more than others, even though he remained largely faithful to the general pattern of the Roman classic. Here as elsewhere in his writings he shows a strong interest in family relations, particularly marriage and the succession of property.[42] There is no doubt that his concentration is upon matters of private law, which compose most of the digest, rather than upon matters of public or political character. He pays little attention to the few references in the Justinian Code to public law. His early interest in private law as well as his life long attention to the civil law was noted by Pierre Solignac in his eulogy of Montesquieu in 1757.[43] Montesquieu's diligence as a scholar, while he was a law student and a judge, is evident in *L'Esprit des Lois*. He shows a high respect for the law and the civil order and the soundest scholarship in the whole work is probably in the books (XXVII and XXVIII) on the history of Roman and French civil laws.[44]

Book VI is very much a criticism of simple government. It deals only with the judiciary and the civil or nonpolitical judiciary at that, but it is as much a condemnation of despotism as any book of *L'Esprit des Lois*. Its title refers first to the effects of principle or special spirit upon the simplicity of civil and criminal laws and the simplicity which it considers is that of judicial systems in despotic governments. It attacks starchamber practices and argues for procedures that permit deliberate thought and a regard for sociological conditions and psychological consequences. Inferentially, the process of adjudication should have the values which characterize natural government, that is, respect for established privileges and rights, a sense of moderation, and a regard for empirical proportions, as well as an institutional structure that assures the freedom of the social order.[45]

The comparative analysis of the spirit of civil laws in different political systems assumes that both monarchies and republics are mixed governments in mixed societies. More attention is given to the former than to the latter and much of the book contrasts the detailed, deliberate judicial processes in monarchies with the simplicity of laws and methods in a despotic state. In this endeavor, Montesquieu throws more light upon the social, legal, and psychological differentiations which he considers to be essential for a tolerant society and a moderate government.

The discussions in Book VI are directed at those who dislike the slow moving judicial procedures in European countries and who envy the quick-moving "justice" in Asiatic countries like China and Turkey. Montesquieu, in defending the more deliberate processes, argues for professional judges. He asserts that "in monarchies there must be courts of judicature" and their decisions must be "preserved and learned, that we may judge in the same manner today as yesterday and that the lives and property of the citizens may be as certain and fixed as the very constitution of the state."[46] He adds that we must not be surprised to find numerous rules, restrictions, and extensions in the laws of monarchical countries. These diverse rules, he says, make for a multiplicity of conflicts and "seem to make of reason itself an art." This last brings to mind Lord Coke's reference to the common law as "artificial reason."[47] Montesquieu's use of the word "constitution" here is also informative. Presumably, judicial protection of property and life is not embraced by the constitution of the state. This accords with indications elsewhere in L'Esprit des Lois that the civil realm differs from the political one and that the judiciary concerns the society more than the state. In other words, the term constitution is used to mean the political arrangement and thus to exclude the civil judiciary. We will find this meaning also in the main portion of the analysis of the English Constitution, to be discussed in the next chapter.

The defense here in Book VI, of the complexity of civil laws in a monarchy, is definitely associated with the social class differentiation which Montesquieu assumes to be natural and necessary in a country like France. He points out the connection between social distinctions and the varying property laws and asserts that "the difference of rank, birth, and condition established in monarchical governments is frequently attended with distinctions in the nature of property; and the laws relating to the constitution of this government may augment the number of these distinctions."[48] Montesquieu explains further that in France goods are divided into real and personal estates, dowries, paternal and maternal inheritances, movables of different kinds, estates held in fee-simple or in tail, estates acquired by descent or conveyance, grounds rents and annui-

ties, and still other more peculiar types. Each class of goods is subject to particular rules which restrict the manner of disposition.
Moreover, a monarch who knows his provinces may allow them different laws or customs. In contrast, a despotic prince knows nothing
and can attend to nothing, Montesquieu declares, so the despot
must take general measures and govern by an inflexible will; "in
short, everything bends under his feet."

The discussion of judicial methods in stratified societies also
brings out ideas on how the legislator and the judge should complement each other, with the legislators in a limited role of making
general adjustments. Montesquieu explains that the laws are so
complex in monarchies that the legislator may need to correct the
deficiencies that arise in the case law. As judicial decisions multiply
in a monarchy, the law is loaded with decrees that contradict one
another because judges may differ in their thinking, because causes
are not always well defended, and because of an infinite number of
abuses "to which all human regulations are liable." This is called a
"necessary evil" which the legislator redresses from time to time "as
contrary even to the spirit of moderate governments," so that the
need for resorting to the courts will arise from "the nature of the
constitution" rather than from the contradiction or uncertainty of
the law. Presumably, the courts should devote themselves to resolving conflicts between the classes and not to unraveling the technical
complexities of the law. Again, constitution seems to refer to an
arrangement of social classes. Countries with despotic governments
may have simple judicial systems because under despotism there are
few distinctions among persons, few privileges, and little regard for
honor. Moreover, there is little private property or commercial activity and thus only slight need for civil laws on property, successions, or commerce. "Despotic power is self-sufficient; round it
there is an absolute vacuum."[49]

The defense of procedural requirements seems to be relevant to
present day controversies over the formalities of prosecution. With
respect to criminal laws as well as property ones, Montesquieu associates simplicity with despotic governments and complexity with
moderate ones. He asserts that Turkey is often held up as a model
in the administration of justice and then scoffs at the idea that this
"most ignorant of all nations" could be the most clear sighted in
this matter. This, of course, may be an indirect attack upon some
recent French methods.

One of the more fundamental premises in Montesquieu's analysis of government, that is, that legislative power concerns liberty of the group while judicial and executive action relates to liberty of the individual, is reflected in his defense here of complex judicial procedure. He asserts that, if "we examine the set forms of justice" for recovery of property or damages, we may find them too numerous, but, if we consider them "in the relation that they bear to the liberty and security of every individual, we shall often find them too few."[50] Accordingly, we will "be convinced that the trouble, expense, delays, and even the very dangers of our judiciary proceedings are the price that each subject pays for his liberty." Thus the complexity of judicial procedure is the basis of this kind of liberty and Montesquieu fortifies his argument with criticism of simplified procedures. In Turkey, he points out that all cases are speedily decided, with little regard for the honor, life, or estate of the subjects. There, the method of determining cases is a matter of indifference; all that counts is that they be determined. The security of a man in a despotic country, Montesquieu asserts, depends upon his being reduced to nothing. On the other hand, in a moderate government, "where the life of the meanest subject is deemed precious, no man is stripped of his honor or property until after a long inquiry," and every man is given "all possible means of making his defense."

The assertions at this point that republics need formalities in judicial procedure as much as monarchies show that Montesquieu is assuming that republics also have stratified societies. Formalities are required here, he says, because of "the value which is set on the honor, fortune, liberty and life of the subject." Among these, at least fortune would differ among various classes of a society. Yet, he uses equality to distinguish republics and despotisms, saying rather dogmatically that in republics men are all equal because they are everything and that in despotic countries they are equal because they are nothing.[51] Equality may be the factor which makes republics less attractive than monarchies when he compares judicial interpretation of law in different kinds of government. Certainly, he argues that there can be more flexibility in monarchies. "The nearer a government approaches towards a republic, the more the manner of judging becomes settled and fixed."[52] The historical support for this is drawn from the classical cities. The Ephori of Sparta were at fault, Montesquieu points out, in passing judgments without having any laws to direct them. Likewise, the First Consuls at Rome began to do the same but soon "they were obliged to have recourse to express and determinate laws." He contrasts legal interpretation in the three kinds of government. In a despotic state, there is no law and the judge is his own rule, while in a monarchy, there are laws but the judge "endeavors to investigate their spirit" when they are not explicit. "In republics, the very nature of the constitution requires the judges to follow the letter of the law." Otherwise, "the law might be explained to the prejudice of every citizen, in cases where their honor, property, or life is concerned." Here again, "the constitution" seems to have a direct relation to the social structure and the attitudes of various classes. Montesquieu goes on to contrast criminal procedure in Rome and in England. In the former the judge determined guilt while the punishment was found in the laws. In England the jury gives their verdict on whether the fact is proved or not and then, if proved, the judge pronounces the punishment inflicted by the law.

Montesquieu's preference for mixed monarchy in contrast to simple democracy as well as despotism is particularly evident in the comparative analysis of the manner of passing judgment. In this explanation he is much concerned with the limits of popular government. In monarchies, he points out, the judges choose the method of arbitration; they moderate their opinions. "But this is not agreeable to the nature of a republic." He seems to be thinking of a classical city democracy with trials before a popular assembly because he says that in early Rome and in the cities of Greece "the judges never entered into a consultation; each gave his opinion in one of these three ways: I absolve, I condemn, it does not appear clear to me."[53] This was, he explains, because the people judged, or were supposed to judge, and "the people are far from being civilians," i.e. trained legal theorists.[54] The method of arbitration is beyond the reach of the people because "they must have only one object and one single fact set before them." They can decide only whether to condemn, acquit, or suspend. The Greeks and Romans had legal forms of action but only to keep the question from changing, and the judges "granted only the simple demand, without making any addition, deduction or limitation." Later, the Roman *Praetors,* who were more professional, devised forms which permitted judicial discretion in pronouncing sentence. This, Montesquieu says, is "more agreeable to the spirit of monarchy." Thus, he seems to say that in the classical republics the people protect themselves by direct action whereas in monarchies they are protected by professionals. This accords with Montesquieu's gradually developing position that mod-

erate government requires trained judges as well as detached intermediaries and a tolerant aristocracy. In other words, the assurance
of personal liberty in modern systems is to be found in proceedings
before selected professionals, such as the Roman civil jurists, more
than in the popular assemblies, such as the citizen court of Athens.

The proposition of this study that Montesquieu is more directly
concerned with the social distribution of authority than with its
functional separation applies to the civil judiciary as well as to the
political legislative, excutive, or administrative powers. It is not
enough for the courts to have some legal or structural isolation
from the political institutions; those who hold judicial authority
must also have professional training, rational detachment, and responsiveness to the natural inclinations of the people and the pattern of the social order. If Montesquieu does not answer the question of who shall be judges as clearly as he elsewhere says who
shall be legislators and administrators, this is probably because he is
less fearful of the judiciary than he is of the tyranny of the political
authorities in France. Reform was much more needed in the areas
of the political legislator and executive. In fact, he makes the civil
judiciary a standard for the reform of other authorities.

What Montesquieu says about the allocation of judicial power
ranges from vague suggestions of popular distribution to a reiterated preference for the use of what seem to me to be trained and
tolerant aristocrats. The popular point of view appears in the
chapter of Book XI on the English constitution where Montesquieu
asserts that the judiciary power should not be delegated to a standing senate and "should be exercised by persons taken from the body
of the people at certain times of the year."[55] In the same chapter he
says that most European governments in which the prince holds
both the legislative and executive power are moderate because the
judicial power has been given to the people. This may mean judges
selected by or answerable to the society rather than the prince. This
discussion is in a book on political liberty rather than on civil liberty and it seems to be concerned with the dangers of a despotic
ruler. Likewise, at this point Montesquieu may assume that the
choice is limited to rule by one or rule by many. Other discussions
develop the idea that the conflict of the prince and the people
might be mediated by what appears to be a professional few.

A dislike for judicial action by the many seems evident in one of
Les Lettres Persanes, where he refers to a tribunal which follows
"the majority of voices." The letter satirizes the litigation of family

disputes and suggests that open trials may weaken the domestic authority of the father, the husband, or the master. In conclusion, it observes that people have "found by experience, that it would be the surer way to determine by the minority." Montesquieu comments that "this is natural enough, for there are very few just reasoners, and all the world agrees that there is a very great number of false ones."[56] Book VI of *L'Esprit des Lois* suggests that the people be the judges when the charge is treason. Support here comes from Machiavelli, who attributed the loss of liberty in Florence to "the people's not judging in a body in cases of high treason against themselves, as was customary at Rome."[57] Florence had eight judges for this decision and "the few were corrupted by a few." Montesquieu adopts the position of Machiavelli and declares that "in those cases the political interest prevails in some measure over the civil." He recognizes that the people might abuse the power to make criminal judgments and calls attention to the plan introduced by Solon for a re-examination of the people's verdict by the Court of Areopagus. Hence, his overall position seems to favor a mixed arrangement: when the people judge, they should be subject to a veto or other check by a professional or aristocratic group.

While Montesquieu would check a popular judiciary with a professional body, he is even more strongly opposed to a judiciary by one. In fact, he often uses the independence of judges to characterize the mixed monarchy which he prefers. Logically, the prince himself would be judge in a despotic government because there are no laws or other limitations upon his rule. But for a prince to act as judge in a monarchy would annihilate the intermediate powers and otherwise subvert the constitution of that form of government. Montesquieu draws upon his legal and judicial training for the basis of disqualification. "In monarchies," he explains, "the prince is the party that prosecutes the person accused, and causes him to be punished or acquited. Now, were he himself to sit upon the trial, he would be both judge and party."[58] Montesquieu notes also that in some states the prince has the benefit of confiscation, and again he could be both judge and party. An added difficulty is that such a prince would have to contradict himself to grant a pardon and thus he "would deprive himself of the most glorious attribute of sovereignty." This shows that Montesquieu's division of executive and judicial powers is not based upon a political doctrine of separation or check and balance but upon traditional procedures which preclude a party from being the judge of his own cause. Hence, separation of executive and judicial functions is not a new political doctrine but an old civil law one. In addition, Montesquieu finds support for his contention a thousand years or more in the past. "Some Roman emperors were so mad as to sit as judges themselves; the consequence was that no reigns ever so surprised the world with oppression and injustice.[59] Inferentially, there were Roman rulers who respected the separation.

Equally condemned with judicial determination by the prince is that by his ministers, even though the latter may be appropriate for advise and counsel. "There is in the very nature of things," Montesquieu points out, "a kind of contrast between a prince's council and his courts of judicature." The one ought to be composed of a few persons and "the courts of judicature of a great many." He explains that the former must undertake affairs with a certain passion and that this can be done when four or five men make it their business. But in contrast, he observes, "in courts of judicature a certain coolness is requisite, and an indifference, in some measure, to all manner of affairs."

France seems to be in the back of Montesquieu's mind throughout his discussion of who should do the accusing of criminal violations. He tends to favor the French method of accusation by a professional official rather than by a private citizen and he impliedly adds another stroke against republicanism for France, I believe, when he suggests that private accusations are appropriate to republics. The Roman rule that one citizen may accuse another, he says, "was agreeable to the spirit of a republic where each citizen ought to have an unlimited zeal for the public good." But, he adds, when the emperors continued this republican maxim there "instantly appeared a pernicious tribe, a swarm of informers." These crafty, wicked men, he says, stooped to any indignity to serve the purposes of their ambition. This is probably designed to warn his fellow Frenchmen because he adds that "luckily we are strangers to it in our country." Then, he declares to be admirable the French law by which the prince appoints an officer in each court of judicature to prosecute all sorts of crimes in his name. If such a "public avenger" should abuse his office he would soon be held to account. Montesquieu also takes exception to Plato's idea that those who neglect to inform should be punished.[60] He considers this improper for his time and his country, thus suggesting again that each national society should find its standards in its own nature.

The proposition that the nature and amount of punishment

should be determined in relation to the psychological consequences upon the accused is first argued in *Les Lettres Persanes*. It arises in a discussion of governmental methods. Usbek, the Persian traveler, is considering "which government is most conformable to reason" and he opts for "that which arrives at its end with the least difficulty" and "that which leads men in a way which best suits their disposition."[61] We may note that he does not make minimum friction the end objective of government but rather the criterion of the means for attaining its goal. "If, under a mild government," he explains, "the people are as obedient as under a severe one; the first is preferable because it is most conformable to reason." Thus, the aim in method is to gain submission with the least severity. Usbek argues further that obedience to the laws of a state does not correspond necessarily to the cruelty of penalties imposed. Rather, the effectiveness of punishment depends largely upon appropriateness to the beliefs and customs of the people. "The imagination conforms itself to the mores of the country in which we live: eight days imprisonment, or a lighter punishment, affects the mind of a European, brought up under a mild government, as much as the loss of an arm intimidates an Asiatic." Men affix "a certain degree of fear to a certain degree of punishment" so that "a Frenchman shall be driven to despair at the infamy of a punishment to which he is condemned, which would not deprive a Turk of his sleep for one quarter of an hour." He doubts that "policy, justice and equity are better observed" in Turkey or Persia than in Holland or England.

The theory of psychologically determined punishment is further asserted in *L'Esprit des Lois,* and it is even more connected with the choice of political systems. "The severity of punishments," Montesquieu declares there, "is fitter for despotic governments, whose principle is terror, than for a monarchy or a republic, whose spring is honor and virtue." There is a tendency in this discussion to bracket monarchy and republic together as "moderate governments."[62] In those systems, he says, "the love of one's country, shame and the fear of blame are restraining motives, capable of preventing a multitude of crimes. Here the greatest punishment of a bad action is conviction." This is a considerable step in the development of sociolological jurisprudence and penal reform. Then Montesquieu gives a characterization of civil laws which clearly shows his esteem for that legal order. "The civil laws have therefore a softer way of correcting, and do not require so much force and severity." This is in relation to moderate and despotic governments but the former have much more respect than the latter for civil laws. The higher value which Montesquieu gives to civil laws is a further indication that he considers civil liberty, by right and in fact, to be distinct from political liberty. Also, it shows the extent to which the liberty of the citizen is based upon processes other than the "political liberty in respect of the constitution" under which he discusses the English governmental structure.

The principle that the legislature is to deal with general situations and the courts with particular ones is also implicit in the remark that in moderate states "a good legislator is less bent upon punishment than preventing crimes." Like Plato and Aristotle, Montesquieu often gives the legislator an educational role. It seems to me that he is saying that the legislator should leave the penalizing business largely to the courts and devote most of his efforts to inspiring good conduct. In fact, Montesquieu suggests that a legislator deeply concerned with imposing penalties might cause increased crime. He finds an example of this among the Chinese; "the more the penal laws were increased in their empire, the nearer they drew towards a revolution." He explains that in China punishments were augmented in proportion as the public morals were corrupted. On the other hand, in almost all governments of Europe, "penalties have increased or diminished in proportion as those governments favored or discouraged liberty."[63] Thus, Montesquieu equates the moderation of punishments with the scope of liberty.

The idea that punishment is to be related to psychological consequences would seem to mean that the amount of punishment may vary with the type of society and government because of the corresponding differences in the general and the special spirit of the people involved. The clearest example of the relation of principle to penal methods is despotic government. The despot must continually take into account that the people are held in obedience by fear and only by fear. Montesquieu points out that such people dread the pain of dying more than the loss of life while in a moderate state the reverse is true. The psychological situation affects also the authors of punishments. Conquerors and monks, who are in the excess of happiness and misery, respectively, are equally inclinable to severity. "It is mediocrity alone and a mixture of prosperous and adverse fortune that inspire us with lenity and pity." Here is another indication of Montesquieu's preference for a position between excesses and his treatment of both extremes as equally bad in much the same manner as Aristotle's arguments in the *Ethics*.[64] Montes-

quieu finds that the tendencies of individuals toward extreme attitudes are observable also among nations. The people of savage and
despotic countries are themselves cruel. "Lenity reigns in the moderate governments." There a good legislator can make anything
serve as punishment. Whatever the law calls a punishment is effective; he notes, for instance, one of the chief penalties at Sparta was
to deprive a person of the power of lending out his wife or of receiving the wife of another man. Again, Montesquieu gives the legislator an educational role and urges him to fit the laws to the structure, mores, and spirit of the national society.

Montesquieu's explanation that punishment should be viewed
for its psychological consequences would seem to be another reminder that at least some of the difference between social classes is
real and natural. The recognition of this is one of the principal elements of what he means by monarchy. The assumption that the earlier monarchy of France was based upon natural distinctions among
people seems to account for his idealization of the older system. "In
the ancient French laws," he declares, "we find the true spirit of
monarchy."[65] In explaining that different kinds of punishment are
appropriate for the common people and for the nobility, he assumes that the two classes have contrasting psychological postures
and would be hurt differently by the same punishment. In the case
of a pecuniary penalty, he says, the common people should be less
severely punished than the nobility because the fine would fall
more heavily upon the peasant. On the other hand, in the case of
imprisonment for crime, the punishment should be less for the
nobleman because by it he loses his honor and his voice, whereas
the peasant undergoes merely a physical restriction.

The recognition of social psychology appears also in the argument that the legislature should employ methods of persuasion or
education rather than coercion. Montesquieu points out that in
Rome the legislator often had merely to specify the right road and
the people would follow. For instance, the Valerian law inflicted no
other punishment than that of being reputed a dishonest man.
Montesquieu argues that, where there is moderate government, the
lesser penalty may be the more effective. "Experience shows that in
countries remarkable for the lenity of their laws the spirit of the inhabitants is as much affected by light penalities as in other countries by severe punishments."[66] The use of cruel punishments to
stop some new type of violence may even cause "the spring of government" to lose its "elasticity." The imagination of the people, he

explains, grows accustomed to severe action and the effectiveness of mild punishments disappears, so that cruel action must be taken in every case. Then even severe punishment loses its force and the evil becomes as common as ever. The proposition is illustrated by the problem of punishing a soldier who deserts. The soldier is accustomed to venturing his life and has less fear of death than of shame. A punishment which brands him with infamy for life, might actually be greater, than the punishment of death.

When Montesquieu undertakes to provide a formula for measuring the degree of proper punishment, he takes "nature" for the determining factor. "Mankind must not be governed with too much severity," he asserts. Instead, "we ought to make a prudent use of the means which nature has given us to conduct them." He explains that, if we inquire into "the cause of all human corruptions, we shall find that they proceed from the impunity of criminals, and not from the moderation of punishments." Then he gives another of the prescriptions which show his deep respect for social psychology. "Let us follow nature, who has given shame to man for his scourge; and let the heaviest part of the punishment be the infamy attending it."[67] This seems to assume a theory of moral society and immoral man. In other words, man's desire to be admired by his fellow man is a strong natural force and this itself should be respected for its deterrent and remedial power. He argues that "if there be some countries where shame is not a consequence of punishment, this must be owing to tyranny, which has inflicted the same penalties on villains and honest men." Again, he says, if there are nations where men are deterred only by cruel punishments, this must arise largely from the violence of the government which has used such penalties for slight transgressions. He admonishes the legislator not to corrupt the minds of the people in this respect. If such a law-maker, seeking to remedy an abuse, thinks only of this object and not of the inconveniences of the action, he may by continuing cruel punishment habituate the people to despotism. Those laws themselves may have a corrupting influence and for Montesquieu this is the greater evil. "There are two sorts of corruptions — one when the people do not observe the laws; the other when they are corrupted by the laws: an incurable evil, because it is the very remedy itself." This is the other side of the twofold proposition which Montesquieu develops as the key to political liberty by right, that is, the obligation of the people to obey the laws and the obligation of the legislator to provide laws which reflect the natural genius of the people.[68]

Japan is given as an example of a country in which excessive punishments corrupted even a despotic government. All crimes were punishable by death, because every disobedience was seen as a crime upon the emperor. "They punish with death lies spoken before the magistrate; a proceeding contrary to natural defense." Even gambling was subject to the death penalty. The Japanese accepted severe laws, Montesquieu points out, because they had become hardened to them. He indicates what the government should have done: "A wise legislator would have endeavored to reclaim people by a just temperature of punishments and rewards; by maxims of philosophy, morality, and religion, adapted to those characters, by a proper application of the rules of honor, and by the enjoyment of ease and tranquillity of life."[69]

For the proposition that mild punishment aids enforcement, Montesquieu finds support in the history of Rome. In preventing intrigue and conspiracy, the Roman Senate rightly determined, he says, that, while immoderate punishments would strike terror, they would also restrain persons from accusing or condemning offenders, whereas when the penalties are moderate there are always accusers available. The idea that punishments are connected with the nature of government, Montesquieu asserts, is shown by the way the Romans changed their civil laws as they altered the form of their government. Under the kings, the regal laws were made for fugitives, slaves, and vagabonds and the penalties were very severe. The spirit of the republic would have required the Decemvirs not to include these laws in the Twelve Tables but those men aimed at tyranny more than at a republican spirit. After the expulsion of the Decemvirs, almost all of the penal laws were abolished, not by express repeal, but by nonuse. Montesquieu points out also that some of the emperors who followed the republic imposed the death penalty for many new kinds of crimes by calling them all murder. But, he notes, having established a military government they soon found that it was as terrible to the prince as to the subjects. They endeavored to temper the rule and "thus drew nearer a little to monarchy." They divided punishments into three classes, mild for the principal persons in the state, more severe for those of an inferior rank, and most rigorous for persons of the lowest conditions. In explaining this practice, Montesquieu seems to be assuming again that persons in the different social classes have varying attitudes with the result that different punishments would have the same psychological consequence in their impact.[70]

The role of civil laws and judicial procedure in assuring the liberty of the citizen is evident also when Montesquieu develops his argument that punishment should be psychologically relevant. In this he is clearly one of the modern pioneers of penal reform. Beccaria acknowledged the influence and contribution of Montesquieu in this respect,[71] and Bentham was, of course, indebted to Beccaria.

The importance of a sense of proportion when imposing punishment is declared first in *Les Lettres Persanes*. One letter asserts that whether the government be mild or cruel, the punishment inflicted should be "greater or less as the crime is greater or less." Another letter declares that the custom, in some states, of putting to death all those who offend them in the least degree, "destroys that proportion which ought to be observed between crimes and punishments." Usbek calls the relationship "the soul of a state and the harmony of empires" and acknowledges that "this proportion, carefully observed by the Christian princes, hath given them a very great advantage over our sultans."[72]

The idea of a just proportion between punishments and crimes is further asserted in *L'Esprit des Lois*. "It is an essential point that there should be a certain proportion in punishments because it is essential that a great crime should be avoided rather than a smaller and that which is more pernicious to society rather than that which is less."[73] In Russia where robbery and murder are punished in like manner, the robbers always murder, whereas in China where robbery is punished less, the robbers never murder. A similar result might come from a difference in the expectation of pardon. In England there are no murders in highway robbery because a robber there has hope of a pardon while a murderer has none. Letters of grace are another means of moderating punishment. The pardoning power of the prince, if exercised with prudence, is capable of producing admirable effects, Montesquieu notes. But not so in despotic governments because there the principle of fear must be maintained. He condemns the practice of racking or otherwise torturing criminals and suggests that, instead of authorizing such methods, a good legislator should use pecuniary as well as corporal punishments and make money penalties proportionate to wealth. The law of retaliation is frequent among despots because they are fond of simple laws, but he argues that monarchies should use retaliation in a limited manner. Punishing parents for the misdeeds of children may vary among countries according to the degree of honor among the people. In France parents may be as severely punished by shame as they would be in China by the loss of their lives.[74]

The explanation of how clemency should vary with the special spirit of the type of government,[75] turns this analysis into another argument for monarchical government. "Clemency is the characteristic of monarchs," Montesquieu asserts, noting that it is less necessary in republics or despotisms. This is related to the roles of the aristocracy in monarchies. In such governments, the great men are governed by honor and heavily punished by disgrace, and there is no need for rigor in respect of them. The remarks here show, I believe, how deeply Montesquieu is concerned with bringing honor-motivated, professional aristocrats into the French government to mediate between the king and the people. This favorite theme is repeatedly forced into the discussion of criminal law and procedure as it is in other subjects of *L'Esprit des Lois*. This analysis also helps to identify who he has in mind when he argues for the privilege of the nobility. He is thinking of the nobles who make positive contributions to monarchy for the honor of doing so and he assumes that by preserving the motivation of honor, monarchy can maintain these necessary contributions. "As the instability of the great is natural to a despotic government so their security is interwoven with the nature of monarchy." The idea of special privileges for the nobility would seem to be tied to the suggestions made earlier that the nobility should make a special contribution to monarchy and that it is honor which motivates this contribution. Montesquieu recognizes that the exercise of clemency involves judgment and that it is guided more by affections than by reason. He warns that there is a danger in punishing no crimes and that a ruler should not forget why he is entrusted with the sword.

The substantial contributions of Montesquieu to sociological jurisprudence, the reform of criminal procedure, and the modernizing of penal methods have not gone unnoticed. Eugene Ehrlich recognizes Montesquieu as a pioneer in the sociology of the law,[76] and a more recent commentator, Wolfgang Friedmann, describes *L'Esprit des Lois* as "an essay in comparative sociological jurisprudence" which "in substance undermined the doctrine of natural law to which Montesquieu still paid lip-service."[77] Another current legal theorist, Julius Stone, credits the writings of Montesquieu and especially *Les Lettres Persanes* with influencing profoundly Beccaria and Bentham, the latter indirectly. Stone declares that Montesquieu's emphasis upon the relations of laws to the mores of a particular people at a particular time is definitely connected to "the break from natural law to utilitarianism."[78]

Montesquieu's endeavor throughout Book VI to make the judiciary conscious of the basic principles of social psychology provides a further definition of what is meant by natural government. Likewise, his insistence upon measuring the seriousness of the crime by the consequences upon the society and adjusting the manner of punishment to the psychological character of the accused are additional demonstrations that "relational pluralism" is both the underlying logic of his method of analysis and the substance of his theory of natural government.

Political Liberty in Fact

Political liberty in respect of the citizen is the express subject of Book XII and the implicit one of Book XIII. Both books analyze output functions, particularly actions of a potentially coercive character. The first deals with penal laws and the other with taxes. The extent to which these books investigate the judicial, executive, and administrative functions adds support to the proposition of this study that the previous book (XI) on political liberty with respect to the constitution is primarily an analysis of legislative and similar control functions. For this reason Books XII and XIII are being considered here in advance of Book XI and its comments upon the English constitution.

The analysis in Book XII concerns criminal laws and procedures, mostly for political crimes, and, like Book VI, it argues for sociological and psychological approaches to prosecution, trial, and punishment. As soon as political liberty is defined to consist of security, Montesquieu turns to methods of prosecution. "This security is never more dangerously attacked than in public or private accusations. It is, therefore, on the goodness of the criminal laws that the liberty of the citizen principally depends."[79]

The inquiry into penal law processes is typical of much of *L'Esprit des Lois* for its emphasis upon natural growth. The perfection of criminal laws is declared to be a matter of long development,[80] and Montesquieu points out that even where liberty is much sought after, the perfection of criminal laws is not always found. Examples are drawn from ancient civilizations in Cumae, Rome, and early France. One defect in Cumae was that the parents of an accuser might be witnesses. In Rome Servius Tullius pronounced sentence for assassination of his own father-in-law. Again, the early French kings had to enact laws against condemnation without a hearing and against false testimony. Montesquieu concludes that when the innocence of the citizens is not assured, neither is his liberty.

The esteem of judicial procedure seems almost overstated when Montesquieu declares that knowledge of "the surest rules to be observed in criminal judgments, is more interesting to mankind than any other thing in the world."[81] When he says that "liberty can be founded on the practice of this knowledge only," I believe that he is talking about liberty with respect to the citizen and not that with respect to the constitution. He highlights the point by declaring that if a state had "the best laws imaginable in this respect," a person tried under that state and condemned to be hanged the next day, would have much more liberty than a pasha enjoys in Turkey. This emphasis upon the method of enforcement is like the remark in his travel notes that his first concern is how the laws of a country are enforced because "there are good laws everywhere."[82] We must recognize that in these instances Montesquieu is absorbed with the immediate issue. The large bulk of *L'Esprit des Lois* is concerned with the means by which good laws can be assured. The comment was made in England and may concern royal dispensation or neglect to execute laws, which Locke says is one basis for dissolving a government.

On the immediate subject of criminal law procedure, Montesquieu presents examples of how good and bad rules may affect liberty in fact for the individual. He asserts that a law which condemns a man to death on the deposition of a single witness is fatal to liberty. There should be at least two witnesses, and he gives a quantitative justification of this requirement. If there is one witness who affirms the accusation while the accused person denies it there would be an equal balance, and a third is needed to "decline the scale." He asserts that the French law in requiring two witnesses is more just than the Greek and Roman rule of only one witness even through the ancient law was deemed to be the work of the gods.

The inquiry into criminal law and procedure provides further instances of Montesquieu's use of differentiation and proportion. In arguing that "liberty is favored by the nature and proportion of punishments,"[83] he classifies crimes according to the degree of their seriousness to society. He explains that "liberty triumphs" when the criminal laws derive each punishment from the nature of the crime because, then, the penalty results not from the caprice of the legislature but from "the very nature of the thing," and in this way "man uses no violence to man." This is similar to the arguments in Book VI, reviewed in the last section, that the legislator should leave penalizing to the judiciary.

Four classes of crime are identified for this purpose. Those of the first species are prejudicial to religion, the second to morals, the third to public tranquillity, and the fourth to the security of the citizen. The punishments inflicted ought to proceed, Montesquieu asserts, from the nature of the respective offense. A crime should be deemed to concern religion only if it directly attacks religion. An example is simple sacrilege. Crimes that merely disturb the exercise of religion should be classed as affecting the public tranquillity or the security of the subject. Crimes of the second class, such as the violation of public or private continence, should be punished by methods of a corrective jurisdiction because they are less founded on malice than on carelessness and self-neglect. Some crimes affecting morals, such as rape, may also disturb the public security and they should be placed in a later category. The crimes of the third class affect the public tranquillity and should be punished by imprisonment, exile or the like. But, if they consist of a simple breach of the peace, they should be considered in the fourth class. This last concerns the security of the citizen and here too the punishments should be "derived from the nature of the thing, founded on reason, and drawn from the very source of good and evil." Montesquieu comments that a man deserves death if he attempts to take the life of another. If he merely breaches the security of property "it would be much better, and perhaps more natural," that such crimes be punished with the loss of property. If the assailant has no property, a corporal punishment might be necessary. This classification of crimes as a basis for determining punishment, Montesquieu concludes "is founded in nature, and extremely favorable to the liberty of the citizen."[84]

The attention of *L'Esprit des Lois* to psychological relationships is evident also in the assertion that moderation and prudence are necessary in respect of certain accusations, particularly witchcraft and heresy. Prosecution of these crimes, Montesquieu warns, is quite injurious to liberty because the charge points not at a person's actions but at his character and "it grows dangerous in proportion to the ignorance of the people." A man of exceptional conduct and pure morals may be in constant danger of being suspected of such crimes. Moreover, he adds, people are disposed to punish with utmost severity any person called a sorcerer; and their indignation increases if he is supposed to subvert religion. Also bad are ill-founded accusations of the crime against nature. Since the crime is naturally secret, prosecution has sometimes been based merely upon the deposition of a child. The crime will make little headway, he says, as long as there are no customs which invite it.[85] This discussion is a further indication of Montesquieu's desire to exclude religion from government and particularly from law enforcement.

The contention in this study that Book XII deals with political and not civil crimes is supported by the considerable attention which the book gives to the crime of high treason. This is clearly a political crime, and the discussion of it extends from Chapter 7 to Chapter 18, with few interludes. The principal theme appears to be that moderation is necessary in enforcement and adjudication as well as in legislation. Thus the inquiry is relevant to the primary objective of the whole of *L'Esprit des Lois*.

First of all, Montesquieu has much to say about how the crime of treason should be defined. The substance of what he asserts is that the term should not be defined too vaguely or too broadly. "If the crime of high treason be indeterminate," he points out, "this alone is sufficient to make the government degenerate into arbitrary power."[86] Examples include the laws of China which make punishable with death any disrespect to the emperor, such as a mistatement by a reporter for the Court gazette. Satirically perhaps, he remarks that those who question a prince's judgment should be prosecuted for sacrilege rather than treason. Likewise, attempts to make false coins or to injure an officer of the sovereign should not be treated as high treason.

The public character of the crimes under consideration is shown by the arguments for free speech and press. Treason, Montesquieu declares, should apply to overt actions and not to thoughts.[87] Likewise, it should not be extended to indiscreet speeches. There is, he says, "a great difference between indiscretion and malice." Words alone are only an idea, he points out, and much depends upon the tone in which they are uttered. When the law treats such speech as treason, "there is an end not only of liberty but even of its very shadow." This he considers to be extremism, I believe. He argues that princes should be willing to moderate their power since "a milder chastisement would be more proper on those occasions than the charge of high treason." There is a position similar to a later one by John Stuart Mill in Montesquieu's declaration that words should not be punished unless they incite action.[88] Then, he says, it is the action in which words are employed that is being punished. The same theme appears in the discussion of satirical writings and their effect upon different kinds of government. Montesquieu issues a general caution at the start, pointing out that when writings are in no way preparative to high treason, they cannot amount to that charge. He condemns a number of rulers for their inability to see above satire. Augustus and Tiberius subjected satirical writers to the same punishment as that imposed for violating the law of majesty. Nothing was more fatal to Roman liberty, Montesquieu declares. He observes that satirical writings are hardly known in despotic governments while in monarchies they are forbidden as a civil wrong and not as a capital crime. In a democracy they are not hindered because "they flatter the malignancy of the people who are the governing party." No government is so averse to satirical writings as the aristocratic. "There the magistrates are petty sovereigns but not great enough to despise affronts." Thus, again Montesquieu shows his dislike of monolithic aristocracy, and he points to the Decemvirs as a horrible example. They punished satirical writings with death.[89]

The apparent digression at this point in which Montesquieu condemns breaches of modesty in punishing crimes is another expression of the underlying theme that coercive measures should meet sociological and psychological standards. The principal objective in punishing crimes, he declares, "ought always to be the establishment of order." The oriental nations which adopt abominable types of penalty are in effect trying "to establish one law by the breach of another." Montesquieu does not express it, but there seems to be two kinds of law here. One is the sovereign command and the other a law of reason or humanity, sometimes called natural law. One specific example concerns the rule of the Romans which forbade the death penalty for girls until they were "ripe for marriage" and Tiberius' expediency of having the executor debauch young females so that they could be given such a punishment. Montesquieu's remark that Tiberius "destroyed the mores in order to preserve the customs,"[90] indicates that he considers mores to be broader and perhaps more ethical in content than are customs. This is significant because Montesquieu uses the term "mores (*moeurs*)" much more than "customs (*coutumes*)" or "morals (*morales*)". For instance, the general causes which give rise to the national spirit include mores and manners but not customs nor morals.

The analysis of conspiracies is another indication that Montesquieu values the civil order more than the political one.[91] In the discussion, he supports individual rights and freedom against political interests by suggesting limitations upon the duty to reveal a conspiracy. He declares that it is natural for a government to allow slaves to inform on their masters about a conspiracy against the ruler, but he insists that the slaves ought not to be admitted to testify. He opposes the law of Augustus that the slaves of conspirators should be sold to the public so that they might depose against their masters, favoring the assertion of Tacitus to the contrary even though that was not inserted in the Justinian Code. Montesquieu opposes the death penalty for nondisclosure, explaining that the Biblical command to kill even relatives who would conspire secretly "cannot be a civil law among most of the nations known to us because it would pave the way for all manner of wickedness." The duty to disclose conspiracies on pain of death should be applied only to "the strongest cases of high treason." Montesquieu concludes that in Japan the laws subvert every idea of human reason because, for example, the crime of concealment applies to the most ordinary cases. He cites the instances of two young ladies being shut up in a torture box because one had a love intrigue and the other did not disclose it. This discussion is another indication of Montesquieu's persistent antagonism to extremes and absolutes in governmental action and his preference for what is reasonable and sensible from sociological or psychological viewpoints.

The final forty per cent of Book XII tells how republics, monarchies, and despotisms should deal with treason, conspiracy, and similar crimes, but I believe that its underlying purpose is to bring out the advantages of limited monarchical government. Montesquieu considers first those republics, presumably democracies which have resorted to tyrannical laws or actions. "Great punishments, and consequently great changes, cannot take place without investing some citizens with an exorbitant power." Accordingly, an excess in lenity is better than an excess in severity; and it is better to banish a few than many and better to leave the accused persons their estates than to confiscate a large number. "Under pretence of avenging the republic's cause, the avengers would establish tyranny." The aim, he says, is not to destroy the rebel but the rebellion and to return to the usual track of government in which all are protected by the laws as soon as possible. In the supporting illustrations, Montesquieu seems to find the Greeks to be more extreme than the Romans in this matter. The former set no bounds to their vengeance against tyrants and so the Greek republics suffered "the most violent shocks." On such matters, he finds that the Romans had more sense. Cassius was put to death for aiming at tyranny but his children were preserved.[92]

The dangers of monolithic democracy may have inspired the assertions that republics sometimes need to suspend certain guarantees of liberty. Montesquieu may fear a tyranny of the majority when he approves the occasional English practice of issuing bills of attainder. "In countries where liberty is most esteemed," he says, "there are laws by which a single person is deprived of it in order to preserve it for the whole community." The bills of attainder, being parliamentary actions, are said to be akin to Athenian laws which condemned a private person provided there was unanimous suffrage of six thousand citizens. Bills of attainder are compared also to the Roman privileges adopted in great meetings. Cicero wished to abolish them because the force of a law consists in its being made for the community, but Montesquieu rejects that argument for the contrary position "that there are cases in which a veil should be drawn for a while over liberty, as it was customary to cover the statues of the gods." This is again a distaste for absolutism, but his objective may be less to qualify liberty than to condemn indirectly popular sovereignty or single-class law-making.

Another difficulty in republics is the danger of excessive use of private accusation. "In popular governments it often happens that accusations are carried on in public and every man is allowed to accuse whomsoever he pleases." This necessitates laws to protect the innocent. At Athens, if an accuser were not supported by one fifth of the votes he was fined a thousand drachmas and at Rome a false accuser was branded with infamy. Likewise, guards were appointed to keep the accuser from corrupting witnesses or judges. Moreover, Athens and Rome permitted an accused party to withdraw before judgment was pronounced. Montesquieu also infers that republican governments are apt to be oppressive to the debtor class.[93]

The further analysis of judicial and administrative practices seems also to be aimed at making monarchies less dogmatic and more attractive.[94] One danger which Montesquieu assails at this point was condemned also in an earlier book. This is the naming of commissioners by a monarch to try a private person. Such a practice, he says, has little advantage to the prince over "the common course of things," meaning presumably, the holding of a judicial trial. Also, the commissioners are likely to be intolerant. Another

practice to be restricted is the use of spies. He considers these unnecessary in a monarchy. Montesquieu seems to make a distinction
between general public order and the behavior of particular individuals and to associate spies with inquiry into private life. He remarks that spies are not required to determine if the people generally are conforming to law and that this is as much as a prince
needs to know. "When a man obeys the laws, he has discharged his
duty to his prince. He ought at least to have his own house for an
asylum and the rest of his conduct should be exempt from inquiry."

Montesquieu's characterization of the ideal prince has some resemblance to the observations of Machiavelli but there are differences. L'Esprit des Lois views the objective of the prince to be
not so much the preservation of power as the maintenance of the
proper spirit. This may reflect the difference between the then
French situation in which the monarch was too powerful and the
earlier Italian times when the danger was instability. Montesquieu's
comments upon the manner in which a monarch ought to govern
are incisive and enlightening. "A prince," he says, "ought to act towards his subjects with candor, frankness and confidence." One
who has "disquiet, suspicion, and fear is an actor embarrassed in
playing his part." Montesquieu's theory of political legal order is reflected here in his attitude toward obedience. A prince should be satisfied with general acceptance of his rule. "When he finds that the
laws are generally observed and respected, he may judge himself
safe. The behavior of the public answers for that of every individual." The prince should not be afraid, "he cannot imagine how natural it is for his people to love him." There may be a slight Machiavellian touch in the next observation that the people will surely
love the prince because "he is the source of almost all bounties and
favors; punishments being generally charged to the account of the
laws." Also, the prince should show himself to his people only with
a serene countenance so that they may share in his glory and be
protected by his power, imagining that what the minister refuses,
he would have granted.[95]

These observations upon the manner of governing in monarchies
have some similarities to the ideas of Plato on the art of ruling.
Montesquieu here would have the prince act in particular situations with justice above the rules. Also, Montesquieu thinks that
the monarch should be the source of inspiration for good habits
and activity. "The royal authority," he asserts, "is a spring that
ought to move with the greatest freedom and ease." He refers to a

Chinese boast that one of their emperors, governed "like the heavens, that is, by his example." Montesquieu assumes that there is a fine art of knowing when and to what extent power should be exercised. He says that sometimes a monarch should use the full extent of his power and other times act only within narrow limits. "The sublimity of administration consists in knowing the proper degree of power, which should be exerted on different occasions."[96] The idea that the use of authority is a sublime art is like the formula for determining which legal order applies in a given situation. There, the answer rests with "the sublimity of human reason." This concept of the monarch approaches Plato's idea of the philosopher who has wisdom beyond that of the laws. Thus, the ideal ruler governs in relation to each specific event, guided by principles too essential or too subtle to be translated into written rules. This interpretation of Montesquieu's ideas on political execution seems to support also his concluding observation that the felicity of monarchies consists in the opinion which the subjects entertain of the lenity of the government.

Montesquieu may combine aspects of Plato and Machiavelli into a system that associates the prince directly with the pleasant matters and leaves the unpleasant ones for indirect action. A monarch, he says, should govern with gracious facility and leave the imposition of order to those charged with the enforcement of law. "There is a certain ease in commanding; the prince ought only to encourage, and let the laws menace." He also asserts that a monarch should be accessible to his people and warns against strong restrictions, recalling that a czar who imposed a death penalty for presentation of an improper petition was never approached by his people.

Montesquieu's advice to rulers on the proper manner of governing may be less cynical than that of Machiavelli because Montesquieu is less concerned about power and more about liberty. This may reflect the difference in their respective situations. The Italian princes of 1500 may have lacked sufficient power, but this could hardly be said of the French monarch of the eighteenth century. Perhaps, Montesquieu is even more aware of the importance of psychological influences and the way of doing things than was Machiavelli. There is much attention to the manner of ruling in *L'Esprit des Lois* at this point. "The mores of the prince contribute as much to liberty as the laws," Montesquieu declares. He explains that the manners of the ruler can "transform men into brutes and brutes into men." If the prince loves free souls, he will have subjects, but, if he loves base souls, he will have slaves. "Would he know the great art of ruling, let him call honor and virtue to attend his person; and let him encourage personal merit."[97] He should not fear the rivalry of men of merit, and he should gain the hearts of his people without subduing their spirits. "Let him render himself popular; he ought to be pleased with the affections of the lowest of his subjects, for they too are men." The common people, Montesquieu asserts, require so little condescension, that they should be humored. Their remoteness will prevent them from giving the prince any uneasiness. Here again is the plea for the monarch to have a democratic attitude toward the people. Likewise, he warns princes to be particularly circumspect about raillery. It may indicate moderation because it borders upon familiarity; it is less excusable in a prince than in the lowest subject. Much less should a prince offer an affront to any of his subjects. Monarchs, he declares, "are instituted to pardon, to punish, but never to insult."[98]

Advice on the moderating and tempering of governance is given even to despots. This is an exceptional instance in which despotic governments are not treated as ideal types of absolute arbitrary rule but are recognized as empirical arrangements which may vary with the situation. In fact, this leads to one of the sharpest statements of the volume on the interplay of the religious, civil, and political legal orders. Montesquieu admits that despotic governments are inherently the same but asserts that circumstances of a religious or cultural character may cause a degree of difference even in despotisms. Such governments do well to establish certain ideas, such as the idea that the prince is the father of the people. Likewise, there should be a sacred book to serve as a rule because the religious code makes up for the civil code and sets limits on arbitrary action. Accordingly, the judges in dubious cases should consult the ministers of religion. "But if it is a capital crime, it may be proper for the particular judge, if such there be, to take the governor's advice, to the end that the civil and ecclesiastical power may be tempered also by the political authority."[99] Thus, in despotisms, which generally depend upon religious power for their force, the political will may be a moderating element. Montesquieu may be a bit cynical in this reordering of traditional values, but again his aim, I believe, is to exclude ecclesiastical dogmas and clerical representatives from the governmental decision-making functions.

While Book XIII, "on the relation which the levying of taxes and the greatness of public revenues bears to liberty," does not expressly specify the type of liberty involved, it would seem to be that type relating to the citizen because the book concerns the effect of executive actions upon the individual citizens rather than the manner in which authority is constituted. It deals more with liberty in fact than liberty by right and, in current terms, more with output channels than with input arrangements.

Book XIII also provides evidence that this portion of *L'Esprit des Lois* concerns political law as distinguished from the civil law and the laws of nations. A taxing statute requires a superior authority and hence comes within Montesquieu's definition of political law. In addition, this book shows the necessity of a third type of executive authority, that, is, one other than the two types of executive power identified at the start of the chapter on the English Constitution in Book XI. At that point government is said to embrace three powers, the legislative, the executive under the law of nations, and the executive under the civil law. These last two cannot embrace the administration of taxes. Taxation rather clearly comes within the political area and has long been the special province of the legislative authority. This is further evidence that Montesquieu assumes the political and legislative realms to be more or less coterminous. The executive authority under political law may not have been mentioned in the first classification of powers at the start of the chapter on the English Constitution because that branch of the executive falls within the area of legislative authority.

The book on taxation analyzes at least six relationships involved in tax policy and administration. These relationships are: between the individual and the state in respect of the burden of taxation, between taxes and economic conditions, between the kinds of taxes and the economic status of the people, between the amount of taxes and the degree of liberty, between the acceptability of tax increases and the type of government, and, lastly, between the nature of the taxes and the kinds of government.

The relationship considered first is that of the individual and the state with respect to the aggregate tax burden. Here, Montesquieu views government to be a common means of protection, and he deems taxation to be the cost of protecting the property left after the payment of taxes. "The public revenues are a portion that each citizen gives of his property, in order to secure or enjoy the remainder." The proper way to fix these revenues, he says, is to consider both the necessities of the state and those of the subject. "The real wants of the people ought never to give way to the imaginary

wants of the state." He may have France in mind when he explains
that imaginary wants flow "from the passions and the weakness of
the governors, from the vain conceit of some extraordinary project,
from the inordinate desire of glory, and from a certain impotence of
mind incapable of withstanding the impulse of fancy." He is speaking of ministers as well as monarchs because he remarks that some
"ministers of a restless disposition" have often imagined that "the
wants of their own mean and ignoble souls were those of the state."
Nothing, he says, requires more wisdom and prudence than the determination of the amount of taxes. "The public revenues should
not be measured by the people's abilities to give, but by what they
ought to give."[100]

The second relationship examined, that of taxes to social and
economic circumstances, is another demonstration of the conditional character of political decisions. Montesquieu declares that "it
is bad reasoning to say that the greatness of taxes is good of itself."
As an example, he asserts that, while in certain monarchies some
petty states are exempt from taxes, such states may be no more prosperous than their neighbors, if they cannot attract industry. Incidentally, this is another instance in which Montesquieu's analysis of
economic matters seems to concern a monarchy composed of small
states or provinces, much like a confederate republic. On the main
point, he seems to argue that economic conditions as well as taxes
may explain the wealth or poverty of a country. Wealth inspires
every heart with ambition and poverty gives birth to despair.
"Nature is just to all mankind and repays them for their industry," but, if an arbitrary prince deprives people of nature's bounty,
the people would dislike industry and indolence, and inaction
would be their only happiness.[101]

The inquiry into the relation of taxes to the economic status of
the people may be an indirect criticism, or perhaps even satire, of
the situation in France because it introduces the idea of a society
under villanage. When a conquered people are wholly under villanage, Montesquieu contends that for the sake of both the slaves and
the masters, the burden of servitude should not be increased. This
applies to a republic, such as Sparta, and also to monarchy and despotic government. For a country in which the people are partly free
and partly under villanage suggestions vary with the type of government. In a republic which has reduced a people to serfdom the
citizens should not be allowed to increase the burden of the serfs. A
case in point is Sparta where the Helots were better workers and

their masters better citizens when an increase in servitude was not
permitted. In a monarchy, the nobles should not have the power to
increase the service or tribute. If the prince wants more taxes,
Montesquieu declares, the lords should pay it and not harass the
serf until he dies of misery or flees into the woods. In a despotic
government, this rule is still more indispensable. When Peter I demanded his taxes in money, he made a very wise rule that the gentleman pays the same tax whether the peasants increase or decrease
so that there is no interest in vexing the peasants.[102] In this analysis,
Montesquieu's attitude seems to be more democratic than aristocratic.

Implications of socially graduated taxes are found in the discussion of a country where all of the individuals are free citizens and
there is no villanage. Three kinds of taxes are deemed possible in
this situation: those on the persons, those on the land, and those on
merchandise, either singly or in combination. "In the taxing of persons, it would be an unjust proportion to conform exactly to that of
property."[103] As an example, Athens divided citizens into four
classes, and for those in the three highest classes the tax was related
to the amount of produce, but for those in the fourth class, even if
they had some produce, there was no tax. In finding this just, Montesquieu remarks that if it did not follow the proportion of goods, it
followed the proportion of needs. Each man, he says, has the same
physical needs, and this requirement ought not to be taxed. Actually, what he describes is a compound proportion, with a basic ex-
emption for minimum necessaries. Elsewhere, Montesquieu asserts
that every person is entitled to certain basic goods.[104] Thus, he
seems to approve the recognition of a lower class, which is under-
privileged and to which special bounty is made directly or indirectly. Earlier in *L'Esprit des Lois* he referred to the four classes of
Athens and pointed out that certain magistracies were filled from
the top three classes.[105] The ineligibility of the fourth class seems to
balance its special consideration in the taxing structure.

In commenting upon the relation of the amount of taxes to the
degree of liberty, Montesquieu seems almost satirical. "Taxes ought
to be very light in despotic government; otherwise," he asks, "who
would be at the trouble of tilling the land?"[106] Maybe he intended
more psychology than economics in the remark. But then he looks
at the other side, that is, at the relationship of the weight of taxes
and the amount of liberty, and he finds a quantitative variable: "It
is a general rule that taxes may be heavier in proportion to the lib-

erty of the subject, and that there is a necessity for reducing them in proportion to the increase of slavery."[107] He declares that this always has been and always will be the case. "It is a rule derived from nature that never varies." Applications of the rule, he says, are found in England, in Holland and at the other end, in every state of lesser liberty down to Turkey. Switzerland may seem to be an exception because the people there pay no taxes, but Montesquieu explains quite sharply that in the barren Swiss mountains "provisions are so dear and the country is so populous that a Swiss pays four times more to nature than a Turk does to the sultan." A conquering people, he admits, might rid themselves of taxes by enslaving the vanquished nation, but he argues that "in this respect, they are no longer a people but a monarch." Still, the general rule holds good: "In moderate governments there is an indemnity for the weight of the taxes, which is liberty," while in "despotic countries there is an equivalent for liberty, which is the lightness of the taxes." Much of this discussion may be subtle criticism of the French rule which imposes heavy taxes while being despotic as well.

Likewise, there is a definite relation between the type of government and the acceptability of tax increases. Montesquieu says that taxes may be augmented in most republics "because the citizen, who thinks he is paying himself, cheerfully submits to them," and is generally able to bear their weight from the nature of the government. In a monarchy "taxes may be increased because the moderation of the government is capable of procuring opulence" and in a despotic government, the taxes cannot be increased "because there can be no increase of the extremity of slavery."[108] This again, may be indirect criticism of simple republics and despotisms and indirect argument for mixed monarchy.

Still another relationship noted by Montesquieu is that between the nature of the taxes and the type of government. Here governments are classed as moderate and despotic and these are considered analogous to slavery and liberty, respectively. "A capitation is more natural to slavery," he explains, while "a duty on merchandise is more natural to liberty, by reason it has not so direct a relation to the person." Thus, to say that a type of tax is relative to the kind of government is to say that it is more relevant than others to the principal conditions which obtain under that government. Again, we find that naturalness means appropriateness to the conditions. Montesquieu gives still another example of this. "It is natural in a despotic government for the prince not to give money to his soldiers, or to those belonging to his court; but to distribute lands amongst them, and of course that there should be very few taxes." If the prince does give money, "the most natural tax" that he can levy is a capitation but it could not be large because there can be no classes of contributors in a despotism.

The proposition of this study that Montesquieu has the viewpoint of the new commercial class as well as that of the old landed nobility is suggested again by his tax recommendation for moderate government. He shows considerable insight into the operation of taxes upon goods. "The natural tax of moderate governments," he says, "is the duty laid on merchandise." That exaction, he explains, is really paid by the consumer although advanced by the merchant to the government. Hence, "the merchant must be considered on the one side as the general debtor of the state, and on the other as the creditor of every individual." Montesquieu explains that the merchant advances the duty to the state when he buys the goods and is repaid by the consumer at some future date. "It is, therefore, obvious that in proportion to the moderation of the government, to the prevalence of the spirit of liberty, and to the security of private fortunes, a merchant has it in his power to advance money to the state, and to pay considerable duties for individuals." He may be speaking from first hand knowledge as as exporter to England when he says that there a merchant really loans the government 50 or 60 pounds sterling for every tun of wine he imports. "Where," Montesquieu asks, "is the merchant that would dare do any such thing in a country like Turkey?"

The adversion to extremes, which we see at many points throughout *L'Esprit des Lois,* is evident for another time in the chapter of Book XIII on "Abuse of Liberty." Here, Montesquieu endeavors to explain how excessive use of freedom may lead to servitude. In the analysis, the terms liberty and moderate government may be used interchangeably and the explanation might seem to involve a paradox or contradiction. He says that the abuse of liberty derives from "these great advantages of liberty." As "a moderate government has been productive of admirable effects, this moderation has been laid aside; because great taxes have been raised, they wanted to carry them to excess." His analysis of this phenomenon amounts to a three stage cycle of decline. "Liberty produces excessive taxes; the effect of excessive taxes is slavery; and slavery produces a diminution of tribute."[109] The argument that liberty causes excessive taxes may be another attack upon extreme tendencies of both prince and people. There is also cynicism in Montesquieu's comments on the practice of some eastern despots to exempt from taxes each year some province that has suffered much. When European princes have done this, he says, their edicts "always make mention of their own wants, but not a word of ours." Probably France is also in his mind when he praises certain oriental ministers whose indolence keeps them from forming new projects and imposing more taxes. "The governors of the state do not perpetually torment the people, for they do not perpetually torment themselves." However, "it is impossible there should be any fixed rule in our finances, since we always know that we shall have something or other to execute, without ever knowing what it is." Still, Montesquieu believes that the monarch should exempt a hard-hit province.[110]

The costly foreign ventures of Louis XIV are probably the target of the criticism of high taxes for military forces. The satire becomes quite pointed when he portrays eastern peoples favoring barbarous rulers who collected a simple tribute in preference to corrupt governments who devise a continual series of extortions. Earlier, Montesquieu complained of too many foreign wars,[111] and here he proclaims that a "new distemper" is spreading over Europe, inducing the princes to keep an exorbitant number of troops. Expressly, he speaks of Europe being ruined. "We are poor with the riches and commerce of the whole world." In Europe, the princes hire troops and pay subsidies for alliances which cause a perpetual augmentation of taxes. Also, he suggests that a sum be accumulated for contingencies. "It is with the public as with individuals, who are ruined when they live up exactly to their income."

The analysis of taxing processes concludes with an attack upon the French practice of farming revenues, that is, the delegation of authority to an individual with only lump-sum responsibility. Montesquieu views such a method as much less desirable than managing the revenues by a commission. The advantage of the commission management is that the prince is more in control and is at liberty to press or retard the levy of the taxes according to his own wants or those of the people. The failure of the Romans to manage revenues by a commission was a great defect in that government, he says, adding that even in a despotism, such as Persia and China, the people are happier with such a system.

The observation here that the unhappiest situation of all is "where the prince farms out his sea-ports and trading cities" may touch upon one of Montesquieu's foremost grievances. The control of provincial cities and regions by the central authority was much opposed by certain commercial classes as well as by the decentralized nobility. The idea that the constituent areas of the nation should be more autonomous and perhaps republican in their government, may be one of the reasons for the proposal of a confederation of republics in Book IX. Likewise, it may be one of the underlying factors in the analysis of commercial and financial activities in Books XX — XXII, as well as some other portions of *L'Esprit des Lois*. The analysis of those books in Chapter III, section one of this study indicates that for economic functions Montesquieu seems to favor small republics rather than large monarchies and perhaps to contemplate a system embodying centralized, limited monarch and decentralized, semi-autonomous republics.

In the further analysis of tax administration, the remarks are obviously aimed at the French system. "The history of monarchies" Montesquieu remarks, "abounds with mischiefs done by the farmers of the revenues." They cause all other orders to become dissatisfied, honor loses its whole value, and the natural means of distinction are no longer respected. The particular lot of the tax gatherers is wealth, and wealth is its own reward. In contrast, he continues, glory and honor fall to those nobles whose life is a continued series of labor and who watch day and night over the welfare of the empire.[112] Again, Montesquieu rests the quality of government upon those aristocrats who have skill and honor. The relevance of Montesquieu's comments to the prevailing situation in France is evidenced by the fact that one of the first and most critical commentaries upon his masterpiece came from a French tax-farmer, Claude Dupin. The critique was hastily conceived and not very sound, and publication was held up for revisions. Nevertheless, the character of the attacks on Montesquieu at the publication of *L'Esprit des Lois* provide considerable proof that what he was saying was directed at the current political situation in France.[113]

Notes

1. *L'Esprit des Lois* (hereafter referred to as *Lois*), XI, 2. For discussions of the meaning of liberty in eighteenth century France, see Emile Faguet, *La Politique Comparée de Montesquieu, Rousseau, et Voltaire* (Paris, 1902), 13-36; Paul Hazard, *European Thought in the Eighteenth Century from Montesquieu to Lessing,* (London, 1954), 174; A. J. Carlyle, *Political Liberty* (London, 1941), 150-157; C. R. Cragg, *Reason and Authority in the Eighteenth Century* (Cambridge, 1964) 3; Guido de Ruggiero, *The History of European Liberalism* (Boston, 1959), 50-66; Kingsley Martin, *The Rise of French Liberal Thought* (New York, 1956), 132-143; John Plamenatz, *Man and Society* (New York, 1963), I, 274-282; Lester G. Crocker, *Nature and Culture, Ethical Thought in the French Enlightenment* (Baltimore, 1963).

2. *Les Lettres Persanes* (hereafter referred to as *L. P.*), CII.

3. *Lois*, III, 3, 11; V, 2-7; see Chapter V, and Chapter VI, of this study.

4. *Lois*, XI, 2, 3.

5. *Lois*, XI, 3.

6. Jean Bodin, *Six Books of the Commonwealth*, Abridged and translated by M. J. Tooley, (Oxford, Blackwell), 60.

7. *Lois*, XI, 4.

8. *Ibid.*

9. John Stuart Mill, *On Liberty*, Introduction.

10. *L.P.*, LXIX.

11. *Lois*, XIX. 3.

12. *Lois*, III, 9, 10; IV, 4; V, 14; VIII, 10. See Chapter IV, second section, of this study.

13. *Lois*, XII, 1.

14. *Ibid.*, XII, 2.

15. *Ibid.*, XI, 6 (Par. 3).

16. Faguet, *op. cit.*, 15.

17. Plamenatz, *op. cit.*, I, 277.

18. *Ibid.*, I, 278.

19. For an analysis of the rule of law in Plato's *Laws,* see Glenn R. Morrow *Plato's Cretan City, A Historical Interpretation of the Laws,* (Princeton, 1960), 544-572; Aristotle's ideas on the rule of law in the *Politics* appear at 1282b, 1287a, b. Even modern legal theorists differ on the meaning of the phrase; see, for instance Julius Stone, *The Province and Function of Law* (Cambridge, Mass., 1961), 262-4, 346-348, 713; and A. J. Dicey, *Introduction to the Study of the Law of the Constitution* (London, 1941), 183-414.

20. Caillois, I, 1217-21; L.P. XXIV, CI.

21. William Farr Church, *Constitutional Thought in Sixteenth Century France* (Cambridge, Mass., 1941), 225, 254.

22. *Lois,* XV, 1 (end).

23. *Ibid.*, XVII, 2-6.

24. Jean Jacques Rousseau, *The Social Contract,* III, 8. Rousseau remarks that Montesquieu originated the principle and that he considers it true. Later in the chapter Rousseau declares that apparently "there are in every climate certain natural causes which seem to mark out the required kind of government." The quotations are from the edition by Charles Frankel (New York, 1947), 69, 71.

25. *Lois*, XVIII, 1,2.

26. *Ibid.*, XIX, 2.

27. *Ibid.*, XIX, 3.

28. *Ibid.*, X, 11.
29. *L.P.* XCIV, XCV.
30. Martin, *op. cit.*, 140.
31. *Lois*, XXVI, 1.
32. Destutt de Tracy, *Commentaire sur L'Esprit des Lois de Montes-quieu* (Paris, 1819), 62.
33. See Chapter III, third section of this study.
34. *Lois*, III, 5 (Par. 4); XXVIII, 24; XXX, 19 (Par. 2). On the distinction between public and private law in Europe, see J. W. Jones, *Historical Introduction to the Theory of Law* (Oxford, 1940), 139-157, 184.
35. This seems implicit in the discussions at *Lois*, I, 1; XXVI, 1, 15-18; and XXIX, 13. Compare the titles of Books XV and XVII.
36. The outstanding present day study by a legal theorist of the relation of law and society is probably Julius Stone, *The Province and Function of Law* (Cambridge, Massachusetts, 1950, 1961). This consists of three parts and the last part includes a chapter on the nature and scope of sociological jurisprudence. Montesquieu's place in this development is described at 399-400. Leading works on the sociology of law include Eugen Ehrlich, *Fundamental Principles of the Sociology of Law*, translated by Walter L. Moll (New York, 1962); G. Gurvitch, *Sociology of Law* (London, 1942); and N. S. Timasheff *Introduction to the Sociology of Law* (Cambridge, Mass., 1939). See also Huntington Cairns, *Law and the Social Sciences* (Baltimore, 1935). The use of the method of sociology by a judge is probably best described by Benjamin N. Cardozo, *The Nature of Judicial Process* (New Haven, 1921). Cardozo seems to reflect Montesquieu's regard for the mores and other nonlegal and nonpolitical aspects of society, as well as his relational pluralism and his dependence upon cautious and comprehensive empirical analysis.
37. This function of the *Parlement de Paris* is treated briefly in most studies of prerevolutionary government in France. A more detailed scholarly explanation of the *Parlement* appears in Franklin L. Ford, *Robe and Sword, The Regrouping of the French Aristocracy after Louis XIV* (Cambridge, Mass., 1962), 79-104.
38. See discussion of laws as a process of facilitating and protecting voluntary arrangements, Harold J. Berman, *The Nature and Functions of Law* (Brooklyn, N. Y., 1958), 375-397.
39. Robert Shackleton, *Montesquieu A Critical Biography* (Oxford, 1961), 18-19.
40. The meanings which Montesquieu gives to *loi civile* and *droit civile* are probably *sui generis*. Also, the meanings may vary slightly from time to time. Mostly they relate to persons and property and usually include domestic law, but Books XV and XVI distinguish civil and domestic servitude. Montesquieu is deemed to have received ideas from Jean Domat, *Les Lois Civiles dans leur Ordre Naturel* (Paris 1694). This appears to be a Corpus Juris for French lawyers. It divides laws as Natural and Arbitrary but is largely concerned with the latter. The primary classification of positive laws is between engagements, i.e., contracts, and successions. There is an English translation by William Strahan (Boston, 1950).
41. *Collectio Juris*, n.a.f. 12,837 — 12,842, *Bibliothèque Nationale.* The biographer Shackleton concludes that the notebooks were prepared during 1716-21, Shackleton, *op. cit.*, 18, 409.
42. For instance, there are seven double pages summarizing Novella

XXII on nuptials and three double pages on Novella XVIII concerning filial succession while others in this sequence are not reviewed, *Collectio Juris* n.a.f. 12, 842, 33-43.

43. Pierre Solignac, "Eloge Historique de M. de President Montesquieu," in *Memoires* (Nancy, 1759) IV, 247-277, at 251.

44. Shackleton, *op. cit.*, 323, 326.

45. The explanation of the spirit of moderation at the start of Book XXIX takes judicial process as the example of the evils of two extremes. It asserts that set forms of justice are necessary to liberty but acknowledges that the number of them might be so great as to be contrary to liberty.

46. *Lois*, VI, 1.

47. See Carl J. Friedrich, *The Philosophy of Law in Historical Perspective* (Chicago, 1957), 79.

48. *Lois*, VI, 1. This is another indication that the term constitution refers to an arrangement involving social classes.

49. *Ibid.*, VI, 1.

50. *Ibid.*, VI, 2 (Par. 2).

51. *Ibid.*, VI, 2 (Pars. 7, 8).

52. *Ibid.*, VI, 3.

53. *Ibid.*, VI, 4.

54. On the role of the Civilians, or Roman law specialists, in the development of French and Continental Law, see Jones, *op. cit.*, 15, 39-35, 37, 42-44.

55. *Lois*, XI, 6.

56. *L.P.*, LXXXVI.

57. *Lois*, VI, 5. The reference to Machiavelli is to Book I, Chapter 7, of the Discourses. The incident concerned Pietro Soderini, and Machiavelli argues that if there had been a tribunal before which the citizens of Florence could have preferred charges against Soderini, their fury might have been assuaged without calling in the Spanish troops.

58. *Lois*, VI, 5 (Par. 6).

59. *Ibid.*, VI, 5, Montesquieu also declares that a single magistrate is appropriate for despotic government and that Roman history shows "how far a single magistrate could abuse his power." *Ibid.*, VI, 7.

60. *Lois*, VI, 8. The reference is to Plato's *Laws*, IX. There at 856 the Athenian says: "Every man who is worth anything will inform the magistrates, and bring the conspirator to trial for making a violent and illegal attempt to change the government." Montesquieu also discusses the role of public prosecutor in the historical review of French civil laws, *Lois*, XXVIII, 36.

61. *L.P.*, LXXXX.

62. *Lois*, VI, 9.

63. *Ibid.*

64. Aristotle, *Nichomachean Ethics*, II, vi., 1107a.

65. *Lois*, VI, 10.

66. *Ibid.*, VI. 12.

67. *Ibid.*

68. *Ibid.*, XI, 4; and XIX, 5.

69. *Ibid.*, VI, 13.

70. *Ibid.*, VI, 15.

71. Beccaria, in discussing the cruelty of punishments and the irregularities of criminal procedures, remarks: "The immortal Montesquieu has cursorily touched upon this subject. Truth, which is one and indivisible has obliged me to follow the illustrious steps of that

great man, but the thoughtful men for whom I write will easily distinguish my traces from his. I shall deem myself happy if I can obtain,
as he did, the secret thanks of the unknown and peace-loving disciples
of reason, and if I can inspire that tender thrill with which persons
of sensibility respond to one who upholds the interests of humanity."
Cesare Beccaria, *On Crimes and Punishments,* translated by Henry Pao-
lucci (Indianapolis, 1963) , 9.
72. *L.P.,* LXXX, CII.
73. *Lois,* VI, 16.
74. *Ibid.,* VI, 17-20.
75. *Ibid.,* VI, 21.
76. Ehrlich, *op. cit.,* 473.
77. Wolfgang Friedmann, *Legal Theory* (London, 1953), 50.
78. Stone, *op. cit.,* 272-3, 400-1.
79. *Lois,* XII, 2.
80. On the development of criminal law in the early history of Europe, see Munroe Smith, *The Development of European Law* (New
York, 1928), 24-28. The comments of Munroe Smith on the early
criminal law recognize that much of what is now regarded as criminal
and public in substance was first dealt with in actions that are now
classed as civil and private. For instance, personal and property rights
were protected merely by actions of tort.
81. *Lois,* XII, 2. The history of criminal law in ancient Europe is
reviewed in part in one of the final books of *L'Esprit des Lois,* XXVIII,
13-36. Montesquieu considers this to relate to the civil laws of France.
82. Roger Caillois, *Oeuvres Complètes de Montesquieu* (hereafter
referred to as Caillois, I or II) (Paris, 1956), I, 879.
83. *Lois,* XII, 4. A similar proposition is asserted in *Lois,* VI, 16,
discussed above. William Warburton in his work on *The Alliance between Church and State,* published in 1736, states the proposition in
almost the same words as Montesquieu.
84. *Lois,* XII, 4 (end).
85. *Ibid.,* XII, 5, 6.
86. *Ibid.,* XII, 7.
87. *Ibid.,* XII, 11.
88. J.S. Mill, *On Liberty,* Introduction.
89. *Lois,* XII, 13 (end).
90. *Ibid.,* XII, 14.
91. *Ibid.,* XII, 15-17.
92. *Ibid.,* XII, 18. Adam Smith observes "That there is a great difference between treason in monarchies and treason in republics." The
first is described as "an attempt on the king's person" while the other
is an attempt "on the liberties of the people." For this reason, the
maxim of assassination became established in republics and not in monarchies. "The laws of monarchy are therefore unfavorable to the
assassination of tyrants" while in a republic, "the definition of a
tyrant is quite clear." He adds that the existing republican governments in Europe do not encourage this maxim because monarchies
now set the fashion. Adam Smith, *Lectures on Justice, Police Revenue
and Arms* (New York, 1964), 55.
93. *Lois,* XII, 19, 20, 21. The servitude and subjection that may
come to the debtors is associated with the laws of classical republics. The discussion points out that Athens and Rome first permitted
insolvent debtors to be sold as slaves. Solon redressed this abuse at
Athens by ordaining that no man's body should answer for his civil

debts. The Decemvirs made no such reform at Rome, even though they knew of Solon's action. As a consequence many cruel laws a-gainst debtors threw the Roman republic into danger. The people wavered between a state of anarchy and tyranny. Later, a law de-prived creditors of the power of confining their debtors in their own houses. This, Montesquieu suggests, gave the Romans their civil lib-erty.

94. *Lois,* XII, 25-30. The distinction between judicial and adminis-trative discretion is not always drawn sharply in *L'Esprit des Lois.* This intermingling is evident also in the commentary of Emile Faguet, *op. cit.,* 259, 266, 267. The difference between Book XII, with its em-phasis upon judicial procedure, and Book XIII, with its focus upon tax revenues, is reflected in Faguet's comment that the general liberty of a country depends essentially upon two things: the independence of the judges and the vote upon taxes by those who contribute, *op. cit.,* 119. The combining of judicial and administrative functions in the *Parlements* and other institutions in the centuries prior to the revolu-tion may have caused the deep running separation of the administrative function in contemporary France, with the civil servant subject only to the administrative court of the *Conseil d'Etat;* see Bernard Schwartz, *French Administrative Law and the Common-Law World* (New York, 1954), 6.

95. *Lois,* XII, 23.

96. *Ibid.,* XII, 25.

97. *Ibid.,* XII, 27.

98. *Ibid.,* XII, 28.

99. *Ibid.,* XII, 29. Other limitations are suggested for despotic governments. The father's disgrace should not be charged against his wife and children. Likewise, the prince should have mediators between himself and the accused to assuage his wrath. It should not be con-sidered a disrespect to the prince for someone to plead with him for a person in disgrace. *Lois* XII, 30.

100. *Lois,* XIII, 1.

101. *Ibd.,* XIII, 2 (end.)

102. *Ibd.,* XIII, 4-6.

103. *Ibid.,* XIII, 7.

104. *Ibid.,* XXIII, 29.

105. *Ibid.,* II, 2.

106. *Ibid.,* XIII, 10.

107. *Ibid.,* XIII, 12. The reference to subjects rather than citizens here may not be significant. Throughout Book XIII, Montesquieu seems to use *"les citoyens"* and *"les sujets"* interchangeably.

108. *Ibid.,* XIII, 13.

109. *Ibid.,* XIII, 14, 15.

110 *Ibid.,* XIII, 18.

111. *Ibid.,* XIII, 16, 17; IX, 7; XIII, 18.

112. *Ibid.,* XIII, 19, 20.

113. Claude Dupin, *Observations sur un livre intitule "De l'Esprit des lois" divises en trois parties."* (Paris, 1757-8). Dupin's analysis and criticism of Book XIII extend over pages 86-135, and considerable attention is given to the farming out of taxes of which he had first hand knowledge.

Chapter VII

The Political Liberty of the Constitution

The book (XI) of *L'Esprit des Lois* that contains the famous chapter on the English constitution is an elaboration of the statement in Montesquieu's definition of the spirit of the laws, that legislation "should have relation to the degree of liberty which the constitution will bear." Presumably, liberty, or at least one kind of liberty, depends for its scope upon the constitution and hence may vary from country to country. He investigates the political systems of England, ancient Germany. Athens, and Rome and at the end remarks that he might have inquired into "all the moderate governments we are acquainted with, in order to calculate the degrees of liberty which each may enjoy." He does not go further, he says, because to exhaust a subject would leave no work at all for the reader. "My business is not to make people read, but to make them think."[1]

Yet he clearly does not intend that his readers should limit their thinking to a few preliminary paragraphs of his analysis. But frequently this is what happens. Montesquieu has come to stand for his few cryptic statements about the concentration of legislative, executive, and judicial powers. The familiar picture, I believe, does not give a true impression of his ideas on either the structure or the spirit of liberty-assuring government. Here a fuller and I hope a more accurate presentation of his political thought on the liberal constitution will be set forth under three headings: the negative warnings, the positive measures, and the historical support.

Political Liberty By Right: Negative Warnings

What Montesquieu says at the start of Book XI about the various meanings of liberty and about the need of power to check power in aristocracies and democracies, was discussed in the preceding chapter. From the suggestions of using power to prevent abuse of power, Montesquieu moves toward his study of the English constitution by inquiring into the ends or goals of different governments. He points out that while all governments have the same general goal, which is preservation, yet each has another particular objective.[2] Rome had increase of dominion for its object, and Sparta had that of war. The Jewish laws had religion as their objective; Marseilles, commerce; China, public tranquillity; and the laws of Rhodes, navigation. The savages had natural liberty as their object. Despotic states have the pleasure of the prince as their object, and monarchies, the glory of the prince and the kingdom. Then the law of Poland, presumably the Liberum Veto, has the independence of individuals as its objective, and, hence, the oppression of the whole results.[3] One nation in the world has political liberty for the direct end of its constitution. This, of course, is England, and Montesquieu says that he will examine the principles on which this liberty is founded.

The chapter on the constitution of England is one of the longest in the whole of *L'Esprit des Lois,* and there is a common tendency to pay much more attention to the first portion of about a dozen paragraphs than to the remaining portion of some sixty or more paragraphs. The first portion is preliminary and negative in character, setting forth classifications of power and warnings against concentration. This is the part most often made to stand for the separation of powers. The remaining portion is essentially substantive and positive in character, but it is seldom drawn upon for support of American doctrines.

The opening paragraphs of the chapter are often cited for the classification of governmental powers to be legislative, executive, and judicial. But I believe that throughout the chapter Montesquieu presents three different sets of powers and that the one usually mentioned, that is, legislative, executive and judicial, is the least essential to his theory of government. That classification may be, perhaps, a given condition for any constitutional analysis and thus necessary in that sense to his theory of government, but I believe that it does not go to the heart of Montesquieu's prescription to assure political liberty with respect to the constituion.

The first trichotomy of powers and the one most peculiar to Montesquieu's analysis of rational and natural government is basically three kinds of positive law. The first paragraph of the chapter on the English constitution is clearly a differentiation of legal realms. "In every government there are three sorts of power," he says, "the legislative; the executive in respect to things dependent on the law of nations; and the executive in regard to matters that depend on the civil laws."[4]

This may appear to be similar to Locke's classification of governmental power as legislative, executive, and federative,[5] even though Montesquieu does not use the term "federative." Like Locke, Montesquieu here makes no express reference to the judiciary, but he divides the executive between the domestic and foreign spheres. Later he calls the domestic executive the judicial authority.[6]

However, this threefold classification may have a basis which is peculiar to L'Esprit des Lois. It may be three sets of relations which correspond to the three types of positive law set forth in Book I and repeated in varying contexts in other parts of the volume. These three are the political law, the civil law, and the law of nations. At the start of Chapter 6 in Book XI, Montesquieu mentions expressly the last two, and the other is surely involved in the functions of government. In Book I, he defines the political law to concern relations between the governor and the governed, the civil law to deal with relations among individuals, and the law of nations to concern the relations among peoples. Most of the time throughout L'Esprit des Lois he considers them to be distinct legal realms.[7] For instance, we have seen in the preceding chapter that Book VI deals with the application of civil laws and that Book XII treats of the enforcement and adjudication of certain political laws. The separate character of these and other kinds of law is clearly expressed in the nine-fold classification at the start of Book XXVI and in the discussions throughout that book.[8] The threefold classification of positive law may have been less novel then than it seems to be now. The division of law into public law, private law, and the law of nations appears in the work of Jean Domat, published near the end of the seventeenth century. It is considered to be one of Montesquieu's sources in the analysis of law.[9]

The separate character of political and civil laws is a key point in Montesquieu's political theory because there is a strong tendency throughout L'Esprit des Lois to make the civil law a guide for the political law and the legislature. Also, Montesquieu tends to expand the scope of the civil law by assuming it to include some property laws which constitutional legists before Bodin call the customary law and which Bodin adds to the natural law.[10] The distinction which Montesquieu makes between political and civil laws corresponds generally to that difference between public law and private law which is much respected by continental legal theorists and much avoided by English and American commentators of the law.[11] Montesquieu emphasizes this distinction and in fact makes it a basic element of his theory of government.

The idea that the first mentioned function of the state, that is, the legislative process applies to the political law and not to the other two types of law has substantial although indirect support through *L'Esprit des Lois*. In Book XXVII one type of political law is associated with enactments by representative bodies and at the same time expressly distinguished from civil laws.[12] Then, the whole work gives a general impression that the civil laws are the product of the judiciary and private agreements whereas the political laws are the product of such political personalities and representatives as the king, the senate, and the assembly. The law of nations also has its peculiar sources. Much of it arises from agreement of the executive authorities of different nations rather than from the parliamentary or legislative organs of particular countries.

This specification of the three powers of a government also raises a fundamental question about the character of the executive with respect to the political law. Montesquieu expressly recognizes the executive with respect to the law of nations and the executive that acts under the civil laws, but makes no direct mention of an executive function dealing with political law. This last type of action can hardly be excluded from government so that Montesquieu must have assumed that it is embraced by or subsumed under the first of the three powers, which he calls the legislative. Thus, we may conclude that here he is not making a distinction between the political legislative and the political executive. Later he may do this but at the start of the chapter on the English constitution I believe that he is distinguishing the whole political realm from the civil order and the law of nations, and that the legislative stands for the whole political realm.

On this basis, the first paragraph of the analysis of the English constitution indicates that the powers of the state are relations arising from three coordinate kinds of positive law, of which the political law is one. At times, Montesquieu seems to consider the political law to be like present day constitutional law but other times he appears to mean a statutory type of law. Moreover, I believe that its content is distinct from that of the law of nations and the civil law. When the legislature enacts a statute superseding some aspect of these other kinds of law, we might say that that aspect becomes a matter of political law but this in my opinion does not eliminate the distinction among the three types of law. There may be areas of either the law of nations or the civil law which are beyond the legal jurisdiction of the parliament. Also, even where the legislature may have potential supremacy there are still considerable areas of the law of nations and the civil law where the parliament has not acted and where action may not be rational, prudent, or feasible. Thus, government under law is not the same as legislative supremacy. The executive and judiciary may and should act under laws which in large part do not derive from the legislature. To summarize, the first three-fold classification of governmental powers in the chapter on the constitution of England can reasonably be considered to represent three distinct sources or kinds of legal authority.

The second paragraph elaborates the first; it specifies the functions within the three areas without changing their character or scope. Also, it makes clear that Montesquieu is assuming a monarchy under law with the prince or magistrate performing all functions. He gives more detail about the three groups of functions which correspond to the three types of positive law. By the first power "the prince or magistrate enacts temporary or perpetual laws, and amends or abrogates those that have been already enacted." By the second, the prince "makes peace or war, sends or receives embassies, establishes the public security, and provides against invasions." Then by the third, "he punishes criminals, or determines the disputes that arise between individuals." This last, Montesquieu now calls "the judiciary power" while he says that the second is "simply the executive power of the state." Even though the third realm is now termed the judicial power, rather than one portion of the executive, it still has the same fundamental character, and it may be considered the area of civil law with sources of law outside the legislative power in the sense that Montesquieu assumes the legislative to be in this discussion. What the civil order includes, I believe, is similar to the subject matter of Book VI, which can appropriately be called "civil liberty in fact." Despite these changes of terminology, the second paragraph, as well as the first, identifies three kinds of legal order and makes them the pattern for classifying governmental powers. Together, these paragraphs constitute the first classification of the three types of power within a state and the trichotomy corresponds to the three types of positive laws which Montesquieu first defines in Book I. Since for Montesquieu laws are relations, the three types of governmental functions may be called political, foreign, and civil relations.

Montesquieu's segregation of governmental functions on the basis of distinct legal realms is not irrelevant to the American system of government. The sources of law for foreign affairs are not the same as those for domestic matter. The President may make executive agreements without either house of Congress and a treaty may supersede a Congressional enactment even though the lower house does not pass upon treaties.[13] Likewise, the American judiciary develops much of our law without direct action of a legislature, and the courts may invalidate statutory provisions that contravene the civil rights of individual persons. Moreover, despite the great increase in administrative law cases and the growing role of the government as legal protector, the majority of judicial actions are between private persons.

Although the first two paragraphs of the chapter on the English constitution each identify three powers of the state, they are not followed immediately by a statement on the separation or other treatment of the three powers. Rather there is inserted a general definition. "The political liberty of the citizen is a tranquillity of mind arising from the opinion each person has of his safety." In order to have this liberty, Montesquieu explains, "it is requisite the government be so constituted as one man need not be afraid of another." Thus, political liberty is "a tranquillity of mind" arising from an individual opinion of personal safety. Moreover, this liberty or state of mind is derived from the manner in which the government is constituted; it appears to be the impression which a person receives in respect of his safety from the arrangement of governmental powers. The test here is not what actually occurs or how the government actually operates but rather the impression that comes from its arrangement. Montesquieu now seems to be judging a constitution by whether its form would give a person assurance that his interests and rights would not be dealt with arbitrarily. This should be borne in mind when considering his explanation of the English constitution.

With the definition of political liberty, Montesquieu marks a change in the focus of his analysis. In the preceding paragraphs, he identified three realms of legal order but henceforth, I believe, he limits the discussion more or less to the internal political realm. This is not surprising because Book XI itself is expressly confined to political liberty. Moreover, the ensuing analysis concerns the legislature more than any other organ, and the legislature is not necessary for either the law of nations or the civil law. There is no discussion about foreign affairs in what follows. Nor is there any direct reference to the civil laws and the only indirect reference is the idea that the judiciary deals with private realms rather than the general will.[14] Also, the discussion of the judiciary terminates rather quickly, and later Montesquieu says that the judicial power is next to nothing. This is so much contrary to the stress upon the judiciary in many parts of *L'Esprit des Lois* that it must mean that the discussion here concerns only the legislature and the executive. This is actually the case because the analysis of the Constitution of England, as we will see, concludes with the idea that the fundamental constitution is a three-class parliament.

Accordingly, when Montesquieu next proceeds to issue warnings against the concentration of powers in one person or in one body of persons, these warnings, I believe, concern principally, if not entirely, the political sphere of government as distinct from the areas of the law of nations and the civil laws. Both of these last two spheres have sources of law outside the political realm of the state, and neither necessarily involves the legislative authority as Montesquieu conceives it. The area in which warnings against the concentration of power would seem to be most appropriate and most needed is that of political law and action. This is where the citizen of France is endangered. He is not likely to feel oppressed by the law of nations. Also, that is a field in which the chief executive traditionally and necessarily acts largely on his own. Even Locke did not attempt to impose parliamentary supremacy or veto upon the foreign affairs; these matters he set aside as the federative power. Montesquieu in the subsequent analysis of constitutional arrangement does not deal with external affairs. Likewise, the civil laws, which arise primarily in a gradual manner through custom, agreement, or judicial action, were not at all as likely to be a source of tyranny as political laws.[15] Montesquieu does not consider the civil laws to be a danger to liberty; in fact, he makes them the principal standard for a free society. The whole tenor of *L'Esprit des Lois* reflects a fear of political actions and a faith in civil laws. Montesquieu is not telling the French people to check the civil realm; rather, he is saying that what threatens them and arouses their fears are the political laws and decisions. Their political liberty by right is a matter of not having to fear the enactment of tyrannical political laws.

Thus, I believe that what Montesquieu says in subsequent paragraphs about the concentration of legislative, executive, and judicial functions reasonably concerns the political laws and not the other types of laws. The three powers, legislative, executive, and judicial, referred to in the ensuing paragraphs, are not the same three powers that were described in the preceding two paragraphs. In the two preliminary paragraphs the three powers, legislative, executive, and judicial referred to the areas of political law, the law of nations, and the civil law, respectively, whereas in the paragraphs that follow they refer primarily to making, applying, and adjudicating the political laws.

The next three paragraphs which set forth the warnings against the concentration of powers are rationalistic and negative in character. They are among the most dogmatic sentences to be found in the whole of Montesquieu's writings. The first two warnings are against the uniting of two powers in the same person or persons. He asserts that "there can be no liberty" when the legislative and executive powers are united in the same person, or in the same body of magistrates. This is "because apprehensions may arise, lest the same monarch or senate should enact tyrannical laws, to execute them in a tyrannical manner."[16] Montesquieu's concern at the fear that apprehensions may arise from concentrated authority shows again that the liberty being discussed at this point is a peace of mind or a belief in security more than an actual freedom. He is preoccupied with absolute monarchy and assumes a situation in which the executive is as despotic as it was in France at the time. Without such an assumption, the idea that liberty is lost because two powers are united runs counter to a later paragraph in which he says that a moderate government is possible despite the uniting of two powers in one hand.

The next warning is against uniting the judiciary power with either the legislative or executive power. If it is joined with the former, "the life and liberty of the subject would be exposed to arbitrary control; for the judge would then be the legislator." On the other hand, if it were joined with the executive power, "the judge might behave with violence and oppression." This shows Montesquieu's strong interest in the character of the judicial function and it also seems to assume a despotic or arbitrary executive.

Having warned against the union of three sets of two powers, Montesquieu then issues what seems to be a superfluous alarm. He attacks the concentration of all three powers in one hand, declaring that there would be "an end of everything," if "the same man or the same body, whether of the nobles, or of the people, were to exercise three powers, that of enacting laws, that of executing the public resolutions, and of trying the causes of individuals."[17] This is a more limited description of the three powers than that set forth in the opening paragraph. The biographer, Shackleton, on the basis of his fine study of the handwriting of Montesquieu's different secretaries, says that this sixth paragraph may have been written as much as five years before the opening paragraph.[18] But there is some evidence that the first two paragraphs were rewritten in order to insert the definition of political liberty in the third paragraph.

Why does Montesquieu warn against the concentration of three powers when he already has asserted that the uniting of any two powers would result in a denial of liberty? Either the warnings against the combining of two powers are not to be taken literally or the one against the concentration of three powers is unnecessary. Yet, *L'Esprit des Lois* is very much a warning against complete concentration of power. Repeatedly this is called despotic. Even the paragraphs that follow are principally arguments against the total unification of powers. In fact, the notorious paragraph against complete concentration of three powers is followed immediately by a statement which seems to cast doubt upon the warning against the union of legislative and executive powers. "Most kingdoms in Europe enjoy a moderate government," Montesquieu asserts, "because the prince who is invested with the two first powers leaves the third to his subjects."[19] Thus, what seems uppermost in Montesquieu's mind at this point is the complete concentration which characterizes despotic governments. In contrast to the moderate governments in which the judiciary is with the people, he gives two examples of complete concentration: "In Turkey, where these powers are united in the Sultan's person, the subjects groan under the most dreadful oppression. In the Republics of Italy, where these powers are united, there is less liberty than in our monarchies." He deplores the plight of the subject when all powers are united in one body. "Hence it is that many of the princes of Europe, whose aim has been levelled at arbitrary power, have constantly set out with uniting in their own persons all the branches of magistracy and all the great offices of state." This, obviously, could be aimed at the French monarchs and adds to the possibility that Montesquieu in describing the English constitution was actually prescribing for his native country. The fear of complete concentration is implicit also in remarks about the Italian republics. "The number of magistrates sometimes moderate the power of the magistracy," which, he says, happened at Venice where there are three organs. "But the mischief is that the different tribunals are composed of magistrates all belonging to the same body; which constitutes almost one and the same power."[20]

What he condemns most is the complete union of powers in a single person or body, and his assertions that liberty is sacrificed by the uniting of two powers is clearly overshadowed by the much greater attention paid to the danger of complete concentration of authority. The warnings against uniting two powers can be reconciled with the principal argument against the union of all power only by regarding them as statements of tendency, that is, that the combining of two powers may tend to endanger liberty. Thus, what appears to be an absolute statement can only be a relative one.

The negative and rationalistic warnings in this portion of the analysis of constitutional arrangement are the principal statements from which the American doctrine of separation of powers has been drawn. For this purpose, Montesquieu has been made to stand for the idea that liberty requires, in effect, a one to one correspondence between a threefold set of functions and a threefold set of organs. The set of functions and the set of organs each have the same three names: legislative, executive, and judicial. This idea can be drawn from Montesquieu only by inverting the warnings against complete concentration into a prescription for complete isolation. Montesquieu himself does not do this, and the concept will be shown as contrary to his positive ideas on constitutional arrangement.

The inversion of a warning against the concentration of three powers into a prescription for the isolation of the three powers is questionable for a number of reasons. It is, of course, not logically necessary. Complete unification of authority can be avoided by partial separation as well as complete separation. Montesquieu himself does not require a full isolation, as later discussions will show, so that his negative statements against concentration are not a good indication of his positive ideas on how the powers should be distributed. He expresses himself much more sharply when he is making negative statements against what to avoid than when he speaks positively about what should be done. For instance, he says later quite definitely where the judicial power should not be lodged but admits that it is a masterpiece of legislation to know where the judicial power should be lodged. Also, *L'Esprit des Lois* is so much concerned with building a case against despotism that Montesquieu tends to dogmatize his warnings on the concentration of authority.

Although the negative statements do not give a good idea of how power should be distributed, they have been much quoted and their cryptic style makes them favorite excerpts for books of readings. But Montesquieu did not rest his case with the negative warnings. He devotes at least three-fourths of the analysis of the Constitution of England to explaining how political powers should be distributed. This principal portion of the analysis is not only the more positive but also considerably more empirical and sociological in character. It gives much attention to the organs of government, particularly the senate, which is not necessarily required by the trichotomy of powers as legislative, executive, and judicial. Likewise, the analysis considers the interplay of social and political classes and suggests pitting social classes against each other according to a formula of quantitative balancing rather than qualitative allocation. Montequieu's ideas on how the powers should be distributed are related to the classical governments of Greece and Rome and the early constitution of the early Germanic nations, as well as the contemporary constitution of England, but the positive aspects of the English analysis will be considered first.

Political Liberty By Right: Positive Measures

Rather fundamental changes occur during the chapter on the constitution of England in Book XI of *L'Esprit des Lois*. The first part of the analysis, as explained previously, tends to be preliminary and negative in character, classifying powers and sounding warnings against their concentration in one person or one group. That portion of the chapter is less than a fourth of the total, but it includes the paragraphs which are usually quoted in support of the American doctrine of separation of powers.[21] The larger portion of the constitutional analysis takes up the more affirmative explanation of how political powers are to be distributed. The shift from a negative to a positive attitude is accompanied by a general change from a rationalistic to an empirical mode of thinking. When Montesquieu assails the concentration of powers, he tends to be conceptualistic or even dogmatic and he uses the terms legislative, executive, and judicial to stand for theoretical types of function. However, when he seeks to show how the powers may be distributed to assure liberty by right, these terms tend to stand for persons or organs. For instance, he uses executive to mean the monarch and legislative to mean the assembly. Moreover, at crucial points he expressly refers to monarch, senate, and assembly, which certainly suggest the one, few, and many pattern of government more than the legislative, executive, and judicial classification.

The affirmative portion of the chapter on the English constitution has three general subjects. The first concerns the judiciary and is surprisingly short. The second is much longer and in fact forms the main body of the chapter. This deals with distributions of powers to the assembly, the senate, and the monarch. The final portion identifies and comments upon what Montesquieu calls the fundamental constitution.

The first thing Montesquieu says about the judiciary power is that it ought not to be given to a standing senate. This is a bit unexpected because previously he seemed to be talking about functions rather than institutions. The casual reference to a senate indicates that he may have been assuming it all along and that he is more concerned with the power of representative institutions than he indicates on the face of the preceding analyses. Also, we may wonder what his comment about not giving judicial power to a senate has to do with England. If Montesquieu is rejecting the appellate power of the House of Lords, he is approaching the English judicial system in a rather peculiar way. There is also uncertainty in his positive suggestions. When he says that the judicial power "should be exercised by persons taken from the body of the people at certain times of the year," he might be thinking about the English jury system without a full understanding of its function. More in line with his general attitude toward the judicial function is his next statement on the need of established procedure. He asserts that the judiciary power should be exercised "consistently with a form and manner prescribed by law, in order to erect a tribunal that should last only so long as necessity requires."[22]

The idea that the power to judge should not be assigned to a single organ, like a permanent senate, but distributed among different persons, may relate to the situation in the preceding paragraph of chapter six. There, as noted at the end of the last section, Montesquieu was discussing the political arrangement at Venice. He had pointed out that in that city the three types of functions were assigned to three different bodies. This, incidentally may be his clearest example of a one to one correspondence of functions and organs. Yet, he concludes that this is bad because "these different tribunals are composed of magistrates all belonging to the same body." Thus, separation of the judicial power helps little unless the authority is properly distributed. With this background, Montesquieu now explains how the judicial power should be allocated.

He asserts that the judges should be drawn from the body of the people at certain times in order that the judicial power, which he says is "so terrible to mankind," is not annexed to any particular estate or profession but "becomes, as it were, invisible." People will not have the judges continually before their eyes, and, accordingly, "they fear the office but not the magistrate." Here Montesquieu seems to be talking about criminal law. In fact, the next paragraph is addressed to "accusations of a deep and criminal nature." In such cases, he believes that the person accused should have the privilege of choosing his judge.

At this point, Montesquieu makes a sharp and interesting distinction between the judiciary and the other two powers. While he is against giving the judicial power to a standing body, he says that the legislative and executive powers may be given to magistrates or permanent bodies because these powers "are not exercised on any private subject." In support of this, he states that the legislative power is "no more than the general will of the state" and that the executive is merely "the execution of that general will."[23] Thus the general will concerns only the legislative and executive. Montesquieu rarely uses the term "general will" and, when he does, it may correspond to at least part of what he calls the political law. The indication in this analysis that the general will does not apply to the courts is further evidence that Montesquieu associates the judges with the civil law much more than with the political law.

The necessity of an established judicial procedure is argued briefly. Even though the tribunals are not permanent, the judgments ought to be fixed "to such a degree as to be ever conformable to the letter of the law." This is developed much more in Books VI and XII, as explained in the last chapter, but the underlying reason is the same. Montesquieu is attacking the absolutism of authority. Here, he says that, if judgments were the private opinion of the judge, "people would then live in society without exactly knowing the nature of their obligations."[24] He is not merely attacking despotism; he is also arguing for a civil order that will be conducive to commercial activity.

But he returns to his favorite theme — that authority should be distributed with regard to the structure of society. "The judges ought likewise to be of the same rank as the accused, or, in other words, his peers." Montesquieu still may be confusing judges with the jurors in England, but his principal concern is as much social psychology as judicial structure or procedure. He wants judges to be of the same class so that the accused "may not imagine he is fallen into the hands of persons inclined to treat him with rigor."[25] This is in line with the definition of political liberty, early in the chapter on the English Constitution, to be "a tranquillity of mind arising from the opinion each person has of his safety." Also, it seems that both of these statements concern political liberty in fact, which is the subject of the next book (XII), rather than political liberty by right, which is the topic of the immediate book. There is the possibility that the warnings against concentration of power and the comments on the judiciary are a bit aside from the main subject of the book. This may be why Montesquieu shortly drops the discussion of the judiciary until Book XII and concentrates upon the relations of the three parts of the English parliament.

The few remaining paragraphs about the judiciary are largely admonitions to the legislature to provide a fair legal procedure. Montesquieu's assertion that the law should not permit the executive to imprison a person who can provide security (or bail) seems to be a recognition of the right of habeas corpus as well as a requirement of prompt arraignment. Those who have been charged with crime and await trial, he says, "are really free, being subject only to the power of the law." But he recognizes that the danger of a secret conspiracy might justify the legislature in allowing the executive to imprison suspected persons for a limited time. He concludes with the declaration that the legal procedures which he has prescribed make up "the only reasonable method that can be substituted to the tyrannical magistracy of the Ephori, and to the state inquisitors of Venice, who are also despotic." Thus, his underlying purpose is still to warn against the despotism of a single class authority, including that of the judiciary.

To summarize, the brief consideration of the power to judge reflects two of the general elements of a natural political system. One is that the judicial power is not simply to be separated from other powers, but rather is to be distributed with some regard to the class character of the society. The other element is that the judges should act in accordance with a legal procedure that is regular and reasonable. These elements contribute to two implicit objectives which receive increasing emphasis in *L'Esprit des Lois,* that is, the sociological distribution of control and the professional mode of operation. The requirements of legal procedure in application and adjudication are dealt with much more extensively in Book XII, as discussed in the preceding chapter. We have noted before that political liberty in respect of the citizen, which is the express subject of that book, relates primarily to enforcement actions, and we will see that political liberty in respect of the constitution, which is the express subject of the book now being considered, relates primarily to the legislative function, and legislative-executive relations.

When Montesquieu cuts short his inquiry into the allocation and regulation of the judicial power, he turns to the distribution of the legislative power, and in a general sense he makes this the subject of the remaining two-thirds of the chapter on the English constitution. The ensuing analysis deals with the division of the parliament and with its relations to the monarch. More and more the discussion indicates that political liberty with respect to the constitution involves the arrangement of political control among the parts of a three class parliament.

Liberty is the value or condition through which Montesquieu approaches the legislative function. He asserts that "in a country of liberty, every man who is supposed a free agent ought to be his own governor," and, accordingly, "the legislative power should reside in the whole body of the people."[26] This sounds like pure or complete democracy similar to that defined at the start of Book II. Yet there he assumes that democracy means direct participation, while here he insists that democracy be representative. He now argues that the assignment of the legislative power to "the whole body of the people" is impossible in large states and inconvenient in small ones. Thus, "it is fit that the people should transact by their representatives what they cannot transact by themselves." Montesquieu seems to favor district representation. He explains that the inhabitants of a particular town know their interests better than those of other places, and he says that the members of the legislature should not be chosen from the general body of the nation but "in every considerable place." The great advantage of representatives is their capacity of discussing public affairs. "For this the people collectively are extremely unfit, which is one of the chief inconveniences of a democracy." The representatives need not have instructions on each particular affair, as in the diets of Germany. This would occasion infinite delays, and a single member could stop the wheels of government. Montesquieu sees a difference between those who "represent a body of people," as in Holland and those who are deputed by boroughs, as in England. The latter would seem to be less directly accountable. His apparent preference for the district representative with discretion to either the national representative or the instructed district agent shows again his underlying support for the professional aristocrat with authority and capacity to mediate and moderate.

Direct democracy, Montesquieu adds, was "a great fault" in most of the ancient republics because "the people had the right to take active resolutions such as require some execution, a thing of which they were absolutely incapable." The people, he explains, should have no share in government except choosing representatives. This they can do. They may not know exactly a man's capacities, but they all "are capable of knowing in general whether the person they choose is better qualified than most of his neighbors." But representatives should not be chosen for the executive part of the government since they are not fit for this. They are fit "for the enacting of laws, or for seeing whether the laws in being are duly executed, a thing suited to their abilities and which none indeed but themselves can perform properly." Thus, Montesquieu is still taking into account the capabilities of people when he prescribes how authority should be distributed. He is assuming the existence of socio-economic classes and may be talking about a model civic culture which he identifies throughout Book XI to be a society directed by law and "a country of liberty." The assumption of political classes is shown quite clearly by his references to a senate. At first, this is mentioned casually but in the analysis of the legislative power, the role of an upper chamber is made explicit.

Even though he has said that "the legislative power should reside in the whole body of people," Montesquieu calls for a senate of nobles with at least the power to disapprove laws adopted by the representative popular assembly. His arguments for the second chamber disclose a number of his ideas about democracy, aristocracy, and liberty. He asserts that in "such a state," presumably meaning a country of law and liberty, "there are always persons distinguished by their birth, riches, or honors." He prescribes that the natural or sociological aristocracy be represented in a separate way, explaining that "were they to be confounded with the common people, and to have only the weight of a single vote like the rest, the common liberty would be their slavery." Hence, he assumes that each class has its own brand of liberty. Continuing, he asserts that without separate representation, the distinguished persons would have no interest in supporting the legislation, because "most of the popular resolutions would be against them." The idea that these people should have more than a single vote may anticipate the suggestion of John Stuart Mill a century later. Mill based his argument upon a difference in education whereas Montesquieu expressly refers to differences in "birth, riches or honors." Yet the two may have much the same thing in mind because in Montesquieu's time education was limited largely to those in families which were distinguished by birth, riches, or honor.

The gist of Montesquieu's contention here is that two classes do exist and that they should have separate representation so that they could protect themselves against each other. The share of the distinguished persons "in the legislature ought to be proportioned to their advantages in the state" and this can happen "only when they form a body that has a right to check the licentiousness of the people, as the people have a right to oppose any encroachment of theirs." Thus, the basic justification of bicameral legislatures is both the socio-economic competition of the classes and the political necessity of each class having a means of protecting its values and interests through veto or compromise. Montesquieu seems to assume sufficient loyalty to class that two channels of representation will furnish adequate protection for the differing kinds of liberty. In this way Montesquieu moves from an initial suggestion of legislative power "in the whole body of people" to a bicameral arrangement in which the people are divided between the nobility and the commonalty. Thus, the legislative power will be committed, he declares, "to that of the nobles and to the body which represents the people." Each body will have "their assemblies and deliberations apart, each their separate views and interests."[27]

His recommendation of a two-class legislature brings a restatement of the three powers. This is the third identification of them in the chapter on the English Constitution. At the start, Montesquieu speaks of the legislative power, the executive power under the law of nations, and the executive power under the civil laws. Later, he designates the three powers to be legislative, executive, and judicial. Now, he suggests a trichotomy comparable to the three parts of the English parliament. He says that "the judiciary is in some measure next to nothing" so that there remain only two. These, presumably, are the people and the king because he says that they "have need of a regulating power to moderate them" and "the part of the legislative body composed of the nobility is extremely proper for this purpose."[28] Accordingly, he is giving the aristocracy a mediating role in the legislative function as he has previously in the administrative and judicial functions. This is another indication that his underlying objective in *L'Esprit des Lois* is to avoid the dilemma posed by *Les Lettres Persanes* in which a monarchy tends to become either a tyranny or a popular republic. Evidence that Montesquieu had this problem in his mind during his visit to London is found in his *Spicilege*. Among the innumerable bits of comment in this notebook is one in English after a reference to *The Craftsman* with the date, June 13, 1730. "Our monarchy," it says "is in the middle point from whence a deviation leads from one hand to tyranny and on the other to anarchy."[29] The *Craftsman* was a critical periodical of Lord Bolingbroke, and about this time there was a debate on the character of the mixed state. Bolingbroke had asserted that the safety of the English constitution depends upon a balance of the parts and that this in turn depends "on their mutual independency on one another."[30] Montesquieu also seems to be on the side of those who view mixed government to represent monarchical, aristocratic, and democratic forces and their joint control of the legislative power. The biographer Shackleton disagrees and asserts that Montesquieu never held this view. It seems to me that Montesquieu makes much of the three class structure of society. He insists upon a senate of nobles because the distinguished persons in a state need separate representation. He is deeply concerned with the conflict of the people and the king and the danger of a nation falling under the domination of one or the other. He repeatedly prescribes a mediating and moderating role for the aristocracy, first in administration, then as a depositary of laws and perhaps other judicial functions, and now in the legislature. Most fundamentally, I believe, he favors the social class distribution of political control not so much to cut authority into small, interrelated bits, but more to provide a means by which each socio-economic class can protect its own peculiar privileges or interests through the veto or compromise inherent in the joint possession of control.

Why does Montesquieu say at this point that the judiciary is in some measure next to nothing, when in other parts of *L'Esprit des Lois* he has attached so much importance to it. The answer seems to be that in this discussion Montesquieu is more concerned with the political constitution than with the civil order. Implicitly here there is the distinction which later is found expressly in Hegel's Philosophy of Right, that is, the difference between the Constitution, which for Hegel includes the monarch, the legislative, and the executive, and the civil society, which for Hegel also includes the administration of justice.[31] Montesquieu seems to regard the constitution to be the social roots of political power. For him, the judiciary is a civil-law maker but not a political-law maker or legislator. The judges may have discretion in applying the political law, but this is a matter which concerns, not the political liberty with respect to the constitution, but rather the political liberty with respect to the citizen which is discussed in the next book (XII).

His further analysis in Book XI of liberty with respect to the constitution and the distribution of power makes increasingly clear that there has been a shift in approach from a conceptual view to an organic one, and from abstract legal differences to concrete political arrangements.

The senate is described largely with respect to its social and political composition. Montesquieu here asserts that the body of the nobility ought to be hereditary.[32] It is so in its own nature but, in addition, "there must be a considerable interest to preserve its privileges," since they are "obnoxious to popular envy," and are always in danger "in a free state." Yet Montesquieu is fearful of placing too much authority in the nobility and would limit its legislative role to the power of rejecting, without the power of resolving. He would deny it the right to ordain on its own authority but would give it the power to annul a resolution taken by another.

Likewise, the executive is considered first with respect to its organic composition. Even though Montesquieu may criticize the exercise of monarchical power in France, he firmly believes that the executive authority should vest legally in a monarch. He has said this before, but he asserts it again in the analysis of constitutional distribution of powers. The executive power ought to be in the hands of a monarch, Montesquieu argues, "because this branch of government, having need of despatch, is better administered by one than by many." He points out that the opposite is true of the legislative power which is "oftentimes better regulated by many than by a single person."[33] This shows again that Montesquieu is guided in the allocation of authority by considerations of operating practicality. The executive power is placed in the monarch apart from any legislative body, not primarily to segregate political power, but because there is need for despatch in carrying out the power, and one can act more quickly than several. His contrast of executive and legislative power in this regard was echoed by James Wilson at the Constitutional Convention of 1787 and by Madison in *The Federal-*

ist.[34] The need for despatch would justify an executive of one person, however selected, and, accordingly, the essential element in this context is the monocratic factor rather than the hereditary one. The monarch of a royal dynasty might be able to inspire glory and honor better than an elected chief executive,[35] but considerable psychological attachment has developed around nonroyal executives at different times in history.

Montesquieu's insistence that a monarch is necessary for the proper functioning of a political aristocracy is one of the continuing features of *L'Esprit des Lois.* In Book II, he declares the two classes to be interdependent and here, in Book XI, he says that "if there were no monarch, and the executive power should be committed to a certain number of persons selected from the legislative body, there would be an end then of liberty." He argues that in such a way, "the two powers would be united, as the same persons would sometimes possess, and would be always able to possess, a share in both."[36] This statement does not appear necessary to the immediate argument or to the warning against uniting of the legislative and executive powers that had been stated previously. The statement might be construed to condemn the cabinet-parliamentary form of government, but Montesquieu probably does not have that in mind. More likely, he is thinking about the corruptive methods of Robert Walpole in placing members of Parliament and making them ministers. That practice was in some formal way an anticipation of parliamentary government, but actually it was the reverse. Walpole was making Parliament responsive to the monarch or his chief minister by use of influence or intervention in elections,[37] thereby destroying the capacity of Parliament to protect the liberty of the nonmonarchical classes and at the same time retrogressing to monarchical domination. This was not what Montesquieu wanted for France. Too much had a chief minister corrupted the French system. Moreover, the warning against a group of legislators holding executive power is another expression of Montesquieu's deep dislike for any oligarchic government. His opposition to closed aristocracies is that they lack moderation and act too much like kings.[38] Also, an oligarchy is not likely to inspire glory nor bestow honor,[39] nor provide the image of grandeur, of which Charlemagne is probably the outstanding example in the opinion of Montesquieu.[40] His condemnation of the Decemvirs, who usurped all authority unto themselves, and his admiration of Charlemagne, who knew how to inspire the nobles into proper channels of action, demonstrate Montesquieu's basic ideas on the necessity of distribution and joint authority.

Having explained the distinctive structure of the political organs, Montesquieu next considers the relations among them, in accordance with one of his basic presuppositions, that is, that each being or realm has both intrinsic and extrinsic relations. In other words, each political organ, such as a chamber of parliament or the monarchy is separate and distinct but at the same time essentially related to the others. What may seem to be a system of checks and balances is another application of Montesquieu's underlying logic of "relational diversity."

A deep dislike of unlimited authority, whether in the monarch or the parliament, continues to be implicit in the subsequent discussion. Likewise, it appears in Montesquieu's fragmentary notes on his travels in England. There is one note that is particularly relevant. It undertakes to explain the reasons for English freedom and in doing so shows Montesquieu's fear of monistic sovereignty, whether in the king or in a popular assembly. "England is at present the freest country which exists in the world," he asserts, adding that he does not except any republic. He explains that England is free "because the prince has not the power to do any possible thing, for the reason that his power is controlled and limited by an act" of parliament.⁴¹ He is talking about the legal structure rather than the corrupt practice. Moreover, he seems to be more concerned about unlimited democracy than about the power of the prince. He argues that "if the lower chamber should become mistress, its power would be unlimited and dangerous because it would have at the same time executive power." In contrast, he says that "at the present the unlimited power is in the parliament and the king, and the executive power in the king, where it is limited." Thus, he makes a distinction between the king as executive and the king as a joint holder of the sovereign, legislative power. Likewise, I believe that he is warning against monolithic democracy, as he did both in the comparative analysis of single-class governments throughout the first portion of L'Esprit des Lois (Books II – X) and, with a different approach, in the first chapters of Book XI. Fundamentally, his objective again is to avoid the two extremes of the irreconcilable conflict of prince and people. In fact, he says as much in the travel notes. "It is necessary then that a good Englishman seek to defend the liberty equally against the efforts of the crown and those of the chamber." The solution, presumably, is to limit both forces. Montesquieu does distinguish between the king in parliament and the king alone, and the general tenor is that a political system consists of the interrelationship of the monarch in his different capacities and the parliamentary chambers representing upper and lower classes. This adds weight to the proposition that the liberty-assuring constitution is most directly aimed at combining monarchical, aristocratic, and democratic forces.

The analysis of the relations of the political organs with respect to each other deals primarily with certain means of limitation and control. The terms "executive" and "legislative" frequently refer to organs, such as the monarch or the parliament, rather than to categories of legal process, and the factor most determining the allocation of functions seems to be the operating capacities of the respective institutions. The monarch is assigned duties that are appropriate for action by one person continuously in office while the assembly has functions appropriate for a collective group which meets only at intervals. Thus, the executive should have power to call the legislature into session. Montesquieu acknowledges that if the legislature did not meet there would be "an end then of liberty," but there are traces of Hobbes and the English civil conflict in the series of observations that a continuous session would interfere with the executive, that the king should regulate the time and duration of meetings, that the legislature should not meet of itself, that it has no will until it meets, and that, if it had the right to prorogue itself, it might never do it.[42] The executive, Montesquieu declares, should be able to restrain the legislature to prevent it from becoming despotic. On the other hand, while the legislative should not have a right to stay the executive, it should have the right and duty to examine the manner in which the laws are being executed. Yet, whatever may be the result of such an examination, he says that the legislative body ought not to have a power of arraigning the person or conduct of the person intrusted with the executive power. "His person should be sacred" because the good of the state requires that the legislative body not become arbitrary and "the moment he is accused or tried there is an end of liberty." In such a case, Montesquieu explains, "the state would no longer be a monarchy, but a kind of republic, though not a free government." Thus, in Montesquieu's theory of political systems, a monarchy may be freer than a republic. Presumably, a monarch is needed to keep an aristocratic or democratic group from becoming arbitrary. But he holds that, while the chief executive may not be accused or tried, his ministers may. *Les Lettres Persanes* depicted the ministers as greater sources of tyranny than the king.[43] Action against the ministers would be sufficient, Montesquieu argues in *L'Esprit des Lois*, because "the person intrusted with the executive power cannot abuse it without bad counselors."[44]

The principle that class interests are more controlling in the distribution of governmental functions than the conceptual categorization of legislative, executive, and judicial powers is evident in Montesquieu's allocation of certain functions to the senate of nobles. There are, he says, three situations "founded on the particular interest of the party accused" in which that body should have judicial authority. First, the senate should try the nobility. The nobles "are always obnoxious to popular envy" and were they judged by the people they might be deprived of "the privilege which the meanest subject is possessed of in a free state, that of being tried by his peers." Accordingly, the nobility "ought not to be cited before the ordinary courts of judicature but before that part of the legislature which is composed of their own body." Next, the senate should have what seems to be the power of penal review, that is, the authority "to moderate the law in favor of the law itself, by mitigating the sentence." Finally, the senate should try high administrative officials. If an administrator of public affairs is to be charged with crime, the ordinary magistrates could not or would not punish, and the legislature should do no more than impeach. Accordingly, "in order to preserve the dignity of the people and the security of the subject, the legislative part which represents the people must bring in its charge before the legislative which represents the nobility, who have neither the same interests nor the same passions." Montesquieu asserts that this is an improvement over the arrangement in ancient republics where the people were at the same time both judge and accuser. It is, of course, the impeachment and trial procedure adopted by the United States Constitution.

The executive veto on legislation is justified more to protect the privilege of the executive than to restrain the legislative assembly. The executive power, Montesquieu says "ought to have a share in the legislature by the power of rejecting; otherwise it would soon be stripped of its prerogative." Again, his underlying interest is with the privilege of a class. He argues that "should the legislative power usurp a share of the executive, the latter would be equally undone." Yet, the power of the monarch is merely to veto. "If the prince were to have a part in the legislature by the power of resolving, liberty would be lost."[45] But it is necessary that he have a share in the legislature "for the support of his own prerogative," and, accordingly, "this share must consist in the power of rejecting." Montesquieu finds support for this conclusion in the history of Rome. He points out that the "change" of the Roman government, meaning no doubt its decline, was due to the fact that neither the senate nor the magistrates, who between them held the executive power, had a right of rejecting legislation. Montesquieu would give both the senate and the executive the power to veto legislation. Thus, their participation in the legislature is not to give them the opportunity to initiate laws, an authority he has placed in the representatives of the people, but rather is to allow the monarch and the nobility the means of protecting their prerogative and privileges.

At this juncture, Montesquieu reaches the high point in his analysis of the relation of laws to political liberty with respect to the constitution. This kind of liberty, in contrast to both political liberty with respect to the citizen and civil liberty, seems to depend upon the proper distribution of political authority among the three classes. He declares that his analysis has developed "the fundamental constitution of the government we are treating of."[46] What he describes is the way in which three forces check each other. "The legislative body being composed of two parts, they check one another by the mutual privilege of rejecting." Now, he sees both the popular assembly and the senate of nobles to possess a power of rejection. Most important is that the checking of power by power is viewed to be the mutual veto which one chamber has upon the other. Then he sees the two checked by the monarch in a mutual arrangement. "They are both restrained by the executive power, as the executive is by the legislative." Here, legislative and executive stand for organs or institutions rather than legal processes. This is an empirical rather than rational approach, a sociological or psychological approach rather than a legal one. Moreover, the designation of this trichotomy to be the "fundamental constitution" indicates that this is the final identification of the three powers. Montesquieu has passed from the trichotomy of legislative, executive, and judicial to that of representative assembly, senate of nobles, and monarchy. The central feature of this constitutional arrangement is not the separation of governmental functions but the mutual right of preservation among political classes against legislation adverse to their respective prerogatives or rights. The basic organizing principle of the fundamental constitution is the joint holding of authority so that there is a "mutual privilege of rejecting." Thus, political liberty with respect to the constitution is class oriented and protective in character; that is, it assumes three political power classes and it gives each such class a means of protecting itself from the enactment of destructive or oppressive laws.

The essential element of mutual restraint in this joint distribution of power is evident in the next statement that "these three powers should naturally form a state of repose or inaction." But with the negative potential of the arrangement, there is a natural source of action. Montesquieu asserts that "as there is a necessity for movement in the course of human affairs, they are forced to move, but still in concert." His recognition that, except for necessity, inaction may result from the mutual veto inherent in a tripartite legislature suggests that his "fundamental constitution" has similarity to John C. Calhoun's doctrine of concurrent majority.[47] However, there would seem to be two essential differences between Montesquieu's ideas and those of the South Carolinian. The former concern only legislative chambers, which would be two, three, or four in number where Calhoun's theory relates to the "interests" within a national society, which might be comparatively large in number. Calhoun does not define "interests," but they would seem to be provincial regions or economic groups if not the particular states themselves. Thus, the doctrine of concurrent majority would allow a veto to each of a large number of groups and hence would be much more restrictive than the joint control of legislation by three parties. Calhoun's scheme would approximate that of a confederation of fully sovereign states whereas Montesquieu's tripartite legislature is not far distant from the traditional English Parliament or the post-1787 United States Congress. A second difference between the systems of Montesquieu and Calhoun is that the former assumes that man and society are naturally action-seeking, while this may not be true of Calhoun, who regards society as more conventional than natural. Thus, for Montesquieu the necessity of action may arise spontaneously within human society while for Calhoun it might result only from special developments or external causes.

Montesquieu may oppose pure, direct, or absolute democracy, which is generally what was meant by democracy in the eighteenth century, but he does not oppose and in fact positively favors limited popular participation in the control processes, which is what Western democracy generally means today. His preference for a mixed government which includes a democratic representative assembly as well as aristocratic and monarchical elements is evident from the discussion of legislative power. At first, he assigns the legislative authority to the body of the people and, when he qualifies this by allowing the senate and the king to participate in the legislative process, he limits these two classes to a power of rejection and maintains the exclusive right of the popular assembly to initiate measures. He acknowledges that in some ancient commonwealths, where public debates were carried on by the people, the executive had the power to propose and debate, but, he says, this was necessary to avoid "a strange confusion."[48]

The distinctive character of the legislative and executive bodies having been explained, Montesquieu takes up the interrelations of these organs with respect to certain functions, particularly the control of finances and the armies. The legislature, he says, should determine the raising of public moneys with consent of the executive, but appropriations should be made on an annual basis. Otherwise, "it would run the risk of losing its liberty." Likewise, there is a danger in "a perpetual command of the fleets and armies to the executive power." Montesquieu, like Machiavelli,[49] seems to favor citizen armies but perhaps for different reasons. The Florentine sought to strengthen the prince, Montesquieu to limit him. The latter asserts that, to prevent oppression by the executive, the armies should consist of the people and have the same spirit as the people. This is possible, he says, only if either the army consists of propertied persons serving for only a year, or there is a standing army composed chiefly of the most despicable part of the nation. To avoid this last, the soldiers should live in common with the rest of the people and not in separate camps or barracks. The immediate control of the army should be in the executive power because its business consists more in action than in deliberation. Also, if the troops depend entirely on the legislative body, it would become a military government, unless, by some extraordinary circumstances, it is kept divided through dependence upon particular provinces or it is opposed by the natural defense of capital towns. Thus, separation of power might then be needed even within the military establishment. Also, there seems to be further recognition of administrative feasibility as a guide for the allocation of functions. The classification of powers and functions as monarchical, aristocratic, and democratic may reflect not only social differentiations but also what is appropriate for the one, the few, and the many.

Montesquieu's final remarks on the fundamental constitution with respect to its origin and how long it will endure, may be more dramatic than historical. The English borrowed their idea he says, from the ancient Germans. "'This beautiful system was invented first in the woods." The remark will be explained shortly. On the possible end of such an arrangement, Montesquieu makes a prediction. "It will perish when the legislative power shall be more corrupt than the executive." If this is relevant to the English situation, it may refer to the contemporary practice of some members of parliament to be controlled through extralegal methods by the king and his chief minister.[50] A system built upon the right of class preservation logically would end when the class representatives do not exercise that right but allow themselves to be corrupted or controlled by the monarchical class. The prediction is a limited one and is consistent with the underlying proposition that the basis of political liberty by right is the social character of the distribution of legislative authority.

The aim of mixed government may be political liberty, but its principle or moving passion would seem to be the spirit of moderation. The final part of *L'Esprit des Lois* makes this the highest legislative guide but even in the discussion of the legislative constitution in Book XI there is recognition of the superiority of moderation even to political liberty itself. Montesquieu says that the "extreme political liberty" of the English constitutional laws should not give "uneasiness to those who have only a moderate share of it," observing "that even the highest refinement of reason is not always desirable and that mankind generally find their account better in mediums than in extremes." Then he ends the chapter on the governmental structure of England with a plea to observe what is at hand rather than to speculate about what might be. He criticizes Harrington's *Oceana* for inquiring into "the utmost degree of liberty to which the constitution of a state may be carried," and observes that "for want of knowing the nature of real liberty" Harrington "busied himself in pursuit of an imaginary one" and "built a Chalcedon though he had a Byzantium before his eyes." Thus, Montesquieu prefers to be guided by the empirical and sociological situation rather than by the product of rationalistic and metaphysical speculation. This is basically so, I believe, even though at this point his aim is to find a legal pattern of constitutional arrangement that would assure liberty by right. Here, he sets aside considerations of how the system is being used or misused, but elsewhere

he points out that the system has depreciated because the English
aristocracy has not kept within their proper place.[51]

My belief that Montesquieu's special analysis of the English constitution in Book XI is a prescription for France, is supported not
only by various aspects of the chapter on the government of England, but also by the chapter which follows immediately. Montesquieu refers to "the monarchies we are acquainted with," and there
is little doubt but that he has France in mind. These monarchies, he
says, do not have liberty for their direct aim and their only objective is the glory of the subject, the state, and the sovereign. But, he
adds, there is a spirit of liberty, presumably latent, which "is capable of achieving as great things and of contributing as much, perhaps, to happiness, as liberty itself." Then his description of these
monarchies shows how they differ from the legal arrangement in
England. "Here the three powers are not distributed and founded
on the model of the constitution above mentioned; they have each a
particular distribution, according to which they border more or less
on political liberty; and if they did not border upon it, monarchy
would degenerate into despotic government." Thus, we may conclude that Montesquieu is suggesting that, while France does not
now have the full freedom to which it is entitled by nature, that
goal is hopefully within reach.

The commentaries upon *L'Esprit des Lois* which appeared in the
decade after its publication do not seem to attach great importance
to Montesquieu's analysis of the English constitution. In fact, they
differ in their accounts of what he said on the matter. The foremost
criticism is deemed to be that of the Abbé le Porte. The portion of
his commentary, in which he considers *la Politique* of Montesquieu's work, is a rather cursory review of the Books II to XVIII
and there is less than average comment about Book XI. The Abbé
restates the paragraph warning against the concentration in one
person or one body of the three powers to make the laws, execute
them, and judge the individuals.[52] His comment is simply that this
is what makes despotism. He has virtually nothing to say about either legislative power or England. Claude Dupin, another critic, expressly interprets Montesquieu's analysis to mean that the English
government is a mixture of democracy, aristocracy, and monarchy.[53] The most attention by a contemporary critic seems to be the
special commentary on the government of England by Elie-Catherine Freron, who was a historian of some note. The title of the
piece suggests that Montesquieu is comparing the English system

with that of France.[54] At the start of the commentary he questions why Montesquieu in his analysis of the English constitution places monarchy in such high esteem when elsewhere in *L'Esprit des Lois,* republican government is preferred. Freron's belief that Montesquieu rates republics above monarchies seems to arise from the statement that virtue is the principle of the former but not the latter. Freron does not seem to take into account the peculiar and limited meaning given to virtue which excludes its application to monarchies. Also, he does not consider what this study contends was Montesquieu's objective in asserting that the principle of republican government is virtue, that is, that such governments are unattractive at least to the French because they require for success such a high degree of self-restraint on the part of the people.

Freron observes that the perfection of the English government is the separation of the three powers which balance themselves, but in that statement he does not identify the three powers. Rather, he adds that England is a mixture of republic and monarchy with the evil of one temporized by the good of the other.[55] He says that the English give the legislative power to the nation and that parliament has the superiority. Yet he goes on to point out the corruption in the English situation by which the king and his minister controlled parliament by "purchasing" many of its members.[56] Corruption of the legal separation had been reported by historians for at least thirty years and quite probably was known to Montesquieu.[57] It may account for the remark, noted previously, that in the analysis at hand he was concerned with the liberty shown by the constitutional laws and not with whether the English actually enjoyed the liberty.

Historical Verification of the Tripartite Parliament

Despite all that Montesquieu wrote about the governments of Rome and England, he finds that the most ideal constitution had its origin among the German peoples. He attributes the "best species of constitution that could possibly be imagined by man" to the early Teutonic nations. This, no doubt, fits in with his ideas on the source of the French civil laws and the privileges of the French nobility, but nevertheless the attribution of the ideal constitution to developments in the German forests cast some doubt on the importance of the English constitution as a source of his ideas.

He finds the model constitution not in the initial governments of the Germanic nations but rather in the ones which developed after certain migrations. The original governments were deficient in Montesquieu's eyes because the assemblies of the whole nation or tribe met directly and not by representation. The more desirable form came when the Germans settled upon lands of the declining Roman Empire. Then the peoples became so dispersed that they gave up the practice of assembling "the whole nation" (by which Montesquieu probably means the whole body of citizens or warriors) and instead acted through representatives. This, he says, "is the origin of the Gothic government amongst us."

At first, the government "was mixed with aristocracy and monarchy," and the mixture was attended with "this inconvenience, that the common people were bondmen." But, Montesquieu explains, the custom developed of granting letters of enfranchisement and this "was soon followed by so perfect a harmony between the civil liberty of the people, the privileges of the nobility and the clergy, and the prince's prerogative," that he believes "there never was in the world a government so well tempered as that of each part of Europe, so long as it lasted." He confesses his surprise and admiration, "that the corruption of the government of a conquering nation should have given birth to the best species of constitution that could possibly be imagined by man."[58]

Thus, Montesquieu describes the best possible political system to be, not an arrangement of legislative, executive, and judicial powers, but rather an arrangement providing representation and protection of the privileges or value interests of different classes. He assumes that, for governmental coordination, the foremost possession of the people is "civil liberty," of the nobility and the clergy their "privileges," and of the prince his "prerogative." We may note that the primary right of the people presumably is their civil rather than their political liberty and that the nobility and clergy are in the same category in contrast to their divided establishment in the French Estates General. I believe that the omission throughout L'Esprit des Lois of any reference to the French Estates General and Montesquieu's esteem of the legal form of the English Parliament results from a belief that separate representation of the clergy in a multi-chambered legislature would impede or distort the political action appropriate to the sociological situation. Previously, in Chapter II, I mentioned that support for this proposition appears in the analysis of English mores and manners in Book XIX. There, he comments upon the fact that the English clergy did not separate itself but supported the same measures as the laity, and Montesquieu seems to approve of that development because he then asserts that the English clergy had the purest of mores in their reserved way of living.[59]

The description of the government of the German nations may or may not agree with historical fact, but there is little doubt that it is another manifestation of Montesquieu's preference for a political system which institutionalizes the basic social classes in a joint legislative authority. Quite clearly, the fundamental or model constitution for assuring political liberty by right is one in which the three principal classes have the joint right to safeguard their respective positions. This is further evidence that what attracted Montesquieu to the English constitution was the political law which gives each of the three classes the right to prevent legislation that might unduly infringe upon their most valued interests.

Montesquieu is not content to rest his case for the fundamental or model constitution upon what he has found either in England or among the early Franks. He also draws upon the political theories of the classical republics of Greece and Rome. Here again he shows his determination to find the operation of certain principles which are not too apparent on the face of recorded history.

The comparative lack of sympathy at this point for Athenian ideas stems from his belief that mixed government should include a monocratic element. The gist of his criticism of the leading Greek theorists is that they did not comprehend class structured monarchy, that is, the sharing of powers by royal, aristocratic, and democratic forces. Aristotle, he says, was greatly puzzled in treating monarchy and distinguished species by "things merely accidental," such as "the virtue and vices of the prince," or by things extrinsic, such as whether tyranny was usurped or inherited. Montesquieu presumably favors standards that are more fundamental and enduring, such as the representation of classes. The ancients, he declares, "could never form a just idea of monarchy" because they "were strangers to the distribution of the three powers in the government of a single person." They could see the distribution of powers only in a government of the many, which Aristotle called a Polity. There, Montesquieu says, the three powers were distributed so that the people were the legislature, and the king had the executive and judiciary powers. This arrangement seems doubly bad to Montesquieu. For one thing, as soon as the people obtained the legislative power, they subverted the regal authority. This helps to explain

Montesquieu's preference for a tripartite legislature. Aristotle's Polity was bad also because the prince held all the judiciary power. "It is a masterpiece of legislation to know where to place properly the judiciary power," Montesquieu remarks, but he adds that the worst place for it is in the hands of the person who has the executive power — "the true function of a prince was to appoint judges and not to sit as judge himself."[60]

These comments show Montesquieu's dissatisfaction with a political system in which power is limited to the people and the monarch. Such an arrangement hardly permits a solution to the problem raised by *Les Lettres Persanes*.

The government of Rome receives considerably more attention throughout *L'Esprit des Lois* than does that of England. Even the book on political liberty with respect to the constitution, which is famous for its treatment of the English government, contains more analysis of the Roman system. Despite his stay in London, Montesquieu probably studied the government of England less than that of Rome. He remarks that it was impossible to be tired of so agreeable a subject as ancient Rome.[61] Some of his earliest essays concerned Roman religion and the ideas of Cicero.[62] In his study of Roman history, he may have used secondary materials, but he seems to have examined them rather thoroughly and not to have drawn conclusions from a few facts or ideas. The scope of his research no doubt was much broader than the illustrations presented in his finished writing. But even in *L'Esprit des Lois* the government of Rome is the most frequent source of illustration for the explanation of political theories.

The analysis of the Roman institutions in the final portion of Book XI provides historical support for many basic tenets of mixed government. Even in the initial period of the kings, Montesquieu finds an example of joint possession of supreme power. He points out that the first five kings were elected by the senate, the people, and the augurs, each with a veto. This arrangement embodies the vital element of joint authority or mutual negative, which is at the heart of the tripartite legislature in the model constitution. Also Montesquieu admires the later Roman constitution for its social roots rather than its legal branches. His observation sounds a bit like Polybius: "The constitution was a mixture of monarchy, aristocracy, and democracy; and such was the harmony of power that there was no instance of jealousy or dispute in the first reigns."[63] So, again a constitution is deemed to be an arrangement of political classes and not a pattern of legislative, executive, and judicial functions. Moreover, the usurpation of power by the later kings, Servius Tullius and Tarquinis, is not described to affect legislative, executive, or judicial power but rather to take authority from the senate and the people, thus upsetting the relative power of the classes.

After the expulsion of the kings, the continuing class struggle between the patricians and the plebians furnishes many conflicts and developments which Montesquieu uses to highlight his ideas on political relations. For one thing, recalling that the patrician families had acquired under the kings great privileges which the jealous plebians sought to reduce, he remarks that "the contest struck at the constitution without weakening the government." Thus, he indicates again that constitution relates to class alignment. Also, he finds in the period of the republic demonstrations of the interplay of three classes even though there is variance in their identification. Sometimes the plebeians are viewed as a separate class and other times as the whole people; sometimes the patricians and the senate are different forces, other times much the same; and then the consuls are occasionally regarded as monarchs but not always. There is a reiteration in the Roman situation of certain principles of mixed government which he asserted in previous discussions. He declares again the proposition first asserted in Book II that monarchy requires the moderating force of neutral intermediaries: "An elective monarchy, like that of Rome, necessarily supposes a powerful aristocratic body to support it, without which it changes at once into tyranny or into a popular state."[64] This is characteristic of the foremost answers in L'Esprit des Lois to the problem raised by Les Lettres Persanes. Here he calls for aristocratic intermediaries even though the monarchy is an elected one. This would seem to make the principle applicable to presidential government. But the election of the chief executive is not, for Montesquieu, sufficient assurance of a moderate attitude in administration.

Montesquieu's analysis of the commencement of the Roman republic provides another demonstration that nature requires political forces other than the monarch and the people. He remarks that a popular state (presumably in the full, logical sense) has no need for distinction among families and that the patricians became a superfluous branch of the government under the consuls because the people could suppress the consuls without hurting themselves. This seems to be another suggestion that without a moderating center

force a government becomes either a tyranny or a simple democracy. He says that while Rome ought to have been a democracy
after the expulsion of the kings because the people had the legislative power in their hands, this did not happen. In times of change,
he observes, all springs of government are tense and "there is a
noble emulation" between those who defend the old and those who
seek the new. Thus, political developments do not follow simple
logical channels but tend to be combinations of natural forces
which preclude sharp rationalistic changes. Montesquieu's observation here would seem to be supported by the developments in the
French Revolution, particularly the failure of the advocates of general will and popular sovereignty to establish a government that
was either moderate or permanent. Their attempt to replace tyrannical monarchy with absolute democracy resulted in a succession of
political systems which has alternated between extremes and never
achieved a continuing stability. Rome was perhaps more fortunate,
it seems, because the republic soon accommodated itself to the
multiple-class structure of the society.

The analysis of power in the Roman republic seems to place a
higher value upon quantitative distribution than upon qualitative
separation, that is, the desired political system is attained more by
adjusting the total amount of authority held or controlled by the
particular classes than by the categorical allocation of particular
types of power to corresponding organs. This is illustrated by comments upon the defects in the Roman government at one period.
Four things, Montesquieu says, greatly prejudiced the liberty of
Rome. These were that the patricians took all public employments
unto themselves, that the consulate annexed an exorbitant power,
that the people were often insulted, and that the people had little
influence in the public suffrage. These defects go much more to the
quantity of power in certain hands than to qualitative allocation.
The abuses were redressed by the people through four measures;
giving the plebeians some of the magistracies, dissolving the consulate into several other magistracies, appointing tribunes to check the
patricians, and increasing the influence of the plebians in the general assemblies.[65] The description of the remedy is another indication that the ultimate test is the relative quantity of power in the
various competing classes, or groups, rather than the conceptual allocation of types of authority.

The apparent interlude at this point, in which Montesquieu condemns again the Roman Decemvirs,[66] is relevant to his general ob-

jective because it verifies the despotic potential of unmixed government even when composed of aristocrats. The Decemvirs, Montesquieu explains, were appointed to compose a set of laws demanded by the plebians. They were given extraordinary power, and the nomination of all other magistrates was suspended; they were vested with the power of the consuls to assemble the senate and with the power of the tribunes to convene the people. But they called upon neither the senate nor the people. Rather they exercised themselves "the whole legislative, the whole executive, and the whole judiciary power." Thus, all of each type of power was concentrated in their hands. This is the essence of despotism.

Montesquieu's picture of the Decemvirs in this analysis of the distribution of powers, illustrates again his tendency to use the terms legislative, executive, and judicial when condemning the absolute concentration of powers. This is similar to the initial and negative portion of the chapter on the English constitution. Likewise, when he considers the more positive matter of how powers should be arranged, he again emphasizes distribution rather than separation. His final view of the English constitution was a three class legislature. A comparable conclusion was drawn about the early Germanic nations in France. Now again he does much the same with respect to the Roman republic. In fact, the contrast may be even stronger in this analysis. His portrayal of the rule of the Decemvirs expressly asserts that they held the whole of the three types of power and then he discusses the way in which each of the three powers should be distributed.

The explanation of the legislative, executive, and judicial powers in Rome associates political ideals with the quantitative distribution of authority among the classes. For instance, a situation in which the plebians allowed the patricians no share in the legislative power is called "the extravagance of liberty,"[67] an action against the principles of democracy. Also, Montesquieu comments that among the admirable institutions of Rome, two were especially remarkable: "one by which the legislative power of the people was established, and the other by which it was limited." What is being limited most fundamentally is not the legislative but the power of the people.

The analysis of the Roman executive power supports the proposition that one objective of mixed legislature is to give each of the principal classes of society a sense of security. The Roman people left the executive power, Montesquieu explains, to the senate and the consuls, reserving only the right of choosing the magistrates and confirming the acts of the senate and of the generals. He interprets this to have a psychological basis: "Thus the people disputed every branch of the legislative power with the senate because they were jealous of their liberty; but they had no disputes about the executive because they were animated with the love of glory."[68] This associates liberty, at least the kind of liberty under discussion, with the legislative rather than with the executive. But while the legislative arrangement should give the people a sense of class security the executive should provide them with a sense of glory. The capacity of monarchy to satisfy the popular desire for glory is recognized in *Les Lettres Persanes* and to some extent in *L'Esprit des Lois*.[69] The latter's emphasis upon the spirit of honor to inspire participation from the nobility is not necessarily a denial of the need for monarchy to supply glory for the people generally. Montesquieu's finding that the Romans were attached to their consuls by a love of glory along with his treatment of Rome to be an elective monarchy shows the breadth of his concept of monarchy. He declares in effect that the psychological attachment of glory is not something peculiar to hereditary monarchy but may be found in any form of government having a strong executive. Thus, his principles of structured monarchy could be applicable to presidential forms of government.

The analysis of the judiciary power in Rome also shows that the key element of mixed government is how a particular power is distributed. "The judiciary power was given to the people, to the senate, to the magistrates, and to particular judges. We must see in what manner it was distributed; beginning with their civil affairs." The power to try civil cases after the expulsion of the kings was first with the consuls and later with the praetors. The annual listing of judges by each praetor is called "a custom very nearly the same as that now practiced in England." In Montesquieu's view "what was extremely favorable to liberty was the praetor's fixing the judges with the consent of the parties." He indicates that this result is achieved in England through the great number of exceptions that can be made, apparently referring to procedural tactics.[70] Montesquieu criticizes the early Roman arrangements which left the criminal authority to the kings and the consuls, and he prefers a later arrangement in which civil disputes were heard by a questor, patricians were tried for crimes by the consuls, and citizens in capital cases were tried by the people. Thus, the principle of distribution for judicial authority is not its separation from other functions but the relevance of the offices to the types of disputes and the social position of the parties.

A number of Montesquieu's ideas with respect to distribution of power and judicial procedure are evident in his comment upon the regulation in the Twelve Tables requiring a law to inflict a capital punishment but only a plebiscitum for pecuniary penalties. This provision, he says, was "extremely prudent" because it "produced an admirable balance between the body of the plebeians and the senate." He explains that "as the full judiciary power of both depended on the greatness of the punishment and the nature of the crime, it was necessary they should both agree."[71] Thus, the objective in allocation of authority seems to be the joint holding of power by representatives of two classes in order that each may protect its position from undue encroachment by the other. The discussion of criminal cases at this point brings out a distinction between private and public crimes which is quite relevant to Montesquieu's distinctions between civil and political law and between judicial and legislative law-making. He asserts that we must distinguish the crimes "which more nearly concern the mutual intercourse of the citizens and those which more immediately interest the state in the relation it bears to its subjects."[72] He calls the one class private and the other public and says that the latter were tried by the people while with respect to the former, a particular commission, named a questor for the prosecution of each crime. Then the questor selected the "judge of the question, who drew lots for the judges, and regulated the tribunal in which he presided." This procedure may have inspired Montesquieu's remarks in the chapter on the English constitution. There he tells about the judges being drawn from the people at different times of the year and about the tribunal being in existence only for the period of trial.

The extent to which Montesquieu finds in Rome his basic ideas about the distribution of governmental functions is demonstrated by his summary of the Roman government. He declares that we must "observe that the three powers may be very well distributed in regard to the liberty of the constitution, though not so well in respect of the liberty of the citizen."[73] He elaborates that "the people had the greatest share of the legislative, a part of the executive, and part of the judiciary power" and that by this means "they had so great a weight in the government as required some other power to balance it." Thus, what is being balanced is not particular functions but the total weight of the various powers held by a class.

Against the total power of the people was that of the senate, that is "part of the executive power, and some share of the legislative." But, he points out, "this was not sufficient to counterbalance the weight of the people." Again, he is concerned with total weight of power in a class. To bring the senate in balance, "they should partake of the judiciary power, and accordingly, they had a share when the judges were chosen from among the senators." Later, the Gracchi took this last power from the senators and then "the senate were no longer able to withstand the people." Montesquieu's comment on this development is quite informative. "To favor, therefore, the liberty of the citizen, they struck at that of the constitution; but the former perished with the latter." Here, again, the liberty of the citizen is associated with the judiciary power, and the liberty of the constitution concerns the distribution of other authority among the conflicting classes.

The mischiefs which arose from the disruption of the Roman constitution were "infinite," Montesquieu observes. He attributes this to the psychological posture at the time. "The constitution was changed at a time when the fire of civil discord had scarcely left any such thing as a constitution." His persistent assumption that in moderate, mixed government the aristocracy must occupy the keystone position of moderator and mediator is implicit for another time in his comment that "the knights ceased to be that middle order which united the people to the senate; and the chain of the constitution was broken."[74] He points out additional reasons for not giving the "equestrian order" the judiciary power and some of these may touch upon the contemporary French situation. He explains that the constitution of Rome was founded on the principle that soldiers should be enlisted from property holders, and the knights, being persons of the greatest property, formed the cavalry of the legions. When their dignity ceased and they refused to serve, the cavalry was enlisted from "all sorts of people" and soon the republic was lost. Besides, he adds, "the knights were the farmers of the revenue; men whose great rapaciousness increased the public calamities." Then, instead of giving them the judicial power, "they ought to have been constantly under the eyes of the judges." This decline would seem to parallel in general the degeneration of the administrative nobility in France. In fact, Montesquieu's next comment concerns France. He commends the "ancient French laws" because they "have acted toward the officers of the revenue with as great a diffidence as would be observed between enemies." His re-

peated opposition to the commonalty having judicial authority over
nonpublic controversies is expressed again. "When the judiciary
power at Rome was transferred to the publicans, there was then an
end of all virtue, polity, laws and government."[75]

The analysis of the government of the Roman provinces, which
terminates the book on political liberty with respect to the constitution, fortifies a number of Montesquieu's principles on the distribution of authority. Also, it throws more light on his opposition to
overexpansion and his belief that the republican form is not appropriate to large systems. The manner of distributing the three powers at Rome was not followed in the provinces. As a consequence,
"liberty prevailed in the center and tyranny in the extreme parts."
The explanation is that when Rome was confined to Italy, "the
people were governed as confederates, and the laws of each republic
were preserved." Here is an example of the confederation of republics, which Montesquieu suggests in Book X. When Rome ex-
panded, the senate no longer had an immediate inspection over the
provinces and the magistrates residing at Rome no longer were capable of governing the empire. Accordingly, they were obliged to
send praetors and proconsuls and with this "the harmony of the
three powers was lost." The persons appointed had a power which
embraced that of all the Roman magistrates. "They were despotic
magistrates," who "exercised the three powers" and were, he says,
"the bashaws of the republic."[76]

What made this system bad for a commonwealth or republic is
that in such governments the same magistrate has both civil and
military power. The conquering republic "can hardly communicate
her government and rule the conquered state according to her own
constitution." The magistrate with both civil and military executive authority must also have the legislative. Montesquieu asks rhetorically, "who is it that could make laws without him?" For these
reasons, the governor sent to a province must be intrusted with the
three powers. Montesquieu also indicates the disadvantage of republican form in such a situation. It is easier for a monarchy to
communicate its government because it sends different officers for
civil and military executive power, "which does not necessarily
imply a despotic authority."[77] Thus, the differentiation of executive power works against despotism in a monarchy, whereas presumably a republic counts upon legislative control to limit the executive. When the latter sends or appoints a provincial governor, he
has the full executive authority without the control of the republi-

can legislative. These statements embody a number of Montesquieu's favorite themes: the distinction between political liberty with respect to the constitution and that with respect to the citizen, the view of the constitution as an arrangement of powers among social classes or their representatives, the emphasis upon distribution of powers among classes or representatives to achieve quantitative balance, and the participation of the aristocracy in each type of function so that it may be an intermediary between the people and the chief executive. What Montesquieu seeks is not a one-to-one correspondence between a conceptual classification of three authorities and a threefold set of organs. Nor does he even seek any kind of mixed allocation involving merely authorities and organs. Rather he seeks a distribution of portions of each of the three powers among classes, with the objective of balancing the total political power of each class with that of the each of the other classes. Thus, the fundamental conclusion is that the limited, restrained government implicit in the idea of political liberty with respect to the constitution is based upon and assured by the institutionalizing of social differentiation. The doubts about the relative importance of the classification of power as legislative, executive, and judicial and the classification among monarchy, aristocracy and democracy, or one, few, and many, seems definitely to be answered in terms of the social class arrangement.

Notes

1. *L'Esprit des Lois* (hereafter referred to as *Lois*) XI, 20.
2. *Ibid.*, XI, 5.
3. Vaughan comments that Montesquieu in effect reduces the uses of the term "liberty" to two, that is, the absolute and the relative. The former, Vaughan observes, is the ideal of extreme forms of democracy and also of a government which enthrones the liberum veto. The latter is "the equal liberty of all to do all that is not forbidden by a rational code of Law." C. E. Vaughan, *Studies in the History of Political Philosophy Before and After Rousseau* (New York, 1960), I, 269.
4. *Lois*, X, 6. In preceding chapters of this book, Montesquieu uses the term "*pouvoir*" but here he introduces the term "*puissance*" as well. The first paragraph reads: "Il y a dans chaque etat trois sortes de pouvoirs: la puissance legislative, la puissance executrice des choses qui dependent du droit des gens, et la puissance executrice de celles qui dependent du droit civil."
5. John Locke, *The Second Treatise of Civil Government*, XII.
6. There is a possibility that Locke considered the judicial authority to fall partly under the executive power and partly under the legislative power. In his days, the judges served for the pleasure of the king and the House of Lords was an appellate court. Colin Rhys Lovell, *English Constitutional and Legal History* (New York, 1962) 403, 425.
7. Compare titles of Books XV and XVII, see also, *Lois*, X, 3, 8, 14; XXX, 16.
8. *Lois*, XXVI, 15, 16, 23.
9. Jean Domat, *Les Lois Civiles dans Leur Ordre Naturel* (Paris, 1689-94). There is a translation by William Strahan (Boston, 1850).
10. When Montesquieu defines civil laws by their content, *Lois*, XXVI, 1, they are described as concerning private rights. This was the principal subject of customary law in the analyses of earlier constitutional legists. See William Farr Church, *Constitutional Thought in Sixteenth Century France* (Cambridge, Mass., 1941), 282-3. Bodin had included the substance of customary law in his concept of natural law, where it lost some of its technical force, see Church, *op. cit.*, 254-5. Montesquieu's treatment of property rights as civil law may have been an effort to strengthen the independence of such laws and rights. The independence of the French civil laws is argued in Book XXVIII on the basis of extended historical inquiry.
11. On the development of the distinction between public and private law in Europe, see generally J. W. Jones, *Historical Introduction to the Theory of Law* (Oxford, 1940). 184, 139-157. Reference is made there to Montesquieu's remark that the rights of nations should not be decided by the same principles as are applied to a dispute over a rain-spout. *Lois*, XXVI, 16. But he does use the civil law as a model for the law of nations, *Lois*, X, 3; XXVI, 20; *L.P.*, CV.
12. Book XXVII (Pars. 11 — 20). The manner in which the early Roman laws were made is said to determine their classification. "Testaments being made in the assembly of the people were rather the acts of political law (*droit*) than that of the civil law, of the public law rather than the private law." Thus, what comes from the legislature may be considered political laws without regard to the content. Moreover, the actions of the legislature are deemed to be commands. "Testaments, being, as I have said, a law of the people, they ought

to be made with the force of a command." This accords with the definition of political laws as relating to the governors and the governed. *Lois,* I, 3.

13.   Edward S. Corwin, *The President, Office and Powers* (New York, 1948), 264.

14.   *Lois,* XI, 6, par. 14.

15.   Montesquieu, in Book XI, 6, par. 14, says that the judiciary is "so terrible to mankind" but he is then within the general area of political liberty and may distinguish political judicial action from civil political action.

16.   *Lois,* XI, 6, (par. 4).

17.   *Ibid.,* XI, 6, (par. 6).

18.   Shackleton, *op. cit.,* 287.

19.   *Lois,* XI, 6, (par. 7). Elsewhere, Montesquieu says that political liberty is found in a moderate government only if there is no abuse of power. *Lois,* XI, 4. The two statements might be reconciled by saying that separation of the judiciary may permit a moderate government, while political liberty is achieved only through the distribution of legislative authority among different social classes. This is what the analysis of the English constitution eventually asserts.

20.   *Lois,* XI, 6, (par. 12).

21.   The Federalist No. 47 interprets Montesquieu's warning against concentration of legislative, executive, and judicial powers to apply only to the whole amount of such power. Moreover, it bases the pattern of the new constitution upon the state constitutions analyzing each to show their pragmatic arrangements of power.

Works on political theory and constitutional form give most attention to the negative warnings. For instance, John H. Hallowell, *Main Currents in Modern Political Thought* (New York, 1950), 148, quotes the first six paragraphs but only one of the remaining sixty-two paragraphs; Leslie Lipson, *The Great Issues of Politics* (Englewood Cliffs, 1960), 299, quotes the same six paragraphs, omitting the definition of political liberty as tranquillity of mind; Alpheus T. Mason and Richard H. Leach, *In Quest of Freedom* (Englewood Cliffs, 1959), quotes the warnings against unity of legislative, executive, and legislative along with the statement of the fundamental constitution as a parliament of kings, lords, and commons without reconciliation or explanation of the two viewpoints; Allan P. Grimes, *American Political Thought* (New York, 1960), merely quotes the sixth paragraph.

22.   *Lois,* XI, 6 (Par. 13).

23.   *Lois* XI, 6 (Par. 16). This is believed to be the foremost use of the term "general will" in *L'Esprit des Lois.* The term is rarely used. Book I says that the civil state requires a union of wills but most of the volume is concerned with the civil society much more than the civil state and to regard it as a psychological unity of sociological forces.

24.   *Lois,* XI, 6 (Pars. 17, 18).

25.   *Ibid.,* XI, 6 (Par. 18).

26.   *Ibid.,* XI, 6 (Par. 22).

27.   *Ibid.,* XI, 6 (Pars 30, 31) (Author's translation).

28.   *Ibid.,* XI, 6 (Par. 32).

29.   Roger Caillois, *Oeuvres Completes de Montesquieu* (hereafter referred to as Caillois I or II) (Paris, 1956) II, 1358.

30. Robert Shackleton, *Montesquieu A Critical Biography* (Oxford, 1961), 299. See also Footnote 50, *infra*.

31. T. M. Knox (Tr.) *Hegel's Philosophy of Right* (Oxford, 1942), 174-6, 126.

32. Elsewhere Montesquieu says that extreme corruption arises when the power of the nobles becomes hereditary *Lois*, VIII, 5, but there he may be speaking of an aristocracy exercising executive power arbitrarily without respect for law.

33. *Lois*, XI, 6 (Par. 36).

34. Jonathan Elliott, *Debates on the Adoption of the Federal Constitution* (Philadelphia, 1888), V, 140, 141, 150. (June 4, 1787).

35. *Lois*, III, 5; IV, 2; V, 9.

36. *Lois*, XI, 6 (Par. 37). See also, *Lois*, II, 4 (Par. 8).

37. See Footnote 50, *infra*.

38. See *Lois* VI, 15; XI, 15; and XII, 21.

39. See Footnote 35, *supra*. One commentator on the separation and balance of powers says that Montesquieu "saw the executive as monarchic" and the "bicameral legislature as aristocratic and democratic" in an effort to balance "economic powers" in contrast to the threefold separation of functions, which he regards as "political." Arthur T. Vanderbilt *The Doctrine of the Separation of Power and Its Present-day Significance* (Lincoln, Nebraska, 1953), 44. For Montesquieu monarchy, aristocracy and democracy are political as well as economic classes while legislative, executive, and judicial are legal and functional more than political. Vanderbilt's analysis seems not to recognize that the fundamental constitution which Montesquieu describes is concerned with the legislative function as distinct from the purely executive and judicial functions. Likewise, his analysis seems not to recognize the distinction between the political and the civil law-making.

40. *Lois*, XXIX, 18; XXXI, 8, 18.

41. Callois, I, 884.

42. *Lois*, XI, 6 (Pars. 37, 41).

43. *L.P.*, CXLVI.

44. *Lois*, XI, 6 (Par. 46).

45. *Ibid.*, XI, 6 (Pars. 52, 53).

46. *Ibid.*, XI, 6 (Pars. 55, 56).

47. John C. Calhoun, *A Disquisition on Government* (New York, 1953), 28, 50.

48. *Lois*, XI, 6 (Par. 58).

49. Niccolo Machiavelli, *Discourses on the First Ten Books of Titus Livius*, I, 21; II, 20.

50. The abuses in elections and patronage, which tended to defeat the legal separation of the ministry and the commons, were pointed out in a dissertation by the historian Paul Rapin-Thoyras published in 1717. The dissertation was accepted as authoritative even in England, see Shackleton, *op. cit.*, 292. It was included in the four-volume history of England by Rapin-Thoyras published in France in 1725. Vol. II, 796-807.

51. *Lois*, VIII, 9; XIX, 27; XX, 21.

52. Abbé Joseph de la Porte, *Observation sur l'esprit des lois, ou l'art de lire ce livre, de l'entendre et d'en juger* (Amsterdam, 1751), 121-168, 147.

53. Claude Dupin, *Observations sur un livre intitule "De l'Esprit des lois" divisees en trois parties* (Paris, 1757-8), 4, 13. Dupin discusses

Montesquieu's analysis of English mores and manners, *Lois,* XIX, 27, more than the chapter on the Constitution of England, *Lois* XI, 6.

54. Elie-Catherine Freron, "Du Gouvernement d'Angleterre, compare par l'Auteur de l'Esprit des Lois au Gouvernement de France," in *Opuscules de M. F.* (Amsterdam, 1753), III, 173-213.

55. *Ibid.,* III, 176.

56. *Ibid.,* III, 185.

57. See *fn.* 27, *supra.*

58. *Lois,* XI, 8.

59. *Ibid.,* XIX, 27.

60. *Ibid.,* XI, 11. This is another instance in which Montesquieu is more definite about what he dislikes than about what he prefers.

61. *Lois,* XI, 13.

62. For a chronological list of the works of Montesquieu, see Shackleton, *op. cit.* 400-408. He wrote the dissertation on the policy of the Romans in religion during 1716 and the discourse on Cicero in 1717. Caillois, I, 81-98.

63. *Lois,* XI, 12.

64. *Lois,* XI, 13. In *Les Lettres Persanes* European monarchy is pictured as an irreconcilable conflict between the prince and the people, with the prince likely to win because he controls the military power. *L. P.,* CII. The idea that an aristocratic group can moderate and stabilize monarchy is, of course, one of the principal points of *L'Esprit des Lois.*

65. *Lois,* XI, 14.

66. *Ibid.,* XI, 15.

67. *Ibid.,* XI, 16.

68. *Ibid.,* XI, 17.

69. *L. P.* LXXXIX, XC; *Lois,* V, 2, X, 2.

70. *Lois,* XI, 18 (Par. 3).

71. *Ibid.,* XI, 18 (Pars. 9, 10).

72. *Ibid.,* XI, 18 (Par. 11).

73. *Ibid.,* XI, 18 (Par. 17). (Author's translation, Montesquieu uses *citoyen* rather than *sujet*).

74. *Lois,* XI, 18 (Par. 18).

75. *Ibid.,* XI, 18 (Par. 20).

76. *Ibid.,* XI, 19.

77. *Ibid.*

Chapter VIII

The Structure and Spirit
of Natural Government

The two preceding chapters, in reviewing the books of *L'Esprit des Lois* on political liberty (XI — XIII) set forth interpretations which differ substantially from those often held about Montesquieu's political thought. The difference probably concerns mostly his remarks about the English constitution. Other commentators often make these remarks the basis for the American belief in the separation of legislative, executive, and judicial powers.[1] In contrast this study contends that Montesquieu's principal guarantee of constitutional liberty is not that allocation but the joint distribution of political control among three classes, such as the arrangement of the tripartite parliament in which monocratic, aristocratic, and democratic forces each have a mutual veto. The difference in these interpretations makes appropriate a further study of Montesquieu's ideas on constitutional arrangement.

This chapter first will analyze the contribution of the English constitution to Montesquieu's theory of government, with particular attention to the limited purpose of that analysis. Then it will make a comparative analysis of the possible means of deconcentrating political power in order to contrast Montesquieu's ideas with other methods of dividing authority. Finally, the chapter will explain my reasons for believing that the spirit of mixed government is moderation and in conclusion will summarize Montesquieu's system of natural government.

The Contribution of the English Constitution

An understanding of how the analysis of the constitution of England fits into the general pattern of *L'Esprit des Lois* and Montesquieu's idea of political system, requires an appreciation of the limited purpose of that chapter and particularly of what it says about the allocation of legislative, executive, and judicial powers.

337

The limited scope of that discussion is shown in half a dozen ways.

First, the analysis of the English constitution relates only to the structure of government while *L'Esprit des Lois* gives more attention to the character of the civil society than it does to the political state. Then, for both government and society, Montesquieu considers the spirit or moving passion as well as the structure. Thus, even the entire subject of governmental structure and legal function is only one part of Montesquieu's system and what he says on that matter can be appraised properly only when viewed in light of his whole sociological and psychological analysis of national society.

Another measure of the limited scope of the chapter on the English constitution is that it concerns only political liberty, and there are many other more direct values and objectives embodied in Montesquieu's system of natural government. This is evident in both the formal and substantive content of *L'Esprit des Lois*. That work has thirty-one books but only three (XI — XIII) are directed at political liberty while nine books (II — X) deal expressly with the nature and principle of governments, five (XIV — XVIII) concern the relations of climate and laws in various aspects, four (XX — XXIII) investigate economic and demographic matters, and six books (XXVI — XXXI) analyze different kinds of legal orders. Moreover, in the substance of the system, political liberty is not the principal dimension, either vertically or horizontally. Montesquieu throughout much of the work implicitly places the realm of civil mores and law on a higher value plane than the political arrangement, and in Book XIX he admonishes the legislators to follow the all-encompassing national spirit which arises from diverse general causes, such as manners, climate, and religion, in order that the people may be free to exercise their natural genius.[2] Then in Book XXIX he tells us that his primary purpose in *L'Esprit des Lois* is to show that the spirit of moderation should be the foremost guide for political decision.

Still further limitation arises from the meaning of political liberty itself. Montesquieu expressly divides it into two parts, which I believe correspond to his underlying division of political relations into the realm of control and the realm of action. The chapter on the English governmental structure concerns primarily only one of these, that is, political liberty with respect to the constitution. This, he calls political liberty by right and his manner of analysis shows that it concerns constitutional laws more than political practices, control more than application, and the political character of the leg-

islative and executive powers, more than the professional mode of
the administrative and judicial processes. Also, he devotes much attention to the other kind of political liberty, which relates to the
citizen and which he calls political liberty in fact. This last concerns
the relations of the citizen to administration and adjudication, and
it is the subject of two of the three books on political liberty. Only
one book of *L'Esprit des Lois* is directed at political liberty by
right, and in this the English constitution is but one of the governmental arrangements which Montesquieu examines. In fact, he
places the source of his model constitution in the ancient Franco-
Germanic nations. This is a brief and perhaps historically questionable attribution, but, nevertheless, Montesquieu makes it definite
and striking, and it does not have the qualification which he
expresses about the English arrangement. Moreover, for sheer volume of analysis, he pays more attention to the Roman republic
than to the English constitution, and his basic principles are found
in Rome even more sharply and broadly than they are in England.

Montesquieu's idea of political liberty by right may be a bit unfa-
miliar to present day theorists of liberty, and this may cause some
difficulty in appreciating the peculiarly limited character of his inquiry into English constitutional laws. But the formal pattern of
L'Esprit des Lois, if we note its breadth and diversity, quite clearly
shows that the study of the English constitution in itself is an ex-
ceedingly meagre basis upon which to build a knowledge of his
theory of government. The first quarter of the chapter, which contains his remarks about the danger of concentrating legislative, executive, and judicial powers, is still less of a basis for his views.
That is negative in character, and conclusions deduced from it can
be quite contrary to the more substantive and positive ideas set
forth in the larger portion of the chapter. In fact, the whole subject
of political liberty deals mostly with freedom from arbitrary political action. The principal elements of Montesquieu's political system concern the positive objectives, such as enhancement of honor
to bring professional aristocrats into public service, regard for the
privileges and interests of classes or social groups, need for legislation that will offset physical and other obstacles to the natural inclination of man for productive activity, potentials of religion for civil
utility as well as supranatural faith, regard for economic and domestic welfare, the idea that legislation should respect the natural
genius of the people and the general spirit of the nation, and above
all that political decision be guided by the spirit of moderation.

His remarks near the end of the chapter show how Montesquieu's focus upon political liberty by right tends to restrict his analysis of the English constitution. "It is not my business to examine whether the English actually enjoy this liberty or not. Sufficient it is for my purpose that it is established by their laws; and I inquire no further." This may be the distinction between legal and political factors more than that between Bagehot's "dignified" and "efficient" ones.[3] Elsewhere, Montesquieu considers the political factors, such as suggesting that English enjoyment of their constitutional liberty declined when the aristocracy became decadent or corrupt.[4]

Two propositions which suggest the limited purpose of the analysis of the English constitution have been noted previously but now warrant more attention. One is that Montesquieu's concept of constitution in Book XI pertains mostly to the area of political law in contrast to the civil law or the law of nations. We have seen that these three kinds of positive law provide a general pattern of much of *L'Esprit des Lois*. The civil law had been discussed in Books V — VII and the law of nations in Books IX and X. Now, Books XI — XIII relate largely to political law. Book XI expressly concerns political liberty with respect to the constitution and inferentially deals with the laws of the political constitution. The remarks about the concentration of legislative, executive, and judicial powers. I contend, relate only to the internal political realm and do not apply to the areas of the civil law and the law of nations.

The second restrictive proposition mentioned previously is that the legislative function, the primary subject of the chapter on the English constitution, is peculiarly the source of political law. Other types of positive law have other primary sources. The civil law is made primarily by the judiciary, and the law of nations involves the executive more directly than the legislative branch. The inquiry into the English constitution considers the judicial power for a brief period but then lays it aside. In fact, it says that the judiciary is next to nothing, and this is so much contrary to Montesquieu's general attitude toward the judiciary that the comment can refer to only the immediate discussion. Likewise, the chapter on the English constitution deals with the executive in only a limited manner. There is no more than a mention of foreign affairs, and the proposals on the distribution of executive authority seem to concern only those matters which relate to the legislative function. Moreover, it is the legislature that is most directly related to political liberty by right in contrast to political liberty in fact. The organization and operation of the judicial and executive branches, and the way in which they may contribute to moderate government, are considered at length in other books, such as Books VI and XII for the judiciary and Books II, III, V and XIII for the executive. What was most lacking in the French political situation at the time was the legislative branch, the Estates General not having met for more than a century. The first step in the assurance of political liberty by right was a legislative branch so constituted as to protect the relevant divisions of the society and to be responsive to the natural genius of the people.

One possible conclusion from this analysis of constitutional arrangement is that there is a constitution for each of the three traditional institutions of authority. Each such constitution would prescribe the way in which the respective power is distributed among the classes of the political society. There is little difficulty in regarding what Montesquieu calls the fundamental constitution to be a constitution of the legislative power because he expressly asserts that it consists of two legislative houses and a monarchical veto power. There is some basis for a judicial constitution because Book XI suggests that the judicial power be distributed among those in different classes. Likewise, the explanation of monarchy in the comparative analysis of different species of governments was to a large extent an inquiry into executive or administrative operations, and Montesquieu laid stress upon the need for intermediaries, and depositaries of law, both drawn from the aristocracy.[5] These various allocations of authority might be considered to make up a constitution of the executive.

The description of the English constitution may be limited also because Montesquieu probably was intent upon saying what the French legislative constitution ought to be. At the time criticism of the French monarchy and church was restricted and a certain amount of concealment was necessary to pass the censor.[6] Actually, *L'Esprit des Lois* was banned for a period.[7] A safe way to tell the French that their government was deficient was to say that the English one was otherwise. England was still regarded as the embodiment of liberty and comparatively speaking it was. The chapter on the constitution of England is a bit peculiar in several ways; for one, there are but two or three references to England in the nearly seventy paragraphs. The facade behind which Montesquieu made his prescription for France was rather thin, but this was the way of censorship at the time.[8]

An explanation sympathetic to this position was expressed in the Romanes Lecture of Sir Courtnay Ilbert in 1904.[9] He admits that Montesquieu was the chief contributor to the authorized version of the British constitution, advanced by Blackstone and Delolme. But he argues that in Montesquieu's time the English Constitution was still developing, that the English Constitution then had more separation than the French Constitution of his time, that Montesquieu was suggesting what the French Constitution ought to be, and that writing under the eye of the index and the censor led him to use indirect methods.

Another reason for believing that Montesquieu is primarily concerned with pointing out those aspects of the English arrangement which he considers most appropriate for France is that he finds much the same ideal pattern in the political systems of the ancient German nations and the Roman republic.[10] These, too, were esteemed by the French and, if Montesquieu's view of England is colored, so much more is his picture of the early Franks and the Romans.

The limited purpose of Montesquieu's analysis of the English constitution is probably more recognized today than it was a half century or more ago when many of the prevailing beliefs about his political ideas first were enunciated. The old views of the constitutional analysis tend to reflect a rather cursory look at *L'Esprit des Lois* and a short view of English history.

There is a traditional belief that *L'Esprit des Lois* embodies a faulty interpretation of the English constitution, and the usual basis of criticism is that Montesquieu speaks of a separation of legislative and executive powers during a period when, it is argued, the parliamentary-cabinet form of government was being developed. I believe that these common beliefs are derived from a number of fallacies and irrelevancies.

Much of the criticism of the analysis of the English constitution seems to assume that what became the cabinet form of government actually existed in Montesquieu's day. A. F. Pollard, author of *The Evolution of Parliament,* may be representative of those who contend that Montesquieu must have been at fault somewhere in his description of the English Constitution. Pollard asserts that "assuredly, there is no separation of powers in the British constitution, and Montesquieu was at fault alike in his observation and in the deductions he made therefrom."[11] Montesquieu was misled, he says, because there was much effort then to keep the crown and the parliament apart "and all connection between the court and commons was considered corrupting." But if, as Pollard says, the unity of the court and the commons was considered a corruption, then it would hardly be part of the constitution laws. Such laws were what Montesquieu said was his sole interest in that analysis, and he may be on sound grounds for what he aimed at and what he did. Pollard goes on to make the rather common criticism that Montesquieu did not realize that the growth of cabinet government was already destroying that separation of powers. But Montesquieu, as he himself said, was concerned here only with the constitutional laws and not with the actual practices. The fact that Montesquieu made this express qualification indicates that he was cognizant of the difference. Moreover, there is independent evidence that he was aware that the separation of legislative and executive powers was being violated and that he was also aware that this was being done by executive corruption and not by parliamentary extension. I say that he knew of such changes and did not wish them for France.

For one reason he opposed them because they meant more power for the English monarch and his chief minister while Montesquieu clearly wanted less power for the French monarch and his chief minister. Knowledge that the separation of legislative and executive powers in England was being violated through corrupt practices of the king's ministers, perhaps as early as 1714-17, during Robert Walpole's first tenure as paymaster and then chancellor of the exchequer as well as after his return to office in 1720, could have come to Montesquieu through at least two sources. One source was the published works of the French historian Rapin-Thoyras, and the other was his acquaintance with Bolingbroke, the leader of the conservative opposition during much of this period. The difference between the constitutional laws for separation and the actual practices against separation had been described by the French historian Rapin-Thoyras.[12] He shows how the interferences by the king and the chief minister in parliamentary elections were breaking down the legal distinction of executive and legislative. The dissertation by Rapin-Thoyras on the Whigs and the Tories, published at The Hague in 1717, was, according to Robert Shackleton, Montesquieu's foremost biographer, accepted as authoritative even in England, and was the "standard textbook on the subject."[13] Dr. Shackleton also indicates that Montesquieu had an interest in the conflict of the Whigs and Tories even though he is silent about the matter in the chapter on the English Constitution.[14] Montesquieu's interest, I suggest, may concern his prescriptions with respect to France more than English history or politics itself.

Evidently, Montesquieu was aware of the corruption which was endangering the independence of the Parliamentary houses. The activities of Walpole were hardly a guarantee of political liberty unless the Lords and the Commons were much more powerful than they seem to have been. Montesquieu surely did not want for France the practice of executive control of the legislature through intrigue and electoral intervention. If he seems to favor the views of Bolingbroke in preference to those of Walpole, this may arise from his ideas about reform in the French situation. What he preferred for his own country, I contend, was what the English constitutional laws provided, that is, the institutional means by which the principal classes of the society could protect their respective rights or interests, in a general framework of circumspection and moderation.

There is positive evidence that Montesquieu was acquainted with Bolingbroke and his writings.[15] While in England, Montesquieu read *The Craftsman,* which Bolingbroke edited, and later he acquired a copy of Bolingbroke's *Dissertation Upon Parties.* The biographer Shackleton says that this last publication was in the library at La Brede,[16] and it records the changes that were occurring. Bolingbroke's ideas on the power of the monarchy are evident in his theory of the balanced constitution, and his doctrine of separation of powers may have influenced Montesquieu. Shackleton maintains that Montesquieu derived the doctrine of separation from Bolingbroke.[17] But it seems to me that they were most in agreement on the need for the co-ordinate authority of the king, the lords, and the commons. Shackleton says that Montesquieu never held the view that the English government is compounded of monarchy, aristocracy, and democracy.[18] On that, as explained previously, I disagree with Shackleton, but neither view excludes the probability that Montesquieu knew of the English political developments through his acquaintance with Bolingbroke and his works. There is evidence that Montesquieu met Bolingbroke in Paris during the latter's exile from England, probably around 1722.[19] Hearing and reading Bolingbroke's version of English politics, Montesquieu was hardly unaware that Walpole was corrupting the constitutional legal arrangement.

But Montesquieu's objective may have differed from that of Bolingbroke as well as that of Walpole. Montesquieu did not wish, apparently, to side with either the Tories or the Whigs. He was interested in providing means for preserving the privileges or interests of all three classes. Moreover, the conflict between the Tories and the Whigs seems to be another version of the dilemma presented to *Les Lettres Persanes* between monarchical and popular extremes.[20] Montesquieu was seeking a means of moderation and mediation, and this was found in the constitutional laws of England but not in the practices or the goals of either English party. English politics had been a series of rather violent swings from one side to the other for a century or more, and Montesquieu seems to have preferred some more stable arrangement.

Yet, he did not wish to deny the activity of the competing parties or at least of the opposing institutions. He may view the basic conflict to be less that of Whigs and Tories and more the Country-Court antagonism.[21] Montesquieu does not wish to eliminate the conflict or try to solve it on a sweeping once-and-for-all basis. His answer is the machinery that will permit an empirical solution to particular problems as they arise. For this reason it seems to me that he prefers the judicial minded nobility of the robe to mediate between the king and the people rather than parliamentary-cabinets designed to eliminate the opposing positions. The recognition of parliamentary estates in France had retrogressed, and the government there was in a worse condition than it had been in England a century before. But what was developing in England was not a return to a natural inter-relationship of social forces nor a new form of constitutional arrangement but rather the political corruption of both the old and the new. This strengthened the hand of the king's chief minister in England, and, while this might have been beneficial for even the Whigs, it hardly appealed to an advocate of limited monarchy in France.

The criticism of Montesquieu's analysis of the English constitution arises, I believe, from two principal failures. One is the unwillingness to recognize that he was describing the constitutional laws and not the political practices. Whatever the merit of such a limited goal, he did say this was his aim, and it seems to me that he did just that. The second cause of misinterpretation is the failure to distinguish between the ministerial control of parliament by corruption, which was going on in his day, and the parliamentary control of the ministers, which developed without corruption at a later period. Among the other eighteenth century commentators of the English government, Delolme and Blackstone do not regard parliamentary ministers to be a matter of constitution.[22] William

Paley may have defended the system on the grounds that it was the only way of preventing the Commons from exerting undue power.[23] Even so, this indicates that there was basic political antagonism between the legislative and the executive branches. Paley indicates that representation was so distorted that patronage and electoral intervention were needed to assure a balance of forces, but this may mean that the parliamentary-cabinet form of government would be workable only if the Commons became considerably more tolerant than it was at the time.

In any event, Montesquieu can hardly be expected to perceive the development of parliament-cabinet types of government even though some formal aspects of that system were already present. In those decades, the ministry controlled the political makeup of the Commons, and it was some time later that parliament determined the ministry. In fact, English scholars did not give the cabinet form of government constitutional status until a century later. The new look came with Bagehot's treatise in the 1860's.[24] By then, the practice of drawing the cabinet from the majority party of the Commons was an openly established part of the English government. But this was not the practice when Montesquieu was writing. At that time the situation was just the opposite. The king and his chief minister were dominating the Commons by patronage, corruption, and interference in elections.[25] This is hardly entitled to the standing of constitutional law.

Some attacks on the analysis of the English constitution seem to assume that this is all that Montesquieu had to say about society and government. To suggest, as Holmes appears to do,[26] that Montesquieu's political theory is no more than what is repeated by Delolme and Blackstone, is to overlook much of *L'Esprit des Lois*. To seize upon one chapter, and largely upon the first quarter of that, is hardly sound scholarship; particularly when it is doubly uncharacteristic of the whole work. This limited perspective seems to be behind the assertion of De Ruggiero that Montesquieu's "rationalistic and legal mind left the inner and more organic aspect of English political life unplumbed, and confined itself to its formal and outward elements, even exaggerating the formalism of its distinction."[27] If this is true, it pertains only to the book on political liberty by right because elsewhere *L'Esprit des Lois* does plumb the inner and more organic aspect of English political life.[28] In the chapter on the English constitution Montesquieu expressly limits himself to the laws and thus intimates that the practice differs.

Other statements, previously noted, show that he was aware of political deviations from those fundamental laws.

The criticism of his comments on the English constitution also seem to assume that liberty arises from the cabinet form of government rather than from the tripartite legislature. There appears to be diversity of opinion on this matter. The comment of Trevelyan that liberty was due to the fusion of the executive and legislative powers rather than to the separate character that Montesquieu suggests seems to overlook a few important distinctions.[29] One is the difference between political liberty by right which Montesquieu was considering in analyzing the English constitution and political liberty in fact which Trevelyan probably had in mind. Also, while the cabinet form of government makes for fusion in some respects it does not in others. Then Trevelyan, like some others, assumes the chapter on the English constitution to be Montesquieu's whole theory of government rather than a fractional part of it. Most of all, there is a general ignorance of Montesquieu's underlying ideas about natural relationship, that is, that diverse objects may be separate and connected at the same time. As noted several times, Montesquieu is not an absolute pluralist; rather things have extrinsic as well as intrinsic qualities so that they are interelated in a working system despite their distinct character.

A recent study raises the possibility that critics of Montesquieu may have overstated the consequences of having parliamentary ministers. The work of Professor Plamenatz suggests that the English government does not involve as complete a fusion of the executive and legislative as others have indicated. Plamenatz tends to accept and justify *L'Esprit des Lois* in this matter. He points to the long-standing distinction between the King in Parliament and the King in Council and suggests that such separation of roles existed in Montesquieu's day and even to some extent at the present time. Plamenatz's analysis may be a bit critical because he does not seem to accept the full distinction between political liberty by right and political liberty in fact. He assumes that Montesquieu rests the rule of law with the independence of the judiciary more than with both that and the distribution of legislative authority. But he does make a careful appraisal of the executive-legislative relations, and he concludes that Montesquieu "understood how England was governed much better than those who accuse him of making a gross mistake about the English system imagine, and that his conceptions and doctrines owe at least as much to French as to English examples."[30]

Plamenatz's explanation is that Montesquieu, after his two year visit in England, knew well that most of the king's ministers were drawn from one or the other of the houses of Parliament. But, Plamenatz points out, Montesquieu rightfully believed that the ministers were primarily responsible to the king and that they were not agents of the legislature even though there were practical advantages in their being members of parliament. This arrangement made for cooperation which was generally regarded as a necessary element of the governmental operation. Nobody imagined, Plamenatz argues, that the executive and legislative powers were not in separate hands even though the ministers belonged to a house of parliament.[31]

The ministers were selected by the king or his nominees. There was yet no convention that they had to include the leader of the majority party of the House of Commons. Constitutionally, the ministers were the agents of the king who could choose his men where he wished. Likewise, Plamenatz points out there is even today a distinction between the cabinet and the House of Commons. The cabinet is a comparatively small group of 15 to 30 whereas the House is a body of 500 or 600. Moreover, I may add, those who are not cabinet or subcabinet ministers are not so many sheep. They do have a voice and a force of their own; the back-benchers are not to be taken for granted. Plamenatz's analysis seems quite sound even though he emphasizes political liberty in fact and may not recognize the full force of what Montesquieu presented as political liberty by right.

The belief, which has developed in the past hundred years, that Montesquieu faltered in not observing the fusion of executive and legislative power in England seems to have reached its peak. During the past two decades commentators have been less critical in their analysis of *L'Esprit des Lois*. The belief was challenged in the Zaharoff lecture by Charles Morgan in 1948 but, as he acknowledges "the legend of Montesquieu's inaccuracy dies hard."[32] Yet it does seem to be declining if not dying. Significantly, this has been accompanied by much more comprehensive studies of Montesquieu. Werner Stark's 1960 analysis of Montesquieu as a pioneer in the sociology of knowledge is a thorough and penetrating study, and the biography by Robert Shackleton published the following year is probably the closest to a definitive biography that has ever appeared.[33] The more favorable attitude of Plamenatz has been discussed. The 1965 commentary by David Lowenthal is likewise something new in its breadth and in its sympathetic understanding of the diverse facets of Montesquieu's theory of government and society.[34] The studies of Montesquieu in the past decade stand in considerable contrast to the more or less sketchy critiques which appeared during the prior half century or so. Above all, there is a willingness to look at more than a few paragraphs and from this there is likely to be an appreciation of the breadth and depth of Montesquieu's system of natural government. The next section of this chapter will attempt to show that what is most often associated with Montesquieu is only a small part of his full set of ideas on the character of modern political systems.

Comparative Analysis of Deconcentration Theories

The doctrines of separating, checking, and balancing or mixing governmental powers with the aim of regulating output functions are in themselves oversimplications, and they lend themselves to the use of simple models to facilitate design, operation, explanation, or persuasion. In this there seems to be a mysterious attachment to the number three. The common approach is to recognize only three functions and three agencies of government and then to use the same terms, that is, legislative, executive, and judicial to designate both the functions and the agencies. But, behind this apparent simplicity, confusion and complexity arise from a tendency to give these terms both a strict, intrinsic meaning and a loose, empirical meaning and pass from one signification to the other without adequate notice or even full awareness.

In endeavoring to classify and define what is involved, I will start with the idea that there are four doctrines. These, I will call, (1) the separation of powers, (2) checks and balances, (3) the balanced constitution, and (4) mixed government. The first two expressly limit themselves to functions and agencies of government and doggedly avoid any open or direct reference to different political classes of the nation. In brief, the separation of powers means a complete, strict one to one correspondence between a threefold set of functions and a threefold set of agencies, whereas checks and balances, as I will use the term, involves an incomplete or uneven correspondence of functions and agencies having the same names. The other two doctrines expressly recognize political or social classes, such as those represented in a tripartite parliament of king, lords and commons, or in a bicameral congress in which there is an aristocratic senate and a popular assembly. The difference between the balanced constitution and mixed government may be slight and many times they have been interchanged. The difference which I intend is that the one aims at static equilibrium while the other esteems the conflict of classes and their motivation of activity. Yet in both doctrines there is a mutual veto gained through the joint holding of controlling power by different classes. I will look more closely at the several doctrines.

The theory of the separation of powers adheres strictly to two premises. First, it assumes that governmental action consists of only three kinds of functions, termed legislative, executive, and judicial, and, second, it assumes that these functions can and should be undertaken separately by three agencies of similar name on a one-to-one basis. This is an enticing ideal for those who wish government to be merely a rational, legal matter without pragmatic, political elements. Any flexibility that it may have, comes, we will see, from ambiguity or even duplicity in the meaning of legislative, executive, and judicial.

The theory of checks and balances is less rigid in its structure. It also assumes three main functions and agencies, but it recognizes subfunctions and involves something less than a complete one-to-one correspondence of functions and agencies having the same general identification. In some respects it may seem to be a modified separation of powers which is accepted as a practical alternative to the first doctrine on the general ground that human arrangements cannot be perfect and that this is as close as one can get to the goal of complete correspondence of threefold functions and agencies. Yet, I believe that the theory of checks and balances is equal and co-ordinate to the separation doctrine. It is embodied in our constitutions and may be a more certain means of deconcentration. As a legal maxim, it can justify any particular arrangement that is contrary to the theory of separation of powers and thus can provide constitutional authority for those adversely affected by a specific application of the separation doctrine. For instance, Congressional intervention in foreign affairs can be opposed on the theory of separation of powers but it can be defended on the theory of checks and balance. Thus, either side in an allocation debate has a constitutional principle in its support.

The distinction between the two doctrines may be confused by the interchange of a strict and a loose meaning of the terms legislative, executive, and judicial. The strict meaning may be intrinsic, simple, or even abstract. By it, the three functions mean only making laws and executing and adjudicating them. This facilitates the belief that there is an ideal separation of powers. But it assumes a very limited concept of government; perhaps confined to merely criminal law processes. Actually, government is more complex; parliament has functions other than law making,[35] and other agencies engage in aspects of law making.[36] Congress has representative, investigative, and communicative functions, and the executive has much to do with statutes and regulations, as well as many functions which are not actually the execution of laws. Such an irregular assortment of functions can be classified by the terms legislative, executive, and judicial by giving them empirical, acquired, or even loose meanings. These result partly from historical accident and partly, I believe, from the tendency of Western theorists and spokesman to name political institutions for their most law-related activity. It makes government appear to be legal rather than political and even idealistic rather than pragmatic. We tend to use the strict meanings in arguing the theory and the loose meanings in describing actual operations but, where there is no exact correspondence of meaning between functions and agencies, I believe that we have checks and balances more truly than separation of powers.

Likewise, the strict, intrinsic meanings may be used in negative warnings against concentration while the loose, acquired meanings are adopted when positive and concrete allocations are described. Montesquieu may have used the two meanings this way in his chapter on the English constitution. At first, he assumed a government by one so that there was no issue of correspondence between functions and agencies and then in his sternest warning against concentration he identifies only three specific functions and these are clearly distinct. But when he comes to positive prescriptions he assumes a rather complex, empirical group of functions as well as historical institutions.[37] He recognizes subfunctions and gives the monarch a share in legislative approval as well as the authority to call sessions, and he allows the parliament to control expenditures and investigate administrative performance. These allocations seem to reflect not intrinsic meanings but rather the factors of historical political conflict, the protection of class interests, and operating feasibility. The right of the king to call legislative sessions helps to check power but it also recognizes his better position to know when sessions may be needed. Insofar as it enters into a balance, it is part of the total power of the monarch to be compared with the total power of another political class. In this part of the chapter on the English constitution, Montesquieu looks upon the legislative and executive powers from an empirical, or political, and operational viewpoint rather than from an intrinsic or conceptual one. The judicial power is dropped early in the analysis but is examined elsewhere with much emphasis upon sociological consequence, and Montesquieu is a recognized pioneer in such jurisprudence.[38]

Commentators generally, I believe, often assume the intrinsic meanings when they speak about functions and the acquired or empirical ones when they talk of agencies, without indicating the differences. For instance, they may consider the legislative function to be simply lawmaking while the legislative branch is assumed to engage also in representative, investigative, and communicative functions. Even the Supreme Court has tried to gloss over the difference by saying that patently non-lawmaking activities are connected with legislation.[39] By such means, we preserve the myth of ideal separation while practicing the irregular allocations of checks and balances. We are able to effect a threefold division of agencies more fully than a true trichotomy of functions, so we give a functional name to an operating agency. We find it easier to confine an official to a single agency than to limit a particular agency to a single kind of function, or to confine one type of function to a single agency.

A threefold typology of these doctrines is recognized by Professor M.J.C. Vile in his recent scholarly work on constitutionalism and the separation of powers. He sets the "balanced constitution" in rather sharp contrast to separation of powers,[40] and he tends to treat checks and balances to be a middle theory. At times he limits this last to the relationship of functions and agencies, but other times he includes the matter of social class distribution as well.[41] As noted before, I use "checks and balances" to mean an uneven allocation in which there is less than a one-to-one correspondence between functions and agencies of similar name. This, I believe, is how the term is actually applied in most studies of American government,[42] when the meaning is at all clear. Professor Vile has some basis for any ambivalence. Sometimes the term is used rather vaguely to label the nonsymmetrical scheme of functions and agencies that actually results from an attempted separation. It is a fitting companion to separation of powers because what one does not designate the other will, in theory as well as in practice. Americans, I believe, satisfy their rationalism with the doctrine of separation of powers and their empiricism with the theory of checks and balances, but allow the facts of a case to decide which doctrine applies.

Professor Vile says that the doctrine of the separation of powers has three principal elements.[43] The first is the division of the agencies of government into three categories: the legislature, the excutive, and the judiciary. The second is the assertion that all government acts are either legislative, executive, or judicial functions. He calls the third element "the separation of persons" or a prohibition of plurality of offices. This requires that there be no overlapping membership in the three agencies of government. The third element, I believe, may be an American emphasis. The Massachusetts Constitution of 1780 probably comes closest to laying down the requirement. The only express application in the United States Constitution is the provision against members of Congress holding executive positions. The requirement is not directly expressed by Montesquieu or Blackstone or the other French and English theorists who have dealt with separation of powers. It may be implicit in the idea of separate agencies and here I will assume that it is. The United States experience before and after 1789, in colonial, state, and national governments generally has placed more emphasis upon separation of agencies than upon separation of functions, and there has been greater success, I believe, in keeping agencies apart than in dividing the legislative, executive, and judicial functions on the basis of their intrinsic meaning.

Nevertheless, the idea that government comprises only three legal processes is, of course, an oversimplification. It is far from Montesquieu's view of things. He may have said, in a negative warning, that there can be no liberty when making law, executing public resolutions, and trying disputes are in the hands of one, but we have seen that his positive prescriptions identify many other functions.

Moreover, he segregates government in several basic ways. For instance, he contends that at one time the government in France was fourfold: religious, economic, civil, and political,[44] and such an assumption seems to run through much of *L'Esprit des Lois*. I have shown previously that he sees government to concern the three realms of political law, civil law, and the law of nations, and that only when he enters the area of internal political law does he talk about the threefold classification of legislative, executive, and judicial. Moreover, when he turns to positive measures, he stresses social distribution. He allocates the legislative authority jointly to the royalty, the nobility, and the commonalty. He assigns executive and administrative authority to nearly autonomous aristocrats as well as to the monarch. The judicial power is somehow to be shared by the people and the nobility so that an accused may be tried by his peers. Montesquieu assigns authority in relation to agencies more than functions, and the agencies have social, political, or professional roots, which he does not try to conceal. Sometimes he divides government and society even more. He divides administration between the civil and the military and between criminal law and tax enforcement. Also, he mentions a number of different economic goals and programs for the government.[45]

Likewise, the American government is threefold only in its architecture and its ideology while its operation is much more complex. The national system and all but one state government have bicameral legislatures. This is hardly a subordinate matter. The great compromise at Philadelphia in 1787 which made the new constitution acceptable was the division of Congress into two houses with differing modes of representation. Even today, we are having a difficult time accepting the idea of a single electoral basis for membership in the two branches of state legislatures. The political division of the legislature seems to be as important as the separation from the executive and the judiciary and perhaps bicameralism is the more important to political and other kinds of liberty. In the national constitution, the separate character of the Senate is more protected against change than the judiciary, the Presidency, or the House of Representatives, even though there could be separation of legislative, executive, and judicial powers without having a senate.

Then the executive branch is a whole bundle of agencies which differ considerably in their relations to the legislative and judicial agencies. In general terms, the political executive differs fundamentally from the bureaucratic administration, and the latter is a multiplicity of professions. There are basic differences between military and civil operations, and between domestic and foreign relations, both at the political and professional levels. Some cabinet members are more policy-makers than Congress in their particular fields while others are just high level managers. Next, we have at least four different merit services among the bureaucracy. Likewise, the judiciary differs on the scope of jurisdiction, functional as well as territorial, and has both civil and political power. Then, trial courts tend to be socially responsive while appellate ones are professionally guided so that we could appropriately elect trial judges and appoint appellate judges.

Having identified the general aspects of deconcentration methods, I will now classify them analytically.

The possible means of allocating political power through the arrangement of legislative, executive and judicial authority may be classified first, for want of better terms, as mechanical and organic.[46] The mechanical is more rational and logical in an abstract sense while the organic is more empirical and operational in a concrete sense. What is being called a mechanical method of allocation is primarily a matter of classifying functions according to the intrinsic meaning of the terms legislative, executive, and judicial. What is being called the organic method of allocation is primarily a matter of classifying functions according to the political character of the institutions, with particular attention to social forces and operating attributes.

There are two general types of mechanical allocations. One is simple and the other is uneven but both proceed from the intrinsic meaning of legislative, executive, and judicial. The first aims at the terminological correspondence of functions and institutions. It calls for the assignment of a threefold set of functions, abstractly conceived, to a threefold set of institutions with similar names on a one-to-one basis. By such method, the legislative branch would be deemed to perform only legislative functions in the strict sense. This is separation of powers in the simplest form.

There is a common belief that Montesquieu prescribes such a method. For instance, R. M. MacIver seems to assume that Montesquieu calls for allocation on a one-to-one basis. He says that Montesquieu could offer only a "mechanical device of separation" and that the "absolute separation of powers prescribed by Montesquieu is obviously impossible."[47] This view also seems to be the cause of what F. T. H. Fletcher calls the "usual objection" to Montesquieu's theory, that is, "that it draws too sharply a line between the three powers and tends to segregate them in watertight compartments possessing neither reality nor utility."[48] Fletcher considers the criticism unjust, but his description of it is fitting. Behind the common criticism is the assumpton that Montesquieu calls for a simple, mechanical allocation of three types of functions to three institutions having comparable names. Actually, as explained previously, the weight of his analysis is for an empirical, sociological distribution of authority among competing political classes. This last is what I call an organic allocation.

When Professor Vile speaks of "the pure doctrine" of separation of powers,[49] he means, presumably, that the three types of functions are assigned to the three corresponding agencies on a one-to-one basis. This is what I call a simple mechanical allocation. Professor Vile finds the purest application of the separation doctrine in the Pennsylvania Constitution of 1776.[50] It provided for a unicameral legislature and placed the executive in a council. Other analysts might see the Pennsylvania Constitution to embody an inadequate recogniztion of the executive, but Professor Vile seems to associate the separation doctrine with a strong assembly and a minimal governor, apparently because this tends to maximize the rule of law. But it seems to me that in the colonial period and particularly near its end, the separation of powers theory favored the legislature as opposed to the other agencies of government because of historical circumstances. More legislative power in the assembly could have had democratic consequences because a good deal of the legislative power previously was exercised by the governor and the council. But the doctrine may work the other way. At the Constitutional Convention of 1789, the separation of powers, i.e. agencies, served to increase the power of the national executive and judiciary and was actually aristocratic in that situation.

The other kind of mechanical deconcentration is an allocation of functions to the three agencies with less than complete terminological correspondence. For instance, the legislative branch may have functions that are not legislative in the strict law-making sense, such as the right to judge the election of its own members or to investigate the actions of the administration. Or the executive may have the authority to call the legislature into session and to pardon convicted criminals. In present day commentaries the simple mechanical allocation is called separation of powers, and the uneven mechanical allocation is usually called checks and balances. The two doctrines can produce contrary results in a given situation, and they tend to coexist in American beliefs, I contend, because in political and legal debate they provide each side with a theory of justification and leave the actual determination to more pragmatic considerations.[51]

This study contends that Montesquieu did not employ either type of mechanical allocation in his explanation of positive measures for deconcentrating political power. The simple, mechanical method might be a possible deduction from his negative warnings but it is clearly contrary to his positive proposals. Some of his prescriptions may have the appearance of a mechanical mixture, but analysis of his explanations shows that he is guided by one or more of the empirical criteria which make for what is being called organic allocation.

The empirical criteria which guide Montesquieu in the organic deconcentration of governing authority may be divided between those which narrow the realm of analysis to the internal political order and those which come subsequent to that point. In the first category are the rather general values by which he excludes the religious order and some of the economic order from the political field. Then there is his express segregation of the realms of the existing civil law and the law of nations. Next, in the deconcentration of internal political power, he recognizes the three categories of legislative, executive, and judicial, and he distributes each jointly or interdependently among two or three classes. This is quite evident in respect of legislative power but also occurs to substantial degree in the areas of executive and judicial power.

There is another empirical criterion which I believe enters into the positive parts of Montesquieu's system of distribution. This is the allocation of political authority on the basis of operational feasibility. To some extent this agrees with the acquired meanings of legislative, executive, and judicial because the functions which the parliament, the king, and the courts have acquired have been determined considerably by operational factors. For instance, the king has the authority to call parliament into session as well as the general executive power because this is administratively sensible. In these matters, the principal guide may be the classification of governmental actions by the one, the few, or the many. There are times when Montesquieu seems to view the legislative as the function of the many,[52] and other instances when he tends to view the executive as the function of the one.[53] Likewise, the few serve as judges, administrative intermediaries, and senators.[54] The main thrust of Montesquieu's ideas on the structure of secular government may be that the few should be interposed in every type of operation as the mediators and moderators between the king and the people. Also, the classification of one, few, and many or of monarchy, aristocracy, and democracy may at times correspond to a classification of mental attributes as political will, reason, and sense, the monarchy being a force of will and decisive action, the aristocracy the embodiment of political reason and deliberation, and the people moved by political sense, interest, and passion.[55]

Each of Montesquieu's suggestions about the distribution of authority among the one, the few, and the many, like his prescriptions for the intermediary roles of the presumably professional nobility, is an answer to the dilemma posed by *Les Lettres Persanes* because each proposal tends to provide means of mediating and moderating the otherwise irreconcilable conflict of the monarch and the people.

The essential factor in Montesquieu's ideas about assuring constitutional liberty is, I believe, more accurately a joint holding of powers than a separation even when this last is combined with a theory of check and balance. The important point of his system in this matter is the distribution of controlling authority among the monocratic, aristocratic, and democratic classes of the nation. This is what I call mixed government and which Professor Vile calls the balanced constitution. I believe this should be distinguished from the theory of checks and balances because that doctrine does not expressly involve recognition of social or political classes or groups and is what I call an uneven mechanical allocation while the mixed government or balanced constitution is what I call an organic allocation because it recognizes social differentiation.

Professor Vile properly sets the separation of powers theory against the doctrine of the "balanced constitution."[56] He applies the later term to arrangements such as a tripartitie legislature with joint participation by the King, the Lords, and the Commons. This is one of Montesquieu's foremost prescriptions, but he does not call it a balanced constituion with any consistency. He is more likely to call it a mixed constitution. Others, such as Bolingbroke, may have called it a balanced arrangement, but the term "balance" is probably more of a myth-word than a real fact. Balance was highly revered because of Newton's achievement and was some kind of ideal in the seventeenth and eighteenth centuries. But those who supported the three-class constitution were, I believe, more interested in the representation of classes and the protection which it afforded than any idea of abstract balance. If balance implies a static condition, then Montesquieu would not be too happy about it because he favored an active and competitive society.

The doctrines of separation of powers and checks and balances are in their formulation ways of allocating functions among agencies without express regard for political class identity and conflict, but I believe that the degree to which they actually restrain arbitrary governmental output depends upon the extent to which they do effectuate a distribution of political power jointly or interdependently among forces that are essentially in conflict. In other words, they must in fact embody the unexpressed elements of joint distribution or mutual veto and of giving the principal socio-economic or political classes the means of countervailing action. Montesquieu's system of natural government embodies both of these requirements, and they come much closer to the essence and substance of his political theory than the separation of legislative, executive and judicial functions in three corresponding agencies. I will examine these matters more thoroughly and specifically.

First, I will consider the need for interdependent or joint authorities. The separation of functions or agencies will not assure against abuse of power unless the output in question requires joint action by two or more power-holders. If a politically unified executive is permitted to act in the matter without either legislative or judicial concurrence, there would be no checking of power with power even though there may be a good deal of separation of functions and agencies in this and other respects.

The realm of criminal punishment is the area in which governmental output is most likely to require action by all three of the legislative, executive, and judicial agencies and where there is most likely to be a close correspondence between the familiar sets of functions and agencies. In its processes we find, both traditionally and presently, that a statute is necessary and that executive prosecution and judicial decree is prerequisite to penal action. Significantly, the doctrine of the separation of powers had its modern origin during a period when criminal coercion was deemed to be the principal and perhaps only area of governmental action. Locke's definition of political power at the start of the Second Treatise is rather much limited to the night watchman theory of government,[57] and this view prevailed during those parts of the modern era when the doctrine of separation of powers was most admired.

Yet, the need for legislative, executive, and judicial action is not equally present in other operations. This is the case with several aspects of foreign relations. Locke, Montesquieu, and the United States Constitution treat that matter differently than domestic relations. In each instance, the legislature has a lesser role for the basic reason given by Locke that foreign affairs are less likely to be determinable by antecedent general rules.[58] Also, the courts have comparatively little to do with foreign policy. Further much of the military policy is determined outside Parliament or the Congress. Still more is it free of judicial decree. Again, there are aspects of mone-

tary and commercial supervision in which the executive or administration acts without legislative direction or judicial review. The
controlling and limiting force of the separation of powers would
seem to be confined at least to those areas in which action is required by more than one conflicting agency. This is true even of
the doctrine of checks and balances. Whatever way in which functions may be distributed among agencies, unless a particular governmental output is under the joint or interdependent authority of
two agencies, there is no assurance of power checking the abuse of
power. The requirement of joint authority warrants analysis of
the relations of the three types of functions.

The trichotomy of legislative, executive, and judicial powers is, I
believe, both historically and logically, two sets of connected
dichotomies.

In the first set, there is a division between general policy and particular action, which may be expressed in a variety of ways, such as
legislative and executive, control and action, or politics and administration. This combines the judiciary with the executive on the assumption that both are engaged in applying general rules enunciated elsewhere. Much of *L'Esprit des Lois* assumes the distinction
between political control and action. In the comparative analysis of
governments (Books II — X) republics concern democratic and
aristocratic means of control while the inquires into monarchy and
despotism deal with opposing modes of operation.

The second dichotomy is that of the executive and the judiciary.
This is largely a matter of making the judicial power independent
of the political executive. Historically, this developed subsequent to
the distinction between legislative and executive. Logically, unless
the difference between general rule and particular application first
is accepted, there is little point in trying to distinguish modes of application. Montesquieu devotes considerable effort and time to improving the character of judicial action by urging that judges be selected with some regard to the class identity of the accused and that
trials and punishment conform to reasonable, established rules. But
he deals with this subject largely apart from the analyses of legislative and executive relations. Books VI and XII are directed primarily at raising the professional standards and practice of the civil and
political judiciary.

The mixed or balanced constitution, which recognizes monocratic, aristocratic, and democratic forces, usually concerns the legislature and legislative-executive relations more than the executive or

the judiciary. This is because, I would say, the development of the theory occurred when the aim was to limit the monarchy in theory by subjecting the monarch to the rule of law and in practical politics by subjecting him to approval by representative bodies who are deemed to have the legislative power of making law. Thus, the rule of law was often a matter of bringing a different set of men into the control of government. Law-making was attributed to those who represented nonmonarchical forces in the parliamentary chambers. Thus, the rule of law as opposed to the rule by men is in some ways a myth-term used to cover the control of government jointly by the principal classes of the national society.

Montesquieu is more associated with the distribution of legislative power among the three classes than he is with the distribution of the executive and the judicial power. The chapter on the English constitution is largely concerned with the legislative agency and its relations with the monarch. The fundamental constitution is said to be a joint arrangement of king, lords, and commons. This is essentially a legislative constitution. However, Montesquieu considers what we might call the executive and judicial constitutions. In Books II — V he urges the distribution of executive and administrative authority to qualified nobles who would act as intermediaries between the monarch and the people. He also suggests a depositary of the laws, like the *Parlement de Paris,* to be staffed by professional aristocrats. His ideas on a judicial constitution are less explicit, but he devotes separate books (VI and XII) to judicial offices, procedure, and practice.

The essential principle of joint distribution of control among competing political classes becomes more apparent in *L'Esprit des Lois* if we approach it with Montesquieu's underlying assumption that government is divided between control and action. The discussion of legislative power deals with political control much more than with political action. The chapter on the English constitution concerns control more than the application or exercise of authority, and there is clearly more analysis of methods of representation than of the processes of law-making. The references in that chapter to the executive power seem to deal with the monocratic institution called executive more than with the executive function, as such.[59] The monarch is made a part of the tripartite legislature and is given power to convene the assembly. Moreover, the "legislative power" is to have authority to examine the manner of execution. This last shows that the legislative branch has control functions other than lawmaking in a strict sense. Likewise, the discussion on the manner of raising money and the recommendations that the legislative branch establish the army while the executive takes immediate charge, deal with control more than action. Moreover, these arrangements tend to distribute control jointly among the monarch and the assembly. Again, his idea that the legislature may investigate the administration is another example of control that is shared jointly by the two political bodies, each in accordance with its operating potential. The monistic chief executive is situated for direct action while the pluralistic or collective assembly is situated for post-review and inquiry.

The control factor is also evident in the extent to which Montesquieu deals with the pattern of representation while analyzing the legislative power. This was the basis for distinguishing democracies from aristocracies when he analyzed different kinds of government in Books II — X, and in Book XI it is the key to the constitutional liberty in the investigation of mixed government. In the chapter on the English constitution, the discussion more and more recognizes class distinctions. The explanation of how legislative power should be distributed first assigns that power to representatives of the people and then adds a senate to represent the aristocracy. The executive power is assigned to a monarch, and the chapter reaches its climax with the declaration that the fundamental constitution for assurance of liberty by right consists of two representative bodies and the executive. This, of course, corresponds to the democratic, aristocratic, and monarchical forces of the society. Thus, the checking of power with power, which is deemed to be necessary for political liberty by right is a matter of pitting against each other the conflicting but complementary forces of the many, the few, and the one.

Most of *L'Esprit des Lois* is directly concerned with differentiations other than that of legislative, executive and judicial. Virtually every book has something to say about monarchy, aristocracy, or democracy in one way or another;[60] the distinction between civil and political laws is a recurring theme,[61] and perhaps the most original part of the volume concerns the interplay of climate, laws, mores, and religion.[62] These differentiations are much more essential to Montesquieu's theory of government than the separation of legislative, executive, and judicial. In fact, this last separation could occur in a way that Montesquieu would not recognize as a guarantee of liberty. For instance, the assignment of functions to three institutions, the roots of which are not socially or politically diverse would not assure political liberty by right.

The specific identity of powers may not be essential to the negative warnings against despotic concentration, but it is essential to the means of avoiding despotism by dispersing authority. Despotism is viewed repeatedly as a unity of all powers in one set of hands, but the identification of the powers being monopolized varies from time to time. Montesquieu may use the trichotomy of legislative, executive, and judicial on some occasions, but even more he defines despotism as a disregard of social values, a commingling of civil and political laws, or a confounding of laws, mores, and religion.[63] When he is merely warning against the concentration of powers or forces, it matters little whether the unification is described with one set of terms or another. But in positive measures the identity of the powers or forces becomes more important. When Montesquieu describes methods of allocation, he seems to use less the terms legislative, executive, and judicial and use more the terms monarchical, aristocratic, and democratic. Likewise, he emphasizes the superior character of social mores and civil law.[64]

There are apparent applications of the doctrine of checks and balances in the positive portion of the chapter on the English constitution. Among other things, Montesquieu gives the monarch a veto on legislation, the legislative body the power to examine administration, and the senate certain judicial powers. But these are really phases of organic, mixed allocation. They reflect the considerations of operating necessity or feasibility as well as the principle that each class should have sufficient power to be able to protect its respective privileges or interests.

When Montesquieu does speak of legislative, executive, and judicial powers, in his analysis of constitutional liberty, he is recognizing, I believe, only one of a number of differentiations. Some of the others may be more fundamental or essential to his theory of natural government. Other differentiations assumed include the priority of the national society to the state, the separation of the economic and religious orders from the political one, and the trichotomy of positive laws, that is, the law of nations, the civil law, and the political law, which control executive action in his categorization of governmental power. When he divides the internal political order into legislative, executive, and judicial areas, he is not stating the end of his theory of political system. There are subsequent as well as prior differentiations, and the additional steps are, I believe, essential features of his theory of government. These are the distributions of authority among the nation's social or political classes. The legislative power is distributed jointly among the monocratic, aristocratic, and democratic classes or their representatives. The executive and administrative power is distributed to at least the monarch and the professional nobility. The judicial power is to be assigned to judges with some consideration of the class identity of the accused. These distributions of governmental authority among the social and political classes or their representatives are, I believe, the essential structural element of Montesquieu's system of natural government. Moreover, there are some pioneering efforts in this differentiation of society beyond the threefold classification of monarchical, aristocratic, and democratic forces. There are occasional references, directly and indirectly, to factionalism,[65] to different types of nobility, both socially and professionally,[66] and to differences among commercial and other economic groups.[67]

Possibly, Montesquieu uses the terms legislative, executive, and judicial to represent some other trichotomy of elements in his theory of political arrangement. For instance, the terms may be indirect designations of social classes or political attitudes. The idea that *L'Esprit des Lois* assumes a correspondence between a set of functions and a set of three political classes is asserted by Joseph Dedieu in his study of Montesquieu's connection with the English political tradition in France. Dedieu finds that Montesquieu combines two theories by "attributing to the royalty the executive power, to the aristocracy the judicial power and a part of the legislative power, and to the democracy, the other part of the same legislative power."[68] This may be an oversimplification, but it does indicate the sociological character of what appears to be a system of legal processes. Likewise, there are occasional indications in *L'Esprit des Lois* that legislative, executive, and judicial may correspond to political sense, political will, and political reason.

The acceptance of the doctrines of separation of powers and checks and balances during the late colonial and early national periods in the United States was, I believe, both the rejection of one pattern of social distribution of political power and the demand for another socio-political arrangement. The colonial governments had separate agencies which corresponded to social, political, or economic differences even more definitely than to legal or governmental functions or processes. The colonial governor was a spokesman of royal policy much more than a sample of pure executive action; the governor's council usually was composed of colonial aristocrats, and it entered into legislative, executive, and judicial actions; and then the assembly was clearly a representative of democratic interests, either the people generally or much of the common, middle class. When the colonial people argued for separation of powers, they were opposing the monocratic and aristocratic elements of the government and the society, and they were seeking increased power for the institution which they controlled. A threefold correspondence of functions and agencies clearly would lessen the authority of the governor and the council, both of which tended to get into all three types of function, and would enhance the position of the assembly by assigning it a greater share if not the entire legislative authority. Such a result is most evident in the Pennsylvania constitution of 1776. But the democratic consquence of the doctrines of separation of powers and checks and balances was, I believe, more the result of historical circumstance than logical necessity. The contrary result could occur in other circumstances. In fact, it did. When the Constitutional Convention applied the doctrine of separating and checking, the result was to establish a national executive and judiciary and to lessen the position which the national Congress had under the Articles of Confederation. Likewise, in the final period of the convention, there was a readjustment in the assignment of powers. This had the aim of achieving a political balance between the total power of the President and that of a house of Congress. This was quantitative, like the adjustments between the plebians and the patricians in Montesquieu's description of the Roman constitutional patterns.

The separation of powers in the United States probably originated in colonial and state politics more than in the pages of L'Esprit des Lois.[69] The selected references to Montesquieu's work and the distortion of these references have been made, I believe, to find a high level disinterested authority for the general pattern of the national and state constitutions. While we may have established three distinct branches in response to political realities, we like to have philosophical support from a non-American theorist, particularly one associated with such values as liberty and constitutionalism. The principal reason for dogmatizing a few paragraphs of L'Esprit des Lois may lie in the professional practices of lawyers and political spokesmen.

The doctrines of separating and of balancing powers in relation to corresponding agencies may provide complementary theories for the two sides in a debate or controversy over the allocation of a particular governmental function. Moreover, the terms legislative, executive, and judicial are much more appealing than monarchical, aristocratic and democratic, or even one, few, and many, to a people who like to believe that they have a government of law and who dislike to think that they have any social or political classes. Likewise, the differentiation of legal orders which means so much to Montesquieu's theory is not well received by many legal theorists today.[70] Political and legal debate needs lofty doctrines from which conclusions may seem deducible by simple logic. The two dogmas of separation and balance can provide between them support for any pattern of allocating authority. What one will not justify as separation the other will justify as check and balance.[71] The process that really determines legislative or judicial decisions on what is proper allocation must of necessity rest ultimately upon something other than these alternative dogmas. The determining factor is most likely to be an unexpressed interest of the relevant groups or classes.

Thus, the American efforts to support the doctrines of separation of powers and checks and balances have seized upon those statements in *L'Esprit des Lois* which are most politically neutral and ethically cogent. We base one theory merely upon a few preliminary negative warnings and the other upon selected bits of his positive suggestions, avoiding his much greater interest in distribution among political classes.[72] We prefer the terms legislative, executive, and judicial to anything that suggests social distinctions. Likewise, we find the negative warnings more attractive than the positive measures. The former embody moral absolutism while the latter tend to be relative and interest motivated. These last are the values that we do not like to admit. As a consequence, we invert a few negative statements in *L'Esprit des Lois* to make it appear that Montesquieu favors the simple, mechanical separation of powers which mark the general pattern of our constitution, whereas most of Montesquieu's analysis calls for a distribution of authority according to the empirical facts of operating feasibility and political class differentiation. If we are limited to mechanical and organic types of order, he was clearly in favor of the latter. In fact, I feel that he strove to find a system of order and activity that is more sociological and psychological than the term organic generally admits. Moreover, we have used the few negative warnings of *L'Esprit des Lois* in political oratory and judicial litigation to conceal the actual determining forces.[73] Behind the dogmatic principles of threefold legal separation, there is most likely to be the interests of political groups or social classes.

Looking in a more general way at the doctrine of dividing governmental functions and assigning them to different persons or agencies in order to ward off abuse of authority, I would say that that theory is meaningful at best only with respect to the aristocracy as opposed to the monocratic and democratic elements of a nation. There is no checking of power in saying that the chief executive, whether king or president, has divided functions. Likewise, there is no real change by dividing the functions of the whole body of the people who act only in a collective capacity. The result of the separation doctrine is to divide the elites, and the theory might better be called the separation of elites.[74] It divides the administrative elite from the legislative and the judicial elites. Or, more specifically, it divides the civil administration, the military elite, the diplomats, the senators, those who compose the lower house, and the judges; each of these elites from the other.

Montesquieu, intentionally or otherwise, seems to have separated nothing so much as the nobility itself. He attempts to moderate the conflict of monarch and people by interposing the aristocracy in various situations, but this involves separating the nobility, mostly along professional lines. The social nobility, the members of the senate, the administrative intermediaries, the depositors of the law, the judges, the civil bureaucrats, and the military officers, are each and all distinct groups or subgroups. This may be a less apparent part of his system of natural government, but I believe that it is one of the most important.

The countervailing American doctrines of separation of powers and checks and balances give little express recognition to the basic psychological and economic factors. Both theories tend to make government appear to be a matter of interrelated legal processes with no regard for social class distinctions or political class conflicts.[75] But these distinctions and conflicts may be the primary forces in abusing and checking authority. The disregard of social classes is what makes these theories attractive, but it also makes them inconclusive except as forensic tools in political and legal debate. In a particular situation what one doctrine will not support the other will. The advocate picks his theory to conform to the desired result and this may apply to the judge as well, even when the judge is the public itself. These doctrines, I contend, have been the front for objectives that were psychologically and sociologically meaningful and which were determined by political, social or eco-

nomic motivations. What success they have had is due to the un-
mentioned factors of class distinction and political conflict. The
separation of function or agency is not conclusive and does not
serve to lessen abuse of authority unless it accompanies the separation of political classes or groups.

Thus, the theory of separation is a protection against abuse of authority only when it involves the separation of something more politically and socially fundamental than the identity of governmental
functions and agencies. In the colonial period, the correspondence
of functions and agencies would have benefitted the democratic
forces because it would have enhanced the power of the agency, that
is, the assembly, which those forces controlled. At other times, separation and correspondence of functions and agencies served to enlarge the power of the more aristocratic forces by establishing or
strengthening executive and judicial agencies. Accordingly, the doctrines of separation of powers and checks and balances are effective
for their purpose only when combined, openly or covertly, with the
doctrines of mixed government or the balanced constitution. This
is evident in Montesquieu's theory of natural government. It contains many principles other than the classification of legislative, executive, and judicial powers. These include the priority of the society over the state, the distinct character of religious and economic
orders, the superiority of civil standards to political ones, and the
regard for class privileges and interests. In the American government, the meaningful separations may be, not so much those among
legislative, executive, and judicial functions in an intrinsic sense, as
those between the political President and the political Congress, between the two houses of Congress, between the commercial and ag-
ricultural interests, between business and labor, and between the
political party that favors collective welfare and the one that favors
individual enterprise.

Moderation — The Spirit of
Natural Government

Montesquieu's system of government embraces a dozen or more
types of function and how these are brought into meaningful relationship with each other may be approached from the viewpoint of
both structure and spirit. Much has been said previously about the
structural elements of natural government, and this will be summarized here in preparation for a deeper inquiry into the spirit of
that system.

Various terms are used throughout *L'Esprit des Lois* to designate

Montesquieu's preferred type of political system. If we are to settle upon one expression that most reflects his own language, it is probably "mixed monarchy," but his emphasis is more upon mixture than upon monarchy. He limits the state or government in a series of ways by recognizing a number of nearly autonomous orders. His system is anything but totalitarian. He considers the economic, the religious, and the civil realms to be largely separate from the political one even though he assumes that they are related in substantial ways. Then the area of inquiry is further reduced when he sets the external political order aside to be guided by the law of nations and perhaps by other standards. When he starts the analysis of internal political relations, he introduces the trichotomy of legislative, executive, and judicial powers. But he soons sets aside the judicial sphere and then recasts the legislative and executive powers into a joint or interdependent combination of an assembly, a senate, and a king.

There is much evidence that the essential process for the attainment of liberty in Montesquieu's concept of government is not legal separation but social distribution. His basic idea of order, which this study calls "relational diversity," assumes that every object or being has both intrinsic and extrinsic relations and that things are both distinct and connected at the same time. Such an underlying theory makes it quite unlikely that Montesquieu contemplated any type of rigid separation. Moreover, in Book V he asserts that to form a moderate government "it is necessary to combine the several powers" as well as to regulate and set them in motion.[76] Then, at the start of Book XII, he says that political liberty with respect to the constitution "arises from a certain distribution of the three powers." Book XI and the chapter on the constitution of England concerns the distribution of the legislative power more than anything else, and it gives paramount emphasis to the related authority of the popular assembly, the senate, and the monarch. There is a slight early consideration of how the judicial power should be allocated, but most of the chapter deals with the distribution of legislative power among the people, the nobility, and the king, and with the division of control between the legislature and the monarch on such matters as the finance and the army. Other books also deal with the distribution of authority. Books VI and XII discuss who should be judges and Books II, III, V, and VIII, and XIII recommend, directly or indirectly, that administrative functions be assigned in considerable part to more or less independent aristocrats.[77]

The importance of class distribution of power is emphasized also in the inquiry into the Roman Constitution. What prejudiced liberty in the Roman republic, Montesquieu says, was that one social class, the patricians, acquired too great a quantity of power of various kinds. The solution, he points out, was to grant the people various portions of different powers so that their total volume of authority could balance that of the patrician class. This was not a matter of separating governmental functions in some qualitative manner but rather that of combining different parcels of power so that the social classes presented an even conflict of forces. The need of a mediating aristocracy is made quite clear in the analysis of the constitution of Rome. "The knights ceased to be that middle order which united the people to the senate; and the chain of the constitution was broken."[78]

The proposition that political liberty with respect to the constitution requires the social class distribution of legislative authority has substantial support in the strong and repeated emphasis upon the role of a senate. A classification of governmental powers in terms of legislative, executive, and judicial would not require a senate, but, when the pattern of government is viewed as a combination of monarchy, aristocracy, and democracy, or a mixture of one, few, and many, a senate becomes an essential part of the structure. The difference between the negative warnings in the first part of the chapter on the English Constitution and the positive measures in the remainder is seen most sharply in the absence of a senate from the former and the repeated reference to a senate in the latter. The aristocracy may also be the keystone of the application of the law. Montesquieu makes the operating character of moderate government depend most directly upon the quality of the elites which serve under the joint control of three political classes in various administrative, military and judicial roles.[79]

De Ruggiero's claim that Montesquieu failed to see that mixed monarchy was really a facade for aristocratic republic can be challenged.[80] Montesquieu was aware that this might be the case in England and he disapproves of it, stressing the need for a tripartite legislature in which all three classes have a mutual veto. He is deeply against a simple aristocratic form of government. He condemns the rule of the Decemvirs in Rome more severely and more frequently than any other particular government.[81] He does not want the aristocracy to be the sole rulers; he wishes them to be a mediating and moderating force. For this it is necessary that there be a mixed constitution. His goal is a structured monarchy in which there are independent intermediaries, a depositary of laws, and a senate of nobles, in order to effectuate a middle course between the king and the people. Both a monarch and a popular assembly are necessary if the aristocracy is to play its proper role.

What Montesquieu was describing in the chapter on England was the constitutional laws, and they did permit a separation of the houses of Parliaments from the King. If the system was being corrupted by bribery or other means, the constitutional laws still remained. The House of Commons and the House of Lords each still had a right to be separate and to provide their constituents the assurance that separate existence could give. The House of Lords legally had an opportunity to play a mediating role. If the Lords were not doing so, it was because, as Montesquieu says elsewhere, the English nobility had forsaken the chance due to corruption or other causes. In effect his comment is that the English aristocracy had become too interested in commerce and had neglected its duties as the professional governing class.[82] On the contrary, the French nobility had remained free of commerce and could play an un-diverted role in the governmental system if given the chance. Montesquieu was concerned primarily with what the English con-stitutional system could mean for France and the English system, as it existed legally, provided for separation and the joint distribution of legislative power among social classes.

What Montesquieu found attractive in the English constitutional structure, was I believe, its recognition of a lower and an upper house with legal power to check legislation desired by the king or the other house. An aristocratic senate like the House of Lords presupposes a tripartite legislature, which combines phases of mon-archy, aristocracy, and democracy, or which otherwise places the forces of the one, the few, and the many in joint control. The theory that legislative, executive, and judicial powers are more or less separate is not irrelevant but, in Montesquieu's theory of gov-ernment, that alone will not assure political liberty by right. There must also be enough recognition of social distinctions to allow the classes separate participation or representation. Any arrangement of legislative, executive, or judicial powers, which does not take into account class representation in the legislative function is simply not Montesquieu.

The guarantee that the legislator will respect the liberty of the civil society and the natural genius of the people is to be found, he says in effect, not in the legal separation of governmental processes but in the social distribution of the political control of those processes. This is the purpose and function of the class divided legislature, and Montesquieu's pattern for this is the legal structure of the English Parliament. Why he prefers this to the traditional Estates General of France is nowhere explained in *L'Esprit des Lois,* but the separate recognition of the clergy to form the first estate would seem to be contrary to his repeated antagonism to religion in politics. If the clergy constituted a separate estate, it could exercise a veto over the whole legislative and governing process, and this is clearly against Montesquieu's principles of government and society and even his ideas of human behavior.

The importance of the social distribution of legislative authority to Montesquieu's theory of government is indicated by his view that political liberty for the society is the basis of liberty for the the individual. He asserts that liberty can consist only of "the power to do what one ought to will and in not being constrained to do what we ought not to will."[83] This makes liberty seem much more of a duty than a right, but he does call it right. "Liberty is the right to do all that the laws permit; and if a citizen could do what they forbid, there would no longer be liberty because the other citizens would all have the same power." The idea that living under laws is liberty may be meaningful if contrasted with either living under despotism or living in anarchy. It is quite contrary to the idea of having unlimited freedom or living without restraint. To live under laws is to live in an ordered society. The idea that the relevant type of liberty concerns societies more basically than individuals is also indicated by the illustrations which precede the analysis of constitutional structure in Book XI. Different societies give varying significations to the term liberty, from the right to bear arms to the privilege of being governed by a fellow nation. Each nation, he says, applies the name of liberty to the form of government which is most suitable to its own customs and inclinations.[84] The important fact is not that liberty is relative but that it is relative to the society as well as to the individual. This, I believe, is another way in which Montesquieu would try to meet the dilemma of tyranny or popular rule posed by *Les Lettres Persanes.*

Further insight into the meaning of political liberty by right is given by Montesquieu when he says in Book XII that it is "the disposition only of the laws, and even of the fundamental laws, that constitutes liberty in relation to the constitution."[85] This would seem to refer to the laws which set up law making processes and institutions as well as the laws which emerge from that authority. Thus, political liberty by right is the assurance which a conforming member of the society has that the legislative authority is so constituted that society may act freely.

Montesquieu's ideas on the social distribution of legislative authority seem designed to both stimulate and protect the society. He believes that the legislature should assure positive as well as restrictive attitudes by both the whole society and that specific class which must furnish the moving spirit of the particular kind of government. This duty is implicit in the admonition to the legislature to follow the spirit of the nation when that is not contrary to the principle of government.[86] Responsiveness to the needs of society would seem to be best assured, in his opinion, when the legislative authority is distributed with reference to the natural divisions of the society. Likewise, the social distribution of such authority, by means of a three class legislature, would provide protection to the classes of society. Any separation of legislative, executive, and judicial functions is merely a take-off point; political liberty by right requires that each of the monarchical, aristocratic, and democratic forces be recognized and that the legislative authority be distributed among classes of this character so that each has such control over legislation by either initiation or veto, that it can protect its respective position if the need arises.

Montesquieu's final and probably most fundamental contribution to the character of mixed, natural government is his identification of its principle, special spirit, or moving passion. He does not state specifically that the spirit of moderation is the moving passion of mixed or natural government, but I believe that this is the necessary import of his analysis of political systems. The essential role of the spirit of moderation arises from the complexity of Montesquieu's concepts of the mixed society and the mixed government. As *L'Esprit des Lois* introduces more and more relations, intrinsic and extrinsic, which affect political decisions, the spirit of moderation becomes more and more a necessity. Its restraining force works upon the objectives as well as the functions of government. There is more than coincidence in the fact that Montesquieu's theory of natural government combines both a limited idealism and a limited authority.

Indeed, the assertion in one of the last books of *L'Esprit des Lois* that moderation should be the primary value for the legislator, is the culmination of a series of high normative standards which appear throughout Montesquieu's writings. In *Les Lettres Persanes* preexisting principles of justice appear to be the highest standard. This is also true of what is known of the treatise on duties that he began about 1725, where the attitude probably reflects the influence of Stoicism and the works of Cicero. But, as noted earlier, a change probably occurred which caused Montesquieu to leave the treatise unfinished and to devote his efforts to the idea of a general national spirit arising from diverse causes.[87] The preexisting principles of justice receive little attention in either the work on the Romans or the *Essai sur les Causes*. They do appear in the first chapter of *L'Esprit des Lois,* but that chapter is a framework of universal realms for the remainder of the volume. The objective principles of justice may be in the background, but Montesquieu is mostly concerned with the positive law of particular societies and the concrete matter of civil life. Throughout *L'Esprit des Lois* what appears to be the highest value changes repeatedly as the volume progresses. Montesquieu moves from transcendent justice to natural sociability, then to virtue, honor, obedience to law, the general spirit of the nation, the rational choice of legal order, and finally, moderation. Yet all of these have some relation to each other because each embraces the elements of order and restraint. In fact, this is true even of justice in *Les Lettres Persanes*. There justice is defined as "the proper relationship really subsisting between two things," and civil justice is laid down as a guide for the relations among nations.[88]

While moderation is not expressly identified as the primary value until nearly the end of *L'Esprit des Lois,* there are numerous references to it in the preceding books and at times it receives rather high standing. In the comparative analysis of the natural relations of different kinds of government, the principle or special spirit which aristocracy ought to have is most definitely identified as moderation.[89] Moreover, the classification of governments is sometimes reduced to two general types, moderate governments and despotic.[90] The analysis of monarchy and despotism in Book V on the relation of laws and the spirit of government includes a penetrating inquiry into the composition of moderate political systems. This helps to explain what is said later about mixed government and the distribution of authority in the chapter of Book XI that deals with the English Constitution. In the earlier book, Montesquieu observes that despotic governments are common because moderate ones are

difficult to achieve. "To form a moderate government, it is necessary to combine the several powers; to regulate, temper, set them in
motion; to give, as it were, ballast to one, in order to enable it to
counterpoise the other."[91] This is clearly in the school that sees
mixed government to be a matter of combining social forces rather
than in separating legal powers. It assumes that the determining
factor is a host of empirical forces that are not clear cut or easily
ascertained rather than a simple, logical definition of legal
processes. Montesquieu reiterates the difficulty of the task. "This is
a masterpiece of legislation, rarely produced by hazard, and seldom
attained by prudence." Here, he finds that prudence is the key to
moderation, and we will see that this thought appears also in the
final portion of *L'Esprit des Lois*. Moreover, the process that is necessary to form a moderate government, he says, is one of combination rather than separation as such. This is another indication that
Montesquieu favors the joint holding of controlling authority more
than its division and isolation.

Likewise, in the portion of *L'Esprit des Lois* which deals expressly with political liberty, there are a number of references to
moderation. Montesquieu asserts that political liberty is found only
in moderate governments, and at the time he is talking about aristocracies and democracies as examples of governments under law.[92]
Presumably, moderation requires something more specific than law
and representation. The underlying interest in moderation throughout the analysis of the Constitution of England is indicated by the
concluding remark that the extreme political liberty in the English
constitutional laws ought not to give uneasiness to those who have
only a moderate share of it, because "even the highest refinement of
reason is not always desirable" and mankind generally finds itself
better off "in mediums than in extremes."[93]

The association of the abuse of power with the absence of moderation also appears in Book XXVIII on the origin of the French
civil laws. There, Montesquieu comments upon the infrequency of
a moderating attitude and the tendency of human beings to seek
greater and greater authority thereby abusing the power they
possess by excesses which take advantage of their rivals. Yet he says
that "we should be often mistaken were we to consider their en-
croachments as an evident mark of their corruption." Presumably,
the quest for more power and the political tactics to gain it are the
natural expectation. "Through a fatality inseparable from human
nature," he says, "moderation in great men is very rare." While we

may believe that the middle road of moderation is a sign of vacilla-
tion and a lack of strength, Montesquieu points out that "it is always much easier to push on force in the direction in which it
moves than to stop its movement" with the consequence that among
"the superior class" there is less difficulty in finding "men extremely virtuous, than extremely prudent." Again, Montesquieu
places virtue below moderation in his value hierarchy. Moreover,
he explains that moderation is akin to prudence, and there is a suggestion that the superior class finds prudence less attractive than
virtue. I believe that in present day approaches we can see that a
leader would develop more charisma with a virtuous position than
with a prudent one.

In investigating the origin of the French civil laws Montesquieu
elaborates on the contrast of virtue and prudence among the political superiors. "The human mind feels such an exquisite pleasure in
the exercise of power" that "even those who are lovers of virtue are
so excessively fond of themselves" and "there is no man so happy as
not still to have reason to mistrust his honest intention." He concludes that "our actions depend on many things that it is infinitely
easier to do good, than to do it well."[94] This is close to the principal theme of *L'Esprit des Lois*. It supports the demand for moderation and also suggests that prudence is rarer than virtue. The depth
of Montesquieu's feeling for moderation and prudence is evidenced
by the way these values come to the surface in a historical study of
French civil laws. Also, the particular situation seems significant.
He is discussing the relations of the civil and ecclesiastic jurisdic-
tions and implicitly deploring the growth of the latter. He points
out the extent to which the church has a part in every event in
human society, and he says that some abuses were redressed by the
parliament, specifically, a French law published in 1409 against the
Bishop of Amiens. Likewise, this quotation provides one footing for
a bridge between Book XXVIII, which is an intensely historical
study, and Book XXIX, which is highly analytical. These two books
are often said to be disconnected, but the quoted statements show
Montesquieu's deep interest in moderation while writing Book XX-
VIII. Then, at the start of Book XXIX he makes the assertion that
he wrote the volume solely to prove that the spirit of the legislator
ought to be that of moderation. Thus, the spirit of moderation is
the connecting link between his most analytical study of legislation
(Book XXIX) and his most historical inquiry into the character of
civil law (Book XXVIII).

This study refutes the idea that the spirit of mixed government is liberty, as one commentator has indicated.[95] Montesquieu's discussion of the principal or special spirit of types of government in Books III — VIII shows that the spirit of a kind of government is the attitude which is needed to make that species of government effective. Mixed government gives each class a veto power, and without moderation one or another class would have such a restrictive viewpoint that hardly anything could be approved. In an emergency the common danger might stir action, but even then the parties must be willing to accept some kind of detriment. Political liberty would not seem to be the principle of mixed government because it would lead to such disregard of others that mutual action would be difficult to attain. Montesquieu makes moderation a higher value than political liberty or virtue. In the book discussing the English constitution he states that "political liberty is to be found only in moderate governments" and that "virtue itself has need of limits."[96]

The means by which Montesquieu seeks to assure the spirit of moderation include the three-class distribution of authority. In this arrangement, functions are performed by an aristocracy under the control of the king and the people, and the sociological and psychological forces which make up the natural genius of a national society are recognized. Mixed government may be inherently negative, and in this respect it is comparable to John C. Calhoun's concurrent majority. Both of these theories of government embody the use of mutual veto to prevent loss of particular privileges or rights. Calhoun acknowledges the restraining influence of the system and indicates that action depends upon a sufficient spirit of emergency. In this respect, Montesquieu's spirit of moderation would seem to be more conducive to a regular and consistent level of action than would a sense of emergency.

The spirit of moderation, along with mixed representation and the mediating role of the professional aristocracy, is much of the answer in *L'Esprit des Lois* to the dilemma raised by *Les Lettres Persanes*. Montesquieu's explanation of why the legislature should be guided by the spirit of moderation is that "political good lies between two extremes." I believe that the extremes to be avoided are evident in his comparative analysis of the structure and spirit of the different kinds of government. One extreme clearly is despotism. The other is described variously as the popular state, anarchy, republic, or democracy, but in each instance it means the mass of the people acting collectively out of self-interest. This polarity is also reflected in his warnings against attitudes of extreme inequality and extreme equality. Whereas, in *Les Lettres Persanes* he sees the monarchies of Europe inevitably degenerating into either despotism or a republic,[97] and he regards the desired equilibrium too difficult to maintain, in *L'Esprit des Lois,* he undertakes to assure the maintenance of an active equilibrium. He not only argues for moderation among the legislators but also moderation by institutional proposals, particularly the establishment of intermediary powers in the executive, a depositary of laws, and a senate with a veto on legislation. In each instance, a qualified aristocracy occupies the mediating role. This is the institutional guarantee of the spirit of moderation, and it is the principal answer of *L'Esprit des Lois* to the problem dramatized in *Les Lettres Persanes* as beyond solution.

With respect to the external relations of national societies, the spirit of moderation and restraint is also an essential element of Montesquieu's theory of government. The idea that each national society provides its own standard means that there is no universally valid political ideology and accordingly no need or justification for one nation to convert the other nations to its way of thought and practice. Then, the fact that it is the civil order and not the political order of a nation which provides the national standard and value may lessen the desire of external expansion. A further restraint is implicit in the idea that large size is conducive to despotism. Montesquieu indicates both in the short work on universal monarchy and in *L'Esprit des Lois* that even Louis XIV himself was happier as the King of France than he would have been as the ruler of Europe.[98] The theory of distinct national standards is another application of the principle of "relational diversity." Harmony and order among nations come not from a concept of universal validity but from a mutual regard for the distinct character of the other national societies.

Though the principal interpretative problem in *L'Esprit des Lois* is whether the separation of legislative, executive, and judicial powers or the social distribution of authority among monocratic, aristocratic, and democratic classes, is the more fundamental, neither nor both of these doctrines constitute all of Montesquieu's system of natural government. There are other important elements. Probably the most fundamental is the recognition that the economic, religious, civil, and political orders have a substantial degree of separate identity as well as a close working connection. This demon-

stration of the relational pluralism lies at the essence of Montesquieu's theory of society and government. The distinction between those four orders is not expressed directly, but it is much
at work in *L'Esprit des Lois*. Montesquieu, I believe, wishes to remove the clergy from participation in the control and operation of
the government. Then he inquires extensively into commerce and
finance and develops principles, policies, and, perhaps, decentraliz-
ing structural arrangements peculiar to those disciplines.

The distinction between civil and political law is basic and the
political realm is divided between the external and the internal.
Most of the time one is represented expressly by the law of nations
and the other is represented by political law. I believe that the trichotomy of legislative, executive, and judicial concerns only the internal political realm. There is a different arrangement with respect to both the civil law order and the realm of the law of nations. Rather clearly, the legislative has less to do with these realms
than it does with the political one. In fact, Montesquieu sometimes
treats the political and the legislative as coterminous. He assumes
legislation to be the controlling power in political government.
Such an assumption has been accepted generally in England and the
United States.

Here is where Montesquieu becomes concerned with political liberty by right, and he endeavors to assure that value by his idea of a
tripartite legislature. This he calls the fundamental constitution,
when looking at the English laws, and the model constitution, when
looking at the structure and function of the German nations newly
arrived on the French soil. But he does not rest his prescription
upon structure and the joint social distribution of control. He is
also concerned with the principle or moving spirit of particular
types of government. He does not specifically identify the spirit of
mixed government, but I believe that this must be the spirit of
moderation because in Book XXIX he makes this value the final
guide to legislative control. The spirit of moderation may provide
the means of reconciling the various forces which enter into the
general spirit of the nation. This is a prescription to the legislature
to take into account social causes or correlations, such as the mores,
the manners, the climate and the religion as well as the laws and
the maxims of government. Thus, the legislature should be responsive to the natural genius of the people and the sociological and
psychological forces of the national society. In fact, we may say that
he makes the legitimacy of government depend upon the degree to

which political decision conforms to the combined effect of the several sociological and psychological forces within the respective national society.

We find here Montesquieu's best answer to the dilemma raised by *Les Lettres Persanes*. There, he pictures European monarchies to fall inevitably into an uninviting alternative of becoming either a tyranny of the one or a popular anarchy of the many. *L'Esprit des Lois* develops various ways of meeting this problem. Among other things, it places the national society ahead of both the state and the individual and puts the civil order ahead of the political order, whether it be monocratic, aristocratic, or democratic. At times, the civil order is divided into domestic, property, commercial, and monetary relations, and at such instances, any one or all are assumed to be distinct from the religious realm and the political one. Montesquieu differentiates civil and political liberty, and emphasizes that there is both a political liberty with respect to the constitution and one in relation to the citizen. He seeks to assure the former, which he calls political liberty by right, through the joint distribution of legislative authority among the social classes of the nation, and to assure the latter, which he calls political liberty in fact, through reasonable judicial procedure and administrative mediation. Likewise, there is deep respect for the several forces, such as climate, mores, and manners, as well as laws and religion, which give rise to the general spirit of the nation. Finally, there is the encompassing prescription that political decision conform to the spirit of moderation.

Notes

1. The foremost study of the separating and balancing of types of governmental power is now M. J. C. Vile, *Constitutionalism and the Separation of Powers* (Oxford, 1967). See also Arthur T. Vanderbilt, *The Doctrine of the Separation of Powers* (Lincoln, Nebraska, 1953); Karl Loewenstein, *Political Power and the Governmental Process* (Chicago, 1957); Malcom P. Sharp "The Classical American Doctrine of 'The Separation of Powers'" *University of Chicago Law Review*, II, 385-456, (1934-35); William S. Carpenter, "The Separation of Powers in the Eighteenth Century," *American Political Science Review*, XXII 576 (1926); and William Bondy, *The Separation of Government Powers in History, in Theory, and in Constitutions*, Studies in History, Economics and Public Law, V, No. 2, Columbia College (New York, 1896). One commentator remarks that "the full meaning of Book XI is obtainable only when it is read together with the rest of the work, for Montesquieu's own spirit appears in one continuous emanation all through the work," Herman Finer, *Theory and Practice of Modern Government* (New York, 1949) 94, but Finer's explanation draws upon only a few chapters of Books XI and XII.

2. *L'Esprit des Lois* (hereafter referred to as *Lois*) XIX, 5.

3. Walter Bagehot, *The English Constitution* (London, 1928), 4 (First published in 1867). In an earlier work Bagehot remarked that "every page of the *Esprit des Lois* proves how much Montesquieu learned from living here." *Physics and Politics* (Boston, 1956), 130. This is hardly pardonable on any count.

4. *Lois* X, 4; XX, 21.

5. *Ibid.*, II, 4.

6. F. C. Green, *Eighteenth-Century France* (London, 1929), 194-221.

7. Robert Shackleton, *Montesquieu A Critical Biography* (London, 1961), 370, 375.

8. See Green, *op. cit.*, 201, 202, 221; and Joseph Dedieu, *Montesquieu et la Tradition Politique Anglaise en France* (Paris, 1909), 228.

9. Sir Courtenay Ilbert, "Montesquieu," *The Romanes Lecture* 1904 (Oxford, 1904), 23, 31, 32, 36.

10. *Lois*, XI, 8, 12, 18.

11. A. F. Pollard, *The Evolution of Parliament* (London, 1920) 235 9, at 237.

12. Paul Rapin-Thoyras, *Dissertation sur les Whigs et les Torys,* (The Hague, 1717) 156. An English translation by N. Tindal appears in the English edition of Rapin-Thoyras, *The History of England* (London, 1732-33) (Four volumes), II, 796-807. The description of abuses includes the statement which indicates that then the ministry determined the political complexion of parliament and not the reverse as developed later: "The first abuse consists in the too great influence of the court in the elections of members of the lower chamber and consequently in their deliberations, . . . We may judge the effect of these intrigues by this single consideration that commonly there is a Whig Parliament when the Ministry is so and a Tory Parliament when the Ministers are Torys."

13. Shackleton, *op. cit.*, 292.

14. *Ibid.*, 296. The controversy is described as between a Court party and a Country party. Shackleton says that Montesquieu derived the doctrine of separation of powers in part from Bolingbroke. Shackle-

ton also says that Montesquieu never regarded the English constitution as a compound of monarchy, aristocracy, and democracy, *Ibid.*, 299; however, that conclusion is challenged in this study.

15. Caillois, I, 881.

16. Shackleton, *op. cit.*, 297-301.

17. Robert Shackleton, "Montesquieu, Bolingbroke, and the Separation of Powers," *French Studies* VII, 25-38 (1949).

18. Robert Shackleton, *Montesquieu A Critical Biography* (London, 1961), 299.

19. Shackleton, *op. cit.*, 54-55.

20. *Les Lettres Persanes* (hereafter referred to as L. P.), CII.

21. Shackleton, *op. cit.*, 297.

22. Delolme asserted that the three particular advantages of the English constitution were the unity of executive power in the monarch, the division of legislative authority, and the regulation of these three legislative powers, Jean Louis Delolme, *Constitution de l'Angelterre,* (Amsterdam, 1771), 142, 161, 176. Blackstone pointed to the distinction between the king and the parliament, the latter consisting of king, lords, and commons, William Blackstone, *Commentaries on the Law of England* (London, 1811), I, 146.

23. William Paley, *Consideration on the Structure of the House Commons* (London, 1794). Also see Vile, *op. cit.*, 107 and *The Works of William Paley,* (London, 1821), I, 432-443.

24. See fn. 3, *supra.*

25. Loewenstein, *op. cit.*, 86; John Plamenatz, *Man and Society* (New York, 1963) I, 286; see fn. 3.

26. "His England — the England of the threefold division of power into legislative, executive and judicial — was a fiction invented by him, a fiction which misled Blackstone and Delolme." Max Lerner (Ed.) *The Mind and Faith of Justice Holmes* (New York, 1954), 381. This comment is a bundle of fictions in itself. It disregards other observations of England, such as *Lois,* XIX, 27, and it pays no attention to the combination of monarchy, aristocracy, and democracy which is far more prevalent in *L'Esprit des Lois* than legislative, executive, and judicial. Likewise, it is not an accurate indication of what Blackstone and Delolme said about the English constitution (ee fn. 22).

27. Guido de Ruggiero, *The History of European Liberalism* (Boston, 1959), 57.

28. *Lois,* XIX, 27. See Chapter II, Section three of this study.

29. C. M. Trevelyan, *History of England* (London, 1926), 511, fn. see comments Charles Morgan, *The Liberty of Thought and the Separation of Powers,* Zaharoff Lecture for 1948 (Oxford, 1948), 13.

30. John Plamenatz, *op. cit.*, I, 282-294.

31. *Ibid.*, I, 284, 286.

32. Morgan, *op. cit.*, 13.

33. Werner Stark, *Montesquieu Pioneer of the Sociology of Knowlege* (London, 1960), 125; Shackleton, *op. cit.*

34. David Lowenthal: "Montesquieu" in Leo Strauss and Joseph Cropsey, *History of Political Philosophy* (Chicago, 1963), 469-490 at 478-482.

35. Woodrow Wilson, while a professor wrote that the "vigilant oversight of administration" is as important as legislation and the informing function is even more important. Wilson, *Congressional Government.* (Boston, 1885), 297, 303, 311.

36. Herman Finer, *Theory and Practice of Modern Government* (New York, 1949), 369, 436, 523, 528.

37. *Lois*, II, 2, 4; V, 9, 11; VI, 1; VII, 2-4; XIV, 5.

38. Julius Stone, *The Province and Function of Law* (Cambridge, Mass., 1961), 400-401.

39. The idea that congressional investigations are a phase of the legislative functions is indicated in *McGrain v. Daughtery*, 273 U. S. 135, (1926), 178, 180. Investigations for exposure were condemned in *Watkins v. United States*, 354 U.S. 178 (1957) but silently treated as unobjectionable in *Barenblatt v. United States*, 360 U. S. 109 (1959).

40. M. J. C. Vile, *Constitutionalism and the Separation of Powers* (Oxford, 1967), 53-76.

41. *Ibid.*, 13-20.

42. James M. Burns and J. W. Peltason, *Government by the People* (Englewood Cliffs, N. J., 1963), 62-3. See also Peter H. Odegard and Hans H. Baerwald, *The American Republic Its Government and Politics* (New York), 311-322, where checks and balances is assumed to be a companion or alternative of separation of powers with little description or definition of the term checks and balances itself.

43. Vile, *op. cit.*, 14-17.

44. *Lois*, XVIII, 10.

45. The distinction between civil and military administration is discussed in *Lois*, V, 19; the difference between criminal law and tax administration involves Books VI, XII, and XIII, while different economic goals and programs are evident in *Lois*, XX, 3, 4, 8, 12, 14, 15, 21; XXI, 9, 20, 21; XXII, 10, 20, 21; XXIII, 29.

46. These terms are much overused but they seem to be the most appropriate for this distinction. The difference is not absolute, of course, but it is substantial. Montesquieu tends to view things more in the organic sense than the mechanical, but his expression often accords with the latter, see Lucien Levy-Bruhl, *History of Modern Philosophy in France* (Chicago, 1924), 144-149.

47. R. M. MacIver, *The Modern State* (Oxford, 1964), 371.

48. F. T. H. Fletcher, *Montesquieu and English Politics* (1750-1800) (London, 1939), 142.

49. Vile, *op. cit.*, 13, 45.

50. *Ibid.*, 136-143.

51. The two principal Supreme Court cases prohibiting activities for violation of the doctrine of separation curtailed the legislative branch, *Kilbourn v. Thompson*, 103 U. S. 168 (1880) and *Springer Government of the Philippine Islands*, 277 U. S. 189 (1928). In each, a contrary argument logically could be made that Congress or the legislature needed the authority as a check upon the executive. Both decisions accord with the general trend begun in the last century to reduce special and particular actions by the legislative branch. On the other hand, the doctrine of separation has had little force in preventing the growth of administrative regulatory commissions which combine three types of powers. On this last issue see Vanderbilt, *op. cit.*, 3., and its reference to James Landis, *The Administrative Process* (New Haven, 1938).

52. *Lois*, II, 2 (last par.); III, 3; IV, 5; V, 2, 3.

53. *Ibid.*, V, 10, 11, 14.

54. *Ibid.*, II, 4.

55. "Intriguing in a senate is dangerous; it is dangerous also in a body of nobles; but not so among the people, whose nature is to

act through passion." *Lois,* II, 2. The executive is able to move with greater expedition in a monarchy than in a republic, *Ibid.,* V, 10. Virtue as the moving spirit of a republic is regarded as a sensation, *Ibid.,* V, 2; and there is reference to the "good sense and happiness of individuals." *Ibid.,* V, 3.

56. Vile, *op. cit.,* 33, 39, 45, 53, 63, 74.

57. John Locke, *An Essay Concerning the True Original, Extent, and End of Civil Government* II, (par. 4 of the Essay is the first paragraph of Chapter II).

58. *Ibid.,* XII (pars. 147, 148 of the Essay).

59. *Lois,* XI, 6, (par. 53, where Montesquieu speaks about the prince being a part of the legislature, par. 54, where he refers to the Roman senate and the magistrates dividing the executive power, par. 57, where he speaks of the part of the executive power in the legislature, and par. 58, where he refers to the executive power in ancient commonwealths engaging in legislative proposal and debate).

60. See, for instance, *Lois,* II: III: V, 7; VII, 2-4; VIII, 5-6, 20; XVI, 9; XX, 4; XXIII, 6; XXIV, 5.

61. *Lois,* I, 3; XXVI, 15; XXXI, 34.

62. *Ibid.,* XIX, 17-19.

63. *Ibid.,* II, 4, 5; IV, 3; VIII, 21; XIX, 17; XXVI, 20.

64. *Ibid.,* III, 8; V, 14; VI, 1, 2; XIX, 16, 17; XXVI, 15, 16.

65. *Lois,* II, 2 (near end); see also *Lois,* III, 7 which asserts that ambition has good effects in a monarchy as it gives life to the government.

66. *Lois,* II, 2 (par. 14-16) 3, 4; V, 8, 9; VI, 1; XX, 21, 22.

67. *Ibid.,* XX, 2, 3, 4, 7, 15.

68. Joseph Dedieu, *op. cit.,* 170, 171. Dedieu points out several similarities in ideas and language between Locke and Montesquieu but asserts that they are fundamentally different in spirit and objective. Locke, he says, aimed at sovereignty of the people while Montesquieu was moved by hatred of despotism. Dedieu also notes Montesquieu's hostility to the social contract theory, *Ibid.,* 168-175.

69. Madison's essay on separation of powers in *The Federalist* No. 47 gives most attention to the constitutional arrangements that had been developed in the various states.

70. The distinction between public and private law is not generally accepted by American lawyers and legal scholars. Compare Edgar Bodenheimer, *Jurisprudence* (Cambridge, Mass., 1962), 169, and G. W. Paton, *A Text-Book of Jurisprudence* (Oxford, 1964), 289-300.

71. For instance, on a question of whether a legislative committee should approve large purchases of land by an executive department, the doctrine of separation could support a negative answer and the doctrine of check and balance could support an affirmative answer. See also fn. 51, *supra.*

72. The American unwillingness to recognize class distinctions is well known. Despite the dislike of concepts of royalty and aristocracy, the American constitution provided for a strong executive when the trend was toward parliamentary government. The United States Senate was originally removed from the people and still is the foremost second chamber. Likewise, the distinction between civil and political law is rarely mentioned in analysis of American government and law.

73. See fn. 51, *supra.* The use of the doctrine of separation to test governmental arrangements in England is reported in a number of situations, Fletcher, *op. cit.,* 141-9.

74. For an explanation of the multiplicity of elites in the American situation, see Arnold M. Rose, *The Power Structure* (Oxford, 1967). Rose distinguishes the "multi-influence hypothesis" from the "economic-elite-dominance" hypothesis.

75. See Vile, *op. cit.*

76. *Lois,* V, 14 (end).

77. *Lois,* II, 4.

78. *Lois,* XI, 18, (par. 18).

79. See *Lois,* II, 4; III, 7; IV, 2; V, 19; XX, 22.

80. Guido de Ruggiero, *The History of European Liberalism* (Boston, 1959), 61.

81. *Lois,* VI, 15; XI, 15; XII, 13, 21.

82. *Ibid.,* XX, 21. This may explain the disputed eighth paragraph in *Lois,* II, 4.

83. *Lois,* XI, 3.

84. *Ibid.,* XI, 5.

85. *Ibid.,* XII, 1.

86. *Ibid.,* XIX, 5.

87. See discussion in Chapter II, section two of this study.

88. *L. P.* LXXXIII

89. *Lois,* III, 4; V, 8; VIII, 5.

90. *Ibid.,* XIII, 12, 13, 14; XV, 12, 15.

91. *Ibid.,* V, 14.

92. *Ibid.,* XI, 4.

93. *Ibid.,* XI, 6 (par. 67).

94. *Ibid.,* XXVIII, 41.

95. Lowenthal, *op. cit.,* 469-90 at 478-9.

96. *Lois,* XI, 4. Later, he says that he thinks "that even the highest refinement of reason is not always desirable, and that mankind generally find their account better in mediums than in extremes." *Ibid.,* XI, 6, (par. 67).

97. *L. P.* CII

98. Roger Caillois *Oeuvres Complètes de Montesquieu* (Paris, 1951), II, 36-7; *Lois,* IX, 7.

Bibliography

1. The Works of Montesquieu

There are two available editions of *Oeuvres Complètes de Montesquieu*. One is published under the direction of M. André Masson, by Nagel, Paris, in three volumes, 1950, 1953, and 1955. The other is presented and annotated by M. Roger Caillois, and published by N.R.F.: Bibliothèque de la Pléiade, Paris, in two volumes, 1949 and 1951. The latter does not include the correspondence but it is more widely obtainable in libraries and references are made to it throughout this study, under the designations Caillois I or II.

For English translations, use has been made of *The Spirit of the Laws,* Hafner Publishing Company, New York, 1949, with the Nugent translation; the *Persian Letters,* published by Alexander Donaldson, Edinburgh, 1773, with the sixth edition of the Ozell translation; and *Considerations on the Causes of the Greatness of the Romans an their Decline,* translated by David Lowenthal and published by The Macmillan Company, New York, 1965. In some instances, the author's own translation has been used, with a notation to that effect. Other works of Montesquieu have been translated by the author, for purposes of this study.

2. Biographies of Montesquieu

The scholarly and definitive biography of Montesquieu by Dr. Robert Shackleton, Fellow of Brasenose College and Librarian of the Bodleian Library, Oxford, entitled *Montesquieu A Critical Biography* and published by Oxford University Press in 1961, has been the principal source of information about the life of Montesquieu. Other biographies considered include Henri Barckhausen, *Montesquieu, Ses Idées et Ses Oeuvres* (Paris, 1907) and Joseph Dedieu, *Montesquieu, l'Homme et l'Oeuvre* (Paris, 1943).

The excellent study by Professor Werner Stark of Montesquieu's epistemology may be considered a specialized biography. It was used extensively and with much help. Entitled, *Montesquieu, Pioneer of the Sociology of Knowledge,* it was published in 1960 by Routledge & Kegan Paul, Ltd., London, in the International Library of Sociology and Social Reconstruction.

3. Other Studies of Montesquieu Consulted

Aron, Raymond. "Montesquieu". In *Main Currents in Sociological Thought, Vol. I.* New York, 1965.

Boase, A. M. "The Interpretation of *Les Lettres Persanes.*" In Will Moore *et al.* (Eds.) *The French Mind — Studies in Honor of Gustave Ridler.* Oxford University Press. 1952.

Carcassonne, Elie. *Montesquieu et le Problème de la Constitution Française au XVIIIe siécle.* Paris, 1927.

Collins, Churton. *Voltaire, Montesquieu and Rousseau in England.* London, 1908.

Courtney, C. P. *Montesquieu and Burke.* Blackwell, Oxford, 1963.

Crevier, Jean-Baptiste Louis. *Observations sur le Livre de l'Esprit des Loix.* Paris, 1764.

Destutt De Tracy, Antoine-Louis-Claude. *Commentaire sur l'Esprit des lois de Montesquieu.* Paris, 1819.

Dedieu, Joseph. *Montesquieu et la Tradition Politique Anglaise en France.* Paris, 1909.

Dupin, Charles. *Observations sur un livre intitule "De l'Esprit des Lois" divises en trois parties.* Paris, 1757.

Durkheim, Emile. *Montesquieu and Rousseau, Forerunners of Sociology.* The University of Michigan Press, Ann Arbor, 1960.

Ehrlich, Eugen. "Montesquieu and Sociological Jurisprudence." *Harvard Law Review.* Vol. XXIX. 1906.

Faguet, Emile. *La Politique Comparée de Montesquieu, Rousseau et Voltaire.* Paris, 1902.

Fletcher, Frank T. H. *Montesquieu and English Politics,* 1750-1800. London, 1939.

Freron, Elie-Catherine. "Du Gouvernement d'Angleterre, compare par l'Auteur de l'Esprit des Lois au Gouvernement de France." In *Opuscules de M. F x x x.* Amsterdam, 1753.

Ilbert, Sir Courtney. "Montesquieu." *The Romanes Lecture* 1904 Oxford University Press, 1904.

La Porte, Joseph de. *Observations sur l'Esprit des Lois, ou l'art de lire ce livre, de l'entendre et d'en juger.* Amsterdam, 1751.

Levin, Lawrence M. *The Political Doctrine of Montesquieu's Esprit des Lois. Its Classical Background.* New York, 1936.

Lowenthal, David. "Montesquieu." In Leo Strauss and Joseph Cropsey *History of Political Philosophy.* Rand-McNally, Chicago, 1963.

Oudin, Charles. *De l'Unite de L'Esprit des Lois de Montesquieu.* Paris 1910.

Plamenatz, John. "Montesquieu." In *Man and Society, Vol. I.* McGraw-Hill, New York, 1963.

Shackleton, Robert. "Montesquieu, Bolingbroke, and the Separation of Powers." *French Studies.* Oxford, 1949.

————— "Montesquieu et Doria." *Revue de Littérature Comparée.* Paris 1955.

————— "Montesquieu and Machiavelli: A Reappraisal." *Studies in Comparative Literature.* I, 1964.

Spurlin, Paul M. *Montesquieu in America.* Baton Rouge, 1940.

Vaughan, C. E. "The Eclipse of Contract: (B) Montesquieu." In *Studies in the History of Political Philosophy Before and After Rousseau, Vol. I.* University of Manchester Press, 1925; Russell and Russell, New York, 1960.

Vyverberg, Henry. "Pessimism in Moderation — Montesquieu". In *Historical Pessimism in the French Enlightenment.* Harvard University Press, Cambridge, Mass., 1958.

4. *Other Works Consulted*

Bagehot, Walter. *The English Constitution.* London, 1928.

Bodin, Jean. *Six Books on the Commonwealth,* Abridged and translated by M. J. Tooley. Blackwell, Oxford.

Bondy, William. *The Separation of Government Powers in History, in Theory and in Constitutions.* New York, 1896.

Carlyle, A. J. *Political Liberty.* Oxford University Press, 1941.

Cassirer, Ernst. *The Philosophy of the Enlightenment.* Princeton University Press, 1951.

Church, William F. *Constitutional Thought in Sixteenth-Century France.* Harvard University Press, Cambridge, Mass., 1941.

Collingwood, R. R. *The Idea of History.* Oxford University Press, 1964.

Comte, Auguste, *System of Positive Polity.* London, 1876.

Cragg, C. R. *Reason and Authority in the Eighteenth Century.* Cambridge University Press, 1964.

Delolme, Jean Louis de. *Constitution de l'Angleterre,* (Amsterdam, 1771).

Dicey, A. J. *Introduction to the Study of the Law of the Constitution.* London, 1941.

Domat, Jean. *Les Lois Civiles dans leur Ordre Naturel.* Paris, 1694. Translation by William Strahan. Boston, 1890.

Ford, Franklin L. *Robe and Sword, The Regrouping of the French Aristocracy after Louis XIV.* Harvard University Press, Cambridge, Mass., 1953, 1962.

Friedmann, Wolfgang. *Legal Theory.* London, 1953, 1967.

Friedrich, Carl J. *The Philosophy of Law in Historical Perspective.* University of Chicago Press, 1957.

Gay, Peter. *Voltaire's Politics, The Poet as Realist.* Vintage Books, Random House, New York, 1965.

Gravina, Jean-Vincent de. *Esprit des Lois Romains.* Paris, 1821.

Green, F. C. *Eighteenth-Century France.* London, 1929.

Halévy, Elie. *The Growth of Philosophic Radicalism.* Oxford Univerity Press, 1928.

Jones, J. Walter. *Historical Introduction to the Theory of Law.* Oxford University Press, 1956.

Knox, T. M. *Hegel's Philosophy of Right.* Oxford University Press, 1942.

Levy-Bruhl, Lucien. *History of Modern Philosophy in France.* Chicago, 1924.

Loewenstein, Karl. *Political Power and the Governmental Process.* University of Chicago Press, 1957.

Lovell, Colin Rhys. *English Constitutional and Legal History.* New York, 1962.

Martin, Kingsley. *The Rise of French Liberal Thought.* New York University Press, New York, 1956.

Morgan, Charles. *The Liberty of Thought and the Separation of Powers.* Zarhoff Lecture. Oxford University Press, 1948.

Paley, William. *Considerations on the Structure of the House of Commons.* London, 1794.

Pollard, A. F. *The Evolution of Parliament.* London, 1920.

Rapin, Thoyras, Paul. *Dissertation sur les Whigs et les Torys.* The Hague, London, 1717.

Ruggiero, Guido de. *The History of European Liberalism.* Oxford University Press, 1927.

See, Henri. *L'Evolution de la Pénsee Politique en France au XVIIIe Siécle.* Paris, 1925.

Smith, Adam. *Lectures on Justice, Police, Revenue and Arms.* New York, 1964.

Smith, Munroe. *The Development of European Law.* New York, 1928.

Stone, Julius. *The Province and Function of Law.* Harvard University Press, Cambridge, Mass., 1955, 1961.

Vanderbilt, Arthur T. *The Doctrine of the Separation of Powers.* University of Nebraska, Lincoln, Nebraska, 1953.

Vile, M. J. C. *Constitutionalism and the Separation of Powers*. Oxford University Press, 1967.

Wormuth, F. D. *The Origins of Modern Constitutionalism*. New York, 1949.

Warburton, William. *The Alliance between Church and State*. London, 1736.

Index

Absolutism: Montesquieu's opposition to absolute power, 9, 59, 77, 87, 305; in monarchy, 9-10, 20, 44, 58, 130; in aristocracy and democracy, 196, 206. *See also* Despotism; Extremism; Mediation; Moderate government; Moderation; Monolithic democracy

Abuse of liberty, 243, 285

Abuse of power, 1, 171, 180, 245, 374, 376

Abyssinians, 138

Action: implicit distinction between action and control, 22, 156, 224, 338. *See also* Control; Political action; Political control

Action and reaction, 22, 26, 60, 69. *See also* Interactions

Active Society: national basis, 40, 45, 56-59; need of predictable order, 40, 46, 241; inner and outer relations, 40-44; social differentiations, 46, 94, 110-11, 239; four orders of group action, 22, 94, 353; natural motion of, 47-48; climatic influence on, 49-53; superiority of moral over physical causes, 53-54; esteem of socially relevant activity, 29, 121-22, 134, 188, 229, 266; social utility, utility test of religion, 118, 133; conduciveness of monarchy to, 189. *See also* Civil society; Competitive activity; Enemies of natural activity; Human attitudes and behavior; General causes of national spirit; National mores and manners; National society; Natural activity; Natural conflict; Relational diversity or pluralism; Social and political power classes; Social class con-

flict; Social distribution of power

Administration. *See* Executive constitution; Executive power; Intermediaries; Mediation; Modes of operation; Operating practicality; Political action; Political liberty in fact; Professional allocation; Professional elites; Taxation.

Affluence, 106. *See also* Luxury

Africa, 32, 107, 109

Alexander the Great, 108

Alienation, 27

Alliance of church and state, 33, 86, 115, 118, 126, 151, 372

Allocation of power: joint, 323, 337, 359-62, 379; mechanical, 355-56, 366; organic, 355, 363; professional 176-79, 224, 234; social, 166-73, 323, 370-73, 379. *See also* Joint allocation; Mixed government; Mixed monarchy; Mutuality; Political action; Political capabilities; Political control; Political responsibilities; Social distribution

Almond, Gabriel, xii

Ambition, 110, 189, 384

American colonization, 85, 109. *See also* United States

Anarchy and tyranny. *See* Dilemma of *Les Lettres Persanes*

Ancient nations. *See* Athens; Germanic nations; Greece; Marseilles; Rome; Sparta

Anticlericalism, 32, 51, 114, 120-22, 125-29

Antimonarchical attitude, directed at absolutism, 9-10, 20, 44, 58-59, 130; later designated despotism, 20, 156

Antipater, 210

Anti-politics, 56

Arbitrariness, 76

Arbuthnot, John, 49, 90

der of social action; Sumptuary laws; Usury

Commercial republics, 100-03, 228. *See also* Marseilles

Commercial theories, 99, 107-09

Common sense, 82. *See also* Collective citizenry; Moral sense; Political sense; Sense

Commonwealth, 174

Communication, 74, 96, 108, 184. *See also* Social communication

Community interest, 10, 141. *See also* Liberty; Living under laws

Comparative analysis, 155, 196, 230, 232, 256, 260, 349. *See also* Classifications

Compensation for seizure of private property, 141

Competitive activity, 69, 170, 189, 203. *See also* Active society; Conflict; Human activity; Natural activity

Comte, August, xii

Concentration of powers, 8, 44, 79, 299-301, 306. *See also* Deconcentration theories; Distribution of powers

Concurrent majority, 317, 377

Confederation of republics, 100, 102, 282, 331

Confiscatory laws, 105

Conflict of: classes, 168, 188; of groups, 102, of interest and justice, 8-12. *See also* Natural conflict; Social and political power classes; Social class conflict

Confounding of general causes, 76-78

Confucius, 118

Conquest, 52, 77

Conquest, law of, 135

Constitution: peculiarity of meaning, 83, 86-87, 98, 178, 188, 248, 290, 341. *See also* Balanced constitution; English constitution; Executive constitution; Fundamental constitution; Fundamental laws; Gothic government; Judicial constitution; Legislative constitution; Massachusetts constitution; *Mémoire sur la Constitution;* Model constitution; Pennsylvania constitution;

Roman constitution; United States constitution

Constitutional law, 296. *See also* Fundamental law

Constitutional liberty, 337. *See also* Political liberty by right

Consumption economics, 95, 97

Contradictions of the human mind, 12-27. *See also* Epistemology; Human mind

Control: distinguished from action, 22, 156, 230, 338, 361; of application of law, 228; of individual and of group, 59; of population trend, 112-14; of thought, 197. *See also* Joint allocation; Political control; Popular control

Conventional modes, 30

Correlations, 22, 54. *See also* Causes; Relations

Corruption, 190, 335, 375

Counsels distinguished from precepts, 122

Counterpoise, 183

Country party, England, 81

Creative will, 70

Crevier, Jean-Baptist Louis, 153. *See also* Criticism of *L'Esprit des Lois*

Crimes, 253, 273, 275. *See also* Private crimes; Public, crimes

Criminal law, omitted from list of legal orders, 252; civil, 137, 148, 271; political, 271-77, 305-06; for religious non-conformity; 129

Criticism, contemporary, of *L'Esprit des Lois,* 76, 116, 136, 172, 179, 193, 197, 210, 238, 287, 292, 320-21, 335

Crown party in England, 81. *See also* Political parties

Cultural influences, 29, 96, 108. *See also* Moral causes

Customary law, 43, 72, 137, 140, 295, 333. *See also* Civil law

Customary liberty, 251. *See also* Civil liberty

Customs, 82, 241, 275. *See also* Civil mores; Mores and manners; National mores and manners; Social mores

International law and relations, 23, 43. *See also* Conquest, law of; Foreign relations; Law of Nations
Interrelationships, 59, 318
Intolerance, 126
Intrigue, 170, 189, 383-84
Invariable laws, 25, 42. *See also* Universal realms
Irish nation, 85
Island residence, 85
Isolation of powers, 302
Italy, 12, 48, 301

Jansenists, 34
Japan, 66, 68
Jews, 28, 109, 127, 294
Joint allocation: of authority, 311, 317, 324, 359-60; of control, 310, 337, 362, 371, 379; of legislative power, 226, 323, 361, 372-73. *See also* Social distribution
Jones, J. Walter, 333
Judicial action, 123, 193, 254, 292, 315
Judicial constitution, 341, 361
Judicial power, 80, 261, 299, 300, 304-07, 310, 334
Judicial procedure, 258-59, 269, 272, 277, 289-90, 306
Judicial systems, 250, 254, 299; popular judiciary, 261; judicial functions, in Senate, 315; despotic, 256-59, 264, 268-69, 274
Jurisprudence, 188, 254, 264, 270-71, 289
Justice, 5, 8-9, 41, 55, 102-03, 139, 145, 257, 259, 374
Justinian Code, 256, 290
Juvenal, 87-88

Kant, 70, 188, 194
Kingship, 11, 205

Labor, 103
Laissez-faire policies, 99
Lamson, G., 38
Land division, 204, 237
Law: definition of law in general, 19; as a general cause of the national spirit, 60; definition of the spirit of the laws, 41-42; *See also* Civil law, Commercial law; Constitutional law; Criminal law; Customary law; Divine

law; Domestic law; Ecclesiastical law; Educational laws; English law; Feudal laws; French law; Fundamental law; Higher law; Human law; Indigenous law; International law; Invariable laws; Justinian Code; Law of nations; Marriage laws, Moral law; National law; Natural law; Physical law; Political law; Positive law; Preservation, law of; Religious law; Roman law; Social law; Sumptuary law
Law and prerogative, 160
Law-making processes, 28, 258, 361
Law of Nations, 43, 144, 252
Law of Nature. *See* Natural law
Legal branches of government, 324
Legal complexity, 256
Legal differentiations, 180, 183
Legal interpretation, 260
Legal orders, classification, 135
Legislation, 34, 80; as coercion and education, 265-66
Legislative: empirical and intrinsic meanings, 349-52
Legislative constitution, 250, 361
Legislative government, 82
Legislative guidance, 66, 78, 209, 258, 267
Legislative power: meaning, 80, 224, 300, 303, 352, 361; special meaning for separation of powers, 349-52; character of generality, 265; popular exercise, 308; bicameral exercise, 309; distributions, 307, 369; functions embraced, 382. *See also* Tripartite legislature.
Legislators, 62, 66, 67, 168
Legitimacy, xiv, 45, 47, 379
Lenders, 111
Lenity and severity, 276
Levy-Bruhl, Lucien, 191
Liberty: classification of, 24, 241, 247; meaning, 145, 241, **333**, abuse of, 243, 285; actual and imagined, 246; relation to cultivation of land, 53, 251; and luxury, 98; and poverty, 102; acquired by political laws, 141, 144; and judicial procedure, 272; relative to social custom, 63-64, 251. *See also* Civil liberty;

Political factions, 81, 170, 239, 364
Political faculties, 236
Political judiciary, 254, 271-81. *See also* Political liberty in fact
Political law: identification, 22-23; distinguished from law of nations, 23, 130-31, 144-45; distinguished from civil law, 23, 130-31, 140-44, 281, 295; associated with legislative power, 128, 132, 254, 295-97, 298-300; related to obedience, 278; general political law not developed, 140, 143
Political l i b e r t y: distinguished from civil liberty, 242, 252-53; general as well as particular, 242; requires moderate government, 245; distinguished from philosophic liberty, 246; distinction between actual and imagined, 246; two types, 247-50, 252; relation to climatic conditions, 250-51; social psychology of, 251-52; relation to types of criminal law, 252-53. *See also* Civil liberty; Political liberty by right; Political liberty in fact

Political liberty by right: relation to degree of liberty in constitution, 293; relation to living under law, 241-46, 372; relation to checking power with power, 242-43, 252, 293; the direct end of the English constitution, 294; classification of powers of government, 299-302; A m e r i c a n adaptation of warnings, 302-03; positive measures, 303-21; allocation of judicial power, 304-07; general will, 307; allocation of legislative power, 307-11, 315-17, 320-21; composition of executive authority, 311-15; fundamental constitution, 315-20; historical verification of ideal legislative c o n s t i t u t i o n, 321-32; constitution of Germanic nations, 321-23; comments upon Aristotle's Polity, 323-24; constitution of Roman republic, 324-32; general principles of liberty assuring government, 332; relevance to present day theories of liberty, 339-40; relation to social distribution of legis-

lative power, 372-73, 379. *See also* Civil liberty by right
Political liberty in fact: distinguished from other kinds of liberty, 242, 246-50, 252-53, 338-39; concerns status of individual in relation t o judicial, executive a n d administrative functions, 271; relation to criminal law procedure, 271-73; dependence upon moderation and prudence, 273-74; in cases of treason and public expression, 274-77; manner of punishment, 275-77; procedural requirements, 277 - 80; ideal prince, 278; method of administration, 278-80; taxes and tax administration, 280-87. *See also* Civil liberty in fact; Judicial procedure; P e n a l reform; Taxation
Political liberty of the citizen. *See* Political liberty in fact
Political liberty of the constitution. *See* Political liberty by right
Political motion, 48, 62, 182, 188-89, 211
Political order of social action, 22, 62, 72, 94, 128, 131, 141, 155-236, 241, 254, 271, 276, 299, 339, 353, 363, 378, 380
Political participation, 204, 232
Political parties, 80, 82, 196
Political power: mechanical and organic allocation, 355. *See also* Allocation of powers; Concentration of powers; Deconcentration theories; Executive power; Government; Joint allocation; Judicial power; Legislative power; Political action; Political control; Power; Professional allocation; Social distribution
Political reason, 179, 183, 233, 235, 364. *See also* Political sense
Political recruitment, 209. *See also* Political socialization
Political responsibilities: popular sovereignty, 195-209; democratic legislative power, 195-209; aristocratic mediation, 209-31; professional aristocracy, 209; political elites, 209; of nobility of the robe, 221-22; of monarchical

power, 177-79, 205, 235; of mixed government, 225, 227, 230; of political control, 224. *See also* Political action; Political control; Political liberty by right

Political sense, 167, 179, 235, 364. *See also* Political will

Political servitude, 53

Political socialization: political education, 24, 197-98, 212-15; of the aristocracy, 209-23; mediation role of professional aristocracy, 209-11; relation to spirit of moderation, 211-12, 217-19; education of aristocracy in monarchies, 212-15; nobility of the robe as moderate elite, 218-22; the role of the aristocracy in mixed government, 210-22, 227, 322-23, 353-54, 369

Political systems, xi, xiii, 85, 190, 223, 226, 306, 322, 363

Political tactics, 56

Political virtue, 205

Political will, 179, 235, 357, 364

Pollard, A. F., 342-43

Polybius, 96, 106, 192, 200, 224, 324

Poorhouses, 113-14

Pope, Alexander, 152

Pope, The (Clement XI), 33-34, 249

Popular absolutism, 45, 173, 196, 206. *See also* Absolutism

Popular class. *See* Social and political power classes

Popular control of executive, 173. *See also* Political action

Popular control of legislative, 166-68, 173, 199. *See also* Political control

Popular democracy, 166, 184, 199, 206. *See also* Monolithic democracy

Popular factions, 170-71

Popular judiciary, 261

Popular participation, 167, 170, 317

Popular sovereignty, 165, 196, 203, 207, 216, 228, 243, 245, 277

Popular suffrage, 169-70

Population trends, 32, 98, 108, 112, 121, 132, 151

Porte, Abbé Joseph de la, 172, 179, 192-93, 197, 202, 237, 320

Portugal, 129, 147

Positive law, 22, 41, 116, 132, 219. *See also* Civil law; Conquest, law of; Domestic law; Human law; Law of nations; Political law

Positive objectives, 339

Poverty, inner and outer causes, 112-13, 207

Power: real and relative, 44; general and particular, 360. *See also* Political power

Practical politics, 56, 81

Pragmatic tests, 119. *See also* Empirical verification

Predestination, 134

Prerogative, 322

Prescriptive method of *L'Esprit des Lois*, 14-16, 341

Preservation, law of, 138

Preservation of government, 116, 238, 294

Presidential government, 312, 328, 365

Pride, 6, 62, 68

Primacy of order, 64

Primitive man, 2, 25

Primogeniture, 220

Prince and people. *See* Dilemma of *Les Lettres Persanes*

Prince's council, 179

Principle of government. *See* Special spirit

Private accusations, 277

Private crimes, 253

Private interests, 188

Private law, 253, 255, 285, 333, 384

Privileges, 322

Production economics, 95

Productive activity. *See* Competitive activity

Profession, change of, 150, 237

Professional allocation of political action; distinguished from social distribution of political control, 156, 166-67, 176; monarchical and despotic modes of operation, 156, 160, 162, 177, 180-83, 224, 230, 279; allocation of operating functions, 176-79, 182, 184, 217; special spirit of intermedi-

aries, 184-90, 209-11, 214-16, 220;
education and reform of aristoc-
racy, 211-15, 218-19, 222; divi-
sions of French nobility, 221-23
Professional elites, 84, 165, 169,
178, 210, 222, 227, 234
Progress, 54, 62
Propaganda, 63
Propagation, 133. See also Popu-
lation trends
Property, law of, 137, 141-43
Property rights, 144
Proportion, sense of, 24
Proselytization, 126-27
Protestantism, 120-21
Provincial cities, 286
Provincial government, 22, 98, 103,
331
Prudence, 220, 273, 282, 375-76
Psychological approach, 200
Psychological attitude, 227, 235
Psychological burden, 195
Psychological factors, 51, 70, 136
Psychological order and change, 62
Psychological relevance, 136, 273
Psychological tests of punishment,
265-66, 269
Psychology, 195, 235. See also So-
cial psychology
Public: crimes, 253; debates, 317;
debts, 110; employment, 184,
220; expenditures, 202; ethics,
105; good, 68, 142, 188; law,
252-53, 255-56, 289, 333, 384;
luxury, 202; order, 278; relations, 279; revenues, 219, 280-87;
service, 84, 220, 354, 383
Pufendorf, Samuel, 16
Punishment, 77, 129, 263-69; psychology, 265-66; relevance to
class, 267; punishing soldier,
267; proportionate to crime,
269; in Russia, 269

Qualitative separation of powers,
326, 370
Quantitative distribution of powers, 303, 326, 379
Quantitative variables, 20, 45, 186,
283

Raphael, 88
Rapin-Thoyras, Paul, 93, 335, 343,
381
Rationalism, 16-20, 170

Rational monarchy, 205
Rational virtue, 10, 12, 17
Reason, 64, 199, 201, 385. See also Political reason; Rationalism
Rebellion, 276
Recruitment, 213. See also Political socialization
Reform of nobility, 213, 218, 232
Reform of penal system. See Penal
reform
Relational diversity or pluralism,
24-25, 42, 61, 74, 107, 115, 117,
134, 181, 229, 313, 369
Relations, internal and external,
23-26. See also Causes; Interaction; Natural activity
Religion: Montesquieu's personal,
115-17; concepts and theories,
13, 31-32, 43-44, 115-17, 125, 215;
effect on civil society, 50, 112,
115-22, 134-39; effect on type
of government, 32-34, 52-54, 120;
separation from politics, 20, 33,
41, 86, 115-20, 126, 151, 215,
273-75, 372. See also Atheism;
Christianity; C l e r g y; Deism;
Ethics
Religious attachment, 124-25
Religious government, 22, 94, 353
Religious law, 32-34, 41-43, 112,
122, 134-39
Religious order of social action,
12, 20, 22, 80, 86, 94, 115, 273-75,
353, 372, 379-80
Religious proselytization and toleration, 126-30
Religious types. See Catholicism;
Christianity; Classifications, religions; Mohammedanism; Protestantism; Roman
Representative government, 8 2,
208, 307, 361
Republican government: one of
two general types, 12, 96; divided into democracy and aristocracy, 156; sometimes mixed,
79, 157, 219, 225-26; classifications, 158-62; geographical factors, 331. See also Aristocracy,
Classical republics; Commercial
republics; Confederation of republics; Democracy; Mixed government; Moderate government;
Provincial government

The typeface selected for the text of this book is Baskerville. Chapter headings are set in Bulmer and subheadings in Baskerville bold. The Benton Review Publishing Company, Fowler, Indiana, did both the letterpress printing and the binding. The books are printed on 60 lb. Warren Old Style paper and bound with Interlocken cloth. Moroni St. John, Purdue University artist, designed the dust jacket. Richard L. Pierce, associate university editor, and Diane Dubiel, assistant university editor, supervised editing and production.

JC   Merry, Henry J.
179
.M8M4   Montesquieu's system
           of natural government

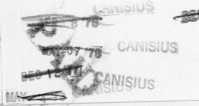